WHEN MISFORTUNE BECOMES INJUSTICE

Stanford Studies in Human Rights

When Misfortune Becomes Injustice

Evolving Human Rights Struggles for Health and Social Equality

Alicia Ely Yamin

Stanford University Press
Stanford, California

STANFORD UNIVERSITY PRESS
Stanford, California

© 2020 by the Board of Trustees of the Leland Stanford Junior University. All rights reserved.

No part of this book may be reproduced or transmitted in any form or by any means, electronic or mechanical, including photocopying and recording, or in any information storage or retrieval system without the prior written permission of Stanford University Press.

Printed in the United States of America on acid-free, archival-quality paper

Library of Congress Cataloging-in-Publication Data

Names: Yamin, Alicia Ely, author.
Title: When misfortune becomes injustice : evolving human rights struggles for health and social equality / Alicia Ely Yamin.
Description: Stanford, California : Stanford University Press, 2020. | Series: Stanford studies in human rights | Includes bibliographical references and index.
Identifiers: LCCN 2019019681 (print) | LCCN 2019021741 (ebook) | ISBN 9781503611313 (electronic) | ISBN 9781503605411 (cloth: alk. paper) | ISBN 9781503611306 (pbk.: alk. paper)
Subjects: LCSH: Right to health—History. | Human rights—Health aspects—History. | Health services accessibility—Law and legislation—History. | Women's health services—Law and legislation—History. | Medical policy—History.
Classification: LCC K3260.3 (ebook) | LCC K3260.3 .Y39 2020 (print) | DDC 362.1—dc23
LC record available at https://lccn.loc.gov/2019019681

Cover design: Angela Moody

Typeset by Kevin Barrett Kane in 10/14 Minion Pro

For Nico and Sam

It is precisely the function of constitutional protection to convert misfortune to be endured into injustice to be remedied.
—*S. v. Baloyi and others (J. Albie Sachs)*
CCT (South Africa) 29/99 (1999), para 12.

Contents

Foreword xi

Acknowledgments xiii

Introduction: Allegorizing the World 1

1 **Indignation and Injustice** 27

2 **The Significances of Suffering** 52

3 **Diverging Parables of Progress** 75

4 **Dystopian Modernization** 102

5 **Globalizing Crises, Pandemics, and Norms** 123

6 **Inequality, Democracy, and Health Rights** 148

7 **Power, Politics, and Knowledge** 175

Conclusions: Turning Toward the World We Want 202

Notes 225

Index 269

Foreword

ALICIA ELY YAMIN'S *When Misfortune Becomes Injustice* is a multilayered work of profound subtlety. Yamin, a leading international human rights scholar and global advocate for health as a human right, has written a book that operates on different levels: analytical, political, moral, and methodological. Most directly, her study is an acute reflection on decades of research, activism, and policymaking at the intersections where human rights and the movement for global health justice meet. Through nuanced discussions of specific moments in the history of health rights mobilization, moments in which Yamin herself often played an important part, she is able to weave a narrative of change, challenge, and modest success that leads her to a set of specific proposals for how to advance the cause of global health justice in the future. Through her experiences as a researcher and advocate in Peru during the late-1990s, to her work as an expert witness in health rights litigation, to her participation in national symposia on rare diseases, Yamin's approach to health as a human right is always grounded in a deep experiential authority.

Yet beyond its various landmark contributions to the field of health rights scholarship, *When Misfortune Becomes Injustice* also ranges much farther afield to consider the most pressing questions of our time—and, arguably, of *any* time. As she puts it, to advance a particular position in relation to health as a human right is at the same time to make a claim "about being human in this ever-changing world." Even more, Yamin's book leaves no doubt that these broader stakes must always be kept in mind even as debates over health rights can become preoccupied with technical problems of legal enforcement, the economics of national health systems, or the quantitative measurement of health outcomes. Instead, Yamin would have us begin and end with a fundamental truth: that we, as humans, are both diverse but equal in humanity, and it is this truth that must shape all our understanding and policymaking, whether in relation to health rights or otherwise.

The application of this first principle throughout *When Misfortune Becomes Injustice* leads Yamin to make several positions refreshingly clear. First, she is compelled to place—or, rather, to keep—the individual at the center of our collective inquiry. This has immediate implications for how the relationship between health rights mobilization and culture is perceived. As Yamin explains, global health justice will never become a reality without a wider "emancipation from predefined social roles," which often work against women and which can embed structural violence across the generations.

Second, the centrality of a diverse but equal humanity to Yamin's approach to health rights has consequences for both political theory and political organization. As she argues, the full realization of health as a human right must go hand-in-hand with the reform of both national and international political systems in order to create the conditions in which democratic deliberation can flourish. On Yamin's view, the tensions between diversity and human equality that have shaped the global health justice movement can only be productively resolved through more robust and pervasive democratic processes.

And finally, the broader philosophical and moral framework of *When Misfortune Becomes Injustice* carries key lessons for the future of human rights. In this, Yamin strikes a salutary balance between sharp critics of human rights and those who have argued that human rights in their current forms should continue to form the primary foundation for global activism and national legal and political regulation. Instead, Yamin argues that the history of health rights mobilization suggests specific models that can be adapted as part of a wider process of reimagining the place of human rights in the face of manifold contemporary challenges.

At the same time, however, Yamin insists that this process of adaptation will prove hollow in the absence of the kind of progressive political and socioeconomic transformations that must precede and accompany it. In this, *When Misfortune Becomes Injustice* is not only a book about the fight for global health justice. It is also an urgent clarion call for global structural change animated by a clear imperative to social action, ongoing struggle, and transcultural solidarity.

Mark Goodale
Series Editor
Stanford Studies in Human Rights

Acknowledgments

JORGE LUIS BORGES NOTED that "a book is not an isolated being: it is a relationship, an axis of innumerable relationships." That is certainly the case with this book, which traces one thread in a tapestry of inspiration, struggle, and solidarity.

I have had the tremendous privilege of having mentors in the United States as well as in the many countries mentioned in these pages who were not just pioneers in international law and public health, but who valued praxis, and showed me how ideas could move worlds. At the very beginning of a career setting out to bridge health and human rights—when we are learning what it means to assimilate professional norms and aspirations—Deborah Maine, Lynn Freedman, and Giulia Tamayo, among others, modeled unwavering integrity as well as the understanding that underpins this book, which is, to paraphrase bell hooks: theory can be and indeed *must* be a laboratory for practice if we seek to use it to change people's lives.

All professional lives, and especially those of women, are inexorably the products of social, economic, and personal contingencies as well as personal aspirations and effort. The many transitions between continents, with children in tow, which once may have seemed sacrifices in terms of traditional professional advancement, in retrospect were inestimable gifts that allowed me to meet and work alongside exceptional colleagues around the world. Only some of these pioneering thought leaders, heroic clinicians, brave judges and parliamentarians, and brilliant activists are mentioned by name. But they are all invariably part of this story and therefore are present in these pages.

Writing this book overlapped felicitously with pursuing an academic study in Argentina. As a result, I benefited enormously from the incisive comments of Roberto Gargarella, a friend, colleague, and leading scholar of comparative constitutional law. Roberto introduced me to new bodies of literature and invited me to re-examine many assumptions and, in doing so, he opened new worlds to me. In addition to Roberto, other friends have been pillars of support at critical junctures, and I am especially grateful to Camila Gianella, Sofia Charvel, Paola Bergallo, Tarek Meguid, Siri Gloppen, Regan Ralph, and Michelle DeLong.

Many people contributed directly to the process of putting this book together. Emily Maistrellis played a pivotal role in an earlier version, which focused exclusively on maternal health. Emily undertook extensive work on that earlier draft, conducted key informant interviews with me, and, critically, helped me establish the temporal sequence in the book.

In turn, I am deeply grateful for the time, knowledge, written notes, and other materials that the following key informants generously shared and whose views are reflected explicitly or implicitly in the text: Jashodhara Dasgupta, Lynn Freedman, Paul Hunt, Deborah Maine, Rebecca Cook, Marge Berer, and Lucinda O'Hanlon.

The current manuscript could not have been written without the dedication of Angela Duger. Angela's thorough research and tracking down of different sources; knowledge of economic, social, and cultural rights; and feedback along the way were invaluable.

Tara Boghosian dove into the project with great enthusiasm, provided thoughtful feedback, and diligently helped prepare the final manuscript for publication under considerable time pressure.

I am tremendously grateful to Sue Goldie, faculty director of the Global Health Education and Learning Incubator at Harvard University, who has long championed the value of bringing multidisciplinary perspectives to global health. Sue provided inspiration as well as enormous personal encouragement and institutional support throughout the time I was researching and writing this book, for which I will be forever thankful.

The institutional support provided at different phases of research and writing at both Harvard and Georgetown was also essential. I am deeply appreciative of both Jennifer Leaning, then faculty director of the François-Xavier Bagnoud Center for Health and Human Rights at Harvard University, and Lawrence Gostin, founding faculty director of the O'Neill Institute for National and Global Health Law at Georgetown University Law Center.

Working with Stanford University Press has been a great pleasure. I was delighted that Mark Goodale embraced the approach of the book for the interdisciplinary, innovative Stanford Studies in Human Rights series he has created.

I am also deeply grateful to Michelle Lipinski for her guidance, support, and even gentle pushback throughout the publication process. I was very fortunate to have the benefit of deep knowledge and constructive critiques from the two anonymous peer reviewers, who accompanied the process from the prospectus through manuscript.

Despite the way creative work by men is often portrayed, it is never an autonomous effort that emerges without contributions and sacrifices by those who share our private lives. As ever, I am endlessly grateful to Nico and Sam, my sons and greatest life-teachers. My partner, Jeremy, has been my traveling companion along this entire journey. As I wrote this book, he shared coffee at sunrise on countless days, and in so doing transformed waking in predawn hours from a dreaded chore to an anticipated pleasure.

Finally, I am forever awed and inspired by the true protagonists of the struggle for health rights: those ordinary women, and men, who carve out dignity and purpose in lives too often shadowed by poverty and discrimination; who make tremendous sacrifices not for their own future reward but to enhance the lives of others; who mobilize collectively to protest tyranny of all forms; and who, despite all odds, change the world time and again.

WHEN MISFORTUNE BECOMES INJUSTICE

INTRODUCTION

Allegorizing the World

> It is hard to understand how a compassionate world order can include so many people afflicted by acute misery, persistent hunger and deprived and desperate lives, and why millions of innocent children have to die each year from lack of food or medical attention or social care. . . . As competent human beings, we cannot shirk the task of judging how things are and what needs to be done. As reflective creatures, we have the ability to contemplate the lives of others [and] the miseries that we see around us and that lie within our power to help remedy. . . . It is not so much a matter of having exact rules about how precisely we ought to behave, as of recognizing the relevance of our shared humanity in making the choices we face.
>
> —*Amartya Sen*[1]

THERE ARE TUNNELS UNDER HARVARD LAW SCHOOL that connect the buildings and are lined with student lockers. Before she became a US Supreme Court justice, as dean of Harvard Law School, Elena Kagan had begun to transform the public space at the law school, not only adding better lighting and framed posters in the tunnels, but also a volleyball court that turned into an ice skating rink in winter outside the student center. As dean, Kagan was famous not just for her brilliant mind, but also for taking the time to stand at the entrance of the annual Thanksgiving reception to personally hand out pies to staff and faculty.

But in September 1988, that was a long way off, and the tunnels were dimly lit and grim. It was the first day of my first year, and I had retreated to this underground labyrinth to contemplate having been the first student called on by a visiting professor of Contracts, who seemed to believe the purpose of the Socratic method was to humiliate as much as edify. A classmate, who on that first day already had established himself as someone to be looked up to, stopped by my locker and said, "Hey, you did great!" Seeing my dubiousness, after another minute he added with a broad smile, "No, really. . . . How'd you know *e.g.* was short for *exempli gratia* anyway?"

Over twenty-five years later, I watched that same former classmate, Barack Obama, who by then had graying hair and furrowed brows, in Dallas as he delivered one in a long line of speeches he had had to give as the first African-American president of the United States after mass shootings and murders of black men by police. Five police officers had been shot dead and nine others were injured in Dallas, Texas, on July 7, 2016, at the very end of a peaceful Black Lives Matter protest.[2] The shooter was a mentally unstable former marine and African American. Many politicians would have used the occasion to pander to racism and fear. President Obama did not. In his speech in Dallas, he asked:

> Can we see in each other a common humanity and a shared dignity, and recognize how our different experiences have shaped us? . . . [W]ith an open heart, we can learn to stand in each other's shoes and look at the world through each other's eyes. So that maybe the police officer sees his own son in that teenager with a hoodie [and] maybe the teenager will see in the police officer [his parents' values].[3]

It was a magisterial speech, one that spoke to the aspiration of recognizing our diverse but equal humanity, which lies at the heart of deploying human rights for social transformation.

It was the kind of speech for which President Obama had become famous, the kind of speech that eight years earlier might even have made us believe in the possibility of a "post-racial America." But after years during which Obama's mobilization of policy had not matched his mobilization of language, and we had witnessed hundreds of killings of African Americans by the police every year, as well as a racially motivated massacre in a Charleston church in 2015[4]—and most of all the election of Donald J. Trump—the "audacity" of that hope seem cruelly naïve.

This book grew out of a critical reflection on a professional career spent pursuing the narrative behind Obama's speech, not just or even primarily in the United States, but around the world: the narrative that all of us are capable of connecting to the otherness within ourselves, and in those around us, and of uniting around ideals of our shared humanity rather than reflexively recoiling in prejudice or fear. Advancing the right to health and economic, social, and cultural rights has entailed making space for not just racial otherness, but the otherness of gender, ethnicity, and our many other axes of often socially constructed identity and confronting the challenges posed to advancing common human interests in contexts of profound social and economic inequalities that foster the process of "othering" and undermine democracy.

An incantation to "look at the world through each other's eyes" can of course produce a hollow tolerance from our own narrow perspectives. Empathy can easily become a way to congratulate ourselves for feeling the sorrows of the world. But if it is taken seriously, the idea that both we as people and our democracies are enlarged by diversity, and that there is value in dialogue among people with distinct views who are treated as equals, has radical transformative potential. Seeing the dignity in the other, ascribing *the other* with our own human qualities—and often ascribing what we see as their human qualities to ourselves—is the basis of all human rights, in relation to health and generally.

It was in many ways during my time at Harvard Law School in the late 1980's and early 1990's that great expectations for the potential role for international human rights rose to prominence on the world stage. Human rights ceased to be just a response to the horrific atrocities in Nazi Germany or dictatorships in Latin America and elsewhere; it also became a discourse that spoke to the aspirations of diverse groups around the world. Indeed, the contrast between international human rights law and US domestic law was striking at the time. On the one hand, hopes of achieving social transformation through the courts had faded in the US as the Warren Court had given way to the Burger and then Rehnquist Courts. At the time I was there, Harvard Law School was dubbed "the Beirut of legal education," for its acrimonious and ideological faculty disputes, largely between the conservative faction (including the dean appointed in 1989) and those who adhered to critical legal studies (CLS), a movement that focused on how the pretension to depoliticize the law and present legal reasoning as a neutral scientific exercise served to entrench the power of the status quo.[5] Many of the insights of CLS theory, in its multiple permutations, both reflected and have been further developed by scholarship from varied legal traditions, as well as other disciplines, which have grappled with the inextricably intertwined relations between law, morality, and politics.

If the domestic US landscape for critical legal advocacy appeared constrained, it was during those same years that international human rights law was exploding—in the news media and as a scholarly field.[6] Although in 1989 the Chinese regime acted with swift repression to put down the protests in Tiananmen Square, we all later sat glued to our televisions watching the fall of the Berlin Wall and Nelson Mandela walking free from Victor Verster Prison in 1990. These events not only shattered assumptions about the global political order, but also opened apparent possibilities for the use of a framework that radically transformed international law to make individuals, and not states, the subject of international legal rules. In short, it was an invitation to enlarge both our legal and political imaginations.[7]

The world was changing before our eyes, and it seemed possible that we could deploy human rights in innovative ways to combat the injustices—by the United States first and foremost—which many of us had until then protested through the politics of the street. When the Gulf War broke out in the spring of 1991, a group of friends and classmates created the International Study Team on the Gulf Crisis to assess the impacts that the US invasion had on civilians in an explicit human rights framework, weaving together legal, public health, and social science expertise to document the resulting deprivations of water, food, sanitation, and health-care access in terms of human rights—economic and social rights.[8] That study team became the Center for Economic and Social Rights (CESR) in 1993, which I went on to contribute to through reports, fact-finding delegations, and then through serving on the board, eventually as vice president (2001–2008) and then succeeding Philip Alston as president (2009–2014).[9] At the time, virtually all international human rights scholars and organizations were still focused on civil and political (CP) rights, such as freeing political prisoners and exposing civil rights abuses. Economic, social, and cultural (ESC) rights were derided if not dismissed by most international human rights organizations as well as scholars. But some of us nonetheless insisted that human rights—understood in its original holistic articulation in the Universal Declaration of Human Rights—could be deployed to regulate economic abuses, just as the expansion of suffrage and other civil rights had diffused political power.

Over the years those of us who have dedicated ourselves to advancing ESC rights, including CESR, have faced at least three challenges in scholarship and advocacy.[10] First, we would have to subvert entrenched ideas about rights: notions that ESC rights were not *real* legal rights, but mere programmatic aspirations. Second, we had to articulate what it would mean to take ESC rights seriously in laws, institutional arrangements, and governance. Finally, we would have to demonstrate that doing so could achieve meaningful progressive social change.

This book is an account about facing those evolving challenges over the last three decades (1991–2019), with respect to the right to health and health-related rights in particular. It is a reflection on the extent to which coming to apply a human rights framework to health, and ill-health, was able to convert a narrative of "misfortune to be endured" to one of "injustice to be remedied."[11] Multiple assessments of international human rights have been written in recent years, both by avowed skeptics and by cheerleaders. This is, however, an insider's account of a particular aspect of the human rights story—applying human rights to global health—in which I conclude there is indeed "evidence for hope" but "not enough."[12]

Framing the Argument

In a previous book, *Power, Suffering, and the Struggle for Dignity: Human Rights Frameworks for Health and Why They Matter* (hereafter referred to as *Power and Suffering*), as well as in other writing, I have suggested that a transformative engagement between health and human rights requires critically rethinking conventional approaches to both human rights and public health.[13] In many ways, this book is the continuation of thinking I did in *Power and Suffering*. The accounts that have been written about the evolution of maternal health, HIV/AIDS, sexual and reproductive health, and other topics into rights issues have addressed pieces of the narrative from different country or disciplinary perspectives. We are missing some of the most significant features of the story of creating *health* as a rights issue. These most revealing, and often most challenging and frustrating, parts of the narrative lie precisely in the points of intersection and friction in the interstices between different fields—law, medicine, and health; human rights and economics—and between their methods and epistemic models. Further, this account tracks the recursive relationships between the "lived experiences" of health rights and the development of supranational and national norms in both law and development—and how these synergies and dissonances evolved over time. Thus, I seek to fill some of those many gaps and to do so in a specific way that enables extracting some lessons about using human rights *critically* for progressive social change in health and beyond. If *Power and Suffering* focused almost exclusively on examples drawn from maternal health to illustrate what applying a rights framework means, this book recounts a narrative that explores the interactions of law, public health, and models of politics, economics, and development.

Some readers may still say this is an account of the struggle for *women's* health rights, and it is true that I focus largely on maternal and sexual and reproductive health. But there is a larger point. As Simone de Beauvoir suggested, not just the world itself, but "representation of the world" is the work of men; reality is described in law, philosophy, and political discourse from the male point of view which they confuse with, and the rest of us are supposed to take as, objective truth.[14] Even well-meaning efforts, such as an opinion survey conducted in 2017 regarding whether feminists have "made traction in campaigning that 'women's rights are human rights,'" reinforce the notion that this is a matter of opinion[15] and that the default human being who possesses rights continues to be a (heterosexual) man, reinforcing deep structures of thought about humanity and society. Many others have noted that those who do not share the dominant racial, colonialist, male, etc. gaze must reconstruct how we represent as well as construct reality if efforts at social change are to be more than palliative gestures. Thus, the argument I make throughout this book is that a truly subversive struggle for health (and other human rights) calls for more than invoking the protected status of an ever-growing list of diverse persons. Rather, it continually calls upon us to think harder about the interlocking structures of power—i.e., racial supremacy, patriarchy, biomedicine, economic constructs—that ratify how we see the world. Doing so cannot mean substituting any other single perspective for the dominant one; my focus on examples of largely heterosexual women is not meant in any way as accepting gender identity and sexuality as binary constructs. Further, we cannot hope to arrive at more a humanized society or world by devolving into lies based on some ostensible immutable "core" which are but fragments of our complex identities. Nor can we hope to do so by reducing questions of moral status to isolated capacities in a vacuum, divorced from social space, as some would now extend to technologies with artificial intelligence.

Instead, I suggest both in my substantive arguments and through the form in which this book is written that we require a more nuanced and less rigidified approach to understanding both our mutual (nondominant) difference and what is essential to our universal *humanness*, given that we are inexorably *embodied social beings*, living together in this ever-changing world. That more fluid approach, in turn, requires accepting that we have not just diverse experiences, but also diverse phenomenologies that structure how we understand those experiences. At the same time, I insist throughout that we are also capable of dialectically humanizing one another and acting on our shared humanity.[16] And much of this book speaks to the conditions necessary to do so.

In reviewing the past thirty years, my argument is that, on the one hand, normative and institutional evolution has been extraordinary in health and other ESC rights and has over these decades advanced efforts to curb traditional forms of tyranny and discrimination, as well as to create new discourses of equality, the purposes of the welfare state, and the boundaries of inclusive societies. Many of these advances indeed have been forged in women's health rights and sexual and reproductive health and rights (SRHR), which have expanded understandings of rights and the liberal state, as well as how power relations influence health *for everyone*. Further, although as this book goes to press many of these advances seem precarious, human rights conceptualization and advocacy have not only achieved normative and rhetorical change, as some critics claim. The application of human rights in health has also been crucial to saving actual lives, from HIV to maternal mortality; improving health outcomes, conditions, and care; and easing burdens of stigma, discrimination, and misery in practice.

On the other hand, even as we advanced new understandings of who got to participate as full members of the polity, and what equal enjoyment of rights meant in practice, the possibilities and political space for deliberation necessary to advance a robustly egalitarian health rights agenda were shrinking. That is, just as health and other ESC rights claims were being theorized and articulated, the global embrace of neoliberalism—and the economic integration of markets and adjustments to internal laws and institutions that ensued—crippled the potential for democratic responses to those claims. Nowhere were the effects of this shifting global political economy more evident than in health and, in turn, the elision of political and moral economies in sexual and reproductive health. Over these decades, trade liberalization, deregulation of private capital flows, and labor market "flexibilization" came to be accepted by many governments as well as intellectual elites as natural or necessary for modernization. Some autocratic regimes eagerly colluded with policies promoted through international financial institutions (IFIs) and powerful governments; others found themselves hamstrung by economic conditions negotiated or created previously. Throughout the book, we will see how this evolution had health effects—whether it was involuntary sterilization justified by a need for economic growth, barriers to medications based on intellectual property regimes, or widely disparate and gendered health outcomes due to increasing privatization of health systems across the world.

Over the course of these years we see the deepening of what Jürgen Habermas has referred to as a "legitimation crisis" in democratic institutions and government.[17] The drivers of this legitimation crisis can be seen in ever-deepening inequality within and between countries, and global crises such as conflict, displacement, and climate change. The results are, among other things, a recent surge of conservative populism, overt attacks on gender equality, and ethnonationalism in elections and referenda that explicitly dismisses the importance of democratic pluralism and rules-based political multilateralism.

To be clear: there is zero nostalgia for some mythical romanticized past in this account; the legal segregation and discrimination within societies, coupled with resistance to decolonization of other societies; the lack of basic civil and political rights; and the existence of inherited privileges that arbitrarily determine life chances are all anathema to the idea of universal dignity I espouse. It is the duality of the narrative that I am interested in: exposing the fact that while we were advancing health and other social rights, the dark side of the multilateral economic order was limiting the very space in which they could be realized; and exploring what alternative socio-legal narratives might have led us down other paths.

I argue in conclusion that in order to use human rights to promote a robust agenda for gender and social justice, in health and beyond, we first need to understand how this twin evolution has occurred. Second, without conceding the critical ground we have gained in so many respects, we can and must re-energize the original human rights aspirations of a social order based upon equal dignity of diverse human beings, which includes economic justice within and across borders. Among other things, rescuing the subversive power of human rights calls for deploying a critical praxis, in which diverse agents create meaning, transgress categories, and do not receive prepackaged truths from elite experts "in the know." Throughout the book, I call for unsettling rather than entrenching orthodoxies, not just in dominant macroeconomic and sociocultural constructs, but also in the constellation of overlapping fields related to health and human rights.

Reflective Methods and Approach

As distinct from important recent additions to the human rights literature regarding neoliberalism and health, or neoliberalism and human rights,[18] much of this book is a critical reflection on what factors triggered reactions and counter-reactions, and how our inherently incomplete perceptions of reality reflected the inexorable movement of history and thought and shaped outcomes described here. Using social science methods of "process-tracing,"[19] I analyze how an array of resources and opportunities ("opportunity structures") were understood by different sets of actors, as over time laws changed, public health evidence was built, economic and political configurations in the world shifted, technologies advanced, and the like.

From the outset, I want to make it clear that my professional life has been inextricably connected with the development of the health and human rights field, as well as advancement of ESC rights. This recounting is therefore a critical reflection on my own motivations, actions, and understandings of rights and power, at different points along the path, and the choices that I made, along with countless other colleagues and movements around the world. It is also inexorably limited and self-consciously subjective, as I adopt what Pierre Bourdieu calls the "the prerogative" of someone familiar with the terrain mapped.[20]

It would be impossible to set out a comprehensive account of the normative developments across regional and national contexts, let alone in international law, and that is not my objective here. Moreover, other scholars and practitioners who have actively carved out this terrain, including many of those with whom I have worked and/or interviewed in the course of writing this book, have already told or would tell a very different story.[21] My hope is that this selective account, and the challenges it raises, will spark discussion in public health, human rights law, and many related fields—and among a much wider public—about the choices we collectively face today.

Part of enabling a broader public, including other fields of study, as well as practitioners, activists and youth, to engage in active debate about using human rights for social change in health and beyond requires democratizing the knowledge regarding what is at stake in how we conceive of rights and how we deploy them. Otherwise we will invariably fall prey to the notion—antithetical to the project I advocate throughout these pages, and in my view toxic to democracy—that only the intellectual elite and so-called experts are able to understand theoretical issues regarding political philosophy or law and the technical issues regarding economics or health. Therefore, throughout this book, first, I explicitly set out my theoretical points of departure and the implications of accepting these views about law, rights, and democracy, on the one hand, and health, health systems, and development, on the other. Second, I go to lengths to synthesize ideas from these different domains, which are all critical to understanding the history of applying human rights to health, but which may be not be equally familiar to all readers.

Finally, I deliberately adopt narrative techniques, which have been used not just by feminists and other nondominant groups in recent scholarship, but also throughout history to elucidate important principles, as well as create a capacity for empathy and self-knowledge. Here I deploy narrative techniques for four distinct reasons, which each relate to a central theme in the book.[22] First, in my own career, listening to others' stories has shown me dignity as well as its denial in people's daily lives, and I share some of those encounters here to bring to life the lived experience of rights and to humanize the often abstract topics addressed, inviting readers to enter into a dialogue with themselves about the narratives they create in their own lives, based on their own experiences. I am well aware that using stories invariably involves the politics of power and representation, especially when the accounts relate to experiences of marginalized and vulnerable people. Thus, I not only take pains to protect identities, but I explicitly situate these interactions as being recounted from *my* subjective perspective, which in no way pretends to reflect their views of the experience, much less the "objective truth" of those interactions. Nonetheless, this form of writing reinforces a central argument I make here which is that even in our inevitable brokenness we can, and indeed must, transcend the monikers we routinely apply to see ourselves in others, and others in ourselves.

A second theme of the book is that what we call "law" is inexorably embedded in a socio-legal narrative, which cannot be understood by its technical workings alone.[23] The language of law, just as the language of economics and medicine, is a way of representing the world. Legal discourses both respond to and shape sociopolitical contexts. Throughout these pages I frequently argue for the importance of legal interpretations, including of international law, setting out coherent rationales, which is another way of saying that legitimacy depends upon authorities—whether courts or legislatures or international bodies—being able to tell a plausible story about why any given measure or rule is reasonable or necessary. Moreover, telling the factual story behind specific cases allows us to see petitioners as more than the positive point of law they are packaged to represent. The political calculations and complexities of selecting litigants and of framing what may be challenged (e.g., marriage need not be between a man and woman) and what may not (e.g., the traditional family structure and/or institution of marriage) underscore the contested construction of normative arguments. Contextualizing these cases, and the evolution of interpretive guidance from the bodies that monitor international human rights treaties (treaty monitoring bodies, or TMBs), also reveals the power struggles and politics between visions of human rights law and between varied national and international groups, which are important considerations for those who wish to pursue legal mobilization for health and other social rights.

Third, in a world where knowledge is often reduced to decontextualized "apps," stories make apparent the *evolution of learning* that has occurred—including the dialogue between my "experiencing self and my remembering self" over these many years.[24] Legal breakthroughs are similarly in dialogue with past events and seeding of norms, even if not strictly judicial precedents. So too are development paradigms. Thus, this juxtaposition of past and present reinforces a third theme: the temporal, inexorably iterative nature of using rights for legal and social change, and the need for a historical understanding of why different strategic moves were made at given times and what we were seeking to advance strategically.

Finally, on a meta-level, the argument I will make throughout these pages is that using human rights for promoting justice in health, and more broadly, itself entails a particular allegory about what it means to be human, in all our diversity, but with equal moral value, coexisting in a world with finite resources to pass onto future generations.

Starting Points I: Law, Rights, and Democracy

My first theoretical starting point is that rights, as opposed to broader conceptions of justice, are inexorably tied to the law, which inherently offers a conservative set of tools for social change. In many ways this is an account about, as the black feminist poet and activist Audre Lorde might say, trying to take up "the master's tools to dismantle the master's house."[25] It is also a contemplation on the challenges to doing so through a particular lens and field: health. Of course human rights are more than law: they are cultural and political idioms; they are tools for social mobilization; they are sites of moral contestation about equality and justice; and much more, as I recount in these pages. Indeed, I will suggest that promising expansions of transforming ideas of rights and dignity into the "immanent regularity of practices," in Pierre Bourdieu's term, lie often in extralegal social practices, vernacularization of meaning in specific contexts, and in a more robust and engaged politics.[26]

Nevertheless, we live in an invariably normativized world where it is illusory to believe that movements for social change can avoid using law. Further, the modern human rights movement was built upon the aspiration that law could equal justice, which I will argue throughout these pages requires grappling with how deeply intertwined the moral, doctrinal, and political aspects of rights are. Sometimes international human rights law is treated as natural law or a positivistic set of rules, as legal facticity above and untethered from politics. The history of using international human rights law to combat abuses under dictatorship and autocracy makes this understandable, as does the desire of women's movements to escape the patriarchal treatment of issues such SRHR in national forums. However, I argue here that the advances we have made in health-related rights, including SRHR, have largely used law in antiformalist and inexorably political ways to broaden understandings of equality and dignity as well as create innovative remedies. Further, specifying the open-textured and evolving meaning of rights in countries, including and perhaps especially health, invariably requires contestation, and to do so justly often requires contesting the bounds of the political sphere and how those bounds are set. Finally, throughout the book I am concerned not just with interpretations of international and constitutional norms, but with how law (and human rights law in particular) functions to (de)legitimate different forms of power within sociopolitical contexts.

My second starting point is that the assertion that all people are "equal in dignity and rights"—as the Universal Declaration of Human Rights states[27]—envisions a world in which everyone's distinctive needs and lives are given "equal concern and respect" in the design and administration of major social institutions, absent some compelling justification for preferential treatment.[28] The notion of dignity that underpins international human rights is drawn from liberal philosophy but has resonance in many other religious and philosophical traditions.[29] In turn, the institutional arrangements that permit dignity are those that free diverse individuals and groups from the hold of entrenched social roles and hierarchies that arbitrarily shape their life chances. The history of the last forty years shows that we need not "fetishize" our current institutional order, as Roberto Unger would say, to uphold health and other human rights.[30] Indeed, I will argue throughout this book that when taken seriously, the claim of emancipation that human rights encodes can be used to challenge ingrained discrimination, religious and cultural ideology, economic exploitation, and inherited privilege that relegate too many people to being placeholders in their societies—and can be extended coherently to begin to address profound inequities in the global order.[31]

In Chapter One, I discuss the origins and grounds for legitimacy of a set of rights that claim universality, which is a precondition to the arguments I will make later regarding building the normative edifice and specifying entitlements in respect of health. Further, I suggest that historically it is not just the idea that such claims are universal that has most contributed to the evolution of human rights related to health over time, but perhaps in practice even more so what Sen calls "the view from a distance."[32] It is precisely the external gaze that allows us to see that the ways things are done in one context, culture, or society need not be the way they have to be done. Understanding the contingency of the accepted order of things opens space for collective intentional action to transform rigidified laws and discourses, which may be imposed by elites in a society at any one point in time.[33] The idea that "human rights overflows its banks"[34] also suggests that contexts—social, cultural, and legal—continually evolve as they interact with one another and are subject to greater internal contestation than is often articulated by political leaders and traditional elites who invoke mantras of cultural exceptionalism from Uganda to Texas.

The ways in which human rights language and tools have been appropriated and deployed over time in relation to health, and more broadly, underscore that rights are not self-standing truths, but loci of contestation over power and evolving values. All rights are "terse formulations of profound arguments about distributive justice and humanity. If we seek to use rights to promote social justice in health, it is a strategic mistake to think that merely using the shorthand is enough to circumvent the argument."[35] The right to health in particular is inherently unstable because of shifting epidemiological trends, demographics, and scientific advances, which in turn lead health systems to undergo constant evolution. Indeed, health, perhaps more dramatically than any other right, calls upon us to continually and collectively reflect on what we owe to one another as coequal members of a polity and as equal but diverse human beings in a globalized world with finite resources. Thus, throughout the book, I emphasize the importance of not just elites or technocrats, but ordinary people coming together collectively to reason with respect to health issues. The legitimacy of this process of collective deliberation is fundamental to the validity of (re)defining a right to health, as well as to the norms that we agree to be governed by more generally.[36]

My third starting point, which follows from the above, is that we should not value liberal democracy merely because of a preset arrangement of state institutions: executive, legislature, and judiciary. Rather the epistemic value of a democratic republic lies in people governing themselves by reasons, rather than power plays between preassigned racial, class, ethnic, gender, caste or other identities. I adopt Seyla Benhabib's definition of democracy as "a model for organizing the collective and public exercise of power in the major institutions of society on the basis of the principle that decisions affecting the well-being of a collectivity can be viewed as the outcome of a procedure of free and reasoned deliberation among . . . moral and political equals."[37] Re-energizing human rights requires linking health and other rights to this more robust idea of deliberative democracy, within but also beyond our official assemblies, where those who are affected—especially marginalized groups—are meaningfully engaged in diagnosing and resolving collective problems.

Starting Points II: Health, Development, and Progress in the World

In advancing possibilities to enjoy health rights in practice, we need to concern ourselves not just with emancipation from predefined social roles, but also with practical progress. Such practical progress includes economic growth as well as technological and medical innovation. Practical progress is, as Roberto Unger argues, a basis for "our power to push back the constraints of scarcity, disease, weakness, and ignorance. It is the empowerment of humanity to act upon the world."[38] In no domain is such progress and empowerment more critical than in health, where scientific advances such as contraception, antiretroviral therapy, antibiotics, and childhood vaccinations, among many other examples, have transformed the life chances of billions of people and continue bringing hope to enhance human flourishing at an ever more breathless pace.

A series of articles and books have recently come out telling us that we are better off now than ever before. These are cheery, optimistic tales about the steady and accelerating march of progress we have made in the world. In 2017, Oxford economist Max Roser noted that "the story that we tell ourselves about our history and our time matters."[39] Roser argues, among other things, that child mortality has declined dramatically, while basic education (intimately related to health) has exploded.[40] Stephen Pinker's 2018 book argues that the Enlightenment worked; we now apply reason and sympathy to enhance human flourishing around the world.[41] Similarly, Gregg Easterbrook's 2017 volume tells us we should be optimistic because the state of the world "is better than it looks."[42]

Indeed, in health there has been tremendous overall progress toward eliminating many preventable infectious diseases and transforming previous death sentences, including from some rare cancers, into chronic diseases.[43] In some forms of cancer, bombardment with a standard assault of chemotherapy, radiation, and surgery increasingly gives way to far more nuanced and targeted "precision medicine" treatments. Scientific communities regularly announce discoveries that offer the keys to greatly expand healthy years of life expectancy, and potentially cure certain diseases through gene editing technologies.

There is, however, a second story, a far darker one, not just about the seeming discounting of our global planetary health and the inequitably distributed effects of climate change, but also about the gaping disparities in the enjoyment of these public health and biomedical advances, and the drivers of those disparities. For example, although the absolute rates of infant death have declined by over 90% due to improvements in nutrition, hygiene, and health care, the gaps between black and white infant mortality in the United States (11.3 to 4.9 per 1,000) is greater today than it was in 1850, before the Civil War that ended slavery.[44]

Similarly, at a global level, despite the thrilling promises of a recent Lancet Commission chaired by Lawrence Summers, the likelihood of "achiev[ing] a grand convergence in health" by 2035 remains a utopian fantasy.[45] The average life expectancy for a child born today in Swaziland is 49 years, while in Japan it is 84 years.[46] For countries such as Finland, 100% of the population has at least reached secondary education, but this attainment drops to 5.5% in Chad.[47] A woman in South Sudan has a greater chance of dying in childbirth than of graduating from primary school.[48] Never before have life chances—and life choices—been so unevenly determined by the arbitrariness of where one is born in this world. Moreover, looking ahead, the capacity for technologies such as germline gene editing—which would enable changes in genes of future generations to prevent disease, as well as potentially make human enhancements, seems technologically possible as of 2018—and raises profound questions not just about inadvertent consequences but about eugenics and equity within and between populations.[49] The story we tell ourselves about progress in the world does matter, as Roser says, and it depends upon certain premises about how we understand health, and development more generally.

My first starting point with respect to health is that inequalities in health matter so much to us because health is so closely connected to a life of dignity, and therefore has special moral importance to us as individuals and to sustaining a democratic society. After all, not all inequalities raise the same concern. Norman Daniels has argued that health enables a preservation of a normal range of opportunities to pursue our life plans, and Amartya Sen has argued health underpins "capabilities" and "functionings" that we value in our lives.[50] In turn, as I will set out further in later chapters, the intimate connection between health and dignity implies that: (1) public health preconditions and access to care cannot merely be allocated by the market as any other commercial goods; (2) the state has a role to play in leveling the playing field in spreading the benefits of scientific progress equitably and providing fair chances to access those preconditions and care; and (3) in a global order, it is increasingly recognized that states have obligations to regulate the transboundary effects on health of state and nonstate actions alike.

My second starting point is that we care particularly about those health inequalities that we understand as *injustices*, which we see as arbitrary, avoidable, and fundamentally unfair. For example, racial differences, which are inextricably bound up with socioeconomic status in the United States, are reflected in the health disparities across a variety of conditions.[51] Race is, according to Jo Phelan, Bruce Link, and Parisa Tehranifar, a "fundamental cause" of health inequalities because of four essential features: (1) it influences multiple disease outcomes; (2) it is correlated with multiple risk factors for disease and death; (3) there is an association between race and health because of a disparity in resources; and (4) new factors that perpetuate the association between race and health are constantly emerging. We need not accept a genetic construction of race to acknowledge that the effect of living as a person of color in the US is associated with increased morbidity and mortality. Indeed, even when specific disease prevalence, such as tuberculosis, is reduced, other diseases such as cardiovascular disease or breast cancer will reveal similar racial disparities because of *patterns of injustice* in society.[52]

Perhaps no public health issue demonstrates the injustice embedded in global as well as national health disparities more than maternal mortality. In the United States, women of color are three to four times more likely to die of maternal deaths in the United States than white women.[53] Globally, 99% of the estimated 303,000 maternal deaths in 2015 occurred in the global South, and maternal mortality remains the public health issue that shows the greatest disparities between economic North and global South.[54] The preponderance of these deaths is preventable. Deaths from unsafe abortions, which account for approximately 11% of maternal mortality worldwide, are overwhelmingly due to legal restrictions on this lifesaving procedure as well as on the medication and necessary information to perform one's own medical abortion safely.

When we stop asking *how* these women died (hemorrhage, sepsis, preeclampsia, etc.), we can see that the reasons *why* they die invariably relate to whether all women and girls have agency in their lives—choices about getting an education; about when and with whom they want to have sex, and whether they want to use contraception; about how many children they want; and how they want their pregnancies and deliveries to be. These choices, in turn, require laws, policies, and institutions necessary to guarantee rights—both decisional autonomy and access to entitlements. But maternal mortality is in no way unique. As the many examples in this book attest, any number of egregious health inequalities and deprivations around the world are the product of "pathologies of power," in Paul Farmer's phrase, as much as biological or behavioral factors.[55] As we will see throughout this book, the understanding of health as reflecting patterns of (in)justice in turn upends traditional biomedical models pursued in clinical medicine and conventional public health approaches that focus on behavior change in isolation from the broader social, cultural, and economic context. It also challenges technocratic assumptions about health systems that understate their normative functions as social institutions.

My final starting point is that meaningful progress in the world—what we commonly call "development"—requires addressing these pathologies of power, or what Amartya Sen calls "unfreedoms."[56] Development requires economic growth without a doubt. Sustainable economic growth can drive practical progress in health and living conditions. Moreover, sustainable economic growth can lead states to enhance public goods. Nonetheless, not all economic growth has equal or equally distributed social benefits and costs, including environmental costs. Thus, economic growth is a means to greater human flourishing; we will see beginning in Chapter Two that societies lose their souls when unqualified economic growth becomes an end in itself.

With these intertwined starting points, I use the lens of health to examine the advances we have made and challenges we still face in using human rights frameworks and tools to promote greater social and gender justice in the world.

Structure of the Book

The chapters of the book are divided into time periods, with some inevitable overlap and circularity to draw out theoretical arguments. Within each time period, although their relative significance varies, I consistently focus on the same set of issues and sets of processes, which are crucial to evolving opportunity structures for different sets of actors. These are the shifts in the arrangement of resources and barriers involved in: (1) the economic and political contexts in which the global order was evolving, with implications for democracy, human rights, and health; (2) the prevailing paradigms of development and their consequences for social mobilization, as well as knowledge and governance discourses; (3) evolving architectures of both international human rights and constitutional law, as well as economic legislation and regulation; (4) the advent of empirical discoveries and innovation with respect to health issues; (5) the appropriation of forums for social and legal mobilizations by different forces at national and international levels; (6) the role of personal and institutional leadership, for good and for ill; and (7) the evolution of technologies, from the internet to the availability of data. Different configurations of these factors influenced trajectories of norm-making and norm implementation, the evolution of global institutional regimes, and the possibilities for mobilization of political consciousness and progressive social change throughout these years.

Chapter One, "Indignation and Injustice," situates the beginning of this story in Argentina under the dictatorship in the 1970's and argues that constructing health rights has required generating a visceral sense of indignation at the abuses that poor people (and women) suffer every day, as well as demonstrating how and when the state is responsible. The turn toward human rights in the wake of reluctant decolonization, disenchantment with more radical politics, and evidence of the brutality of authoritarian regimes had three central implications. First, human rights offered a more confined legal approach to change as opposed to radical social aspirations and movements. Second, at the time, human rights law focused on CP rights violations in the public sphere, a product of a particular vision of rights and responsibilities in the traditional liberal state, promoted by the West. Third, human rights focused on individuals, and the aspirations of newly decolonized states for a New International Economic Order were substantially displaced to other domains, despite continuing interest in a "right to development."

The 1970's also saw the advent of widespread access to oral contraception and safer methods of abortion in some places. This practical progress led to social and legal mobilization to emancipate women from predefined social roles across the world. The struggle to advance women's health rights would require shifting understandings of both who was entitled to be full subjects of rights and what that required from the government. The 1979 adoption of the Convention on the Elimination of All Forms of Discrimination against Women (CEDAW) was a milestone in expanding rights paradigms to address women's realities. Nevertheless, empirical data was still needed to vindicate women's rights from abuse and discrimination.

In Chapter Two, "The Significances of Suffering," I recount how due to shifts in global economic arrangements and the beginning of market fundamentalism in the 1980's, the prevalent narrative in many countries became that the private sector was more efficient at economic management than the state. The state would be left with a residual role of targeting the needy that could not fit into the market as a matter of charity, upon whom conditions could be placed, as in the case I describe of Latonya, a young African American whose welfare aid was conditioned upon her "fitness" as a mother. In the US, health systems were increasingly treated as marketplaces, and care as a commodity, which is anathema to understanding the inherent connection between health and dignity. Whether an individual having a health or economic problem or a whole country's economy stalling, failure ceased to be a social problem and came to be seen as the result of inept governance or individual defects or deviance, with disproportionate gendered impacts. These views of private versus societal responsibility supported justifying the restructuring of national economies and domestic governance by multilateral IFIs, which took on expanded roles.

The central argument I make in this chapter is that it is not possible to theorize health rights without exploring understandings about who suffers and why. In the 1980's, UNICEF's child survival revolution led to the Convention on the Rights of the Child and the notion of children, previously treated as chattel or partial adults, as full subjects whose dignity needed to be cultivated as much as protected. At the same time, new epidemiological data on maternal mortality led to understandings that women had separate needs from children, which in turn was necessary to give content to women's rights to be free of avoidable death in pregnancy and childbirth. It was also in the 1980's that HIV/AIDS spread across the world as a modern-day "plague," which revealed the ambivalent relation between biomedical innovation and social emancipation for LGBTQ activists.

In Chapter Three, we see two "Diverging Parables of Progress" propagated by the multilateral political institutions of the UN, on the one hand, and on the other by the evolving roles played by the multilateral economic institutions of Bretton Woods. At the global level, in the wake of the groundbreaking Vienna World Conference on Human Rights in 1993, which reaffirmed the interdependence of CP rights and ESC rights and called for establishing the Office of the High Commissioner for Human Rights (OHCHR), feminist networks achieved enormous mobilizations and advances in sexual and reproductive health and rights (SRHR) and women's rights at UN conferences. As Carmel Shalev wrote of the International Conference on Population and Development (ICPD): "For the first time, the international community focused on the needs of individuals, the empowerment of women, and the emergence of an evolving discourse about the connection between human rights and health that linked new conceptions of health to the struggle for social justice and respect for human dignity."[57] The Beijing Conference reinforced the understanding at ICPD—but we did not anticipate the virulence of the backlash that would follow.

At country-level, in the 1990's "transformative" or "social" constitutionalism swept many countries, from South Africa to Colombia, enshrining a new social contract based on rights to material conditions necessary for dignity, as well as traditional CP rights, and a new form of more engaged and less formalistic adjudication. The developments gave us hope for using ESC rights and law to create more egalitarian social orders.

The second narrative, which became evident while I was living in Mexico during those years the North American Free Trade Agreement (NAFTA) was being negotiated in the early 1990's, was intensifying economic integration, and new legal norms were also being propagated regarding trade, deregulation, and the securitization of debt, which hardly aligned with the goals of social justice and human dignity. The General Agreement on Tariffs and Trade (GATT) was replaced by the World Trade Organization (WTO) in 1995, which had binding enforcement mechanisms and would quickly expand its jurisdiction into intellectual property as well as issues previously preserved for domestic sovereignty, from health and safety regulations to agricultural and environmental standards. All of these issues, central to the enjoyment of health rights, were thus no longer subject to domestic political negotiation and justification. Rather, the rules of the game were exercised through hidden power, justified in technocratic terms as necessary for the "modernization" of economies and societies, and monitored using abstracted indicators. I argue that this framing of modernization based on dictates from technical knowledge experts was critical to making these neoliberal policies seem neutral and unchallengeable.

In Chapter Four, "Dystopian Modernization," drawing on experiences in Alberto Fujimori's autocratic Peru, I recount how the utopian aspirations of the UN development conferences became a dystopia in the involuntary sterilization of hundreds of thousands of overwhelmingly indigenous women in Peru in the late 1990's. There was a toxic synergy between the hypercentralized regulatory states in many countries and the delegation of decisions over fiscal and other governance policies that affected health and other ESC rights to technocrats in international institutions. Perhaps nowhere can this be more clearly seen than in Fujimori's zealous and antidemocratic implementation of the IFI strictures through almost 1,000 decrees, including in health sector reform. Moreover, the conservative backlash against Fujimori's "modernization" after the sterilization scandal reflected and was refracted at the global level. SRHR were excluded in the next development framework, the Millennium Development Goals (MDGs), which only included one depoliticized goal on maternal health.

Nonetheless, the new theorizations of rights and ensuing state responsibilities, for example with respect to violence against women, made redress possible in the involuntary sterilizations case, as well as social and political mobilization, and further law reforms. I set out a scheme for considering the impacts of rights strategies that includes a broad array of direct and indirect, material and symbolic effects, noting that doing so was not possible until the mid-1990's. Although the results of using rights strategies in Peru are mixed, and sometimes backlash must be considered as part of impact, I argue that the most powerful aspect of health rights can be a deeper one. That is, rights offer a story of changing the way in which not just political and judicial decision-makers think about issues, but also the way subaltern groups—including women marginalized by the state—create what Nancy Fraser calls "counterpublics."[58] It is in these counterpublics that women and others often come to deliberate about our bodies, our health, our dignity—and our relationship to political and social institutions, including health systems.

In Chapter Five, I turn to "Globalizing Crises, Pandemics, and Norms." By the first decade of the 2000's it was clear that diseases such as HIV/AIDS could move across borders, creating in many ways a new era of global health security and catalyzing the creation of new global health institutions. It was also clear that the rapid movement of capital had facilitated economic volatility and contagion around the world, culminating in the crash of 2008, which turned into a global economic crisis. South Africa, newly democratic and needing to participate in the global economy, was deeply affected by the economic strictures imposed by the IFIs and the United States among others, including with respect to access to medicines.

Continuing the argument begun in Chapter Four about assessing impacts of human rights strategies, I argue the TAC PMTCT litigation in South Africa, which established a right to receive nevirapine, was so successful because it was a part of a much broader social and political strategy. The HIV/AIDS case study demonstrates it was possible to establish affirmative health entitlements as legal rights and assets of citizenship, as opposed to commodities the price of which could be set by pharmaceutical companies or international largesse.

In Chapter Five, I also note that the MDGs were intended to be global norms, but in fact ended up being used as national planning targets, by which governments were held accountable for narrowly defined outcome metrics, as opposed to institutional and social change. I contrast the technocratic top-down approach to health outcomes of the MDGs with the very different view of health systems of the MDG Task Force on Maternal and Child Health, which I argue is consistent with health systems centered around a right to health. That is, rather than apparatuses for delivering goods and services, just like justice and education systems, health systems inexorably constitute fundamental institutional arrangements in a democratic society, where women in particular, due to reproductive and socially constructed caretaking roles, experience their rights and equal inclusion, or alternatively the indifference of state institutions, as exemplified in a maternal death I describe in Malawi.

Finally, around the turn of the millennium, there was also a proliferation of international human rights norms, institutions, and procedures related to health and other ESC rights. This rapid expansion led to fragmentation that was used by conservative opponents of human rights, and in particular SRHR, to undermine international law. Further, there was a trend toward expansive policy guidance in TMB statements; using the CESCR's General Comment 14 on the Right to Health to illustrate this trend, I argue that it distances TMBs from the imperative of coherent justification and dialogue with states, as well as blurs the lines between progressive realization and minimum thresholds in human rights law.

In Chapter Six, "Inequality, Democracy, and Health Rights," we see that the extremes of economic inequality reached by the second decade of the millennium were undermining not just health, but the possibility of democratic governance. Focusing on Brazil and the *Alyne da Silva Pimentel* case from the CEDAW Committee, which established an affirmative right to maternal health care, makes clear that we had achieved tremendous advances in both judicial enforcement as well as in the development of human rights–based approaches (HRBAs) to health, which could facilitate understanding the laws and policies and institutionalization required by taking health rights seriously. Using the example of the UN's "Technical Guidance on the Application of a Human Rights–Based Approach to the Implementation of Policies and Programmes to Reduce Preventable Maternal Mortality and Morbidity" (UN Technical Guidance)[59] and its use in a Technical Follow-up Commission to the *Alyne* case, the chapter sets out critical definitional issues in an HRBA to health, and argues for preserving space for ground-up critical problem-solving, in which local actors in the health system and beyond collectively identify and pose solutions to problems, such as obstetric violence in Brazil.

Further, judicial enforcement of health rights had gone beyond one condition, such as HIV/AIDS, or one medication to add to the formulary; in Latin America, the question had become how to use adjudication not to grant privileges to those who happened to have access to justice but to promote systemic equity across systems. Using the context of Brazil, the chapter considers polarized claims about the impacts of judicialization of health rights on formal and substantive equality, as well as democratic oversight of health. Moreover, by the second decade of the millennium it was possible to evaluate impacts of the innovative use of dialogical remedies introduced by various courts—from India to Argentina to Colombia—in matters relating to health, which had been creative responses to the institutional constraints posed by dysfunctional politics and regulation. It is clear that meaningful participation of civil society has proven critical in all of these processes. Yet, ultimately, the use of HRBAs and dialogical remedies depend on catalyzing the political organs of government, which often limits the extent they lead to transforming the socioeconomic and gendered realities that undergird health inequities.

Chapter Seven, "Power, Politics, and Knowledge," begins by setting out the enormous challenges we face in the post 2016 context, from vast socioeconomic inequalities, the looming climate crisis, conflict and displacement, and the new challenges to democracy posed by a wave of populism and ethnonationalism, in both candidate elections, including Donald Trump, and in referenda.

Amid this chaos, in 2016, the world embarked upon meeting the UN's Sustainable Development Goals (SDGs). The SDGs emerged out of a reassessment of the MDGs and proposed a universal development agenda for rich and poor countries alike, aimed at tackling inequalities within countries as well as between them, and linking goals in social sectors to access to effective institutions and justice. Unlike the small group of donor countries and UN bureaucrats who chose the MDGs, the SDGs were created by a broader coalition of states and an open process that allowed for significant input from civil society. Among other things, SRHR were included across goals, and rather than silo-ized health issues, universal health coverage (UHC) was the centerpiece of the health goal.

Yet, despite the transformative rhetoric of the political narrative, I argue that some of the indicators chosen to measure progress, such as inequality and SRHR, are ill-suited to creating the transformative change promised in the political document. Since the 1990's we have recognized that quantitative indicators have an important place in facilitating the measurement of progressive realization and compliance with empirical dimensions of health and other ESC rights. However, the use of abstracted data to measure the indicators in the SDGs reduces and distorts the meaning of inequality and SRHR, respectively, and potentially saps energy from contesting attacks on gender equality that are on the rise. Thus, this representation of knowledge through abstracted, quantified indicators calls for vigilance by advocates, as well as the use of complementary qualitative, contextual information.

The importance placed upon UHC opens possibilities for convergences with the right to health. Nonetheless, the imperatives of fair financing, which includes undocumented migrants; fair and democratic priority-setting; and meaningful oversight must be taken seriously. We have examples of models to follow in regard to all of these, and I emphasize the conditions necessary for meaningful citizen participation in the process for setting health priorities in a democracy.

At every stage of this history, groups in the diverse human rights community have been adapting their arguments and strategies to the realities in which they find themselves. In Chapter Seven, I note promising if nascent efforts to expand social contracts to extraterritorial obligations (ETOs) of states over transnational corporations and through multilateral and direct initiatives, among other things. These potentially offer more fruitful ways of promoting global health justice than relying on international assistance to meet subsistence needs.

In the Conclusions, "Turning Toward the World We Want," I synthesize four central threads that have been intertwined throughout the book to understand how we got where we are and what might lie ahead. These relate to dimensions of power regulated by rights, shifting relations between public and private domains, evolving conceptions of the social contract, and the imperative of democratizing health systems. In short, these two truths coexist: on the one hand, we have achieved transformations of laws—and lives. On the other hand, we have too often accepted episodic victories in ESC rights, including health, achieved in the context of institutions and assumptions that were too often unchallenged—and not fully understood by most of us, including me.[60]

Yet far from an account of despair or fatalism, this book is a call to re-envision our collective efforts at social transformation, in health and beyond. Throughout this history, it has been possible to continuously push the bounds of what seemed once impossible in human rights. There is no reason that with reflective, critical praxis that spans multiple fields, human rights cannot join with other progressive social movements to reimagine our institutional possibilities in order for diverse people around our globally interconnected world to enjoy dignity and greater well-being.

Concluding Reflections

In 2016 I was in another set of far more sinister tunnels than those under Harvard Law School: the labyrinth of the Mangapwani slave caves on Zanzibar. We had lived in Tanzania for three years, so this visit with my teenage son was returning to familiar terrain. It was rainy season and there had just been a pelting, bruising downpour. The caves were half inundated and the coral was extremely slippery. I made my way carefully, half crawling, half wading and hiking simultaneously, through the watery blackness. Our guide, Abdul, was a tall, lanky young man, about the same age as my son Sam, and they quickly moved on ahead of me. Abdul looked back from time to time, "Sawa Mama?" he asked in the familiar Swahili. "Sawa, asante—OK, thanks," I said, meaning I was managing physically. But emotionally it was impossible to be all right, not to viscerally feel the oppressive heat and humidity magnified in the almost total blackness of these tunnels, not to shudder at the terror and anguish the men, women, and children must have felt having been ripped away from their lives and loved ones and everything familiar to them, made to travel miles under brutal conditions, to be held here in these hidden tunnels before being sent onward, shackled together in long rows with heavy bronze anklets, twenty-four hours a day.

Zanzibar was a shipping point for slaves from all over Central and Eastern Africa, from Kenya and Uganda to the Congo and Tanzania.[61] The British had officially outlawed the practice in 1897 when Tanganyka and Zanzibar were protectorates. But a famous Arab slave trader named Tippu Tipp continued to use the caves and tunnels clandestinely until as late as 1905.[62] Indeed, it is not inconceivable that some ancestor of President Obama's father, whose family is from Kenya, might have been enslaved and passed through these very caves.

When we got out of the cave, Sam and I stood catching our breath, adjusting to the light and taking in what we had experienced. I said, "What a torture!" Abdul asked me what the word meant and for me to type it into his cell phone. "I have learned something," he said, smiling broadly and repeating, "too-chur." Yes, torture. "Very heinous ('hee-ness') things man does to man," Abdul said, looking at his feet. And added, "For greed." Indeed.

Abdul was filled with curiosity about the world beyond the shores of Zanzibar; he had taught himself English by listening to the BBC News that came on twice a day. He and my son Sam had hit it off during the day. As we walked to the car, Adbul asked Sam why Donald Trump hated Muslims. "What does he think we are? Why does he say those things?" Sam shrugged, looking down at his own feet now, embarrassed, and then said, "He just makes stories and stuff up" and added, "and he's crazy." We all nodded and repeated together, "Yes, he's crazy."

I grew up in a house of many coexisting truths and many lies, much like every home and every family, everywhere. And as in every other case, truths were transmuted into lies and vice versa. But I was fortunate to have a background of mixed national origins and social classes and religions. The gift of being forced to struggle consciously with multiple and sometimes conflicting identities and truths from an early age is that sense of slight unease that causes us to pause, rather than reflexively accept any prepackaged narrative of our identity. It invites us to examine more closely the stories we tell ourselves and others—in private spaces, from generation to generation, and as societies—to shape the boundaries of normality and deviance, and justify policies and political discourse. These are the stories that become the invisible scaffolding that contains our personal narratives, as well as socio-legal and development paradigms, defining both our knowledge and humanity in the process.

As human beings, our responses to facts, events, and conditions are uniquely conditioned by our beliefs about what things mean—which is a function of history, origins, values, law, and the like—and thus fundamentally about the stories that we choose to believe. The slave trade justified its nefarious commerce based on a story about who was (and was not) human. Colonialism justified its economic exploitation based upon a narrative of what deities and cultures—and people who looked and acted a certain way—were "civilized" as opposed to "barbaric." Nazi atrocities were based on another racialist story about the need to protect the Aryan population from subhuman Jews, Roma, nonheteroconforming individuals and persons with intellectual disabilities, among others. Throughout history, elites—from royals to the intelligentsia—have affirmed that they are more capable of creative thought, reasoned argument, and better able to govern than ordinary people. Ethnonationalism is yet another construction of difference based on the lie of ethnic purity and its significance. Of course women have been perpetually socially and legally constructed as *other*, and less than—as fragile virtuous maidens confined for our own protection; dangerous seductresses to be controlled through more brutal means, or deviant lesbians whose lack of sexual attraction to men is seen as imperiling the natural order.

In turn, the development of modern international human rights law, and a system to promote it, was founded on a story about the equal dignity of all people, in all our messy diversity. In many respects, more than the development of legal norms, institutions, and procedures, or new empirical discoveries, the struggle to apply human rights to health invariably involves competing allegories of what it means to be human and why it matters.

CHAPTER 1

Indignation and Injustice

Massive human rights violations involve what Kant deemed "radical evil"—offenses against human dignity so widespread, persistent, and organized that normal moral assessment seems inappropriate.

—*Carlos Santiago Nino*[1]

The family is the basic cell of the government: it is where we are trained to believe that we are human beings or that we are chattel, it is where we are trained to see the sex and race divisions and become callous to injustice even if it is done to ourselves, to accept as biological a full system of authoritarian government.

—*Gloria Steinem*[2]

IN AUGUST 2015, I stood in the cramped attic rooms of what used to be the Naval Mechanics School (ESMA, for its Spanish acronym) which is now a museum and cultural center,[3] listening to the tour guides tell school groups from around Buenos Aires that it was here, and later in the basement, that military doctors delivered the babies of women who were being held by the military dictatorship that ruled Argentina by terror between 1976 and 1983.[4]

The ESMA was the most notorious of the clandestine detention and torture centers used by the Argentine junta. A junior official in Task Force 3.3.2 later recounted that they had adopted a technique the notorious Josef Mengele had used in Nazi Germany: "They put a spoon in the vagina until it touched the fetus. Then they give it 220 [volts]. They shock the fetus."[5] It was also at the ESMA, among other places, that the systematic plan to steal and sell the babies of female prisoners took place. Dozens of young women who were alleged to be subversives gave birth in the ESMA and other detention centers only to have their newborns taken from them. Virtually all of the women who delivered were subsequently murdered, often dropped from planes into the Río de la Plata, which runs between Argentina and Uruguay. The infants were given false birth certificates and, for the most part, adopted by military families.

I became involved in human rights originally because my mother's family is from Argentina, and I was deeply affected by the horrors of the state-sponsored terrorism in Argentina. Claiming to be the defenders of "tradition, family, and property," the military categorized all opposition as subversive, which had to be eradicated to restore a nostalgic notion of what Argentina had been in a mythical past. Establishing a polarity between defenders of "law and order"—an elite class structure and a "natural order" of the traditional patriarchal family, on the one hand—and the "dangerous" uncontrolled masses and unregulated sexual desires, on the other, has been used not just in Argentina but, as we will see in these pages, in many contexts to mobilize reactionary impulses over time.

However, the military took their fundamentalist economic and social visions to a hideously violent extreme. Quickly the junta became notorious for the atrocities it committed, including abduction by death squads that trolled the streets in unmarked cars, torture, mass murder, and the estimated forced disappearance of as many as 30,000 Argentines—many of whom had been imprisoned and tortured in clandestine centers, such as the ESMA.[6]

On that cold, rainy day in 2015, I was a mother, standing alongside my teenage sons in that attic, watching their faces as they read the letters that these women had written to their families about their deliveries just before they were murdered. I left the cramped room hurriedly and went to the stairwell, fighting back simultaneous urges to sob and to throw up.

The genesis for this book was in no small way driven by the revelations that flowed from those twin impulses. That is, I set out not only to document evolving understandings and responses to the massive, widespread, persistent violations of dignity around our world that occur simply because people are desperately poor, or women, or come from disadvantaged minorities, or all of the above. I also set out to explore what factors are required for these outrages to elicit the stomach churning quality of profound injustice rather than merely be lamented as misfortune.

In the ESMA case, it is impossible to not be revolted by this ultimate embodied injustice of reducing women's bodies to reproductive instruments by their oppressors, completely erasing their humanity and dignity. It is readily apparent that the patriarchal values and gender subordination that the dictatorship openly called for played out in the institutionalized domination and violation of real women's bodies. And at a human level it is unimaginable not to empathize with the pain of delivering a baby under those circumstances, only to be wrenched away from one's newborn child in that manner.

Yet, what is equally important for understanding different responses to the widespread degradation of dignity we will discuss in these pages is that the harms people suffered under the Argentine dictatorship, including pregnant women in the ESMA and elsewhere, were clearly organized and directly committed by state agents. Indeed it was in part because of indignation spurred by what the Argentine junta did to pregnant women, as well as others, that the world community was galvanized around the human rights abuses of the military in Argentina and the whole Southern Cone of Latin America, which was overtaken by brutal dictatorships. As, since the 1970's, the responsibility for the injustices we will discuss in these pages becomes more diffuse and complex, deploying rights claims and formulating transformative remedies also has had to shift, and must continue to do so.

Although this account really begins in the 1970's when human rights arguably became the dominant language of human emancipation, it is important from the beginning to set out the conceptual foundations and legitimacy of international human rights law, as well as some of the limitations embedded in that conceptualization. Further, the postwar multilateralism on which human rights was based also included an economic multilateralism of the Bretton Woods institutions. Civil and political (CP) rights—e.g., stopping those violations that the military junta in Argentina had committed—were privileged by the West during the Cold War. The term *human rights violation* was not yet applied to the clandestine abuse of women and children that goes on behind closed doors in private spaces every day of the week in every country in the world. As a result of the marginalization of economic, social, and cultural (ESC) rights by the West, nor was the term used to describe a lack of access to public health conditions or health care across the globe, or other entitlements.

It was also in the 1970's that the scientific advancements of the 1960's regarding contraception became widespread. Social and legal mobilizations to obtain access to these advances began to erode the inextricable identification of "'woman as womb,'" as Simone de Beauvoir had described it earlier,[7] and therefore to create space between the biological fact of sex, on the one hand, and the meaning and power dynamics involved in gendering identity on the other. The early advances of the women's movements around the world also made visible connections between equality and control over women's bodies as fundamental to their life plans and dignity. In 1979, the UN Convention on the Elimination of All Forms of Discrimination against Women (CEDAW) was promulgated. It was also in the 1970's that two leading abortion cases, in the US and West Germany, charted very different courses for one of the most contentious issues in health rights.

The Beginnings and Rise of Modern Human Rights: Context, Concepts, Process

Multilateralism

It is impossible to separate the international human rights enterprise from the Janus-headed aspirations and concepts that spawned it. In the first place, the creation of the United Nations was aimed at avoiding the catastrophe of another Holocaust and the breakdown of peace, democracy, and security that World War II had entailed. Yet, from its inception, international human rights law also contained within it the Utopian notion of a world of equal dignity, with the elusive promise of an international order necessary to sustain it. It also represented a faith in multilateralism—rule-making through international organizations. The primary organization to project this vision in human rights was, of course, the United Nations, which took the place of the much weaker and failed League of Nations.

However, the larger postwar vision of multilateralism that would secure a lasting peace within and between nations included economic commerce, and multilateralism was equally important in the original design of the "Bretton Woods institutions": the International Monetary Fund, the World Bank,[8] and shortly thereafter, the General Agreement on Tariffs and Trade (GATT), which, although not formally institutionalized, maintained a small secretariat in Geneva.[9] Thus, from the outset in the postwar order, there was a division between political multilateralism and economic multilateralism. In retrospect, the rule-making and rule-enforcing authority of the Bretton Woods institutions would come to legitimate global inequalities in power in a way that the naked brutality of colonialism could no longer effectively achieve. Throughout these pages, we shall see efforts to reinforce mutual aspirations in human rights and development, as well as evolving conflicts between the two multilateral regimes.

Dignity and Rights

The Universal Declaration of Human Rights reflects manifold philosophical, cultural, and other influences, but the central notion of rights emerges from a liberal philosophical tradition. In this paradigm, the capacity for reason and conscience enables dignity and gives each human life distinctive moral value. Thus, human beings are not merely instrumental to larger social goals, nor are mere containers of "utility," however defined. This fundamental idea of what being human means distinguishes the human rights field from conventional public health and mainstream economics, which are deeply influenced by utilitarian, or consequentialist, values, as we shall see throughout this book.

The liberal philosopher Immanuel Kant emphasized the intrinsic and incommensurable value of dignity: "Everything has either a price or a dignity. Whatever has a price can be replaced by [an] equivalent; on the other hand, whatever ... admits of no equivalent, has a dignity."[10] Kant went on to note that this quality of having incommensurable intrinsic worth makes those with dignity ends in themselves, while those things that have a price only have relative worth. Thus, when we understand health as a right because it is essential to people's dignity, it follows that public health and health care cannot merely be allocated by price as any other good in a market.

Moreover, our own dignity is bound up in a mutual recognition of others' dignity and treating each other not as means but ends. This web of mutuality might be articulated in many ways, in reference to our myriad dimensions of identity. The African-American feminist Audre Lorde stated it as "I am not free while any woman is unfree, even when her shackles are very different from my own."[11] In turn, the legal philosopher, Ronald Dworkin, underscores the obligation *to ourselves* that flows from this understanding of being human: "It matters that we live up to our freedom as much that we have it. Freedom of conscience presupposes a personal responsibility of reflection, and it loses much of its meaning when that responsibility is ignored."[12]

The imperative of dignity does not require unfettered autonomy or mean that people's interests can never be negatively affected. However, fundamental rights should not be overridden by an ordinary policy goal, whether economic, such as stemming inflation, or demographic, such as increasing/decreasing population growth. The exercise of rights is bounded by others' exercise of rights. Thus, acknowledging a right to health as intimately connected to dignity does not mean that we have a right to claim any existing medical treatment regardless of cost, including opportunity costs to others. I will argue throughout this book that treating health as a right requires, first, addressing the inextricable connections between health and broader social policy and, second, adopting decisions within the health system with respect to financing, priority setting, and regulation/oversight in a manner that takes seriously the moral consideration to which each human being is entitled.

Universality and Legitimacy in International Law

In the aftermath of World War II, where manifestly unjust national laws had facilitated the Holocaust, a critical mass of scholars and policymakers believed that a supranational rules-based order was necessary to protect all people's dignity, as well as international peace and security. The founding document of international human rights law, the Universal Declaration of Human Rights (UDHR), which contained both civil liberties and economic, social, and cultural rights, was promulgated without dissent by the United Nations General Assembly in 1948 as a "common standard for all humanity." The nature of a body of "higher law" that aspires to enshrine a universal vision of justice is subject to debate.

The Argentine legal theorist Carlos Nino has argued that historically the notion of depoliticizing law began with the French Declaration of the Rights of Man and Citizen, where rights emanating from popular will were to be separated from the corroded law of the Ancien Régime, and this new secular but superior law could be infallibly interpreted through human reason. Thus began a tradition of attempting to isolate law from politics, which led to what we generally call "positivism" and "formalism" in different contexts.[13] Despite what we know about the historical context of the UDHR, as well as the peculiarities of a supranational set of norms, there have similarly been tendencies to treat international human rights law as a set of revealed truths, whether as "natural rights" or as positivistic sets of rules.

On the one hand, with claims to universality, and by providing what Sen calls "the view from a critical distance,"[14] this body of international norms has enabled people to see their own laws and situations as neither just nor inevitable, and it was arguably in the 1970's that oppressed groups throughout the world found moral agency in the idiom of universal human rights. On the other hand, in my view the only way to understand the achievements and challenges to deploying health and ESC rights since the 1970's in particular is by analyzing the political contestation and power dynamics involved in the evolving interpretations at both the international level and in the localization of the meanings of these rights in different countries.

But let's start at the beginning. Considering the normative grounding of a universal set of human rights from the outset will help us evaluate later developments. Many rights recognized in the UDHR were disregarded in practice within the countries represented in the negotiations, including racial equality in the United States. Representation of sub-Saharan Africa, still struggling under colonialism, was notably missing—and the drafters were virtually all men.

Nevertheless, the UDHR did bring together leading jurists and thinkers from European, Latin American, North American, Islamic, Jewish, and Chinese philosophical, cultural, and legal traditions to establish a set of rights that would be valued across cultural contexts.

Prominent critics of a universal code of rights, such as Alasdair MacIntyre, argued that without fundamental agreement about cultural values, abstract principles could not sufficiently guide state practice and were open to both reinterpretation and outright rejection.[15] Jacques Maritain, the French philosopher who had played a central role in the drafting of the UDHR, was aware that it was difficult to conceive of a global agreement among people from different cultures and civilizations, spiritual families, and schools of thought.[16] But Maritain argued that the aim was not to agree on an affirmation of "the same conception of the world, man, and knowledge, but on the affirmation of the same set of convictions concerning action. This is doubtless very little. . . . It is, however, enough to undertake a great work."[17]

Thus, philosophically, the UDHR was arguably based on what the liberal philosopher John Rawls referred to as an "overlapping consensus" among many schools of thought.[18] Evidence of shared concepts of human dignity and equality can be found in sources from Confucianism and Islam, to Christian teachings and Enlightenment liberalism, to the Mexican Constitution of 1917, to Franklin Roosevelt's 1941 "Four Freedoms" speech. That is, as suggested by Maritain, precisely by refraining from disputes over fundamental arguments regarding religious and philosophical conceptions of justice, an overlapping consensus on a set of rights as basic tools for dignity and equality could be reached, even when the grounds of this support may have differed.

In social choice theory, the UDHR might also be called an incompletely theorized agreement (ITA). Cass Sunstein applied the concept of an ITA to show how US judicial decisions function to establish constitutional rules even in the face of profound disagreements.[19] Indeed, perhaps the UDHR was the archetypical ITA, given the daunting social pluralism that needed to be overcome to arrive at one universal declaration. To illustrate how an ITA works, Sunstein notes that people who accept a general principle—e.g., murder is wrong—need not agree on what this principle entails in particular cases, such as abortion or euthanasia.[20] Thus, for example, the "right to life" did not have to specify the reasons for valuing life or metaphysical understandings at the time the UDHR was agreed upon.

John Tobin and Jennifer Prah Ruger have applied these ideas of an ITA in relation to health rights specifically.[21] Ruger notes that the ITA approach "is well suited to human goods that are plural and ambiguous" as it allows for different but converging paths to agreement. "In matters of public philosophy concerning inherently plural and indistinct concepts, and in dealing with collective choice involving numerous views and disagreements, ITA can help bring participants in a public policy and human rights discussion to agreement on certain specific outcomes."[22]

As Amartya Sen argues, the fact that an agreement, such as the UDHR, is incompletely theorized does not reduce its merit, but it does point to a necessary process of deliberation on these norms in order to refine the particular agreements and reach specific outcomes.[23] In respect of health rights, this underscores the importance of the process of negotiating the contours of the right to health in light of how it functions in diverse people's lives, in specific constitutional, historical, and social contexts.

Human Rights as Politics: The Cold War and Beyond

Philip Alston has noted that the inclusion of both civil and political (CP) and economic, social, and cultural (ESC) rights on an equal footing in the UDHR "reflects a hard-fought ideological and political compromise ... between capitalist and communist approaches in the 1940s."[24] However, this "glue" arguably did not "hold the package together" in political terms during the Cold War, when the primacy of CP rights was championed in the West, and ESC rights were championed by the former Soviet bloc and others.

The 1970's: Context for the Ascendancy of Rights

According to the legal historian Samuel Moyn, it was in the 1970's that we saw "the ideological ascendancy of human rights."[25] Against the backdrop of decolonization, the civil rights movement in the United States, the rise of military dictatorships across much of Latin America, and the glaring failures of the Soviet Union, violations of individual rights were elevated in the global order, and the idea of human rights as a "common standard of achievement" for all peoples and all nations, which was set out in the Universal Declaration of Human Rights took hold.

There were important early efforts to connect the promotion of human rights and a more egalitarian global order. For example, dependency theories focused on the effects of historically contingent power dynamics between countries in the "center" such as the US and Western Europe and countries in the "periphery."[26] Moreover, this was not merely an issue confined to scholarship. In 1964, the UN Conference on Trade and Development (UNCTAD) had been created as a forum to conduct research and advance a greater basis of equality of exchange between nations.

There was equally recognition both by some human rights scholars and at policy level of the need to connect the two worlds. In 1968, the first World Conference on Human Rights, held in Tehran, declared that "the achievement of lasting progress in the implementation of human rights is dependent on sound and effective national and international policies of economic and social development."[27]

A coalition of representatives from postcolonial states and the nonaligned movement were arguing at the time for a New International Economic Order (NIEO), which aimed to reduce inequalities among nations.[28] NIEO was announced in a special session of the United Nations in 1974; later that year the UN set out a "Charter on the Economic Rights and Duties of States."[29] However, anticolonial and egalitarian aspirations embedded in the NIEO were espoused by some governments that were decidedly authoritarian. When, in 1977, the UN Commission for Human Rights called for a report on the "right to development,"[30] it provided encouragement for countries in the global South to argue for expanding human rights to include issues of international development. At the same time, there was an obvious conceptual tension in how individual rights coexisted with states' claims to self-determination in the eventual non-binding UN "Declaration on a Right to Development."[31]

Moreover, disillusionment with revolutionary politics and linkages between Marxism and the Gulag among left-leaning intellectuals in the West grew more prominent in the 1970's.[32] For example, it was after the crushing of democratization hopes in the Prague Spring in 1968 that the "new philosophy" took the French intellectual and political worlds by storm and, in turn, spread. By the late 1970's, many of these thinkers, including Michel Foucault, had come to question the premises of emancipation through revolution, which concentrated solely on the question of political sovereignty and not on the many other faces of a more continuous "disciplining" power that Foucault asserted acted through technologies and knowledge to both control our bodies and identity, and structure our field of action, and which was particularly relevant to thinking about health and the possibility of health rights.[33]

Another important thread to understanding this shift is that the postwar years into the 1970's had also been an era of prosperity, which saw unprecedented growth, high employment levels, and a dramatic rise in living standards among the working class in many countries, especially in the economic North. The world's economy had grown at approximately 3% per capita per year between 1950 and 1973.[34] In the United States, for example, the poverty rate declined to its lowest point—11%—in 1973. Income tax was progressive; the top marginal rate was 88% in 1942, 91% from 1951 to 1963, and above 70% until 1981. Economic growth and diminished inequality undoubtedly reduced the perceived urgency of the class struggle.[35]

Different groups began clamoring for inclusion within societies and a right to their identity—including women and racial and sexual minorities—not just an end to class exploitation. It was a decade of catharsis and confrontation, from the emergence of LGBTQ movements to women's liberation. Not surprisingly there were also backlashes to the sweeping social movements that threatened to disrupt the very core of patriarchal society. Antimodernist religious groups—in democracies as well as dictatorships such as Argentina—constructed imaginary monsters in response to this social and domestic dislocation. For example, women's unrestrained desires were associated with moral decline; thus regulating them became an integral, if tacit, aspect of efforts to control women's bodies through law.[36] We will see that dynamics of mobilization and countermobilization have characterized fights for sexual and reproductive rights since the 1970's for heterosexual women and LGBTQ populations.

In 1979, as the UN Convention on the Elimination of All Forms of Discrimination against Women was promulgated, and the Argentine dictatorship was proclaiming its defense of Western Christian values, the Shah of Iran was toppled by a revolution that swept Ayatollah Khomeini's particular brand of fundamentalist Islam into power.[37] Across religions and regions, all of these fundamentalisms traded in dogmas regarding women's essential roles in the family and reproduction.

In short, it was in this world that protecting the rule of law and personal freedoms for women and a multitude of oppressed groups came to seem more than just a sleight of hand as Marxist critics of liberalism and legalism had long asserted.

Human Rights and the Liberal State: Conceptualizations and Challenges

During the Cold War, CP rights were separated from ESC rights not only ideologically but also legally, being drafted into two separate treaties—the International Covenant on Civil and Political Rights (ICCPR) and the International Covenant on Economic, Social and Cultural Rights (ICESCR), which both entered into force in 1976. Largely aligned with political interests of Western Europe and the United States, the dominant human rights paradigm was inextricably tied to the traditional liberal state and the understanding of how power is exercised that it entails.

The conventional canon of civil and political rights, based on an understanding of the functions of the traditional 19th-century liberal state, might be divided into the following categories: (1) protection of individual physical integrity, including provisions against torture, arbitrary detention, and arbitrary deprivation of life; (2) procedural fairness when a person is deprived of liberty, such as due process of law, conditions of imprisonment, etc.; (3) formal legal equality or equal protection of the law based on race, gender, etc.; (4) freedoms of conscience, expression, association, political activity, and assembly; and (5) freedom of political participation.[38] In the traditional liberal state, the subjects of rights were assumed to be equal, autonomous individuals (property-owning, heterosexual men), who were free to pursue their own notions of "the good" in private, to be distinguished from protections for the limited set of rights described above. These protections were conceived as negative liberties based on what the state could potentially do *to* individuals.

These rights protections in turn were based upon a notion of power as domination over, "getting what one wants," whereby A has power over B if A can make B produce a certain outcome, even against her will[39]—e.g., restrain movement, association, speech, the exercise of conscience, or forcefully take property away. The archetypical example is torture by state agents, as in the ESMA. Thus, traditional liberal views of the way in which rights serve to regulate power is by protecting against such domination.

That the edifice of international human rights has largely been built upon this quite narrow conception of regulation of power within the liberal state has had substantial implications—from the sets of rights recognized to the conceptualization of those rights, including CP rights. For example, political participation has largely been conceived of as episodic voting for political representatives, who in turn are delegated responsibility to decide on a wide array of complex issues. This need not be the case. In a notion of democracy that emphasizes a more robust deliberation and set of social practices, political participation could be understood to be a positive right, which is, as other rights are, "dependent for [its] normative force on the engagement and commitment of an active citizen body."[40] Analogously, realizing the right to health in particular, given its inherently indeterminate and evolving borders, depends not just on freedom from interference in choices and access to a preset menu of interventions set by technocrats.

Rather, it requires active *will-formation* in Habermas' term[41]—ongoing collective deliberation about what we owe to each other as diverse human beings, with equal dignity, in light of constant technological progress and epidemiological and demographic change.

The ethicist Norman Daniels notes that because reasonable people can disagree on how to allocate resources for population health, the task of justice is to create a choice situation that is procedurally fair to all, where the outcome in the allocation of resources is seen as fair because the process for deliberation is seen as fair.[42] I agree, and we will come back to the importance of procedural justice in health time and again. However, as this and every other choice situation occurs in an inexorably political space, the struggle for health rights has required continually expanding the subjects who get to participate in decision-making processes regarding health, what issues get considered and decided, in accordance with which overt or hidden rules.

The traditional liberal conceptualization of rights is further ill-suited to the full realization of health rights because it prescribes a remedy that re-establishes a *status quo ante*. For example, if a person is arbitrarily detained, or an election is stolen, remedies entail restitution, compensation, and guarantees of nonrepetition. We have seen over these three decades that claiming health rights can seek remedies for regulatory and compliance failures aimed at re-establishing a *status quo ante*. Also, international law has been used to fill gaps in the oversight of national health systems. We have also seen uses of international law to remedy impunity at national levels. Nonetheless, the broader struggle to advance social and gender equality in health has required constant efforts to destabilize and transform the status quo and the legal frameworks that sustain it.

Situating the Right to Health under International Law

Due to the politics of the Cold War, ESC rights, such as health, were marginalized in both the normative architecture of international human rights and the practice of the mainstream international human rights movement/community. The right to health was defined as a social right under international law and included in Article 12 of the International Covenant on Economic, Social and Cultural Rights (ICESCR).

There are numerous differences between the phrasings of the International Covenant on Civil and Political Rights (ICCPR) and the ICESCR. For example, Article 12(1) of the ICESCR states not that "everyone has a right to" health (as the rights in the ICCPR are framed), but that "States Parties recognize the right of everyone to the enjoyment of the highest attainable standard of physical and mental health."[43] This phrasing also differed from the definition of health as a "complete state of physical, mental and social well-being" which had been set out in the WHO preamble.[44]

Indeed, the ICESCR does not actually define health per se but in Article 12(2) sets out steps to be taken "to achieve the full realization of this right" including: "(a) reduction of the stillbirth-rate and of infant mortality and [provision for] healthy development of the child; (b) improvement of ... environmental and industrial hygiene; (c) prevention, treatment and control of epidemic, endemic, occupational and other diseases; and (d) [creating] "conditions which would assure to all medical service and medical attention in the event of sickness."[45] While the ICCPR requires states to realize CP rights immediately, Article 2 of the ICESCR set out that each State party "undertakes to take steps, individually and through international assistance and co-operation, especially economic and technical, *to the maximum of its available resources*, with a view to *achieving progressively* the full realization of the rights recognized in the present Covenant by all appropriate means, including particularly the adoption of legislative measures"[46] (emphasis mine).

In practice, these differences were long used to justify indefinite postponement of implementation of ESC rights by states, which is clearly unacceptable under international law. Scholarship emphasizing that the language differences were inserted to distinguish the "real" legal nature of CP rights and the programmatic nature of ESC rights inadvertently or deliberately legitimated this view. Nonetheless, this need not be the way we think about health, or indeed other ESC rights. There is another plausible manner to interpret "progressive achievement" based both on the *travaux preparatoires* for the ICESCR and purposive interpretation in light of the continually evolving nature of the right to health. That is, in the words of the Danish representative reflecting views similar to other state delegates at the time, "[progressive achievement] introduced a dynamic element, indicating that no final fixed goal had been set ... since the essence of progress was continuity."[47] Indeed, if progressive achievement were not taken as a fixed path to a set destination, we might reorient the interpretation of health rights to focus more on the necessary conditions for the choice situations, to which Daniels refers, to function continuously and fairly. This approach in no way denies the need for continuous improvement or the need to address disparities between countries or international cooperation and assistance, but it makes clear that even the most advanced countries require dynamic efforts to continually realizing the right to health.

The language "international assistance and co-operation," was also not included in the ICCPR. In conjunction with the language of "maximum available resources," these framings have given rise to many theories about how limitations based on resources would affect not just the reality but the legal standard in, for example, Cameroon very differently from Canada. In practice, of course wealth disparities and levels of development also affect CP rights. Nevertheless, some health rights scholars have attempted to construct specific levels of affirmative international assistance obligations based on this language and other political commitments.[48] In my view, such an approach may reinforce debunked distinctions between CP and ESC rights, as well as power imbalances in the global political economy. By contrast, as I argue in later chapters, greater promise for achieving greater global health (and social) justice in the world order lies in addressing deepening economic governance and constructing norms to deter negative actions by states in the economic North directly, through their transnational corporations and through multilateral institutions.

The two sets of rights were treated distinctly not just in international law, but also in practice by an international human rights advocacy community dominated by northern nongovernmental organizations (NGOs). Aryeh Neier, who played an influential role in shaping the international human rights movement as "apolitical" and "classless," first as founding director of Human Rights Watch in 1978 and later as president of the Open Society Foundation, long argued that ESC rights were essentially political questions, not suited to judicial decision-making and, in turn, emphasizing the connection between rights and juridification, not *real* rights.[49] Although barriers to justiciability have been eroded in international and constitutional law in many settings,[50] this narrow view of human rights that prevailed in the 1970's continues to dominate many official political as well as legal discourses today. At the same time, recent critiques of human rights writ large too often take this stance from prominent "international" nongovernmental organizations as synonymous with the much more diverse global human rights community.[51]

The Evolution of International Human Rights: Women's Rights

What Simone de Beauvoir first referred to as women's "lived realities" have challenged an array of notions in traditional liberal thought.[52] Other feminists have also suggested our bodies are not so much autonomous entities as situations.[53] In the most extreme example, women's bodies become evidence in sexual violence cases. In our daily lives, the way women appear—from the clothes and makeup we wear to the obvious visibility of pregnant bodies—was (and still is) inextricably wrapped up with public judgments of virtue and worth, in a way that male identities largely are not. Rights in conventional liberalism are generally thought to regulate "intersubjective" conduct—e.g., disputes between property-holders, or when freedom of speech becomes interference with others' rights. But for women, this is especially complicated. Just by wearing a short skirt or going topless, a woman can be construed as engaging in *intersubjective conduct* and perhaps inciting sexual harassment or assault. Moreover, the relationship between a woman and the embryo growing inside of her body has been treated as intersubjective and therefore subject to regulation even by criminal law, that most blunt of legal controls.

The rigid dichotomy between public and private realms in the traditional liberal state also excluded many of the most pressing issues in women's lived realities from being considered as questions of justice and rights at the time.[54] In the 1970's, "public" and "private" appeared as two extremes in international law. Actions by state actors under a dictatorship—as in the torture and disappearances in Argentina—were recognized as human rights violations. By contrast, physical and sexual violence in the private domain of the home was not considered, nor discussed publicly, as an issue of equal dignity.

Moreover, even when, in the early 1990's, human rights law and constitutional law began to acknowledge that human dignity is intrinsically related to nondependence—"no citizen shall ever be wealthy enough to buy another, and none poor enough to be forced to sell himself," according to Rousseau[55]—they did not include women's lived realities. Sexual divisions of labor and power are intertwined and reinforce each other. When men are breadwinners in the public labor market and women are caregivers in the private domestic space, it belies the nondependence to be able to pursue one's life plans, including leaving a certain job—if that job is wife and mother. For women, sex work is criminalized in many societies because women are not allowed to use their sexual labor for financial independence. At the same time, de facto transactional sex in loveless and even abusive unions around the world is justified as part of the traditional family; indeed, marital rape is still not typified as a crime in many settings. Thus, addressing women's diverse needs for protection and agency across spheres has required creatively reinterpreting the canon of constitutional and international human rights law over these years.[56]

However, it was in the 1970's that women's lived realities were beginning to change as a result of women's liberation movements in countries around the world and the advent of scientific progress, which together offered the possibility of emancipation from preset social roles.

Convention on the Elimination of All Forms of Discrimination against Women: The Emergence of New Frameworks

In the 1960's and 70's, as mentioned above, women began seeking increasing freedom from oppressive gender roles and the control of their bodies, desire, and lives, through social and legal mobilization. In December 1975, the UN Secretary-General announced that 1976–1985 would be known as the "UN Decade for Women," to advance the equal rights of women.[57] In 1979, the concerted organizing of women's movements around the world led to the promulgation of the Convention on the Elimination of All Forms of Discrimination against Women (CEDAW). CEDAW, the first human rights treaty to enshrine women's issues relating to discrimination in private as well as public spheres, contributed to an understanding of the need for substantive as well as formal equality and illuminated the lack of data on discrimination against women.

Bridging the Public-Private Divide

For the first time, a binding international treaty acknowledged the role of the state in setting the parameters for behavior across public and private spheres, political and sociocultural domains. For example, Article 5 called on states parties to "modify the social and cultural patterns of conduct of men and women, with a view to achieving the elimination of prejudices and harmful traditional practices which are based on . . . stereotyped roles for men and women."[58] In the late 1970's this language was groundbreaking for international law; the patriarchal family and traditional gender roles were not only widespread, but vigorously defended by conservative regimes from the military in Argentina to the new revolutionary government in Iran, and largely taken for granted in public discourses around the world. Breaking down "stereotyped" roles for men and women also opened the door to integrating into international law understandings of "gender" as a social construct based upon custom and power relations as much as biological sex.

Formal and Substantive Equality

Some feminist scholars have critiqued CEDAW for trying to fit women into a male model (the liberal inclusion model) rather than focusing on "structural biases that prevented women's assimilation."[59] That is no doubt true in hindsight, as is the exotification of non-Western culture in the CEDAW Committee's interpretation of harmful traditional practices. Nonetheless, CEDAW played a fundamental role in the iterative reformation of the architecture of international human rights law.

CEDAW began to enlarge our understanding of women's need for not just formal but substantive equality. Formal equality seeks to eradicate arbitrary legal differentiation, which had often excluded women from both many forms of formal employment *and* the public deliberative arena.[60] A quintessential example of women's exclusion from civic space was not allowing them to sit on juries in all fifty states in the US until 1973; this required changing the legal (and social) conceptualization of women *as people* who should be treated as equal members of a community of peers, able to participate in deliberations based on rational arguments.[61]

Yet formal equality often ignores the sociopolitical contexts that underpin actual, lived realities, as noted above. Granting substantive equality requires legislative, regulatory, and institutional measures that enable the effective enjoyment of rights by diverse women on an equal footing with men, across both economic and political realms as well as private, familial spheres. For example, in terms of health care, CEDAW stipulates that women's differential reproductive and other health needs need to be considered in policy and programs in order for them to fully enjoy meaningful equality in health rights with men.[62] Thus the treaty recognized that differential obligations flow to achieve substantive equality for women, which would become theorized far more over coming decades, in constitutional law and in general comments from treaty monitoring bodies, including General Comment 20 from the CESCR.[63]

Need for Empirical Data

Although women faced both formal and substantive discrimination in every country of the world when CEDAW was promulgated, there was virtually no data available to show how bad things were. Indeed, even as late as 1991, a report by the UN entitled "The World's Women 1970–1990: Trends and Statistics" called for data on domestic violence, which it described as "unmeasured but almost certainly very extensive."[64] Without the most basic empirical information about the discrimination that different groups of women faced, it proved difficult, if not impossible, to mobilize the political branches of government to address issues conceptualized in CEDAW. It was not until 1994, for example, that the United States passed the Violence Against Women Act,[65] by which time a global mobilization had occurred.

In women's health the situation was equally stark. In the 1970's women's health was measured in terms of fertility and treated largely as an appendage to child health. It would take another decade before evidence began to accumulate to illustrate that women's health needs to survive pregnancy and childbirth were entirely different from those needed for babies' survival. But the normative notion enshrined in CEDAW and circulating in advocacy and academic circles that women required different health care was pivotal to creating the urgency around data collection and practical progress in the 1980's and beyond.

The Ambivalent Relation between Biomedical Innovation and Women's Liberation

If CEDAW helped to generate urgency for collecting empirical data on women, scientific innovations were critical to the social and political movements for women's liberation generally. The oral contraception pill had been approved in many countries in Europe and in the United States in the 1960's, and by the early to mid-1970's tens of millions of women around the world were using oral contraception, which was a game changer.[66] In 1969, the UN Fund for Population Activities (now the UN Population Fund, UNFPA) had been created, and the era of state-sponsored family planning programs began.[67] Access to oral and other forms of woman-controlled contraception unquestionably advanced women's reproductive autonomy and sexual agency in the 1970's.

Nonetheless, the entanglement of contraception with state control of women's fertility is a theme that we will see played out in synergy with colonialist impulses in global health throughout this story and one that continues to this day. Indeed, it is not possible to understand the struggle for women's health rights without understanding the ambivalent relationship between women's health and androcentric biomedicine, which has both freed women from traditional roles and been used time and again to regulate and "discipline" diverse women's bodies.[68]

In the 1970's, when doctors were virtually all male and female patients were denied the most basic autonomy as well as information, women's health movements took on the mission of educating women about their bodies. These were feminists who saw the connections in their own lives and those of others between controlling, and enjoying, their physical bodies—and their dignity. The Boston Women's Health Book Collective's iconic *Our Bodies, Ourselves*—which has been translated into half a dozen languages—explained clearly issues of sexuality and reproduction (including abortion, even before it was legal) in political, cultural, and social context.[69]

The same phenomenon of connecting the personal and political was occurring throughout the world but took on different issues in the global North than in the South. Women's movements in much of the global South were inextricably tied to broader social movements as women played distinctive roles in health care and social provision, ranging from traditional healers and birth attendants in rural communities to managers of "food kitchens" (*comedores populares*) in periurban slums. In parts of Latin America, women's movements were shaped by resistance to authoritarian regimes, and many were critical in fighting for democracy. For example, in Brazil, women's struggles included not just contraception or reproductive agency, but fighting for reforms to enable affordable and nondiscriminatory access to basic housing and childcare, as well as the universal health system ushered in after the military dictatorship ended.[70]

Abortion: Courts, Politics, and Women's Equality

Contraception can fail, is often unavailable, or is not negotiable with male partners or predators. Pregnancy is too often the result not of loving creation but of brutal subordination.[71] Abortion therefore entails a right to security from the unwanted appropriation of a woman's own body—a kind of imposed slavery[72]— and the often irreparable damage to a girl's or woman's life plans from a forced pregnancy, or even maternal death when abortion is performed under unsafe conditions.[73] Yet, the issue of abortion also illustrates the complexity of using rights to secure women's full equality across public and private domains—not just to protect girls and women from the life-changing consequences of predation, but also to enable us to experience sexual pleasure without the implications of procreation, which men are free to take for granted.[74]

Legislatures were not inclined to pass laws liberalizing abortion at the time, and women then turned to courts as more favorable opportunity structures. The two leading early cases on abortion are: *Roe v. Wade* in the US Supreme Court in 1973 and *BVerfGE 39,1—Abortion I* from the Federal Constitutional Court of (West) Germany in 1975. In *Roe*, the US Supreme Court ruled that a right to privacy under the Due Process Clause of the 14th Amendment included a woman's decision to have an abortion, but finding that the state's interests in preserving life became stronger over the course of a pregnancy, the court linked the right to terminate a pregnancy to fetal viability.[75] Some prominent legal scholars, such as Ronald Dworkin, have argued that what was really at stake was "whether state legislatures have the constitutional power to decide which intrinsic values all citizens must respect, and how [if so, they] may prohibit abortion on that ground."[76] Responding to that question would have entailed complex public deliberations about grounds for abortion in theory and practice, the legitimate reasons we should accept as diverse people for when women should be entitled to abortions, and the limits to delegating decision-making authority to elected representatives regarding the contours of women's legal obligations to allow their bodies to be used to support a potential life.

But those were not the conversations to be had in the United States in the 1970's nor largely to date. The biological and often religious debate about when life begins and in turn the (im)morality of women who would choose not to be mothers, conveniently lent itself to reductionist rhetoric and polarization for politicians and religious leaders alike, and does to this day.[77] Even when resulting in logical and legal incoherence—such as allowing for embryos (i.e., "people") outside of women's bodies in labs to be destroyed—these tropes have been deployed by those seeking to curtail abortion rights to provide *the only* acceptable answer: to stop reasoned discussion, not foster it. Further, as Thomas Keck has written, the political backlash to the *Roe* decision shaped the history of not just abortion wars but party configurations and debates about the relative validity of vindicating rights through courts or through legislatures in decades to come in the United States[78]—and elsewhere as well.

The history of abortion jurisprudence illustrates the effects on women's health rights of law reifying the distinctions between the private/personal and public/economic spheres. The *Roe* case followed an earlier case on contraception, *Griswold v. Connecticut* (1965), in which the US Supreme Court established the basis for the right to privacy with respect to certain intimate practices, as a right to "protect[ion] from governmental intrusion,"[79] i.e., a classical notion of rights as shields. However, as many have noted, including Robin West, "Women need the freedom to make reproductive decisions not merely to vindicate the right to be left alone, but often to strengthen their ties to others."[80] Locating abortion rights entirely in the private sphere, as opposed to recognizing what West calls the "web of interlocking, competing and often irreconcilable responsibilities and commitments"[81] faced by women allowed the US Supreme Court in later decisions to preclude state funding for abortion for poor women as well as to place significant restrictions on access to abortion, as long as they did not "unduly burden" the exercise of the right.[82] The structural constraints on accessing abortions—from racial barriers to needs for child care or leave from work to geographic distance and transportation costs, let alone fees—were systematically organized out of the fictional legal narrative that women made these choices in an autonomous vacuum.[83] That, in turn, led to the emergence of a separate discourse and movement for "reproductive justice" in the United States, which perceived rights, and sexual and reproductive health and rights (SRHR) in particular, as overly associated with individualistic "choice."

The trajectory of abortion has been very different in other countries. In *BVerfGE* 39,1 - *Abortion I* (German: *BVerfGE* 39,1—*Schwangerschaftsabbruch I*) in 1975, the Federal Constitutional Court of (West) Germany held that respect for human dignity required criminalization of abortion in all but a few exceptional circumstances called indications (*Indikationen*).[84] This regime of indications included cases where the life or health of the mother would be at risk if she had to carry the child to term[85] and sexual assault.[86] The court specifically rejected the reasoning in *Roe* based on the guarantee of human dignity extending to the unborn, influenced by the limitations on who was considered worthy of dignity in light of the former history of Nazi Germany.[87] However, the court recognized the sui generis condition of pregnancy—a positive obligation of a very intensive nature to care for the future child with her own body. The German court, and later other courts, such as Portugal's Constitutional Court[88] and Chile's Constitutional Court most recently in 2017,[89] found the intensity of that obligation—unmatched by any other—makes the duty to carry a pregnancy to term unenforceable under certain circumstances. The German Court held that prevention of abortion through counseling and provision of social protection would be far better than conceptually separating the woman from the fetus and criminally prosecuting the woman for a termination that fell beyond the indications.[90] With the reunification of Germany in the early 1990's, after abortion had been available on demand in the East, the *Bundestag* significantly loosened restrictions further, and the state publicly funds abortions.[91]

Over the last forty-plus years, abortion battles have been proxies for contestation over the role of courts versus legislatures in defining boundaries between private morality and public policy, international and national law, and the role of women in society. But it was in the 1970's that abortion rights were first articulated by courts in terms of rights. It was also in the 1970's that conservatives seized on the issue, which they perceived as permitting them to claim a moral high ground when they could no longer be openly against equal rights for racial minorities and women generally.

Concluding Reflections

The atrocities committed by the military in Argentina epitomized the use of public power to instrumentalize other human beings—inscribing their bodies and obliterating their agency—to achieve given sociopolitical objectives. But one of the most striking elements of the ESMA when I was there in 2015 was the suffocating intimacy of the abused and the abusers. The concentration camp was located in the officers' club. Throughout the dictatorship, naval officers slept on the first and second floors, while prisoners slept on the third floor and in the attic and were routinely tortured in the basement.

Rear Admiral Rubén Jacinto Chamorro, the director of the ESMA for most of those years, lived with his family in quarters attached to the officers' club.[92] Chamorro's own daughter grew up in the ESMA. She had friends over, who later testified about seeing the moving of people from one section to another. It is unclear what the girl knew at the time, but either a sense of guilt or inability to reconcile her childhood memories with what had happened must have become unbearable, as she later committed suicide. On the other hand, Coca Bazán, a former member of the Montoneros insurgent movement, who had been a prisoner in the ESMA, eventually married Chamorro. After the dictatorship fell, she moved with him to South Africa until his death, when Bazán then reportedly entered an ashram in India.[93]

I thought about how we invariably construct our own and others' personal narratives in relation to political perspectives when in 1986 a classmate from Harvard College and I went to interview José Alfredo Martínez de Hoz, minister of the economy for much of the dictatorship, about the ties between business elites and the Argentine military. Martínez de Hoz would soon be tried for human rights violations he committed during and prior to the military regime, and eventually forced to live out his last years under house arrest.[94]

But on the day we went to see Martínez de Hoz at his posh apartment in the historic Kavanagh building overlooking the Plaza San Martín, that was all yet to happen. The Plaza San Martín is circled by beautiful 19th- and early 20th-century European-style palaces and low buildings, and the art deco style combined with what was in the 1930's the tallest building in Latin America still made the Kavanagh building stand out even fifty years later. The walls of the high-ceilinged room in which we sat were decorated with an astonishing number of heads of large game animals that he himself had killed—elephant, giraffe, zebra, wildebeest, and the like—that all stared out disconcertingly, if not accusingly.

There was a surreal dissonance in that room, and not just because we were surrounded by dead and dismembered bodies of animals, as he served us tea and *alfajores* on imported china.[95] It was hard to square the thin, genteel, elegantly attired man sitting across from us with the monster who had crushed labor movements, organized murders of trade union members, and who had so often been the external face of the brutally repressive regime in Washington and London. Having studied at Cambridge University in England, he clearly assumed, as elites sometimes do, that our shared privileged educations meant we would see the world in much the same ways: we'd see the heads on the wall as evidence of great conquests on his world travels and similarly would accept his narrative of conquering subversion by the masses to enable progress in Argentina. We did not.

In addition to legitimating the dictatorship abroad, Martínez de Hoz did his part in destroying the Argentine economy, instituting wage freezes, which both hurt the working class and drove people into poverty, while rescinding the inheritance tax, which enormously helped the wealthy. Perhaps the most long-lasting effects would be felt from deregulating financial markets and the banking industry, and having the state assume over 100,000,000 USD in debt (in 1970's dollars), triggering effects that very much continue to haunt Argentina today.[96]

I have a telling photograph from the afternoon I left the meeting with Martínez de Hoz of men congregating around benches in the Plaza San Martín—ranging in age perhaps from 50 to 70 years of age, sporting tweed jackets, caps or fedoras, ties or cravats tucked into their cashmere sweaters—and engaged in animated conversation. Looking at the photo today, I am struck by the absence of women in the Plaza that afternoon. Public space was still reserved for men, and when women did come out they sat separately. At the time, however, I had been deeply shaken by the interaction with Martínez de Hoz, and I recall wondering what had *they* done, what roles had these well-heeled men played during those dark years?

The controversial "Punto Final" law was passed later that same year, putting an end to the trials of military leaders, until it was subsequently overturned.[97] The trials of members of the military regime were crucial not solely or even primarily for the punishments perpetrators received. Just as with the Nazis, the atrocities that had been committed in the ESMA and elsewhere were beyond normal moral assessment or human punishment.[98] The trials were essential to engender a broad public reflection on what made the dictatorship possible and to try to overcome the poison to democracy that stems from ingrained mistrust of others—others who share not just park benches and public spaces, but also our social worlds. The trials were also part of a broader project to lay the foundations for a more democratic society, the meaning of which would evolve over time. The post-dictatorship amendments to the Constitution, included not just CP rights but also ESC rights and incorporated international human rights norms at the highest level of Argentine law.

However, at the time, the long-lasting affronts to massive numbers of people's dignity precipitated by the economic policies of the military were not categorized as human rights violations. Nor did the brutal sexual and physical violence against women every day in Argentina and all over the world generate the same moral indignation as revelations of abuse committed directly by the state.

In short, by the 1970's, there had been three trends that had shaped the face of modern human rights and would influence the ongoing struggles to use human rights for social justice. These were distinct but related. First, we see the rise of a less radical, more contained politics of rights that largely accepted the "rules of the game" in the traditional liberal state. These rules included a specific understanding of the exercise of power as well as distinctions between political and economic, and public and private realms, with particular impacts on women's lives. Second, rights inexorably stood for the rule of law, and in turn opened a role for juridification, whereas extralegal or primarily political mobilization had traditionally been seen as the path to social transformation. At the same time, under the cloak of Cold War politics, economic entitlements were excluded from being "real rights" subject to legal enforcement and were converted into social aspirations. Third, the division between the political and economic domains was reinforced by the institutional governance cleavage between the political United Nations and the economic institutions of Bretton Woods at the global level. By the end of the 1970's, a sharp separation between human rights as individual claims against the state, on the one hand, and global economic and development issues, on the other, had been clearly drawn, despite some efforts to link them.

Yet even as the international human rights framework may have constrained aspirations for social change, human rights activists quickly began to tinker with the bricks of traditional liberal democracy—"like master *bricoleurs*," as Carlos Forment suggests[99]—in order to contest both the boundaries of the public arena and the issues that were to be decided within it. Nowhere was this more true than in the struggle for health rights, and women's health rights in particular.

The white kerchiefs that became the symbols of the mothers and grandmothers of the Plaza de Mayo who began protesting the forced disappearances of their children and grandchildren under the dictatorship gave way to green kerchiefs to symbolize feminist struggles for SRHR in the second decade of the 21st century. Persistent feminist mobilization around femicide and gender-based violence in Argentina, which built on incremental changes in national and international law, in turn led to much broader deliberations, within official assemblies and beyond, on legalization of first-trimester abortion beginning in 2017–2018. Moreover, as this book went to press, some of these activists—young and old, heterosexual women and LGBTQ alike—were at the forefront of linking claims for SRHR and gender equality with broader demands for social justice and connecting current austerity policies with the handling of Argentina's debt by international financial institutions.

CHAPTER 2

The Significances of Suffering

There are successful countries and people, and there are failed countries and people because the efficient deserve rewards and the useless deserve punishment. . . . Broken memory leads us to believe that wealth is innocent of poverty.

—*Eduardo Galeano*[1]

"Plague" is the principal metaphor by which the AIDS epidemic is understood. Plague . . . has long been used metaphorically as the highest standard of collective calamity, evil, scourge. . . . And these mass incidences of illness are understood as inflicted, not just endured.

—*Susan Sontag*[2]

The inconvenient truth, and let us face it, is that the tragedy of maternal mortality is that . . . mothers are not dying because of diseases we cannot treat. They are dying because societies have yet to make the decision that their lives are worth saving.

—*Mahmoud Fathalla*[3]

IN ANOTHER SETTING, Latonya would have seemed much like any other petulant teenager who had little interest in being tied down to a baby. But her starting point in life had not only led to a lack of life choices from a very young age, but had now also enabled the state to regulate even the most intimate aspects of her life. Latonya had dropped out of high school before she was 16, developed an addiction to drugs, which led her to engage in transactional, if not commercial, sex—and had a baby. When I met her in 1988, the baby's father was not in the picture. Latonya's mother, Annie, had been raising the baby during Latonya's recent stint in prison. Annie, whose accent betrayed she had moved north as an adult, probably to escape Jim Crow laws, and whose face showed some of the hardness of her life, was, as any mother might be, both angry at her daughter and defensive of her.

Apparently, Latonya had bathed her baby with Ajax detergent the night before, a cleanser used to scrub pots and pans, and the infant had been taken to the emergency room with skin abrasions and burns. This was before cell phones and Peggy, the caseworker whom I was assisting, did not have details. Before we shared information instantly, people had to piece together truths through multiple phone calls and personal interactions, which in turn implied a different relation to knowledge, time, and physical reality. In this case, we went to Latonya's home to figure out what had happened.

Latonya had to have legal custody of the baby in order to receive Aid to Families with Dependent Children (AFDC), the federal welfare program administered by states that was meant to support single mothers. That's why we were there: to evaluate whether Latonya could plausibly assert her "fitness" as a mother. The Women's Employment Project (WEP) was meant to secure employment and/or welfare benefits for formerly incarcerated women, such as Latonya, most of whom were in prison for drugs or sex work, or both, and some of whom had HIV—which was as lethal as it was stigmatized at the time.

Annie and Latonya lived in a nondescript building among many housing projects in Roxbury, a neighborhood where at the time two white women in business attire stuck out. Boston was still subject to compulsory busing for school desegregation in early 1988, stemming from federal district court orders that followed from the US Supreme Court's *Brown v. Board of Education* decisions in 1954 and 1955.[4] But by most accounts, busing to overcome separate and unequal educations had not worked as planned in Boston, a story that points to the enduring impacts of racial segregation in people's lives in the US long after it ceased to be legally imposed. To this day, despite its reputation for progressive politics, greater Boston remains a profoundly racially segregated city, with educational opportunities as well as health statistics determined largely by zip code.[5] The neighborhood Latonya lived in exuded the bleakness characteristic of urban poverty in much of the United States at that time, as if the so-called housing projects were deliberately designed by government planners to deaden any grand hopes or dreams that managed to sprout in a child of these streets.

In the apartment, the walls were strikingly bare—no books or art that might suggest how Annie and Latonya wanted to see the world. We sat on the one sagging couch facing a television set—which at the time was still a box shape with "rabbit ears"—while we listened to Annie and Latonya tell us their versions of events. Peggy, who I believe was genuine in her religious faith, explained to me that employment was often not possible, so the focus of WEP was on getting our clients AFDC benefits for the sake of the innocent children who suffered, if not the mothers. Latonya was still a girl herself, but innocence implies that guilt and blame lie somewhere and that not all suffering merits the same response from governments or society.

AFDC began under FDR's New Deal, as Aid to Dependent Children in 1935—as Roosevelt said about those programs at the time, "not as charity, but as social duty."[6] AFDC had continued in different forms until 1996 when President Bill Clinton enacted the so-called Welfare to Work Act: The Personal Responsibility and Work Opportunity Reconciliation Act.[7] Billy Bulger—better known for being the brother of the brutal mob boss James "Whitey" Bulger—was the president of the Massachusetts state senate when I met Latonya in 1988, and he spearheaded a welfare reform proposal that largely foreshadowed the national law, conditioning welfare payments upon employment in many cases. By then, attitudes about personal responsibility versus the duty of the state to free people from want had changed dramatically since the New Deal. President Clinton later argued the national law would "transform a broken system that traps too many people in a cycle of dependence to one that emphasizes work and independence."[8]

AFDC drew particularly scathing critiques about perpetuating laziness and dependency because it fed so many racial and gender stereotypes. It was denounced in the 1980's for leading poor women, and by implication if not fact, *women of color*, to have additional children in order to get benefits.[9] When social protection is viewed as charity as opposed to part of the social contract, it facilitates placing moral judgments, as well as demands, on the behavior of poor people and especially women such as Latonya.

Latonya's life, as were so many others, was caught up in a sweeping change in how poverty was conceived and addressed in the 1980's. In 1980 the former actor Ronald Reagan had been elected president of the United States and declared it was "morning in America"—as in a fresh new start to embrace after the chaos and unrest of the 1960's and 1970's (e.g., civil rights and women's liberation movements). Morning in America—and the equivalent under the Iron Lady of Great Britain, Margaret Thatcher—translated into a series of policies that set the stage for dramatic market expansions and financial deregulation, and increasing wealth inequalities, both within the US and UK and around the globe.

It is impossible to use human rights to effect meaningful social change in health and society without first understanding the implications of doing so for construing the meaning and determinants of health. In Chapter One, I argued for the need to expand traditional liberal conceptions of rights, and in turn to enlarge the contours of "the political" and the responsibilities of the state, in order to advance the health rights of all people, including women. In this chapter we'll see that treating health as a rights issue entails specific understandings of the goals and means of development, as well as of health and health systems. Health is perhaps the most complex subject to address through human rights law as doing so requires challenging not just economic and political discourses, but also scientific paradigms, to discern whose and what suffering should be treated as a societal responsibility by the state.

First, the chapter examines the dramatic changes in political discourse and economic policy that occurred in the 1980's, which ushered in changes to the role of the state vis-à-vis expectations of establishing a "level playing field" for its citizens. For example, from 1951 to 1982 in the US, the wealth of the top 10% never exceeded more than one-third of total wealth. This relative social equality was only possible because in addition to the state actively generating employment opportunities, and college and home subsidies, income tax during this period had been progressive: the top marginal rate was 91% from 1951 to 1963 and above 70% until 1981. But this was all about to change, as states and financial institutions embraced neoliberal policies that expanded the role of markets to allocate social as well as private goods, while leaving only a residual role for the state. In both the US and the UK, tax reforms that benefited the wealthy[10] were coupled with deregulation and privatization across many domains of the economy.[11]

On the global level, the neoliberal faith in markets to drive economic growth came together with untenable debt burdens in the global South in the 1980's. As a result, international financial institutions and banks called for dramatic restructuring of economies in the global South (structural adjustment programs, or SAPs), which meant adopting a new set of imperatives that came to be called the "Washington Consensus."[12] Reviewing some of the premises and effects of SAPs, the chapter contrasts this dominant paradigm of *development as economic growth* with Amartya Sen's understanding of human development as expanding substantive freedoms, which influenced thinking about health rights in general, and my own in particular.[13] In global development, the dominant neoliberal paradigm that began to be actively pushed by international financial institutions (IFIs) overshadowed UN ideas of a right to development and ushered in new notions of the role of international trade.

Second, the chapter moves from broadly examining the changed paradigms of state responsibility for societal well-being (and the lack of it) to how we conceptualize the specific effects on health of these and other policies. Patterns of health and ill-health are only questions of justice if we understand them to be causally related to social relations and institutional arrangements. In the 1980's increasing empirical evidence emerged to support the link between social inequality and health status. Yet ideas of health as a social construction, which were set out in international conferences, were competing with other paradigms. Indeed, the entrenched biomedical understanding of disease in terms of pathologies in isolation from social context lent itself to neoliberal efforts to privatize responsibility for health and in turn allow states and commercial actors to label suffering as deserved. This commodification of care, inconsistent with a right to health, began to be imposed through structural adjustment on countries in the global South where fees were even charged for essential services. I contrast this understanding with one in which health systems are understood as spaces to construct democratic inclusion, and in turn enshrined rights to care and public health measures as part of the social contract.

Finally, I turn to two cases where specific populations' health was beginning to be construed in terms of rights in the 1980's. The distinct trajectories of child survival and child rights and maternal health and women's rights both indicate that using human rights for social change requires conceptualizing the person who suffers as a subject of dignity. In turn, for historically dehumanized groups doing so requires the alignment of opportunity structures to advance both empirical knowledge and normative frameworks.

Conceptions of Development and Progress in the World

How we understand the purpose of development affects what policies we pursue, and in turn how we evaluate the impacts of those policies, for good and ill. The decade of the 1980's was marked by a shift in thinking, both as to what constitutes the aim of macroeconomic policy and the political economy of development in an unequal world.[14] The SAPs that swept the global South in the 1980's and later economic reforms we will discuss are referred to as *neo*liberal because they were understood as a resurgence of the 19th-century ideas of laissez-faire capitalism and economic liberalism. Over the course of these decades, neoliberalism has come to be associated with an unassailable faith in markets, which has ended up marketizing not just economies but societies, down to the most intimate of social interactions, with significant gendered impacts.

The Ends and Means of Development

The consequentialist goal of development in what I shall loosely refer to as "mainstream economics" is maximizing economic growth. Economic growth over time is presumed to reduce poverty levels, measured in income. Neoliberalism was based upon the idea that efficient economic outcomes were best produced without government intervention, through "free" markets. Nobel Prize winning economist Joseph Stiglitz and many others have written about the empirically disprovable assumptions regarding markets and their failures, which were built into neoliberal policies.[15]

Many human rights scholars have also written of how impacts of neoliberal policies undermine health rights.[16] Yet it is important to be clear about the relationship between the *goals* of development and human rights before we examine the means through which economists and policymakers have sought to achieve them. As I noted in the Introduction, economic growth can be *and indeed should be* beneficial to human flourishing and rights. Sustainable economic growth should enable individuals to have greater choices in making and executing life plans, recognizing the finite resources of the planet; sustainable economic growth should also provide the government with greater revenues to enhance social welfare for living members of society and to maintain a situation where future generations enjoy an equal degree of freedoms and entitlements.

However, economic growth is a means, not an end in and of itself from a human rights perspective. Not all economic growth enhances meaningful choices or produces social value. As many economists have recognized—including Adam Smith in *The Theory of Moral Sentiments*[17]—the value of economic growth is inherently dependent on the distribution of its benefits, as well as social costs. For example, the so-called natural resources curse refers to the fact that state reliance on extraction of natural resources for economic growth generally: (1) does not require or yield equitable investment in education, independent institutions, or population health; and (2) has high costs in terms of both health and environmental consequences, which will affect future as well as living generations.

Further, economic growth alone does not capture what is essential about progress in the world from a human rights perspective. In the 1970's and 1980's,

Amartya Sen, along with others, such as Mahbub ul Haq, was putting forward a very different understanding of development. Sen's "capabilities theory" proposed that that what is really valuable to people are freedoms people have to be and do certain things with their lives, and that promoting the aim of development should be to promote "the capabilities that a person has, that is, the substantive freedoms he or she enjoys to lead the kind of life he or she has reason to value."[18] Sen's landmark theory had been inspired in part by his study of the Bengal famine of 1943, where rural laborers' negative freedom remained unaffected, but they did not have the "functioning" of nourishment nor, in turn, the "capability" to escape morbidity.[19]

Sen argued that traditional development that focused too narrowly on increased average income was inadequate because diverse people differed in their capabilities to convert income and wealth into the functionings they actually valued.[20] In one famous example, Sen, who had suffered a severe illness as a child and remained concerned with questions of health equity throughout his lifetime, noted that a person with a disability would face a "conversion gap" in transforming income into valuable functionings.[21] Sen's insights have been crucial in examining the demands of justice in health equity and prioritizing health needs, as diverse people are invariably more or less well-off not just in terms of socioeconomic status, but also in health status. Further, such conversion gaps are invariably affected not just by "immutable" biological traits, but by the institutional arrangements in a given society.

Thus, it follows from the goals set out that the *means* to attain "human development" call not just for growth incentives, but for removing "unfreedoms"—including infringements of civil and political rights—which interfere with capabilities. The process of human development calls for respecting rights, rather than using whatever means was thought by economists of the time to promote maximum economic utility. As set out in the Introduction, human development is closely aligned with holistic understandings of human rights, which emerged with greater force in the 1990's.

Sen's notion of development was institutionalized in 1990 by the United Nations Development Programme (UNDP) in the Human Development Index (HDI) and the annual *Human Development Report*. The *Human Development Report* was an alternative—a dissent by some development economists—to the World Bank's *World Development Report*. The HDI, instead of focusing exclusively on economic growth to gauge development, measured "a long and healthy life [life expectancy], being knowledgeable [education] and having a decent standard of living [income]."[22] In the year 2000, UNDP's *Human Development Report* focused specifically on human rights and human development.[23]

Structural Adjustment and the Washington Consensus

Despite work by Sen and others, in the 1980's the dominant economic model focused on the goal of economic growth, and free market ideology coupled with events in the world changed the approach to securing that growth. Since their creation, the Bretton Woods institutions—especially the International Monetary Fund (IMF) and the World Bank—had generally solved temporary balance of payments problems through short-term loans that would enable states in the global South to repay debts. However, in the 1980's far more ambitious policies were introduced to address what was perceived as structural instability. States in the global South, often under newly decolonized regimes or dictatorships—as in Argentina during the tenure of Martínez de Hoz—had borrowed heavily to maintain levels of imports and consumption. Eventually, unsustainable borrowing produced deteriorating balance of payments on increasingly large debt.[24] In 1982, Mexico defaulted, which led to the fear that many other countries in the global South would follow suit, thereby crippling banks in the North and causing the global economic system to collapse.[25]

The World Bank and IMF—pushed by their most powerful shareholders, and in particular the US—developed a set of more drastic interventions in the internal governance and economies of countries in the global South to address this perceived threat. "Structural adjustment" meant that in exchange for rescuing them from default, indebted countries were required to adopt a menu of neoliberal policies which included: (1) privatization and deregulation; (2) trade liberalization to open markets to foreign investment; and (3) reduction or elimination of social subsidies to balance budgets.[26] The logic the SAPs followed became known as the "Washington Consensus."[27] These market-friendly reforms prioritized fiscal discipline and balanced budgets, and almost universally involved replacing broad universal social programs (often largely aspirational at the time) with targeted programs for the neediest, including in health, to meet "basic needs."

In the ends-justifies-the-means logic of SAPs, those populations who could not fit into the productive sectors—e.g., rural peasants in the informal economy—were not treated as subjects with rights but as externalities on the road to modernity. Moreover, economic policies, like all policies, are gendered. SAPs, and neoliberal policies more broadly, have had outsized impacts on women.

Women are disproportionately not employed in the formal economy and at the same time bear the burden of unremunerated care work for those who were no longer receiving government services.[28] Further, men's lost livelihoods and reduced sense of masculinity frequently translated into increased substance abuse, shifts in intrafamily food distribution, and domestic violence.

Women also are more dependent on health systems, both for their own reproductive health needs and for their children's care, which at the time in much of the global South largely involved preventable diseases of poverty. Under SAPs, most government expenditures for health were reduced to a mere 2% of gross domestic product (GDP), which is very low and was a considerable reduction from the 1960's and 1970's.[29] In one study examining the effects of SAPs on the health sector in multiple countries, the authors conclude that the data show that "the incidence of preventable diseases rises and [over the course of children's lives, there is an] irreversible deterioration in health status."[30] In the 1980's and 1990's, many countries following SAPs increased fees for childbirth at health facilities and other reproductive services, including contraception, which disincentivized women (who often had no control over financial resources) from interacting with the health system altogether.[31] Studies based on measuring nutritional indicators for children argued the adverse effects of SAPs on the health of the poor would continue to be manifested for decades.[32]

The SAPs dramatically showed how closely health patterns reflected social policy choices. In 1987, UNICEF published the first major institutional critique of SAPs, entitled *Adjustment with a Human Face*, which pointed to their adverse effects on the health of women and children in particular.[33] By the 1990's, the World Bank itself conceded that "women have borne the brunt of SAP-induced poverty," and that even "where growth has occurred its benefits have been unevenly distributed."[34]

A New View of Multilateralism Takes Hold

Structural adjustment also required changing the relationships between countries through economic integration. In the 1980's, multilateralism, which was supposed to be the key to propagating norms of equal dignity through the UN, was quickly becoming, through transformed Bretton Woods institutions, the key to entrenching norms of neoliberalism throughout the global order.

As noted in Chapter 1, growing tensions between models of human rights and economic development were not uncontested by the organs of the United Nations. Among other things, the UN Commission on Human Rights commissioned

Philip Alston to prepare a report on "the international dimensions of the Right to Development," which noted the crux of the challenge would be translating a right to development "into a notion capable of providing practical guidance and inspiration, based on international human rights standards, in the context of development activities."[35] In 1986, the UN General Assembly adopted a non-binding Declaration on the Right to Development based in part on that earlier work, which attempted to combine language on state self-determination and sovereignty over natural resources of the New International Economic Order (NIEO) with the rights of individuals to "participate in, contribute to, and enjoy economic, social, cultural and political development, in which all human rights and fundamental freedoms can be fully realized."[36] But, just as Alston's report had signaled, the right to development remained a nebulous concept with inherent tensions between individuals' and states' claims.

More importantly, however, powerful actors in mainstream economic development were interested in taking a very different turn during the 1980's, including a sharp rupture with previous understandings of the purpose and nature of international trade. At the Uruguay round of negotiation in 1986, the General Agreement on Tariffs and Trade (GATT), which had moved away from protectionism but still permitted significant flexibility in global trade for political imperatives at national level, was significantly expanded. The GATT had previously afforded maneuvering room for distinct approaches to corporate governance, labor markets, tax regimes, business-government relations, and welfare state arrangements. In short, it allowed for what Peter Hall and David Soskice termed "varieties of capitalism."[37] For example, the German social market of economy differed from the Scandinavian welfare state which differed from the French indicative planning model. Dani Rodrik argues that "GATT's purpose was never to maximize free trade. It was to achieve the maximum amount of trade compatible with different nations doing their own thing."[38]

That made sense. A regime of international exchange is enormously preferable to protectionism for many reasons, from dramatic economic efficiencies to the interpenetration of and exposure to varied social and cultural forms it permits, which in turn can drive creativity, spread practical progress, and encourage emancipation from traditional cultural and social roles, alongside greater mutual cultural understanding and human rights. It is no coincidence that the height of protectionism in the US, reflected in the Smoot-Hawley Act of 1930, which was a dismal failure and exacerbated the Great Depression, coincided with deeply nationalist fear mongering in public discourse.[39]

Nonetheless, the economic boon of competitive advantage reaped from international trade—just as other economic growth—is proportional to how a country distributes benefits and costs, including social and environmental costs,. Without this condition, it was entirely foreseeable that among other things, certain sectors of the economy would benefit from trade liberalization while others, usually workers in other sectors, would be systematically left out of "globalization."[40]

Indeed, according to economist John Ruggie the defining features—i.e., the "generalized norms and conduct"—of the postwar international economic order "rested on a grand domestic bargain."[41] Based on Keynesian economic principles widely accepted at the time, "societies were asked to embrace the change and dislocation attending international liberalization, but the state promised to cushion those effects by means of its newly acquired domestic economic and social policy roles." Thus, "[u]nlike the economic nationalism of the thirties, ... the postwar international economic order was designed to be multilateral. ... But unlike the laissez-faire liberalism of the gold standard and free trade, its multilateralism was predicated on the interventionist character of the modern capitalist state."[42] Nonetheless, in the 1980's, as trade liberalization came to take on an almost religious zeal among economists of the day, GATT came to encompass trade not just in goods but also some services, and subsequently intellectual property. And the grand bargain gave way to a neoliberal multilateralism that began to look a lot like a framework built for a global elite.

In short, in the 1980's the narrative of poverty as personal failure of people such as Latonya was coupled with one of political ineptitude of the governments in the global South. Ideas of a more just international economic order evaporated as states in the global South were blamed for their lack of economic development and instructed as to how to reform their economies.

Conceptions of Health and Health Systems: Implications for Health Rights

First, a right to health does not and cannot mean a right to *be healthy*. Full stop. Being healthy is affected by an array of factors, including personal behavior and luck. However, to construe health as a matter of rights, as Amartya Sen has suggested, we must understand health as being (1) inextricably connected to dignity, and (2) subject to social influence.[43] This second condition is essential because we cannot have rights to personal talents, such as a beautiful singing voice or mastery of the violin; nor can we have rights to matters that lie outside of social influence. Health is perhaps the most contested of rights in the sense that many issues require navigating and redefining the boundaries between individual responsibility, divine will, and social responsibility.

Second, how we understand health in turn determines what we do to protect and promote it. To be clear: not everything that affects health can or should be encompassed by the right to health, which includes both public health preconditions and care. In health rights advocacy we should always keep in mind that the right to health is indivisible with and interdependent on an array of rights, CP and ESC, which are together necessary for a life of dignity. Nonetheless, if we understand health to be subject to social influence, as well as biological or behavioral factors, we cannot isolate an individual or population's health from the sociopolitical and economic contexts, including the design of health systems, that produce patterns of (ill-)health. In turn, understanding health this way allows us to assess the dramatic, and gendered, impacts of SAPs as having been not just unfortunate, but the foreseeable result of unjust social policies.

Paradigms of Health: Reflections of Social Structures versus the Biomedical Paradigm

Ironically, at the same time as the implementation of neoliberal policies was creating greater social inequalities in the 1980's, the empirical evidence about the predictability of the impact of such structural forces on health was becoming irrefutable. The Black Report in the UK followed an earlier Whitehall Study on gradients in health among British civil servants, and showed that there were "marked differences in mortality rates between the occupational classes" and concluded that "[m]uch . . . can be adequately understood in terms of . . . consequences of the class structure: poverty, working conditions and deprivation in its various forms."[44] This nascent but growing body of empirical evidence emerged as Thatcher was shredding the social safety net. Nevertheless, it was crucial to arguing later that patterns of health and ill-health are the predictable results of laws, policies, and programs. In turn, these laws and policies that drive health and social inequalities—such as SAPS—are subject to change, in just the same way that the drivers of civil and political rights violations are.

At the global level, in 1978 the WHO had adopted the Declaration of Alma-Ata (Alma-Ata Declaration).[45] Alma-Ata represented a Utopian idea of health as a "fundamental human right" and contended that "the attainment of the highest possible level of health is a most important world-wide social goal whose realization requires the action of many other social and economic sectors in addition to the health sector."[46] Alma-Ata's "health care for all"—although referring to health *care*—conceptualized patterns of health and ill-health as socially constructed, and therefore called for changing institutional and social relations not just in health sectors but within and across societies, including embracing the idea of a NIEO.

Alma-Ata's conception of health as a collective good was reaffirmed in 1986 at the First International Conference on Health Promotion in Ottawa. The Ottawa Charter stated that "at the heart of [the process of health promotion] is the empowerment of communities—their ownership and control of their own endeavours and destinies."[47] Community control of "their own destinies" and "empowerment" over their lives resonated strongly with understandings of the purpose of human rights and would be integral to the development of some human rights–based approaches to health in later years. However, both Alma-Ata's view of health as a social construction and Ottawa's focus on health promotion through community empowerment contrasted sharply with mainstream discourses of health at the time and today.

In Western medicine, despite its relatively recent dominance in the 19th century, the so-called biomedical paradigm has become so widely accepted that it is almost universally taken for granted. In the biomedical paradigm, health is construed as *the absence of* disease or pathology, or stated positively, "species-normal functioning." In this paradigm, *disease* is separated from *illness*. The meaning of illness, and the complex effects it produces in the individual sufferer, can only be understood in social context.[48] By contrast, in biomedical research and clinical practice, diseases and the individual bodies they play out in are divorced from the social context in order to isolate and study their pathophysiology through, for example, randomized controlled trials.[49] Thus both the social *causation* of health revealed by studies, such as the Black Report, and the social *meaning* of health phenomena are peripheral in the biomedical paradigm in which health is deemed an objective technical issue. Moreover, these objective technical issues are to be deciphered by scientific and clinical experts. In turn, these expert judgments are taken to be not only neutral and detached but unchallengeable by ordinary laypersons, even as they exercise what Michel Foucault called "disciplining power" in defining the contours of "species-normality."[50]

The emergence of HIV/AIDS in the 1980's highlighted the ambivalent relationship between the construction of health rights and mainstream biomedicine. In the West, HIV/AIDS was associated initially with homosexual men; it was sometimes labeled the "gay plague" and portrayed widely as evidence of their sexual deviance as well as promiscuity.[51] Other sufferers, such as sex workers and IV drug users were also deemed to have merited their punishments for transgressing social norms. Within a decade, biomedical research had discovered the mechanisms of the retrovirus that caused HIV and produced effective therapy. At the same time, this research would not have advanced at the pace it did but for the tenacious and often confrontational mobilization by HIV/AIDS activists in the 1980's and 1990's—which in turn likely could not have happened but for the emergence of LGBTQ rights movements in the late 1970's. Fighting not to be beaten by the police for holding hands in the street became fighting to collectively stay alive.

It would take, and still requires, far more advocacy, by human rights activists and others, to convey that HIV/AIDS is a social phenomenon driven by and perpetuating discrimination based on all kinds of stigma and stereotypes, including that very concept of species normality.[52] In the 1980's popular narratives of deviance both drove and were reinforced by the passage of laws that excluded HIV-positive people from entry into countries (including in the United States); forbade blood donations from "high-risk populations," such as gay men; permitted discrimination in employment and housing; and in some cases criminalized HIV transmission.

Indeed, the self-denominated "health and human rights movement" was founded in the early 1990's in large measure out of the unreflective discrimination so widespread in public health in the HIV pandemic. Jonathan Mann and others argued that to truly address HIV/AIDS required addressing the underlying human rights violations in law and institutional practice, as opposed to treating the biological virus and secondary infections alone.[53]

Health Systems: Charity, Marketplaces, or Sites for Constructing Citizenship

No right can be realized without institutional arrangements. The way in which we conceive of patterns of ill-health and suffering shapes how we understand broader social policies, but it also shapes how we conceive of health systems. Dating back to medieval times, many hospitals and health institutions (e.g., "infirmaries") were historically organized by religious or charitable organizations in both Europe and Islamic societies. When George Orwell famously recorded his account of time spent in a public hospital in France in 1929, "How the Poor Die," public hospitals were often still filled with the impoverished and others who had no other way to avoid being there.[54] Those who could afford it were attended at home by doctors with little black bags. However, health and health care evolved tremendously over the 20th century, with broad sanitary measures and occupational safety and newly discovered vaccines to prevent formerly deadly diseases, as well as the advent of antibiotics for infection control and the near universalization of access in countries across Western Europe. In the global South, there has historically been a deep synergy between missionary charity and colonialist and neocolonialist enforcement of Western conceptions of hygiene and social norms.[55]

It was in the 1980's that the idea of health systems as marketplaces governed by business incentives began to advance greatly in the United States, and through SAPs in other countries. The idea that health care should be allocated by markets was not new and indeed had been roundly criticized by even leading economists. In a famous article in 1963, the Nobel Prize–winning economist Kenneth Arrow had pointed out that the unique extent of asymmetries of information in health and the fact that providers set both supply and demand made health a particularly poor sector to be set up along market principles.[56]

Nevertheless, by the 1980's market fundamentalism was sweeping social policy, including understandings of health systems. Moreover, by the 1980's ever more reliance on health-care technologies for diagnosis and treatment had made the doctor with the little black bag a thing of the past in the US and created ballooning costs.[57] In the US, where private health care was largely tied to employment, health maintenance organizations (HMOs)—insurance groups that contracted with providers—began requiring so-called managed care to separate financing and administration from provision of care to reduce costs.[58] Patients were increasingly treated as customers engaging in commercial transactions, and the individualism of biomedicine lent itself to this privatization of responsibility for care, as social context for patterns of health and disease were systematically marginalized.

Political shifts toward increasingly treating health systems as marketplaces depended on disseminating a public discourse of health as a matter of individual behavior and therefore a personal responsibility. Some economists argued that at the "margins" people would take risks that were bad for their health if care were paid for them, thus promoting perverse incentives—i.e., "moral hazard." Conversely, individuals would make better "choices"—about smoking, eating, sex, and the like—if forced to pay the full costs of their own personal health care.[59] Just as in the legal fiction regarding abortion as a private choice in the US, the social norms and material constraints on individual agency were disregarded.

The two narratives of individualistic choice in law and health policy are deeply intertwined, but in relation to health systems, the insurance, pharmaceutical, and other industries directly profited off this view.

Moreover, through SAPs, the logic of treating system users as *consumers*, and separating financing from organization and delivery of care, was also applied in poor countries across the global South. As noted above, SAPs introduced user fees even for essential child and maternal health services, such as emergency obstetric care, where the concept of moral hazard was patently absurd. Women suffered disproportionately in that they invariably have greater reproductive health needs and are the only ones at risk of dying due to pregnancy and childbirth.[60] Rural women in particular almost never controlled household resources and thus were subject to the discretion of a man as to whether he would be willing to sell an animal or liquidate other assets to buy the blood to save a woman's life.

Even as SAPs imposed cost-reduction logic on health systems, there were alternatives. In Western European countries that adopted universal schemes during the 20th century, health systems were understood not as markets but as sites to reflect as well as promote inclusive democracy as part of the social contract. Legislation that enshrined these schemes across Western Europe would not have been possible without the active political mobilization and clout of organized labor movements, which changed understandings of modern democracy and rights in the welfare state.[61]

Health systems were also sites of democratic contestation in much of Latin America, where immigrants from Europe had ushered in demographic shifts as well as claims for social benefits, even when those systems often showed the fissures between formal labor and nonformalized sectors.[62] President Salvador Allende of Chile was a physician himself who had famously championed social medicine before he was overthrown in 1973.[63] The post-dictatorship Brazilian Constitution of 1988 explicitly enshrined a broad right to health, understood as part of social citizenship in a democratic state of law and a factor of social and economic policies, not just medical care.[64] The relentless march of neoliberalism would, however, challenge these views of health systems in much of Latin America beginning in the 1980's.

Making the Suffering of Women and Children Matter: Connections between Health and Rights

It seems axiomatic, but it is worth stating explicitly that for individuals and groups to enjoy health rights, they need to be seen in legal and political discourse, and in turn to see themselves, as subjects of dignity. In the 1980's normative and empirical developments shifted opportunity structures and enabled understanding of both children and women, separately, as possessing the "right to have rights."

Children's Health and Children's Rights

In 1982, the new director of UNICEF, James Grant, launched a "child survival revolution" which was intended to reconceptualize reduction of infant mortality and morbidity as integral to development in line with broader notions of human development discussed above.[65] The initial reaction to Grant's declaration was overwhelmingly skeptical, both from those who thought it a distraction from economic development and from those who believed Grant had deferred too much to the IFIs. Critics such as Halfdan Mahler, then director general of WHO, argued Grant's endorsement of "selective primary health care" as a package of interventions—growth monitoring, oral rehydration techniques, breastfeeding, and immunization—undermined the understanding of the social construction of health put forth in the Alma-Ata Declaration.[66]

Nevertheless, Grant—and UNICEF as an institution—persisted. The child survival revolution is believed to have saved twenty-five million lives between 1980 and 1995 through immunizations, oral rehydration therapy, growth monitoring, breastfeeding promotion, family planning, and food supplements.[67] In 1982, child mortality and infant mortality killed 40,000 children per day.[68] In 2016, when the world's population had expanded exponentially, child mortality killed 15,000 children per day.[69]

For James Grant the idea of child *rights* was integral to the promotion of children's health. The promulgation of the groundbreaking UN Convention on the Rights of the Child (CRC) in 1989[70] and UNICEF's adoption of rights-based approaches to child health were the first application of rights specifically to health. The CRC adopted a groundbreaking "best interests of the child" standard. Accordingly, all policy decisions, as well as parental decisions in the privacy of the home, were to be taken in the best interests of the child, understood as "the holistic physical, psychological, moral and spiritual integrity of the child and promot[ing] his or her human dignity."[71]

Although children could benefit from the protections of other treaties, the CRC enshrined a new understanding of children as full subjects with "evolving capacities" as they grew, which in turn implied shifting the boundaries of human rights law. In addition to continuing to erode distinctions between public and private spheres begun under the Convention on the Elimination of All Forms of Discrimination against Women (CEDAW), a central consequence of acknowledging children as subjects of rights and citizens is that parents (and other private actors) should be able to *justify* their decisions regarding their children based on *reasons* that consider the children's best interests. At the time that was revolutionary as it inherently reframed parent-child relationships and the meaning of family. Evidence of withholding vaccinations and other health care suggests that it remains so today. Just as with women, children had historically been treated as chattel, not as citizens or subjects capable of developing self-governance and reason.[72]

The CRC not only challenged the unquestionable authority of parents, it implicitly adopted a new developmental and relational perspective on rights. By the late 1980's when the CRC was being drafted, the insights of social constructivism and developmental psychology had been widely disseminated. Jean Piaget, one of the pioneers of developmental psychology, argued that knowledge structures—including perception children have of themselves—are not preformed but develop through dialectical interactions with parents and peers, and their social environment.[73] In its references to "evolving capacity" of the child, the CRC adopted this developmental perspective, implicitly recognizing in turn that rights are not solely a matter of protecting fully-formed individuals from interferences with the dignity they have a priori, as a strictly Kantian perspective might suggest. That is, the arbitrary detention of someone in the military dictatorship in Argentina was a life-interrupting violation of fully-formed personhood and dignity. But for girls such as Latonya, and all children, their sense of themselves as being subjects with dignity results from the way they are treated at home, and in their communities and societies.

By the 1980's, a growing body of critical theory permitted understanding that this dialogical construction of identity was not neutral and often far from benign. People created themselves through internalizing external race, class, caste, sexual orientation and gender identity norms, and the like. As but one example, for some girls in some places, the process of internalizing oneself through the reflected "male gaze" as simultaneously inferior or insignificant compared to males, and as sexual objects or instrument of reproduction, had—and continues to have—life and death consequences.[74] Those girls whose lives are shadowed by poverty, patriarchy, and prejudice are not just limited by external barriers as to what they can do in life, but grow up believing that they do not deserve to have choices in their life.

In this vein, Suruchi Thapar-Björket and her coauthors write that domination of women "is less a product of direct coercion, and more a product of when those who are dominated stop questioning existing power relations."[75] This invisible internalized domination, which begins with becoming who we are within specific contexts, entails a completely different exercise of power than we saw in the ESMA. Yet it has been essential in promoting women's and girls' health rights, as well as those of gender-nonconforming kids and children with disabilities, as well as of discriminated racial and ethnic minorities and other marginalized groups. It is simply too late to introduce the idea that people are subjects of their lives when they reach the magical age of 18, and the CRC took the momentous step of acknowledging the implications of that insight for human rights law.

Re-envisioning Maternal Health, and Implications for Women's Sexual and Reproductive Rights

If in the 1980's children were being normatively reconceptualized as subjects of rights as opposed to partial adults or even chattel, adult women were also being reconceptualized as more than instrumental to children. As mentioned in Chapter One, in the 1970's and early 1980's there was an almost total lack of data on women's health, except for World Fertility Surveys (WFS), which were the precursor to the Demographic and Health Survey (DHS).[76] But this was beginning to change.

In 1985, at the global review of the UN Decade for Women, it was announced that half a million women across the globe were dying each year from obstetric complications.[77] A few months earlier, a game-changing article had been published in the *Lancet* by the late Allan Rosenfield, then dean of the Mailman School of Public Health at Columbia University, and Deborah Maine entitled "Maternal Mortality—A Neglected Tragedy: Where is the M in MCH?" In that article, Rosenfield and Maine asserted that despite the focus of maternal-child health on child well-being, "not only are the causes of maternal death quite different from those of child death but so are the potential remedies."[78]

While the infant mortality that most concerned Jim Grant improved with declining rates of poverty, maternal mortality did not.[79] Looking at child survival, it is possible to see a confluence of factors from nutrition to housing conditions to infectious diseases, etc., which weaken the child and ultimately can lead to death. Thus, it was easy to make the case that child survival was an indicator of human development. But maternal mortality does not follow that pattern.[80] Either a woman experiences an obstetric complication or she does not, and if she does, she needs access to emergency obstetric care. Even if a woman is weak, malnourished, anemic, etc., it is more likely than not that she will experience an uncomplicated delivery. On the other hand, even if a woman is well nourished, well educated, and has access to antenatal care, etc., she can still have a severe obstetric complication that can lead to death without access to a package of services that have been available in industrialized countries since the 1940's.[81]

Thus, as late as the 1980's what global health was promoting to address women dying in pregnancy and childbirth was not based on empirical evidence, but on a deeply ingrained ideology that *what was good for children had to be good for the pregnant women*.[82] Maine recalls being inundated with negative reactions when in the 1980's she tried to persuade public health programmers across Asia that traditional birth attendants and antenatal care could not solve the problem of maternal mortality; "it was like saying there was no God."[83]

In 1987, two years after the global review found that half a million women were dying each year from maternal deaths, a global Safe Motherhood Initiative was launched in Nairobi, Kenya, where the target of halving maternal mortality by the year 2000 was set.[84] For the first time there seemed to be political traction around maternal health. However, as Jeremy Shiffman and Stephanie Smith write regarding the "protracted launch" of the Safe Motherhood Initiative, that commitment dissolved as uncertainty regarding proper measurement of maternal mortality, the absence of an institutional base to lead the initiative, and lack of "coherent thinking" untainted by ideologies about what was required to address maternal deaths stalled momentum.[85]

Unlike child survival, maternal health had neither a personal nor institutional leader akin to James Grant and UNICEF, and there was contestation as to interventions. Maternal mortality lay at a complicated political and empirical intersection of needing to see women as separate from children, and yet to acknowledge advancing maternal health required health systems and medical care. Indeed, in the 1980's, many feminists were not interested in the emerging Safe Motherhood Initiative paradigm because they were actively working on reproductive autonomy and abortion, and saw a focus on safe motherhood as supporting an essentialist political discourse that constructed women as reproductive vessels. Moreover, women's health movements were challenging the power of the biomedical establishment, and pushing for emergency obstetric care in global health seemed antithetical to de-medicalizing reproduction.

Nonetheless, transnational mobilization around women's rights in the 1970's and 1980's had produced CEDAW and other normative efforts to combat discrimination, including in health care. The lack of lifesaving services required only by women, whether abortion-related or emergency obstetric care, was beginning to be understood as discrimination and in turn as matters of reproductive rights. For example, the Women's Global Network for Reproductive Rights started as an abortion campaign and became the first organization to call itself a *reproductive rights* group. In the 1990's these same groups would come to actively appropriate international human rights mechanisms and frameworks.

In short, changing empirical approaches to both women's and children's health in the 1980's had important implications for rights paradigms and vice versa. Jim Grant's child survival revolution was integral to the development of the CRC. The CRC in turn introduced the transformative notion of children as full subjects with rights, with evolving capacities, and challenged traditional authoritarian norms within the family. In those same years, efforts to combat maternal mortality revealed empirical data that pregnant women had distinct health needs from the fetuses they carried in their bodies. Yet, it was only possible to visibilize how gaps in programming led to women's needless suffering because researchers had a normative premise that women *should be seen* as individual subjects with dignity, as opposed to mere appendages to children.

Concluding Reflections

If Latonya had contracted HIV around the time I met her in the late 1980's, she almost certainly would have died by now. Almost forty years after HIV/AIDS first came to light, it is now a chronic disease and not a death sentence for many in upper- and middle-income countries, as well as for some low-income countries. This transformation is a consequence of both practical progress in biomedical research and clinical practice, and human rights and other advocacy on behalf of people living with HIV/AIDS. Nonetheless, patterns of HIV/AIDS to this day still illuminate structural inequalities between and within countries, and too many people whose lives are not invested with social and political value still suffer in the shadows.

In 2013, I was living in Tanzania while overseeing a study based at the Harvard T. H. Chan School of Public Health on the intergenerational impacts of maternal mortality. By then, there were few publicly funded AIDS orphanages remaining in East Africa, and those that existed were woefully underfunded, since foreign donors had revised their views about the cost-benefit of charitable aid to fund orphanages. That was the case with the Kurasini Children's Home, the only public orphanage left in Dar es Salaam, Tanzania, by 2013, which housed over a hundred children from infants up to the age of 18, some of whom were children of women who had died in childbirth, as well as AIDS orphans. By 2013, I was able to look at photos of Kurasini on the internet to see what to expect. But the afternoon I arrived, it little resembled the cheery photos someone from afar would have seen. Few children were playing in the open dirt expanse between buildings; a group of younger children quickly congregated and clung to me and my Tanzanian colleague as if starved for human affection. The rooms were sparse and barrack-like, and the bathrooms grim; the food gruel-like; the children's heads shaved to keep down lice; and even where posters had been pasted to walls, there was no evidence of anything that children there had created themselves. The atmosphere was inescapably bleak; these children were growing up in a gray world where it was difficult to see how they might develop a sense of their own distinct moral value.

In the last building we visited, we met Janet, who was approximately the age Latonya had been when I met her, and who also had an infant. She was surrounded by other girls, who were playing with the baby as if it were a doll, and she seemed happy to have the attention of visitors. Janet wore a mask of bravado that concealed what she was really thinking, as much as it revealed an apparent underlying fragility. We learned that she had been escaping from the grounds at night for months and having sex with men in the area (which was near a commercial port) for small amounts of money that were enough to buy alcohol or marijuana. I noted to myself the baby had signs of being HIV-positive—fevers, diarrhea, skin infections. But neither she nor the baby had been tested. Kurasini did not test the children, for fear of creating stigma and because even if they were found to be positive, they couldn't treat them there. If Janet and the baby lived until she turned 18 in two to three years, they would be pushed out into the streets and, as she had no particular skills as well as a child for whom to care, it was more than likely she would become a commercial sex worker.

Janet—far more than Latonya—was never given any choices about her life, and by this stage she had no plans, no hopes beyond feeding and clothing herself and her baby, and not being brutalized in her next sexual encounter or being evicted from the orphanage in the short run. Children cannot question the world into which they are born. She had been born desperately poor in a very poor country, her parents had both died of AIDS, and she might be HIV-positive now too. She had no relatives who wanted to take her in, no resources to draw upon—in short, she had no plan B. To say Janet had somehow deserved the suffering in her life for having sex and doing drugs seems a callous and patronizing view given her life chances from the time she was a baby. As we have seen, girls and women (along with other marginalized groups) often are systematically trained not to see the profound deprivations and abuse they are forced to endure. Yet, as Martha Nussbaum notes, this kind of social conditioning makes them more, not less, worthy of the societal support necessary to achieve essential capabilities and functionings in their lives.[86]

In sum, in this chapter we have discussed how the significances that we attach to suffering, in our own lives and those of others, inexorably shape the possibilities for using rights to advance social justice in health. Health rights continually call for interrogating and contesting what disease and illness are "natural" and where the boundaries of individual and societal responsibility lie. In the HIV/AIDS pandemic, we saw the ambivalent relationship between advancing health rights and biomedicine, which is both an engine of practical progress and at the same time often reinforces notions of normality and deviance. Further, the individualism of biomedicine lends itself to treating health as a technical issue, divorced from social context and, in turn, to commercializing care without regard for the wider conditions of people's lives. In the 1980's, even as empirical evidence began to mount that health was deeply influenced by social inequalities and power structures, marketization of health systems was sweeping the US and, through SAPs, increasingly the global South.

More broadly, the overarching lesson to extract from the narrative of the 1980's is that moral conceptions about justice influence how we come to think about ourselves (as we grow up and as adults), as well as the institutional arrangements we come to take for granted in our societies.[87] The neoliberalism that was ushered in during the 1980's, and imposed through structural adjustment on the global South, began to transform moral conceptions of the role of the state, as well as its capacities for ensuring levels of social well-being. As Galeano would later write, when it stopped being seen as the "fruit of injustice," poverty might arouse pity, but it no longer caused indignation.[88] At the same time, we also saw how the 1980's witnessed new moral conceptions of children and women, respectively, as subjects of rights, which would lead to changes in laws and in the lives they, and future generations, could lead

Since the 1980's, in applying human rights in health we have had to address both how we can come to think of ourselves as diverse but equal human beings, and the laws and institutions and discourses that shape the lives we can lead. The challenge was, and remains, nothing less than to reshape the political economy of avoidable suffering.

CHAPTER 3

Diverging Parables of Progress

The proposal that promoting and protecting human rights is inextricably linked to the challenge of promoting and protecting health derives in part from recognition that health and human rights are complementary approaches to the central problem of defining and advancing human well-being.
—*Jonathan Mann et al.*[1]

Neoliberalism's financial bomb . . . not only destroys the polis, imposing . . . misery on those who live there, but also transforms its target into just another piece in the puzzle of economic globalization.
—*Subcomandante Marcos*[2]

ON JANUARY 1, 1994, the Zapatista National Liberation Army (Ejército Zapatista de Liberación Nacional, or EZLN) declared war on the Mexican government. On that day, the soon-to-be-famous "Subcomandante Marcos"—complete with his black ski mask and pipe—read the First Declaration of the Lacandón Jungle: "They do not care that we have nothing, absolutely nothing, not even a roof over our heads, no land, no work, no health care, no food nor education. Nor are we able to freely and democratically elect our political representatives. . . . But today, we say ENOUGH IS ENOUGH."[3] This dramatic rebellion and manifesto were timed to coincide with the entry into force of the North American Free Trade Agreement (NAFTA). Although there was intense fighting for twelve days after the announced rebellion, the EZLN revolt was based not on older revolutionary notions of armed struggle and class warfare. Rather, it was explicitly based on human rights and inclusion of diverse identities in a meaningfully democratic society. "Todos los derechos para todos"—"all rights for everyone"—became the slogan of the first post-Cold War insurgency.[4]

I had lived in Mexico in the early 1990's after law school, and I had seen firsthand both the extreme destitution and the government indifference to massive suffering, which were at the root of the Zapatista rebellion. Despite Mexico having a theoretically democratic government (as opposed to a military dictatorship as in Argentina), the Partido Revolucionario Institucional (Institutional Revolutionary Party or PRI, for its acronym in Spanish) had held uninterrupted power since the 1917 Revolution. In the early 1990's, the PRI had its corrupt tentacles in every aspect of political and communal life in Mexico—which is precisely what the Zapatistas were seeking to change.

The "autonomous communities" the EZLN established were prototypical "counterpublics" in Nancy Fraser's term: groups excluded from politics vis-à-vis the state, gathering together to "[understand] themselves better, forging bonds of solidarity, preserving memories of past injustices, interpreting the meaning of those injustices, working out alternative conceptions of the self, of community, or justice, of universality . . . deciding how to act individually and collectively."[5] And unlike in many insurgencies, women assumed important leadership roles in the EZLN.

The Zapatistas set up autonomous health systems based on ideas of health as a social construction and community empowerment, echoing the Alma-Ata and Ottawa declarations.[6] I have a photo from 1997 of a teenager working in the makeshift *consulta externa* (outpatient) health post, wearing a stethoscope over his T-shirt. Nailed to the loosely bound wooden boards on the wall behind him was a piece of paper listing names of those who took turns manning the post throughout the week, as well as those responsible for all preventive public health activities. On that trip in 1997, we met traditional birth attendants (TBAs) who managed care for pregnant women and deliveries and were accorded respect for their knowledge and skill. Unlike doctors and nurses in the formal health system, the TBAs were intimately familiar with their patients as people, and in turn they communicated with their patients horizontally—woman to woman, human to human—as opposed to treating them as anonymous patients.

Nevertheless, these counterpublics faced impossible odds in converting their resistance into practical progress in people's health and lives. After the initial days of armed conflict, there was a halting process of peace negotiations with the government. Political affiliations and religious differences (Catholic versus Evangelical) were exploited and manipulated, and paramilitary groups with Orwellian names, such as "Peace and Justice" in pro-government communities began attacking EZLN communities in resistance to dispossess them of land and livelihoods.

The state health system was actively deployed as part of the counterinsurgency, with government health workers both discriminating against and collecting information on EZLN sympathizers when they came to facilities or during public health immunization campaigns.[7] As a result the EZLN rejected health services.[8] A study done several years later in the conflict zone—where communities were divided—found astronomically high estimated maternal mortality (over 600 per 100,000 live births), as well as alarming child health statistics.[9] As discussed in Chapter Two, overwhelming evidence in public health had shown that without timely referral to adequate emergency obstetric care in the event of a severe complication, women died. But the formal health system was hostile, and even had they wanted to do so, TBAs could not refer patients in need of blood or surgery. Notably, many of these maternal deaths had gone unrecorded by the Mexican state, which did not care about how poor indigenous women died, much less how they were forced to live.

Advancing the EZLN aim of "all rights for everyone," required more than enabling indigenous communities to reimagine society without the injustice they had long been forced to bear, as important as that was. It also required access to the benefits of scientific and material progress—including emergency obstetric care as an essential part of control over their bodies and reproductive lives. It was in the 1990's, in the years just before and after the EZLN rebellion, that promoting women's reproductive health, including maternal health *as a matter of human rights*, was acknowledged as a global imperative.

This chapter tells the complicated story of those extraordinary years. The 1993 World Conference on Human Rights in Vienna broke down barriers between civil and political rights and economic, social, and cultural (ESC) rights, and resulted in transformative shifts in thinking about violence in the private lives of women. UN conferences in Cairo and Beijing, in 1994 and 1995 respectively, pronounced bold programs of action for political, social, and economic changes to promote reproductive health and rights, and gender equality. These UN conferences, and others throughout the 1990's, advanced concepts of human development and fed into the emergence of a nascent health and human rights movement, which sought to connect the fields of human rights and public health in both theory and practice.

Further, ESC rights, including health rights, were finally being recognized at international and national levels. The UN Committee on Economic, Social and Cultural Rights (CESCR) adopted the concept of a minimum threshold level of ESC rights, without which the meaning of ESC rights as rights, and in turn the ability to live with dignity, was lost. Moreover, a wave of new transformative constitutions and constitutional amendments, as in Argentina, replaced the outdated social contract of the traditional liberal state, which included enumerations of ESC rights often based on or directly incorporated from international law. This social rights constitutionalism meant a multitude of national actors, and especially high courts, were negotiating and vernacularizing rights set out in international law, including health. Human rights advocates also increasingly turned to regional and international legal forums to combat government impunity in countries such as Mexico, as well as to set standards in newly pronounced sexual and reproductive health and rights (SRHR).

At the same time, the early 1990's also saw deepening economic integration, with enormous impacts on the relationship between domestic politics and international law. Growing financialization (the increasing share of national and global economies dominated by financial sectors) accompanied and encouraged the expansion of trade and foreign investment, which required significant legal and regulatory changes. Mexico exemplified both the new wealth opportunities and the structural exclusion of unproductive groups created through neoliberal policies. Less than six months before the Zapatista uprising, in July 1993, *Forbes* magazine applauded the eleven new billionaires who had been created in Mexico since 1991.[10] Yet even while opening markets for trade and increasing exports were framed as unchallengeable elements of "modernization," what had previously been political issues regarding debt and trade in those same countries were converted into technical issues, to be managed by lawyers, economists, and bankers in the North beyond the purview of the public.[11] Many presidents, including Salinas in Mexico, embraced their roles as implementers of modernization and used the powers of the executive branch to pass significant reforms with virtually no meaningful democratic discussion.

In retrospect, it is easier to see not just the incompatibilities between these two diverging parables, but also how they dialectically interacted. But in the early 1990's we were filled with enthusiasm about the possibilities of human rights, both in the visions at the UN and as tools on the ground.

UN Conferences on Human Rights and Development: Emergence of New International Norms, and Institutions

The 1980's had been marked by development policies that would meet basic needs only for those who could not fit into productive sectors in the newly trimmed-down state. In 1990, the United Nations Development Programme's (UNDP) launch of the Human Development Report and the Human Development Index, based upon Sen's capabilities theory, put institutional force behind addressing the multi-dimensional aspects of poverty as the starting point of development, rather than as an afterthought. The 1990's UN conferences—the Vienna Conference on Human Rights, the Río Conference on Sustainable Development, the Jomtien Conference on Education, the Cairo Conference on Population and Development, the Beijing Conference on Women, the Copenhagen Conference on Social Development, the World Food Summit in Rome—all reinforced "people-centered," "sustainable," "social," and always transsectoral development, which required legal and institutional changes for diverse people to live flourishing lives. At the same time, in these UN conference declarations, earlier notions of a New International Economic Order (NIEO) were displaced by the imperative of international assistance and cooperation to help people in postcolonial and low-resource countries achieve their rights.

Reaffirming the Universality of Human Rights, and the UN's Role in Setting and Institutionalizing Norms

In their chronicle of the history of the human rights movement, Roger Normand and Sarah Zaidi assert that in the early 1990's "after a long period of neglect, the fractures within human rights could be redressed by all three levels of the United Nations: the peoples of international civil society; the agencies, institutions, and operational programs of the organization itself; and the community of states."[12] At the World Conference on Human Rights (Vienna Conference) in 1993, an unprecedented 171 governments recognized that "all human rights are universal, indivisible and interdependent and interrelated"[13]—civil and political (CP) and ESC rights—and committed to strengthening the machinery of the United Nations to support this holistic understanding of human rights. Then UN Secretary-General Boutros Boutros-Ghali called the Vienna Declaration and Programme of Action "a new vision for global action for human rights into the next century."[14]

Indeed, it was. The Vienna Conference affirmed that "extreme poverty and social exclusion constitute a violation of human dignity and that urgent steps are necessary to achieve better knowledge of extreme poverty and its causes, including those related to the problem of development, in order to promote the human rights of the poorest, and to put an end to extreme poverty and social exclusion and to promote the enjoyment of the fruits of social progress" and called on states to foster participation of poor people in decisions and plans to combat poverty.[15]

At the same time, earlier aspirations for an NIEO had fallen to the side as the world stood witness to the collapse of previous dictatorships and at the same time catastrophic civil conflicts which were beginning to unfold in Africa and Europe. Thus, human rights were described as "birthrights" and "their protection and promotion" as "the first responsibility of Governments."[16] The state's right to development became largely focused on individuals within states: "All peoples have the right of self-determination, [to] freely determine their political status, and freely pursue their economic, social and cultural development."[17] In turn, the Vienna Declaration called for "enhancement of international cooperation."[18]

The Vienna Conference also signaled a growth in global civil society, which would be sustained by the UN conferences throughout the decade. In 1993, the Vienna Conference was attended by an unprecedented number of civil society actors, numbering over 7,000 participants and representing 700 nongovernmental organizations (NGOs).[19] A year later, there were 4,000 NGOs represented from 133 countries at the NGO Forum at the International Conference on Population and Development (ICPD) in Cairo.[20] In 1995, almost 30,000 attended the NGO Forum at the Fourth World Conference on Women in Beijing.[21] Civil society involvement at all levels—from preparatory meetings to the NGO forums at the conferences themselves—proved crucial to the outcome documents.[22] Given that these forums were organized before widespread use of the internet, and when international travel was relatively much more difficult and expensive, the strength and impact of this new global civil society was extraordinary.

As Normand and Zaidi suggest, the agencies of the United Nations also took on more robust roles in promoting human rights. In the new geopolitical environment, the UN system seemed unfit for purpose. Critics noted the lack of human rights–based policies in its institutional actions and shallow permeation of human rights across the UN.[23] The Vienna Programme of Action led to the establishment of the Office of the High Commissioner for Human Rights (OHCHR) to coordinate human rights activities throughout the UN agencies and to strengthen the UN system in knowledge and actions regarding human rights.[24] Part of the OHCHR role is accomplished through its oversight of "Special Procedures," which include experts chosen to raise awareness of and understanding of specific human rights issues. For example, following on Vienna, in 1994, the UN Human Rights Commission (predecessor to the UN Human Rights Council) appointed the first Special Rapporteur on Violence against Women.[25]

The Vienna Programme also led to the creation of National Human Rights Institutions (NHRIs) in countries around the world, as well as an international coordinating body (now the Global Alliance of National Human Rights Institutions).[26] NHRIs' effectiveness in acting as checks on executive power is inexorably dependent on budgets, mandates, capacities and independence.[27] But the emergence of new institutions at the UN and national levels illustrates how institutional architectures have been constantly reshaped to meet evolving governance imperatives and political realities. Indeed, this history reminds us how unnecessary it is to fatalistically accept global or national institutional governance as it exists today.

Women's Rights Become Human Rights

In addition to the reaffirmation of the interdependence and indivisibility of all human rights, a hugely successful global mobilization by feminist organizations "helped to establish the specificity of women's human rights, including their right to bodily integrity and freedom from violence."[28] Vienna was the beginning of international human rights norms being interpreted in a gender-sensitive way whereby the state would no longer be responsible just for eliminating discriminatory laws or traditional practices, as CEDAW had recognized; now *to the extent that the state failed to prevent or sanction* abuses of women in the private sphere, these failures could be characterized as human rights abuses.

The Global Tribunal on Violations of Women's Human Rights, which took place as a parallel nongovernmental activity at Vienna, was the symbolic culmination of efforts to make governments recognize the impacts of violence against women, and the gendered nature of experiences of injustice. Thirty-three women provided testimony, and a panel of "judges" assessed accountability for the abuses presented, explaining how the acts denounced could be interpreted as violating given human rights principles, and making concrete suggestions on redress for these violations of women's rights.[29] Just as the public spectacle aspect of trials to try to bring together fragmented societies after dictatorships, such as the one in Argentina, was critical—what Mark Osiel has denominated as a "self-conscious dramaturgy" aspect[30]—so too was it here. The tribunal showcased women and their voices asserting theoretically private issues in a very public space, as the world and government representatives looked on. Enacting that process in public not only explicated interpretation of norms and state responsibilities in ways that responded to women's lived realities; it also empowered women to see themselves as claimants, mobilized enormous support for changing paradigms of rights, and generated pressure to create the mandate of the Special Rapporteur on Violence against Women. At the same time, the symbolic tribunal also reflected the shift from social mobilizations to a court-centric approach to establishing accountability for violations of women's rights.

This new understanding of the state nexus to the systematic subordination of women was reflected in the nonbinding Declaration on the Elimination of Violence against Women, which was adopted by the UN General Assembly just months after the Vienna Conference.[31] Further, feminist activism in Latin America led to the promulgation by the Organization of American States (OAS) of the binding Inter-American Convention on the Prevention, Punishment and Eradication of Violence Against Women, the Convention of Belém do Pará, which expressly recognized the state's obligations to prevent and sanction acts of violence against women committed by individuals whether in the public or private sphere.[32]

But the impact of the Vienna Conference on women's health rights cannot be understood in isolation from the subsequent conferences of the 1990's. As discussed in Chapter One, since the 1960's and 1970's, women's movements in the economic North were largely concerned with reproductive autonomy, domestic violence, and formal equality in employment. In the global South, women faced different social, cultural, and economic issues, different environments, and different possibilities for mobilization. Moreover, many feminists in the global South had also been concerned about the inequalities spawned by the global economic order. Bringing together networks of feminist activists from North and South alike, starting in Vienna and repeatedly during the 1990's for a series of transsectoral UN conferences, was invaluable for forging new understandings and—at least temporarily—bridging distances in political agendas around a set of gender equality goals.

ICPD and Beijing: What Was at Stake in the Paradigm Shift in Development?

The ICPD Programme of Action reflected a dramatic shift from population policies based on demographic goals to policies based on sexual and reproductive health and reproductive rights, including maternal health rights. The Fourth World Conference on Women at Beijing in 1995 extended the paradigm of ICPD and noted the need for political and institutional change to achieve women's equality.

ICPD: Women at the Center of Development

The significance of the shift from utilitarian population policies designed to suit imperatives of labor forces and economic growth to reproductive rights is central to the argument I make throughout this book. Population debates were nothing new in the 1990's. Amartya Sen has written of the debates between Malthus and Condorcet at the turn of the 19th century, which Sen argues marked the original framing of what he calls the "collaborative" and the "override" approaches.[33] Condorcet was confident that the potential of overpopulation could be solved by reasoned human action: "through increases in productivity, through better conservation and prevention of waste, and through education, especially female education, which would contribute to reducing the birth rate."[34] When ordinary *women* were educated and given the necessary information and conditions, they would see the value of limiting family size through voluntary family planning "rather than foolishly . . . encumber the world with useless and wretched beings."[35] Malthus, on the other hand, did not trust the ability of ordinary women to reason and favored "overriding" their will to control overpopulation.[36] ICPD achieved many things, but perhaps above all it reflected the triumph of the "collaborative approach," of placing trust in *women*—ordinary women—to be able to make reasoned choices about their lives and their potential children's lives when given information and supported by social institutions. Thus, ICPD was based on a view of women as human beings with reason and conscience, which is the basis for dignity and all rights—as opposed to population policy based on demographic end-goals to meet through instrumentalizing women and their fertility.

ICPD was not just an upheaval of thought; it implied the need for revolutionary changes in policy, program, and practice, within and beyond the health sector. Programs that were previously administered separately, such as family planning, sexually transmitted infections, and maternal health, were now joined together under the umbrella of the newly defined "sexual and reproductive health."[37] Whenever a field comes to draw contours around itself, it implies certain understandings of the issues in that field and the populations affected. In ICPD, reproductive health was based on people's—and *women's*—agency over their reproductive lives, and that implied "that people are able to have a satisfying and safe sex life and that they have . . . the freedom to decide if, when and how often to [reproduce]."[38]

Needless to say, ICPD was not all "peace, love, rainbows and unicorns."[39] Advances made by an extraordinary convergence of LGBTQ, abortion, and women's health advocates from North and South alike met with staunch opposition by conservative groups, and difficult choices had to be made in lobbying for the outcome document. Sexual rights were dropped from the final outcome document.[40] Abortion was mentioned in terms of "the health impact of unsafe abortion."[41] But expanding abortion legalization was not included in the final outcome document.

Nonetheless, it is fair to say that ICPD was a milestone in the conceptualization of reproductive rights and women's decisional capabilities as a basis of human development, and in bringing together women's movements from North and South. It has also been a driving factor in "promoting the use of law, policy and rights in the service of reproductive health."[42]

Beijing: The Social Construction of Gender and Power

The Fourth World Conference on Women, held in Beijing, China (Beijing Conference), in 1995, enabled the SRHR movement to continue mobilizing around an expanded platform for women's health and human rights. The Beijing Platform reiterated and strengthened what had been stated in Vienna regarding violence against women as a violation of human rights.[43] Beijing also reiterated the paradigm of ICPD and emphasized "gender stereotypes" and "gender bias" as inequities in power to be overcome: "Health policies and programmes often perpetuate gender stereotypes and fail to consider socio-economic disparities and other differences among women and may not fully take account of the lack of autonomy of women regarding their health. Women's health is also affected by gender bias in the health system."[44]

By the mid 1990's Judith Butler and other important scholars had theorized the social construction of gender and how gender subordination functioned in women's lives. Butler distinguished "between sex, as biological facticity, and gender, as the cultural interpretation or signification of that facticity."[45] Butler argued that the "script" of gender performance is conveyed through socially established meanings, enacted repeatedly in our lives and transmitted from one generation to the next. These theories proposed that as gender roles were socially and culturally established, not fixed and immutable, their meanings were subject to alteration and subversion. The Beijing Platform reflected these advances in thinking and recognized that realizing women's health rights, among others, required subverting limited gender roles as much as treating women as equal to men, as CEDAW had set out only fifteen years earlier. Challenging the power of internalized gender stereotypes—naturalized shortcuts to understanding how *women should act and what they should want*—called for multiple strategies beyond breaking down legal discrimination against women, including basic education to reach young generations. It was at this time that international legal mobilization was taking hold as the strategy to forge women's rights.

The idea of *gender as a social construction* was a red flag for religious conservatives; it was "interpreted by religious conservatives as a code for the disruption of cherished certainties about human relations."[46] Coupled with ICPD having put women's choices and agency over their lives at the center of development, Beijing's platform for action lit a match under conservative opposition to gender equality, especially from the Vatican, conservative Islamic states, and Christian evangelicals in the United States. At the time, however, most of us were eager to put these new framings of our identities in practice; we did not foresee all the forms the backlash would take or what the long game would be.

Health and Human Rights Movement Founded

New linkages between human development and human rights, as well as growing attention to the barriers discrimination posed to health, created momentum to form a scholarly field that formally drew together health and human rights. In the early 1990's Dr. Jonathan Mann was named founding director of the François-Xavier Bagnoud (FXB) Center for Health and Human Rights at what is now the Harvard T. H. Chan School of Public Health. Mann was a hugely charismatic figure, and he asserted that the FXB Center was not merely to do academic research; it was to catalyze "a global movement."[47] Mann and colleagues set out three relationships between health and human rights: the impact of public health policies and programs on individuals' human rights, the health consequences of human rights violations, and the inextricable linkage between the promotion of public health and the promotion of human rights.[48]

Coming out of the HIV/AIDS world, the first dimension of Mann's paradigm emphasized potential infringements of rights from health policies, practices, and programs, such as the deliberate or inadvertent kinds of discrimination we discussed in Chapter Two, which he argued were built into the long-standing infectious disease control principle of limiting the "rights of the few" in order to preserve the "good of the many,"[49] among other things. The second dimension of the framework that Mann and his colleagues developed underscored the long-lasting social, physical and mental health effects of violations of human rights, such as torture.

But it was principally the third dimension described by Mann and colleagues—the "inextricable linkages" between health and human rights—that had been the focus of women's health movements and SRHR advocates for some time, and could be seen reflected in the UN conferences of the decade. It was women's lack of power—cultural, social, political, and economic—that reflected systematic human rights violations, and was in turn reflected in health access and outcomes. Issues such as violence against women made it clear that health was not just a product of biological factors, but of power relations in society, across public and private domains. And, in turn, the changing patterns of health and ill-health for diverse women required institutional shifts and transformation of those power structures, not just biomedical interventions.

Social Rights and New Social Contracts

The changing geopolitics that had permitted reaffirming the indivisibility and interdependence of human rights at the Vienna Conference also played out in the construction of international human rights norms and in constitutional law. In 1990, the UN Committee on Economic, Social and Cultural Rights (CESCR) adopted General Comment 3: *The Nature of State Parties' Obligations* in which it established the notion of an essential minimum level of ESC rights: "A State party in which any significant number of individuals is deprived of essential foodstuffs, of essential primary health care, of basic shelter and housing, or of the most basic forms of education is, prima facie, failing to discharge its obligations under the Covenant."[50] Thus, the CESCR argued protecting the worst-off in society from the grinding degradation of extreme poverty was not a programmatic aspiration or a laudable effort, but a *legal obligation* of parties to the International Covenant on Economic, Social and Cultural Rights (ICESCR) without which each of these rights "would be largely deprived of its raison d'être."[51]

The notion reflected in General Comment 3 was that an essential minimum was necessary to guarantee a person's nondependence, so that no one could be converted into a mere instrument for other ends. Accepting an essential minimum *as a matter of rights* also implied recognizing the causes of extreme poverty as being subject to change through political choices, including enactment and implementation of laws, policies, and programs, which would be echoed in the Vienna Declaration.

For the CESCR, disentangling the causes of poverty due to national political choices from those embedded in international relations would obviously pose a challenge, as would the concept of a minimum core that transcended a particular context.[52] Nevertheless, I believe setting out a minimum threshold level was fundamental for the advancement of ESC rights as *real rights* in the world that existed in 1990. First, the *illustrative* list provided by CESCR was never intended to be understood as invariant. Second, the contextual dimension was meant to be addressed through a dialogue with states parties—a "scoping and benchmarking" process—with whatever limitations and defects that had in practice. Shifting the burden of proof, including when a state alleged an economic downturn, allowed CESCR to require states parties to present reasoned arguments and valid evidence to justify the actions in place to redress any extreme denial of ESC rights within their countries, as well as the resource limitations and other constraints on state action. Thus, the dialogue would theoretically differ with respect to the absence of essential primary care for excluded minorities in a middle-income country—such as indigenous groups in Mexico at the time—or the absence of ESC rights in situations of mass deprivation.

Second, and equally important, this minimum level was never meant to substitute for, nor be read in isolation from, obligations relating to the progressive realization of ESC rights under the ICESCR.[53] Maintaining this understanding of minimum core obligations was crucial if ESC rights, including the right to health, were not to end up serving as palliative remedies for egregious instances of degradation, rather than as scaffolding for creating more egalitarian societies.

At National Level: "Transformative Constitutionalism" and New Roles for Courts

The essential minimum originally sprang from sociological concepts around the obligations of the Bismarkian state.[54] Indeed, many constitutional formulations explicitly linked the notion of an essential or existential minimum to the purposes of the modern welfare state or democratic state of law that were enshrined in recently adopted constitutions. From the late 1980's through the mid-1990's a wave of new and reformed constitutions—from Argentina to South Africa—included CP rights but also generous enumerations of ESC rights and reflected a new vision of the social contract. This "transformative" or "social constitutionalism" which "aspired to large-scale social change through political processes grounded in law"[55] thrived in post-dictatorship and transitional contexts where these constitutions reflected emancipatory aspirations to transcend historical oppression.

The Colombian Constitutional Court eloquently captures the changed conception of the state under its Constitution of 1991: "The realization of freedom and equality requires measures, actions, entitlements and services that a person by himself cannot achieve. The social state of law thus evolved from a liberal state of law, animated by the purpose of ensuring that the material prerequisites of freedom and equality are effectively guaranteed."[56] Thus, while still grounded in a liberal view of rights, these new constitutions reflected a much more egalitarian nation-building project.

Transformative constitutionalism also implied a more politically and morally engaged adjudication and the idea that courts, especially high courts, could be engines of democratization. Constitutional reforms were accompanied by structural reforms and, in some cases, the creation of a constitutional court (e.g., Colombia and South Africa) or specialized chamber of a constitutional court (Costa Rica). High court judges were no longer seen as mere custodians of legality, but as the guardians of the new egalitarian aspirations in constitutions—and in practice the chief bricoleurs of new legal architectures.[57] Ciro Angarita, a justice on the iconic first Constitutional Court of Colombia, created through the 1991 Constitution, stated this view powerfully:

> The Constitutional Court guarantees the coherence and wisdom of rights interpretation and enforcement. This new relation between fundamental rights and judges is a sharp departure from the previous constitution; a change that can be defined as a new strategy for rights enforcement that consists in granting to judges, and not to the administration or to legislators, the responsibility of promoting the development of fundamental rights. In the previous system rights only had symbolic force. Today, with the new constitution, rights are what judges say they are [and can be enforced].[58]

In the 1990's, this new constitutionalism seemed to promise social transformation through rights and the rule of law, through courts taking seriously the deprivations of dignity of the poor that were being ignored or fostered by the political branches of government.

Judicial interpretations of law became less formalistic in this more engaged adjudication, which was critical to advancing ESC rights as real rights. In some countries, such as Colombia, courts began to systematically erode categories of rights paving the way for enforcement of ESC rights, such as health, which were listed not as fundamental rights but as public services or as part of directive principles. In other countries, the right to life was interpreted broadly to include access to health care. Barriers to judiciaries addressing social policies that had been grounded in doctrines of "political questions" began to fall away as new understandings of the capacities of courts in democratic states of law were advanced.

The erosion of formalistic approaches to interpreting constitutional rights according to rigid rules of doctrinal interpretation was accompanied by judge-made procedures that were equally essential to the judicial enforcement of health rights. For example, innovations in court practices, such as the expansion of amicus curiae, allowed for third-party advocates as well as scientific expertise to be introduced in health rights cases. Standing rules were loosened to varying degrees to allow NGOs and other groups to bring claims on behalf of directly affected plaintiffs in collective cases, such as water rights or effects of pollution on health.

In many countries in Latin America, the introduction or modification of protection writs (e.g., *ámparos, tutelas*) under newly reformed constitutions transformed access for individuals to courts to resolve complaints—in health and other ESC rights—that had suddenly become constitutional matters. These protection writs decreased or eliminated costs and greatly reduced waiting times (to a matter of days, as opposed to months or years). In some countries these writs could be presented orally—and famously on banana leaves in Costa Rica—and often required no legal representation.[59] Suddenly the legal opportunity structures became far more appealing for resolving what had been daily complaints about the indifference of the administrative state, but were now constitutional issues. Health complaints were far more easily individualized than, say, education. Individual protection writs to secure health rights in particular would increase exponentially over the next decades, and eventually, as we will see in Chapter Six, come to raise questions about the role of the courts in health policy in Latin America.

The Relationship between International Human Rights and National Law

It is not surprising that the dramatic shifts in countries and at the international level affected the relationship between international human rights law and national law in the early 1990's, both through social constitutionalism and through new approaches to using supranational forums by rights advocates.

Social Rights Constitutionalism, Vernacularization, and Power Dynamics

Social constitutionalism was deeply influenced by international human rights language and law, in some cases by the adoption of an expanded catalog of rights and in some cases by the incorporation of international human rights treaties into constitutional frameworks through "constitutional blocs," such as in Argentina's post-dictatorship amended constitution of 1994. The idea of a constitutional bloc originated in the doctrines of the French Constitutional Council and jurisprudence from other European countries but was widely adopted in the newly reformed constitutions in Latin America.

The process of adopting and adapting norms in one space and legal system from another is far from linear, as Terence Halliday and Bruce Carruthers note.[60] The relationship between international law and constitutional law raises challenges that are very distinct from legal interpretation arising in federalist systems, where rules of hierarchy and conflict-of-laws are navigated on the same legal field. The inherent indeterminacy of rights definitions, contradictions between national and international norms, contestation over interpretation, and the multiplicity of actors engaged in interpreting and applying norms in any given context pose challenges for advancing all human rights, and especially health-related rights.

Anthropologist Sally Engle Merry first used the term *vernacularization* to describe the cultural process through which human rights ideas are translated from "the discourses and practices from the arena of international law and legal institutions to specific situations of suffering and violation."[61] After constitutionalization of ESC rights, such as health, Daniel Brinks, Varun Gauri, and Kyle Shen argue that they undergo "a process of vernacularization that selectively translates apparently universal aspirations into a much more localized version deeply grounded in local social and political realities. The extent to which they are universal, or particular, or effective, is a function of this process of vernacularization."[62] Focusing on vernacularization as localization of legal norms, Brinks, Gauri, and Shen assert that "[t]he comparative literature on social rights, and especially the judicial enforcement of social rights, can be read as an account of how the universal language of rights is transformed by and transforms particular contexts."[63]

The process of localization has been especially complicated in health rights. The right to health was defined broadly in Article 12 of the ICESCR to include both medical care and public health preconditions, as noted previously. Within countries, ministries of health are responsible for certain issues, while other ministries might be responsible for nutrition and public health measures. In federalist systems, health duties are divided between federal and subnational governments—each with specific budgetary responsibilities and the need to identify priorities among diverse populations. Further, nonstate actors often provide and greatly affect access to care and health status, and commercial private actors increasingly have come to exercise enormous power in health sectors. Finally, the subject of health includes both technical issues regarding scientific evidence and issues of gender stereotypes and "sensitive ethical" matters, as SRHR are often deemed. All of these issues have been contested repeatedly since health rights began being constitutionalized in the early 1990's.

Thus, the notion that the right to health can be progressively elaborated through soft law and interpretive declaratory statements at the international level, and then merely be *operationalized* in countries by policymakers or courts, is inaccurate, and discounts the importance of this process of vernacularization. And it is important to be explicit as to why this is the case. As Jean Dreze noted of the right to food, and equally if not more applicable to health: "the entitlements and responsibilities associated with the right . . . are far from obvious."[64] That inherently incompletely theorized nature of human rights, and the lack of obviousness of the right to health in particular, *requires* a process of deliberation about trade-offs, which takes into account scientific evidence but is also invariably contextualized. Finally, such "implementation strategies" often misread the relative significance of the obstacles faced within countries, which lead to ineffectual approaches.

As Roberto Gargarella aptly notes, the "transplanting" or "grafting" of social rights into constitutions in Latin America has produced complicated results.[65] On the one hand, the incorporation of social rights reflected a new imagination of fundamental principles binding a democratic state of law, but on the other hand it did not change the hardwired architecture of the state institutions necessary to realize them. Indeed, as health rights were incorporated into national constitutions, judicial interpretations of these rights increasingly conflicted with neoliberal reforms of health sectors in the region, as we will see in Chapter Six. Addressing these structural barriers calls for a distinct set of strategies to challenge the agenda-setting dimensions of power and to advance health and social equality.

Using International Forums to Define State Responsibility

At the same time as post-dictatorship and transitional contexts gave rise to transformative constitutionalism, they also gave rise to an anti-impunity turn in international human rights advocacy. Unlike earlier human rights advocacy focused on denouncing the acts of the state that intruded in people's lives and stopping outrageous abuses—as in the ESMA in Argentina—human rights advocates now often sought punitive accountability for violators of rights and the regimes that had dictated those abuses. Trials were no longer exclusively or primarily opportunities for collective reflection and social reconstruction, they were intended to punish the very acts that eluded normal moral assessment. This trend was visible not just in the international criminal tribunals after the genocides in Rwanda and Bosnia[66] and later an International Criminal Court.[67] It was also true more broadly of human rights, in that advocates turned to newly strengthened regional and international forums when national institutions were seen as ineffective in bringing justice for victims of state abuse. New human rights NGOs, such as the Center for Justice and International Law (CEJIL), were founded in the early 1990's, with the mission of bringing human rights cases to supranational forums to combat impunity.[68]

The Echoing Green Foundation fellowship for social entrepreneurship I had to work with Mexican colleagues in bringing cases to supranational forums in the early 1990's reflected the growing consensus among human rights lawyers regarding the importance of using international mechanisms as escape valves for impunity and democratic dysfunction. For example, colleagues and I documented a pattern of transfers and reassignments, and even promotions, for Federal Judicial Police officers involved in systematic abuses of human rights, including torture and extrajudicial execution, which we brought to the UN Committee against Torture reviewing Mexico's compliance with the Convention against Torture.[69] At the time much human rights work in Mexico entailed continually bearing witness to the disproportionate effects of predatory policing and military activity on poor and marginalized populations, in rural and urban areas alike: the *campesino* who was shot by police to get him to leave his parcel of land to make way for large landholders; the parents whose son was detained, tortured, and murdered in Mexico City for no reason; the young woman who was killed by her abusive husband and disappeared by complicit police; and the like. Thus, along with many of my Mexican colleagues, I understood taking actions against impunity as seeking to protect the rights of powerless individuals and groups against arbitrary abuses and extortion, sometimes directly related to the restructuring of the economy.

However, a growing body of recent scholarship has critically examined this "anti-impunity turn" in human rights.[70] In retrospect, the construction of justice as *criminal justice* targeting individual actors in human rights writ large played into the global neoliberal narrative denying state responsibility for systemic social injustice. However, in describing the human rights movement, it is important to distinguish between contexts, as well as between international NGOs and local NGOs working on the ground. In Mexico, as Asa Laurell, the Mexican physician and health scholar, notes, the state played a decisively repressive role in dismantling former institutions to "diminish the intervention of the state" in pursuit of neoliberal modernization.[71] For example, official unions were used to violently squelch clamor for wage increases and grievances over privatization and lay-offs. Human rights lawyers took those highly unpopular cases, seeking to expose another side of the structural injustice against which the Zapatistas were rebelling. They also diligently documented abuses against the Zapatistas by the military and paramilitaries in Chiapas. Human rights NGOs in Mexico were in no way oblivious to what was happening politically and economically. They were not opting for a classless struggle, as international NGOs may have been; as a practical matter, in order to avoid the direct repression of the state—which was sadly often not possible—they had to project "political neutrality."

The turn toward anti-impunity had particularly complex effects on gender equality and women's health rights. Some prominent legal scholars have been deeply critical of this anti-impunity turn by feminists. Janet Halley, for example, writes, "Criminal law is their preferred vehicle for reform and enforcement; and their idea of what to do with criminal law is not to manage populations, not to warn and deter, but to *end impunity* and *abolish*" (emphasis in original).[72] On the one hand, as we saw in Vienna, calling for the prosecution of perpetrators of violence against women in private as well as public spaces had become central to redefining the role of the state in protecting women's rights as human rights. On the other hand, the strengthening of criminal prosecution against those deemed perpetrators as a matter of protecting women lent itself equally to the administrative state criminally prosecuting women and providers for abortion, for example.

Moreover, this turn in the use of international mechanisms to establish rules and accountability necessarily implied—and began to establish in practice—a hierarchy between international law as interpreted by international and regional bodies and tribunals, which was conceived as "pure," and national law interpreted by national courts and legislatures. This evolving distinction also had especially complicated implications for women's SRHR advocacy and gender equality.

In the early 1990's, establishing the hierarchy of international human rights law was appealing precisely because many of the issues that most affected women's health and rights had been marginalized in domestic politics and law as private moral and ethical concerns, which were excluded from the arena of public "political" deliberations. Thus in the early and mid-1990's supranational litigation was seen as a way to bring in that "view from a distance" and create new standards around the reproductive rights that had been articulated in international conferences. In 1992, the Center for Reproductive Rights (CRR)—then the Center for Reproductive Law and Policy—was founded and would become the single most important "norm entrepreneur,"[73] in Finnemore and Sikkink's term, in relation to reproductive rights in the world. Luisa Cabal, Monica Roa, and Lilián Sepúlveda wrote a few years later about CRR's work in Latin America, saying it had "pioneered the use of international litigation as a strategy to ensure that national-level legislation, policies, and jurisprudence better reflect the international community's recognition of reproductive rights [and] to push for development of new standards for the protection of reproductive rights under international law."[74] This turn toward international mechanisms in SRHR and faith in "the international community" took many more years to adequately consider the need for follow-up to this norm entrepreneurialism—the building of social and normative legitimacy necessary for what Finnemore and Sikkink term "internalization" of norms in national spaces, including among youth—which is essential to using rights for sustained political and social change.[75]

The Other Story: Deepening Neoliberalism and Depoliticizing Debt and Trade

The other narrative of neoliberal "modernization" is crucial to understand the timing of the EZLN rebellion coinciding with NAFTA. In contrast to some other countries in the region, in 1992, constitutional reforms were enacted to change the *ejido* system (property owned and farmed communally) to strengthen private property, because it was deemed necessary for foreign investment under NAFTA.[76] The constitutional reform was a piece of a much larger story of the agreements and legal reforms undertaken by Mexico, as well as other governments, starting in the early 1990's.

The Other Commitments Countries Made: Debt and Trade

By the early 1990's the IMF had become the world's leading promoter of market-liberalizing reforms through structural adjustment.[77] Kentikelenis and Babb argue that the radical transformation of the IMF in less than a decade—and all of its implications for global economic governance—occurred "through a process of *norm substitution*—the alteration of everyday assumptions about the appropriateness of a particular set of activities."[78]

There was no formal renegotiation of treaties, for example, that signaled a break with the postwar "grand bargain," as it had been negotiated regarding the Bretton Woods institutions. As Kentikelenis and Babb note, " Such de facto but not de jure institutional change preempts overt contestation or lengthy negotiations and masks underlying politics through symbolic work. In other words, these processes are clandestine, taking place away from public scrutiny that would undesirably politicize issues intended to appear apolitical and technocratic."[79]

Once the IMF transformation was achieved, together with similar transformations in the ecosystem of international financial institutions (IFIs), the issues they addressed were deemed to be within the purview of IFI technocratic expertise, and therefore inherently technocratic, which is what they were seeking to achieve.

By the end of 1991, 75 countries had received structural adjustment loans worth more than 41 billion USD,[80] and the effects of SAPS had become politically untenable in many of these countries. In 1989, riots had broken out in Venezuela due to austerity measures the government had imposed to repay creditors, and an estimated 300 people were killed.[81] Succeeding James Baker, who had been a major architect of the transformation in the IMF and structural adjustment in the 1980's, then US Treasury Secretary Nicholas Brady proposed what would later come to be called the Brady Plan. Indeed, Mexico was the first country to convert its debt into these bonds under President Salinas de Gortari, who was president when I lived in Mexico. In order to ease Mexico's debt burden, Salinas privatized 85% of state-owned industries. Other debt was securitized and converted to "Brady Bonds." After Mexico, Brady Bonds were issued by over a dozen other countries. Unlike huge chunks of debt, Brady Bonds could be traded on capital markets rather than sit on the balance sheet of any particular creditor. Brady Bonds signaled the beginning of securitizing debt more broadly and turning to global financial markets to address structural problems in national economies.[82]

Thus, debt, which had previously been understood as a political issue—and which had made countries susceptible to political protest, as in Venezuela—increasingly became the domain of technocrats at the IMF and other IFIs. The causes and legitimacy of sovereign indebtedness were displaced from political contestation, and the mechanics of payment were worked out by specialized lawyers, economists, and investment almost always in the global North.[83] Debt was now cloaked in technocratic language, and the political risks of buying this sliced-up debt were reduced to disclosure statements in securities prospectuses.

Multilateral trade rules were also being redefined and in turn disrupting national economies significantly. When new trade regimes did require formal treaty negotiations, they not surprisingly coincided with political backlash. On the day the EZLN revolted, January 1, 1994, NAFTA created the largest free trade block in the world between Canada, Mexico, and the United States. A year later, on January 1, 1995, the General Agreement on Tariffs and Trade

(GATT) was superseded by the World Trade Organization (WTO), and the so-called TRIPS agreement began to show its teeth.[84] TRIPS had been negotiated as part of the Uruguay Round of the GATT in 1994, among other issues such as the General Agreement on Trade in Service (GATS). Under the WTO the trade preferences and other benefits that came with membership in the WTO, which were significant enticements, were conditioned upon ratifying the TRIPS (Trade-Related Aspects of Intellectual Property) Agreement. Second, as states were subject to discipline through the WTO dispute resolution mechanism, TRIPS had real enforcement power.[85] TRIPS required additional changes in tax regimes, corporate governance, and welfare state arrangements—which often contradicted basic premises of ESC rights, including access to medicines as part of a right to health.

The packages of deepening reforms were dictated by the IFIs, which undertook systematic reviews of the commercial regulation and financial systems of countries in the global South in order to make them serve the larger goals of free trade and deregulation of capital markets. In the 1990's, as we saw the transsectoral and institutional agendas in UN conferences, Terence Halliday argues that the "ideational shift in development theory towards the importance of institutions, with law prominent among them, began to propel in-house lawyers [at the IFIs] away from the implementation tasks of contract writing and regulatory oversight towards law reform as a bulwark of macroeconomic development."[86] But this notion of macroeconomic *development* contrasted starkly with the human development lauded in those UN conferences, and this *law reform* was pushing in precisely the opposite direction of transformative constitutionalism and the enlarged conceptions of the social contract set out in international human rights law.

The Other New Institutions

Just as there were new human rights institutions to address expanded scope and interpretation of rights, so too were new institutions necessary to incorporate the growing importance of trade in services and intellectual property. Intellectual property was removed from the World Intellectual Property Organization (WIPO) in the UN and situated in the technocratic, and "non-political," WTO. Protecting intellectual property (IP) was different from the WTO's other roles regarding liberalization of trade because the WTO required adopting far more invasive IP rules, which largely did not exist in the global South—as opposed to "freeing up" trade in goods.[87]

In turn, enforcement of trade disputes, including IP disputes, was shifted to the WTO and specialized dispute resolution tribunals in regional and bilateral trade agreements, and systematically removed from democratic space. These dispute resolution mechanisms were ostensibly intended to shield technocratic decision-makers from political influences, but they also performed the symbolic function of transforming the relevant grounds for making determinations. For example, Chapter 11 of NAFTA guaranteed investment protections that were stronger for foreign investment than domestic investment and subjected disputes to an arbitration tribunal set up under the agreement. Thus, even had they sought to do so, local legislatures in Mexico would have been limited in their capacities to promulgate legislation protecting public health and the environment. As but one example, in 1997, a Mexican municipality's refusal to provide a permit for the construction of a toxic waste dump was challenged by a US firm as obstructing the provisions of NAFTA, and the US firm was awarded 15.6 million USD in damages.[88]

Framing Knowledge and Governance Discourses, and Displacing Democratic Debate

This tectonic change in national laws and macroeconomic policy required a specific framing of neoliberal progress in the world as natural and rationally uncontestable, which was achieved through internal norm substitution within IFIs, as noted above. It also required executive branches in countries to accept these new rules and to wield their disproportionate power to rearrange laws and institutions, not in the service of human dignity but in the service of capital markets. That delicate politics of legitimation was facilitated by the use indicators, which allowed complex processes to be reduced to simple metrics.[89]

Adjustment targets and numerical indicators were developed so that the IFIs—and in turn private lenders and investors, and credit rating agencies—could assess any given country's progress. These included some substantive issues such as inflation, budget deficits, balance of payments, and the like, as well as implementation of laws and regulations, such as rules for orderly insolvency. As Halliday argues, the use of these indicators for aspects of legal architecture also produced cycles of recursivity in norm-making at international levels and law making at national levels—often with significant gaps but nonetheless in the opposite direction from social constitutionalism.[90]

More broadly, the crystallization of evaluation into seemingly neutral unchallengeable numerical indicators played an important role in sustaining global governance and the knowledge discourse promoted by the IFIs and their major member states about what progress in the world entailed. As Bøås and McNeill argue:

> Powerful states (notably the USA), powerful organizations (such as the IMF) and even, perhaps, powerful disciplines (economics) exercise their power largely by framing: which serves to limit the power of potentially radical ideas to achieve change. A successful framing exercise will both cause an issue to be seen by those who matter, and ensure that they see it in a specific way. And this is achieved with the minimum of conflict or pressure. For the ideas appear to be "natural" and "common sense."[91]

Key to this framing was referring to neoliberal progress as "modernization," which was eagerly picked up by many governments and elites across the South, including in Mexico.

It was in the name of modernization, which he touted even in his inaugural address,[92] that Salinas took executive actions to deregulate, privatize (including in health), and open the country to foreign investment. Modernization was the new frame for making deepening structural adjustment policies which had been acknowledged as causing disproportionate suffering to women and children's health, as discussed in Chapter Two. The reality of modernization was no better for women who occupied more of the lower-paying jobs in health sectors and were thus more affected by flexible contracts that eliminated benefits. Women were not at the center of this development; the institutional and cultural shifts called for in ICPD and Beijing were a far cry from the reality of this "modernization."

In Mexico, Salinas used the hypercentralized executive power to achieve the ends of the IFIs, which he had adopted as those of his own government. The parts of the modernization project that could not be accomplished directly through executive action faced little resistance from the PRI-dominated legislature. But Mexico was not alone in displacing the neoliberal agenda from democratic contestation. Juan Arroyo has dubbed the health reforms that took place across Latin America during the 1990's "silent reforms" precisely for the lack of public or democratic discussion involved in determining the shape of the system.[93]

There is no question that powerful executive branches in undemocratic governments embraced their new roles as champions of "modernization" together with the new opportunities to exploit for economic and political advantage. But it is also true that deepening global economic integration made it increasingly difficult for indebted nations to resist the neoliberal framing of the world. As Thomas Friedman suggests, the range of political choices became reduced to fit within that framing: mainstream opposition parties offered "Pepsi" while incumbents offered "Coke."[94] More radical proposals were pushed to the fringes of the democratic spectrum and delegitimated as unserious. Also, political systems in North and South alike confined participation to sporadic voting for representatives of political parties, which hardly allowed for meaningful collective reflection that could untangle the multitude of issues arising out of the neoliberal organization of the economy. When the first non-PRI president was elected in 2000 after more than seven decades, the government continued to follow the same neoliberal playbook. By 2018, a more progressive (center-leftist) government took power in a very different global scenario, which may (or may not) open opportunities for other policies.

Concluding Reflections

In 2016, I participated as a judge in a Symbolic Tribunal on Maternal Mortality and Obstetric Violence in Mexico City, modeled in aim and style after the first Global Tribunal in Vienna, and others that had followed. We wore robes and sat behind a panel in the enormous Siqueiros Polyforum in Mexico City; we heard twenty-seven testimonies from women and widowers around the country, each more harrowing than the last, and made concluding comments placing their specific suffering in the framework of human rights law.[95] "Obstetric violence"—including both disrespect and abuse and unnecessary medicalization of the natural childbirth process—was now articulated as an issue of human rights, just as violence against women had been named in Vienna. As in Vienna, this was a symbolic tribunal; we were not prescribing redress, and by this time we knew more about the pitfalls of promoting punitive accountability in reproductive health. Nonetheless, I was struck by the deeply cathartic effect for people whose lives and loved ones' deaths had been dismissed with indifference of sharing their stories in a public arena, and of having their profound personal suffering acknowledged as injustice by those invested with symbolic legal authority.

Much had changed in terms of using human rights to advance women's SRHR in the years since the early 1990's when women's rights were first explicitly acknowledged as human rights in international law. In a 2017 survey, residents of Mexico City said they were "very likely" (6.3 on a 1–7 scale) to associate human rights with women's rights.[96] Moreover, through the work of advocacy organizations such as CRR and many others, as well as scholars, we had built the scaffolding of international law. We had also seen many aspects of women's health rights become judicially enforceable. Yet many challenges remained, and new ones had emerged, which reveal much about the path that SRHR advocacy embarked on in the 1990's and the effects of the diverging neoliberal narrative on women's health rights.

At the end of the 1990's the world would pursue a very different approach to development than that set out in the transsectoral UN conferences. SRHR would be displaced by a global imperative to reduce maternal mortality, which appeared depoliticized. But the evidence-based argument for access to emergency obstetric care became deformed, translated into monitoring institutional births as the indicator that drove policy and funding. Birth attendants had to operate within the formal health sector to be considered "skilled"; TBAs could bring patients into facilities but were subject to prosecution for delivering themselves. By 2016, the TBAs from Chiapas who had come to Mexico City for the Symbolic Tribunal spoke in a private meeting of being subject to suspicion, threats, and violence in the same communities that had venerated their skills twenty years earlier, due to community fear of state retribution. At the same time, the coerced institutionalization of delivery by the state had not been accompanied by commensurate increases in budgets, staffing, and facility space. This environment was a breeding ground for obstetric violence and abuse within the health system— the root of the reason for the Tribunal.

We had also learned much more about the need to address social determinants of health beyond the health system, including those increasingly driven by the power of private actors and transnational corporations, which had been promoted by neoliberal reforms throughout the years. Since NAFTA, huge tracts of land and rights to both surface water and aquifers had been privatized, used by beverage conglomerates that sold cheap soda and blocked community access to water use. As a result, diabetes had become a larger health threat than infectious disease in Chiapas.[97] The manifestations had changed. But the social exclusion and deprivation of rights that the EZLN had denounced long ago—"fundamental causes of disease" that are preventable through structural reforms[98]—had not changed much for the indigenous peoples of Chiapas, despite the aggregate economic growth and other development progress that had been made in Mexico.

In retrospect, it may be easy to see the limitations of our tools and strategies for achieving greater health and social justice in the face of encroaching neoliberalism and the structural drivers of health and social inequality. It is not true that all of the diverse actors in the global human rights movement, which extends far beyond the large international NGOs, were blind to the degradations wrought by these economic reforms or ideologically complicit. What is true—as we have seen throughout this chapter and will continue to see in the book, and is a critical lesson about using human rights for progressive social change—is that the process is iterative, messy, and nonlinear. In rights advocacy we are inexorably dealing with multiple actors, plural perspectives, and partial knowledge, and responding to the shifting opportunities and barriers that present themselves at a given point. Those responses have often unexpected positive as well as negative consequences.

We can—and indeed must—acknowledge the daunting and even Sisyphean nature of the struggle for equality and dignity in health and beyond, as well as where we have failed in our efforts. But at the same time, we need not diminish the value of the ongoing struggle. Further, it would be a mistake to discount the real changes in diverse people's lives that resulted from the 1990's expansion of rights struggles to include more people—e.g., women—as well as the substantive freedoms necessary for diverse people to live with dignity, including health. Ideas do not create change by themselves. The proliferation of human rights norms around health and SRHR in the early 1990's inspired the creation of countless NGOs, multiple fields of scholarship including "health and human rights," and legal and social mobilization to claim different populations' rights to health in Mexico and around the world, which is ongoing today.

CHAPTER 4

Dystopian Modernization

The majority of the country, bombarded by the skillful propaganda by the government of Fujimori and Montesinos, opted to turn their backs on [what had happened]. It was the era of neoliberal illusion.

—*Carlos Iván Degregori*[1]

Although the so-called negative rights (including the right not to be an object of coercion or sexual violence) constitute an appreciable advance, those of us who see ourselves as part of movements of emancipation do not merely aspire to rights as curbs on power. This tradition has . . . not served to dismantle the hierarchies that permit the continuation of abusive policies and practices, nor has it been useful in addressing the challenge of enlarging and extending capabilities and human freedoms to all people.

—*Giulia Tamayo*[2]

THE MISTY *GARRUA* THAT BLANKETS Lima for much of the winter was thick on the morning in August of 2014 when Camila Gianella and I interviewed Augusto Meloni at his parish church in Lima. Meloni had not always been an ordained priest. Indeed, he had been a high-ranking official in the Ministry of Health under President Alberto Fujimori when I had lived there in the late 1990's. Meloni was director general of the Office of Finance, Investment and Foreign Assistance (Oficina de Financiamiento, Inversiones y de Cooperación Externa), in charge of garnering foreign assistance for the family planning program, which had systematically sterilized over a quarter of a million, overwhelmingly indigenous, women.[3] Some of the officials involved in Fujimori's family planning program had gone on to work for the United Nations Population Fund, or hold other important positions, but that was not the case with Meloni. Now, years later, he was representing conservative Catholic views against abortion rights. The truth is that women's bodies and lives are all too often trampled in the name of larger social goals—whether neoliberalism or traditional family values—as those years around the turn of the millennium in Peru so dramatically showed.

When I first met Giulia Tamayo, just after moving to Lima, she was already in the thick of compiling evidence and writing a report for the women's rights group CLADEM[4] regarding a systematic policy of sterilizing indigenous women. One morning we sat on her floor amidst piles of documents as Giulia went through the evidence for bringing a case to the Inter-American Commission on Human Rights (IACHR). That case involved María Mamérita Mestanza, a 33-year-old indigenous woman from Cajamarca and mother of seven children, who underwent bilateral tubal ligation (BTL) just months earlier in 1998. Mamérita and her husband had been subject to years of continual harassment and threats of criminal prosecution by personnel at the local health center, on whom they depended for all of their family health needs. Mamérita was not examined prior to the surgery, and despite postsurgical nausea and headaches, she was sent home from the health center the next day. The health center dismissed daily pleas from her husband about Mamérita's worsening condition, and nine days later she died at home. After her death, the Ministry of Health paid a nominal fee to Mestanza family, and regional health authorities convened a pro forma "investigative commission," which exonerated the health personnel from all responsibility.[5]

Giulia and other colleagues not only uncovered the full circumstances surrounding Mamérita's death; they also framed what had happened to her as the result of a national policy that set targets for BTL for health facilities throughout the country. In 1999, CLADEM, together with another women's rights group, DEMUS,[6] and a mainstream human rights NGO, the Asociación Pro Derechos Humanos (Association for Human Rights, APRODEH), took Mestanza's case to the IACHR as emblematic of the systematic violations of the rights to life, bodily integrity, and equal protection of the law, as well as violations of state obligations to prevent, sanction, and eradicate violence against women under the regional Belém do Pará Convention, which had entered into force only a few years earlier.[7] Both the Center for Reproductive Rights (CRR) and the Center for Justice and International Law (CEJIL) later joined as co-petitioners. In 2002, a new administration agreed to pursue a friendly settlement, which was reached in 2003, whereby the Peruvian government acknowledged legal responsibility and agreed to compensate Mestanza's surviving family.[8] Thousands of other women and their families were not compensated and did not receive any physical or psychological counseling. In 2017, DEMUS asked the IACHR to reopen the friendly settlement for lack of compliance.

This chapter tells the story of the events in Peru in the years leading up to and around the turn of the millennium, which made it clear that using human rights to advance the health of diverse women, and women's sexual and reproductive health in particular, faced a distinct set of challenges. Alberto Fujimori had campaigned on rooting out the Maoist Sendero Luminoso (Shining Path) and the smaller Marxist Movimiento Revolucionario Tupac Amaru, and he did so by relying heavily on the National Intelligence Service directed by Valdimiro Montesinos, in addition to military campaigns. Fujimori implemented neoliberal doctrines with the same authoritarian zeal that he used against the suspected terrorists. However, initially Fujimori had championed the ideas set out in International Conference on Population and Development (ICPD) and Beijing and had stood up to the conservative Catholic Church, which left the women's rights movements divided. By 1998, it was clear that Fujimori's notions of a modern Peru did not include rural subsistence farmers and, in contrast to the fundamental message of ICPD, Fujimori did not trust these indigenous *women* to make basic choices over their bodies and lives. Thus, with the support of multiple international donors, the Fujimori administration decided to "override" personal agency and control their fertility for them.

After Fujimori fled to Japan in 2000 to escape liability for corruption and crimes against humanity, the health policies put in place by President Toledo's administration sought to restore traditional Christian values to Peru and, ironically, framed women's SRHR claims as reflective of an amoral modernity. The conservative Catholic administration in Peru's Ministry of Health in the Toledo administration coincided with a global backlash against women's SRHR. The Millennium Development Goals (MDGs), launched by the UN in 2001, revealed the enormous conservative resistance to SRHR that had been mobilized after ICPD and Beijing. At the same time, the MDGs also revealed that the Bretton Woods institutions were now directly and indirectly shaping the newly technocratic UN development agenda.

Finally, in this chapter, I begin to discuss the impacts of deploying human rights to advance women's reproductive health, and health more broadly, in light of what happened in Peru. Previously, such an analysis would not have been possible. It was only in the wake of naming health and reproductive health matters as *rights*, and the new opportunity structures created by these new normative understandings, coupled with new institutions and actors, discussed in Chapter Three, that it became possible to consider the meaning of deploying human rights for health and what progress would entail. Extrapolating from Peru, I argue that assessing progress on health and economic, social, and cultural (ESC) rights more broadly requires a framework that includes but goes beyond conventionally used civil and political (CP) rights metrics, such as judicial decisions and direct compliance with black-letter orders. Indeed, the ESC rights community quickly recognized that we also needed quantitative indicators, such as budgetary efforts, and health inputs and outcomes to evaluate effective enjoyment of health rights. We also needed, and still need, to explore less quantifiable metrics, such as institutional and political shifts at multiple levels, as well as the discursive effects of different framings of rights. I conclude that the most significant and lasting impacts of deploying rights in health may not be the most visible, but rather lie in the largely unrecorded appropriation of agency over their bodies and lives by subaltern groups, including indigenous women.

Peru: "Stark Utopia" Breeds Dystopia

As the economist Karl Polanyi had suggested decades earlier, the illusion of self-regulating markets implied a "stark utopia," which could not exist for any length of time without becoming a dystopia that destroyed human aspects of society.[9] As discussed in Chapter Three, in the 1990's, governments across the global South converged around a set of "best practices" regarding economic restructuring, based on the "expertise-based authority" of the international financial institutions (IFIs). As discussed, this authority had been carefully constructed based not just on mobilizing resources, but also on a new framing of the world and the role of IFIs in it. The World Bank started calling itself a "knowledge bank"; the Organisation for Economic Co-operation and Development (OECD)—the club of wealthy donor countries—became a "policy bank." In the late 1990's Thomas Friedman referred to these best practices as the golden straightjacket: "If your country hasn't been fitted for a golden straightjacket, it soon will be.... As your country puts [it] on [two things happen]: your economy grows and your politics shrinks."[10]

But in Peru and elsewhere, authoritarian executive branches embraced the shrinkage of politics just as they welcomed economic growth. Shortly after taking office in 1990, despite promises made during his electoral campaign, the democratically elected Alberto Fujimori instituted the so-called Fuji shock. The Fuji shock included fiscal and monetary reforms, drastic reductions in public spending, sweeping privatization of state enterprises and "flexibilization" of labor, which introduced short-term service contracts without benefits across the economy, including in the health sector.[11] The consumer price index rose 7,650% and real salaries fell precipitously. Inflation in the health sector was among the worst, where the cost of care rose an average of 8,400% between 1990 and 1991. The population living in poverty went from seven to twelve million almost overnight. By 1994, almost 60% of the Peruvian population was living in poverty, with poverty among rural populations far higher.[12]

Nonetheless, donning the "golden straightjacket"[13] did produce rapid economic growth, which boosted Fujimori's popularity among the classes that benefited from financial deregulation, and lowered worker protections and free trade. Just as importantly, Fujimori became a poster child for the IFIs. In the first years of the 1990's, Peru received more than a billion USD for structural adjustment loans from the World Bank, as well as additional complementary loans from the Inter-American Development Bank (IDB). These included, for instance: a 400 million USD "Financial Sector Adjustment Loan"; a 300 million USD "Structural Adjustment Loan Project;" and a 300 million USD "Trade Policy Reform Project"—all of which were aimed at "state modernization."[14] Modernization became synonymous with these formulas, including in health sector reform, just as it had in Mexico. Thus, any opposition was invariably characterized as anti-*progress,* which in the case of Peru extended to those who raised objections to Fujimori's tactics in fighting the armed insurgency.

As Friedman suggests, the strictures of neoliberalism also narrowed the available political and economic policy choices. But shrinking politics suited Fujimori's authoritarian mode of rule. The dramatic structural adjustment achieved in Peru was almost entirely through supreme and ministerial decrees—at least 923. Thus, just when ESC rights were being recognized in international law, Fujimori was following very different international prescriptions for law and institutional reform. And he was able to implement the IFI's restructuring program for Peru with almost zero democratic discussion. When it appeared that he would face political resistance, in April 1992, Fujimori carried out the "auto-coup." In other words, he dissolved Congress, the Court of Constitutional Guarantees, and the National Council of Judiciary, arguing that these institutions were blocking his attempts to combat terrorism, which by the late 1980's had spread to Lima.

Fujimori portrayed himself as a savior of the country, both economically and in terms of national security. Before populist despots could even dream of social media, Fujimori and his infamous advisor, Vladimiro Montesinos, expertly used the popular *chicha* press to spread fake stories, create constant distractions, and erode faith in democratic institutions.[15] With shrinking oversight from other branches of government, his administration was able to trample human rights without facing massive popular protest for almost a decade. In 1991, the Grupo Colina death squad assassinated fifteen people in Lima, including an eight-year old, on the alleged (erroneous) belief they were terrorists. This massacre, carried out on Montesinos' direct orders at the behest of Fujimori, together with another at La Cantuta University, became symbolic of the impunity under Fujimori's regime. This case, *Barrios Altos*, was not investigated until April of 1995 and even then, was thwarted by Congress passing an amnesty law, which was supported by military courts. The case went to the IACHR and eventually the Inter-American Court of Human Rights, which in 2001 abrogated the amnesty law. The Inter-American Court ordered the Peruvian government to reopen the investigation and to adequately compensate the victims.[16] After he fled in 2000, Fujimori was later extradited from Chile in 2007 to face charges of crimes against humanity in Peru. *Barrios Altos* was the first time that the international law had influenced an internal criminal case against an ex-president.

Family Planning Program in Sociocultural Context

Anti-natalist population policy was an integral part of Fujimori's restructuring from the beginning. Rural subsistence farmers in Peru—often indigenous—were left out of his vision of modernization. Thus, their numbers had to be contained to align with Fujimori's aspirations for employment and economic growth. Despite these goals, Fujimori made it appear he was supportive of the transformative agendas of ICPD and Beijing. The Fujimori government participated in a technical committee to monitor the implementation of the ICPD's Programme of Action, in collaboration with international agencies and women's rights NGOs. Fujimori personally attended the Beijing Conference, where he publicly declared the commitment of his administration to implementing the Beijing Platform for Action,[17] and at the beginning of his second presidential term in 1995, he declared that "women were going to be in charge of their own destiny"[18]—all of which indicated to some women's rights NGOs that Fujimori could be an ally in their struggle against the conservative Catholic Church and patriarchy more broadly.

Indeed, Fujimori had stood up to the Peruvian Catholic Church beyond promoting access to family planning. For example, in 1991, he initiated changes in the Penal Code to criminalize marital rape and introduce the term of "offenses against sexual liberty." In 1997 at his administration's urging, a law exempting rapists from criminal penalties if they married their victims was repealed.[19] These actions aligned with struggles against impunity for violence against women that were gaining ground at the time.

In the aftermath of ICPD, Peru received support from the US, the UK, Japan, and even the United Nations Population Fund (UNFPA) to "bring Cairo home." Indeed, between 1995 and 2000, Movimiento de la Mujer Manuela Ramos (Manuela Ramos, for short), one of the most important feminist NGOs in the country, received a major grant from the US Agency for International Development (USAID) to implement the project ReproSalud in coordination with the Ministry of Health. Through ReproSalud, local community members were trained and spread awareness about reproductive health and rights, including but not limited to family planning.[20]

When in 1996, Fujimori's administration decided to prioritize permanent and long-acting contraceptive methods the implications were not immediately clear to the public. Soon thereafter though, Giulia and other investigators heard reports of abuses, and quotas for BTLs, in the department of Huancabamba in northwestern Peru. It turned out that health workers across the country—who were now operating on flexible contracts rather than stable employment—had to meet certain quotas each month for surgical sterilization.[21] The punitive placement of targets on workers predictably produced a cascade of coercion, manipulation, and abuse, as in Mamérita's case. Other women were told that they would receive a free health check-up at the clinic and were then threatened with fines, denial of future medical care, or even imprisonment if they refused the procedure. Between 1996 and 2000, an estimated 300,000 people were surgically sterilized in Peru through the family planning program.[22] More than 272,000 sterilizations, the overwhelming majority, were BTLs performed on rural indigenous women from the poorest quintiles of the population, often under conditions that did not meet basic standards of hygiene and care, let alone informed consent.

The Peruvian Health System: A Site for Reinforcing Social Exclusion

The story of the sterilizations in Peru is ineluctably tied to the systematic dehumanization fostered by the health system. The Peruvian health system was historically developed in the urban coastal areas, where the state saw the diffusion of Western hygiene and biomedicine as part of a process of civilization and colonization of the indigenous population, especially women who were supposed to be "limpias y modernas" (clean and modern).[23] The individualistic biomedical approach—a sharp contrast from indigenous cosmologies—was coupled with the long-ingrained ethos of "modernizing and civilizing" and became grossly abusive in the family planning program. Investigations done by activists found that providers' conceptions of indigenous women, as less than fully rational and dominated by their husbands, facilitated the sterilizations.

The structural reforms made to the health system during the 1990's acted in synergy with historical patterns of discrimination and biomedical approaches to care. The health sector reforms designed in keeping with World Bank and IDB guidance, required shrinking government expenditure by abandoning universal programs in favor of "targeting" reduced packages of basic services to "the poor."[24] In light of the ravages of other structural changes in the economy, and over half the population living in poverty, a 1993 document from the Ministry of Health, "Guidelines for Social Policy," had even stated: "It is considered that the state should guarantee access to the entire population to health services *because that is a basis for equality between people which sustains the exercise of citizenship and modern democracy*" (emphasis added).[25] Nevertheless those aspirations, which echoed the notions of ESC rights being set out at the international level, were discarded in favor of "targeting," out of efficiency concerns. But even on their own terms, experts from the IDB calculated that Peru could not finance even 20% of the needs of women and children in *extreme poverty* with the budget Fujimori assigned, for example, to cover maternal-child health between 1995 and 2000.[26]

Numerical targets were not just applied to identify eligibility for coverage; they were also used to increase "efficiency" in programs. Thus, targets were instituted in relation to prenatal checks, institutional deliveries, and other services, in addition to family planning. In the family planning program, coverage goals for surgical sterilizations increased every year between 1996 and 2000 according to the policy. Quotas for BTL "recruitment" and performance were even broken down by cadre of worker at facilities.[27] As many health workers had been placed on service contracts, as opposed to fixed salaries, in line with "flexibilization" of labor, it was far easier to manipulate their behavior. Failing to meet a monthly quota meant having compensation reduced or potentially being dismissed and not rehired elsewhere. Health establishments, and workers, were evaluated on whether they met quantitative goals.[28]

Punitive treatment of workers did not just lead to direct abuses, most extremely illustrated by the family planning program; flexible service contracts also created high absenteeism among workers doing other jobs on the side. Absenteeism, in turn, posed significant costs to the system, not just in Peru but across the countries in which salaried positions were replaced with service contracts.[29] But the costs of these effects of health system design were "externalized"—borne by workers and patients—and not included in health system evaluations used by the World Bank and IDB.

Other aspects of health reform, from decentralization to separating financing and administration from delivery did not work as planned either. Decentralization without adequate attention to governance and accountability produced inequities and local capture more than democratization. Separating financing from service delivery led to parallel "apolitical" institutions being created for professionals with technical expertise to work directly for PARSalud, the Spanish acronym for "the Project for Support to Health Sector Reform." Fujimori's administration was indeed shown to be responsible for scandalous looting of public coffers, but there is no evidence that these parallel structures prevented corruption in the health sector. Indeed, there is evidence that bids put out to private contractors fostered collusion and new configurations of cronyism, and created sandcastle institutions that did little to strengthen the country's health system in the long term.[30] And PARSalud was based on loans, not aid, so failures were borne by poor Peruvians, not by the protected creditors.

Human Rights Advocacy for Women's Health: Framing, Alliances, and Strategies

The mainstream human rights community was among the few groups that persistently stood up to Fujimori, and appealing to supranational forums was a key part of their strategy in resisting the autocratic state. After the Inter-American Court declared null and void a faceless military trial of Chileans accused of being terrorists, Fujimori unsuccessfully tried to withdraw unilaterally from its jurisdiction under the American Convention on Human Rights in 1999. Martha Chávez, a leading member of Fujimori's party in Congress stated at the time: "A covert left-wing ideology has taken over [the Inter-American Court]."[31]

Moreover, the use of supranational forums—the Inter-American System and shadow reports to treaty monitoring bodies—was not limited to CP rights violations stemming from the regime's disregard for the rule of law in fighting terrorists. NGOs fought the regime's destruction of labor rights, which they saw clearly as the unshackling of capital to advance the neoliberal agenda. APRODEH and another NGO, the Centro de Asesoría Laboral (CEDAL) brought cases such as *Five Pensioners v. Peru* and *Lagos del Campo v. Peru*, and set precedents in international law over the years.[32] Moreover, APRODEH, CEDAL, and other groups dedicated much of their outreach and advocacy to ESC rights, including health, education, and the rights of indigenous populations. Peruvian NGOs were leaders in mobilizing for ratifications of the Additional Protocol to the American Convention on Human Rights on ESC Rights (Protocol of San Salvador), which entered into force in 1999.[33] During the years I lived in Peru, human rights NGOs were among the few voices battling against and decrying the regime's exploitation of the disadvantaged in the wake of economic and social reforms.

However, the mainstream human rights movement in Peru, just as in many parts of Latin America, had historically maintained strong ties to the progressive side of the Catholic Church, which has created a complicated relationship with women's struggles for SRHR.[34] Indeed, in Mexico, when the then-governor of Chiapas liberalized abortion under the state penal code, Bishop Samuel Ruiz, the hero to the indigenous EZLN, threatened those who supported the revised code with excommunication and was able to get it changed.[35] Similarly, in Peru, when the Fujimori regime attacked Catholic Church leaders' opposition to the family planning program, the mainstream human rights movement initially reacted by supporting the Church position and its right to express opinions about public policies in the context of profound autocracy. But when the revelations of forced sterilizations came out, APRODEH signed onto the *Mamérita Mestanza* petition, and other NGOs also put their weight behind denouncing the administration.

Advocacy around the forced sterilizations construed the sterilizations as structural violence against impoverished women of indigenous descent, which was embedded in the Peruvian health system—and society as a whole.[36] The government and USAID had portrayed the issues as lapses in quality of care, so a major part of the advocacy involved framing the sterilizations *as human rights issues* relating to rights to health, bodily integrity, equality, and dignity. Giulia was outspoken about the need to dismantle what was by then commonly called "intersectional discrimination" faced by indigenous women in the interlocking systems of power based not just on gender, but on class, race, and ethnicity.[37] By sketching new understandings of what full equality demanded for diverse women across Peru, the face and makeup of women's movements also shifted. Advocates such as María Esther Mogollón, coordinator of the Movimiento Amplio de Mujeres-Fundacional (Foundational Broad Women's

Movement), sought to create a moment of truth and self-appraisal not just in Peruvian society, but also in traditional feminist advocacy circles. Mogollón was a fierce activist but later came to write and teach about sexual pleasure and sexual citizenship of diverse women with disabilities, as someone with a physio-motor disability.[38]

Indigenous women were able to amplify their voices across this deeply hierarchical society, organize movements, and even enter politics. Hilaria Supa, who led protests and lobbied against the sterilizations from early on, was selected to be the coordinator of the Women's Federation of Anta (Federación de Mujeres de Anta), a region of Cusco. Supa was later elected to the national Congress in 2006 and became the first parliamentarian in Peru's history to take the oath of office in Quechua. And in 2011 she was elected into the Andean Parliament.[39] Moreover, the reproductive health and rights of campesinas across the country became not just a political issue, but an issue on the agenda of the democratization movement, which eventually led to President Fujimori fleeing to Japan and faxing his resignation in 2000.[40]

The *Mamérita Mestanza* case, together with political and legal advocacy around involuntary sterilizations, also reflected the sea change that was occurring in normative understanding of violence against women in the 1990's, not just at the level of legal norms binding on countries such as the Belém do Pará Convention, but also in social norms. As Sally Engle Merry writes, human rights were so powerful in reshaping violence against women because they provided a "radical break from the view that violence was natural and inevitable."[41] And it was not just in functioning states and political orders; at the time, rape against women in armed conflict was being recharacterized under international humanitarian law as a war crime through the International Tribunals for the former Yugoslavia and Rwanda.[42]

In this light, *Mamérita Mestanza* and another Peruvian case involving sexual assault by a doctor in a health facility[43] were groundbreaking in using the new paradigms of violence against women. But the *Mamérita Mestanza* case in particular was not just pursuing the larger human rights turn toward combatting impunity, but affirming women's bodies and health as integral to women's full equality in society. DEMUS, CLADEM, Movimiento de la Mujer Flora Tristán (Flora Tristán, for short), and other organizations mobilized around systemic changes—legal reforms to promote education and prevention—as well as sanctions for violence. As Rebecca Cook wrote at the time, women's health represents a metaphor for the (non-)fulfillment of women's rights "in the body politic and in influential community institutions, whether political, economic, religious, or health care." Cook argued that "development in legal doctrine" in international human rights law could provide remedies for violations of women's health rights.[44]

In retrospect, the expanded turn toward supranational forums in the 1990's, both to develop new legal doctrine and to combat impunity, promoted the increasingly reflexive acceptance of a hierarchy of international law over domestic law and politics—especially perhaps in the jurisprudence of the Inter-American Court.[45] For example, Roberto Gargarella has written about the *Gelman v. Uruguay* case, which involved an Argentine woman who was disappeared during the time of military dictatorships across the Southern Cone and whose daughter was born in captivity in Uruguay.[46] The Inter-American Court invalidated the Uruguayan amnesty and called upon the state to remove barriers to prosecution of those responsible. In so doing, Gargarella argues that the court did not distinguish between amnesties imposed by autocratic regimes to cover themselves, such as in Peru, and the Uruguayan amnesty law passed in 1986 under a democratic government and reaffirmed twice by popular referenda with meaningful citizen participation.[47] This distinction matters because through its jurisprudence the court is setting up a template for deciding what counts in rights adjudication, what arguments are persuasive or not—and in this case, it is sidelining democratic decision-making and fostering rights as a modular project.[48]

Nevertheless, finding an appropriate balance between democratic process and a "higher law" is not a simple issue, especially for women's health, SRHR, and the rights of marginalized and excluded groups. As noted in Chapter Three, appealing to an international law positioned as hierarchically superior to politics was attractive in SRHR advocacy precisely because many SRHR issues fell outside of the boundaries of traditional "political deliberation," or were intentionally marginalized by legislatures dominated by religious forces, even in "democracies." For example, when Peru theoretically returned to democracy after Fujimori, in two later cases relating to denials of therapeutic abortion to adolescent girls who had been victims of sexual violence and faced threats to their health, CRR and PromSex, an SRHR group in Peru, pursued the supranational litigation arguing the futility of domestic remedies.[49] Of note in these cases is that, first, the solidarity of the mainstream human rights community to combat violence against women did not extend to enabling them to seek therapeutic abortions. Second, CRR carefully shopped for venues other than the Inter-American System in both Peruvian abortion cases because of the conservative religious leanings of the judges on the Inter-American Court, belying the notion that international human rights law is "pure" and above politics of its own. Third, the same opportunity structures that make supranational litigation appealing to set SRHR standards present barriers when it comes to the inexorably political implementation of judgments.

Anti-SRHR Backlash: National and International Developments

Just as the events that played out in Peru were inextricably tied to developments at the global level and global institutions, so too did the revelations have international reverberations. The involuntary sterilizations in Peru were capitalized on by antichoice religious movements around the world, including in the US government. With strong lobbying from Representative Chris Smith, among others, in 1998 the US passed the Tiahrt Amendment, which, among other things, required that countries receiving US foreign assistance funds ensure their family planning programs were "voluntary" and precluded any use of quotas or targets.[50]

The revelations in Peru coincided with a vicious countermobilization to undermine reproductive rights in the aftermath of Cairo and Beijing. The conservative opposition believed that the "reproductive health and rights" approach of ICPD and Beijing was morally wrong because "it promote[d] 'abortion on demand' (the main concern of the Holy See and other Christian conservatives), homosexuality, pre-marital and extra-marital sexual relations, and greater control for women over sexual and reproductive behaviors."[51] Consolidation around these objectives became a rallying cry for the backlash against ICPD and Beijing, which framed women's reproductive rights as hedonism in an amoral, materialistic modernity.

By 2000, when the then UN secretary-general's report "We the Peoples: The Role of the United Nations in the 21st Century" was launched, setting out global priorities for consideration by member states in setting the next development agenda, the only commitments to health care made were within the context of infectious diseases; the only target related to gender equality was meekly housed under the education goal.[52] The UN secretary-general's declaration reflected the fact that the G-77 (the UN's informal association of developing countries), the Holy See, conservative Islamic States, and evangelical Christians in the United States deliberately joined forces to block potential mentions of SRHR in the new development agenda.[53]

In the fall of 2000, the Millennium Declaration, which outlined the new development agenda through 2015, was signed by 189 countries. Filled with language reaffirming values of dignity and equality, member states resolved to "spare no effort to free our fellow men, women and children from the abject and dehumanizing conditions of extreme poverty."[54] But only seven years after Cairo, no mention was made of the role of reproductive health and rights in doing so.

Translating the Millennium Declaration into eight global development goals (MDGs) was an opaque process controlled by a tiny group of technocrats who were mostly economists and statisticians from UN agencies.[55] The contrast with the social mobilization at the UN conferences of the 1990's could not have been more dramatic. Among other consequences, as Barbara Crossette has written, "This [more] streamlined procedure also meant . . . that those delegations who would have fought hard to include reproductive rights and services had limited input. NGOs and even government experts were barred entirely from the process."[56] Reproductive health and rights was reduced to MDG 5, related to the depoliticized goal of "improving *maternal health*." A major opportunity for advancing women's health rights had closed almost without people knowing it had happened. As Marge Berer explained, "Thus does 25 years of international work for women's health vanish into thin air, not with a bang but a whisper."[57]

It was in this climate that the pendulum in Peru swung back to a denial of reproductive rights based on these same conservative objectives. In 2001—the same year that the MDGs were adopted—the new administration of President Alejandro Toledo launched two investigations into the national family planning program, even using the rhetoric of "genocide." The new minister of health under Toledo, Luis Solari (and his successor) were both part of the ultraconservative Catholic sect, Sodalitium Christianae Vitae. Surgical contraception, which had been subject to strict regulation after the scandals, was entirely eliminated as a contraceptive method option by ministerial decree—affording no more democratic discussion than Fujimori had. Under the new regime, women's fertility was determined by the "will of God"; thus, all contraception was heavily restricted, and criminal penalties for abortion were increased and enforced with greater regularity.[58] At the same time, as Peru was in danger of losing USAID funding, the idea of "safe motherhood" in MDG 5 was the perfect noncontroversial goal and discourse for the conservative Catholics who had taken control of the Ministry of Health. Cecilia Costa, who in the early 2000's directed the "Contingency Plan for Reduction of Maternal Mortality" told me in an interview, "They can criticize us for what we did with family planning, but look at what we're doing now on maternal mortality. . . . This is a priority for the country and we're going to set our sights on this, and saving women's lives is an *unquestionably* good goal."[59]

Ironically—or not—the neoliberal model of development which had produced the anti-natalist abuses lent itself just as easily to the depoliticization of women's health. In the MDG agenda, progress or lack of progress was to be measurable through nested sets of quantitative goals, targets, and indicators.[60] The reductionism of the MDGs was in direct reaction to the transformative aspirations of institutional, legal, and political change in the earlier UN conferences; the MDGs were clearly narrow technocratic goals pasted onto neoliberal economies within countries and in the global order. Indeed, with the MDGs, the nature of the political UN development process came to look much more like the technocratic governance-at-a-distance used by IFIs to ensure appropriate "modernization." Marge Berer writes that it was not just that the women's movement was sidelined: "[t]he global agenda . . . was taken over by the World Bank and the International Monetary Fund. . . . This 'coup' was a by-product of the consolidation of power by these new stakeholders, who asserted their leadership at the expense of the United Nations, whose leadership was previously responsible for global governance."[61]

Assessing Impacts of Applying Human Rights Frameworks and Strategies in Health

The way we choose to measure the effect of deploying human rights in health depends upon epistemic, empirical, and normative premises. Doing so, in my view, has required going beyond both traditional legal and health metrics.

In the newly created health and human rights field, some scholars, such as Sofia Gruskin, argued for programmatic health measures to assess progress and contended that rights, such as nondiscrimination, education, information, and privacy "can help focus programmatic attention and promote health-related interventions."[62] By contrast, Audrey Chapman argued, "The monitoring of human rights is not an academic exercise; it is intended to ameliorate human suffering resulting from violations of international human rights standards."[63] The first approach tended to instrumentalize rights to improve health programs as opposed to seeing improved health as instrumental to a life of dignity.. Chapman's suggestions, by contrast, were in line with the newly agreed Maastricht Guidelines for assessing violations with ESC rights in international law.[64] Giulia Tamayo and colleagues had effectively used fact-finding methods to gather testimonies, medical records, and policy documents to build their case for both direct policy infringements of rights and discrimination, in keeping with the Maastricht Guidelines.

Over the next decades, scholars and institutions would devise methods to measure not just violations but progress in health and ESC rights, by turning to indicators and statistical data to measure outcomes and policy efforts, including budgets. Importantly, those of us who argued early on for the use of indicators in measuring compliance and progress with health rights imagined them as useful complements to qualitative evidence in revealing what governments were or were not doing in health policies and programs.[65] However, the use of public health indicators evolved over the years toward tools for increasingly instrumentalizing rights, obscuring power dynamics as much as revealing them, as we will see in Chapter Seven.

In traditional legal assessments of human rights impacts, emphasis is placed upon the norms established and the direct impacts on litigants. Thus, for example, we can identify direct impacts, which stem directly from court-mandated actions as part of the friendly settlement. These entail material changes, such as reparations to the Mestanza family[66] and the general class of affected women. In Peru, the sterilized women were given access to the state-funded health insurance, which by law they were entitled to in any case. As noted above, the women who were sterilized were not additionally compensated for the physical injuries or mental trauma they suffered.

However, to look only at direct material impacts on litigants of legal cases or human rights campaigns fails to capture some of the most important effects of using rights—and legal claims—such as institutional changes. In Peru, protocols for informed consent and policies in health requiring surgical sterilization to be performed under certain (hospital-like) conditions were indeed adopted. Moreover, there were major changes in the actors and power relations within the Ministry of Health when the scandal broke, as well as ultimately in the government.

In their work on impacts of judicial decisions, Cesar Rodríguez Garavito and Diana Rodríguez Franco emphasize the need to examine "symbolic effects" as well as material effects, which can be either direct or indirect. These include discursive effects and transformation of people's attitudes.[67] In this case, there is no question that political discourses changed at the time, due not just to the Mestanza case but the scandal and social mobilizations that surrounded the revelations: the issue of the sterilizations became an issue on the democratization agenda of civil society organizations as well as political parties. Moreover women across Peru—even if others more than campesinas—began to internalize the idea that violence against them, in domestic settings or health centers, was not inevitable.

Civil society activism for health rights beyond SRHR also evolved. A Civil Society Forum on Health (Foro Ciudadano en Salud, FOROSALUD), which was formed not exclusively due to the sterilizations but also because of other health rights activism occurring, created a large civil society network of health professionals and human rights advocates across the country. As a result, the notion of health rights was more broadly disseminated, and over a period of years different legislation was proposed by civil society and passed in subsequent years, including Law 29414, which established patients' rights in healthcare facilities.[68]

Moreover, although it ended in an "amicable resolution," the *Mamérita Mestanza* case triggered profound effects on normative development not just in the region, but across the world over the next few decades. The case in Peru paved the way for framing involuntary sterilization as a violation of an array of rights, including bodily integrity and freedom from inhuman treatment.[69] Courts at both national and international levels have also been deeply influenced by the events in Peru, but judging that impact can take years if not decades. The European Court of Human Rights (ECtHR) found that sterilizations of Roma women in Slovakia, performed without full and informed consent, had amounted to inhuman and degrading treatment in violation of the European Convention on Human Rights.[70] In a 2016 case in the Inter-American System, *I. V. v. Bolivia*, involuntary sterilization of an indigenous woman was found to constitute intersectional discrimination.[71] Recent cases brought in national courts in Africa have also cited the *Mamérita Mestanza* case precedent in briefs and amici.[72]

On the other hand, within Peru, even when issues were brought onto the health agenda and actors changed, decision-making about interventions remained tied to goals and targets, and the Peruvian Ministry of Health remained authoritarian and punitive in subsequent administrations. As Giulia Tamayo noted in the prologue to my 2002 book on maternal mortality and health sector reforms in Peru, the same structural and gender inequities that had underpinned the sterilization abuses continued to disproportionately result in the neglect of obstetric care for poor, rural, indigenous women "making manifest and unquestionable [the underlying and continuing] discrimination against them."[73]

The events in Peru demonstrated that, as Alice Miller asserts, "taking a 'rights approach'" to women's SRHR calls for moving beyond the naming and shaming found in traditional human rights reporting and litigation. Advancing SRHR requires engaging "with the much messier and more context-specific questions of how rights are made real, how services are revised and policy makers and local authorities are convinced that their practice must change, and how affected persons are moved to act as if these rights can in fact underpin their actions and demands."[74]

Table 4.1. Analytical Categories for Impacts of Strategies

FORM/CATEGORY	IMPACTS
Order(s) by decision-making institution (court, Ministry of Health, etc.)	Direct material impacts for affected individual(s)
Norm-setting and diffusion	Adoption and diffusion of legal standards across other jurisdiction(s)
Institutional/policy	Institutional and/or policy changes and changes in relation to health issue(s) including through budgets
Actors and power relations	Processes of decision-making; mobilization of new political actors/coalitions relating to health (including and beyond specific issue) and health-related planning, priority setting, programming, and monitoring
Political discourses and social values	Societal goals, political discourses, and social values in relation to health and/or specific health-related issue(s)
Ideational/symbolic	Appropriation of subjectivity and agency over health/lives by marginalized groups/individuals (including but not limited to directly affected groups); changed relationship vis à vis community/society/state

In short, as Table 4.1 indicates, to the extent that we can capture the impacts of deploying human rights in strategies for social change, we need to enlarge our frame. Impacts cannot be measured purely in direct compensation or even guarantees of nonrepetition or law reform. Discursive understandings of issues such as sterilization in health facilities as being *injustices* are critical to sustained social change. In SRHR, as well as many struggles for health rights, progress is far from linear and often produces backlash, as in this case.

Further, as I argue throughout this book is that we cannot look at impacts without considering the structural limits that were being imposed on SRHR and ESC rights by the neoliberal restructuring of the economy. Even after Fujimori's draconian adjustments in the early 2000's, Peru's foreign debt represented 38% of GDP, and the country was spending four times more on debt service than on health annually.[75] Moreover, 40% of Peru's debt was in variable rate instruments and almost two-thirds in US dollar-denominated instruments. Thus, the Peruvian government—as were other governments literally across the world—was extremely vulnerable to exchange rate fluctuations and risks. As we shall see in Chapter Five, this was at the very same time that the deregulation of financial markets was encouraging fluctuations and volatility, which not only led to contagion of economic crises quickly, but also precluded governments from being able to predict what resources they could allocate to health and social sectors for long-term investments.

Yet, in Peru as well as elsewhere, the most profound ideational shifts may follow idiosyncratic pathways, which although not easily measured can be profoundly transformative over time. Evaluation of those consequences is a much trickier enterprise, which acknowledges the incommensurability of certain effects and requires the capacity to accept "learnings" at multiple levels that are not always equivalent to "impact."

Concluding Reflections

In 2017, after then President Pedro Pablo Kuczynski pardoned ex-President Fujimori on Christmas Eve, human rights groups brought a challenge to the Inter-American Court arguing it was not possible to pardon crimes against humanity, such as *Barrios Altos*. Women's rights groups, informed by evolving norms in international law over twenty years, argued that the sterilizations also constituted crimes against humanity. In November 2018, Fujimori and some of the other high-level officials involved in the family planning program were criminally charged in Peruvian court for orchestrating the sterilizations. Moreover, less than two years after our conversation with Augusto Meloni—after continuous struggle by women's rights organizations—Peru adopted a protocol for therapeutic abortion, in compliance with the CEDAW Committee's findings in the *L.C. v. Peru* case brought by PromSex and CRR.[76]

Reflecting on those years in Peru and applying human rights to women's health yields a complex story. On the one hand, Fujimori's brutal sterilization program betrayed the idea that women's rights had been accepted broadly as human rights and that diverse women's decisions should be at the center of reproductive health and development policies. On the other hand, those same UN conferences, together with other significant normative developments, had allowed advocates in Peru to use international law to frame the violence of the involuntary sterilizations as human rights violations and as structural injustice staining Peru's claim to democracy, which previously would not have been possible.

More broadly, Fujimori was a poster child for the neoliberal policies being foisted upon governments across the global South. His antidemocratic dismantling of institutions was also reflected in the health sector and in the way he used the family planning program as a tool for his economic "modernization." But Peru was far from unique. Demands by the IFIs and northern governments for adherence to the tenets of economic globalization interacted toxically with highly centralized power in executive branches and weak democratic institutions. At the same time as ESC rights were being theorized and articulated, the "golden straitjacket" was systematically closing democratic policy space. Moreover, women's struggles for SRHR, which had been ravaged under Fujimori, were caught in a backlash that framed secular "modernization" as antifamily, antitradition, and antireligion.

Nonetheless, there is another equally important story about health rights in Peru, which goes to what Eleanor Roosevelt noted over sixty years ago: that it is in small spaces in which rights need to be recognized in order to be made real in the larger world.[77] As but one example, during the years I lived in Peru, among other things, I worked with Dr. Mario Ríos in creating a program on human rights in health within APRODEH, a reflection of a quickly burgeoning field. Together and separately, we traveled throughout the country, working with local groups, and doing workshops regarding what considering health as a right might mean in practice. These conversations were not about Human Rights in capital letters. Far from being "experts" there to edify community members, we were in these diverse communities to listen to the stories of the health-related struggles in people's lives, and to facilitate an opportunity for collective discussion as to their priorities. Issues ranged from abusive treatment at a specific health center, to user fees that should not have been charged, to lack of potable water and sanitation; in each case, they had the agency to create the meaning of health rights functioning in their specific context. As an outsider, I found I was often able to offer a "view from a distance," surfacing issues that might not have arisen, or mentioning ways specific challenges, such as transporting pregnant women to health centers, had been addressed by communities elsewhere.

In all of these spaces, and especially those that were just with women, conversations threaded the personal domain and issues of public policy. It is in these sometimes intensely intimate conversations about our complex sorrows and our anger that people excluded from official public arenas, and women in particular, begin to think about our socially constructed vulnerabilities, and how to navigate power individually and together, in the health system and beyond.

We all understand ourselves in relation to the society and social institutions under which we live. Yet we are also constantly being fed certain narratives about ourselves and our societies, from promises about neoliberal modernity to religious stories of sin and redemption. When appropriating rights allows indigenous women and other marginalized people to collectively create alternative allegories about themselves and their worlds, those "impacts" are not easily measurable or comparable across contexts. But ultimately, the human capacity for seeing ourselves, and others, differently is not only what enables new possibilities for political action.[78] It is the most potentially transformative aspect of deploying human rights strategies—with lower case letters—not just to advance women's SRHR or health rights, but more broadly for social justice.

CHAPTER 5

Globalizing Crises, Pandemics, and Norms

[G]lobalization is under trial, partly because these benefits are not yet reaching hundreds of millions of the world's poor, and partly because globalization introduces new kinds of international challenges as turmoil in one part of the world can spread rapidly to others . . . as demonstrated by the dramatic spread of AIDS around the globe.
—*WHO Commission on Macroeconomics and Health*[1]

[A] vast amount of resources are being devoted to the [MDG] Campaign, which has indeed reordered priorities across the development spectrum. If human rights are not seen to be part of that agenda, the rhetoric of the past couple of decades about the integration or mainstreaming of human rights into development efforts will have come to little.
—*Philip Alston*[2]

[O]ur post-war institutions were built for an inter-*national* world, but now we live in a *global* world."
—*former UN Secretary-General Kofi Annan*[3]

I HAD BEEN LIVING in East Africa for several years when I interviewed the family of Elva, a woman in southern Malawi who had died in 2012 delivering her sixth child after her husband had infected her with HIV. Elva's husband, Christopher, was by all accounts emotionally and physically abusive to her and the children. He had full-blown AIDS, which he contracted in South Africa where he did occasional jobs. Over 80% of the population in Malawi was living on subsistence farming, and it is common for men to do seasonal labor in South Africa.[4]

123

According to Elva's mother, Pauline, Christopher had been taking antiretroviral therapy he obtained in South Africa but stopped at some point. He would not allow Elva to use condoms or any contraception for that matter. Indeed, Elva only found out she was HIV-positive in her last pregnancy, which had been the product of marital rape. But marital rape was not a crime in Malawi, and there was no question of Elva getting an abortion. She was given nevirapine to prevent mother-to-child transmission (PMTCT), which spared the baby, but not her.

The health center where Elva delivered was not equipped to manage an obstetric emergency, let alone one that required surgery. Nor was there any referral network—no ambulance, no provision for vouchers for private cars, not even stable communication between the health center and the hospital. Pauline managed to take Elva to Blantyre District Hospital, which was hours away on the only paved road in the district. But when they arrived, there was no one to treat Elva. After more delays, a desperate Pauline brought her daughter all the way back to the health center, where she died.

When Elva died, Christopher disappeared. There was no question that the children would end up being raised by Pauline. Christopher never offered support or came to visit; when he died of AIDS shortly before my interview with Pauline, the news had reached them through another community member. The children were all struggling: flies in their eyes, lice and skin conditions, not eating, not sleeping, not able to pay attention in school as well as other less perceptible but no doubt equally profound ways. By 2012, had they lived in South Africa, they would have had access to a social protection allowance for HIV/AIDS orphans; in this remote corner of a remote province in southern Malawi, they had access to nothing.

In this chapter we trace the continuing struggles for health rights after the turn of the millennium, focusing on the evolving recursive relationship between global and national events and realities. The global economy remained ever more firmly gripped by neoliberal policies and, by the turn of the millennium, a "global web-enabled playing field" allowed corporate actors and investors to work across the world in real time.[5] Deregulation led to vastly expanding capital markets which left governments in the global South with little control over basic economic policy and planning. It also meant that economic crises in one part of the world were quickly felt elsewhere, which culminated in 2008 with the global economic crisis.

The conflict between deepening global economic governance and national political imperatives was acutely illustrated in South Africa. After the advent of combination therapy using protease inhibitors (now known as antiretroviral therapy, or ARVs) was announced at the 1996 World AIDS Conference in Vancouver, Canada, global advocacy around the HIV/AIDS pandemic changed the paths of both development and health rights. In 1996, Brazil became the first country from the global South to provide universal access to ARVs after activists, NGOs, central and regional governments, and development agencies came together and framed the demand for access to ARVs as a human right.[6] Other countries followed, from Argentina to India. But nowhere was HIV/AIDS more devastating and has the narrative of what occurred been more analyzed than in South Africa, where litigation was used in combination with other social mobilization to obtain the right to medications under the Constitution.

The prevalence of HIV in southern Africa changed calculations of the imperatives of addressing HIV through the new development agenda, and HIV funding became the success story of the Millennium Development Goals (MDGs). In general, however, the MDGs shifted dramatically from the aspirational view of development through institutional and political change to a technocratic approach to siloed interventions, where goals and targets could be set and measured at the global level. Against this background, the UN attempted to define "human rights–based approaches" in relation to development cooperation. The MDG Taskforce on Child and Maternal Health also argued for the importance of human rights in achieving the MDGs and articulated what treating health as a right meant for health systems.

In general, however, the human rights community was largely disconnected from the development world. And there were both advances and missteps in using human rights law to advance health rights in the first decade of the millennium. On the one hand, additional population groups, such as persons with disabilities and, increasingly, LGBTQ persons, were acknowledged as subjects of dignity with equal rights, which called for reassessing what makes people fully human and what the social contract means. New standards were also created in women's SRHR, but at the same time there was tremendous countermobilization around a conservative religious agenda both at national and international levels. On the other hand, at the UN the institutions and procedures of human rights proliferated exponentially, fostering a bureaucracy which required a cadre of more professionalized human rights advocates. A shift *to professional expertise* in health and human rights, and human rights more broadly, accompanied by an exponential increase in courses, in turn lent itself to legalistic strategies, often disconnected from local struggles as well as sociopolitical realities.

The Globalized Economy: Inequality and Instability

By the early 2000's growing economic inequalities, within and between countries, were also widely apparent. Together with other authors, in 2000, Jim Yong Kim, who would serve as president of the World Bank from 2012 to 2018 and appear to change his views significantly, questioned the International Monetary Fund (IMF) and World Bank narrative of the time, arguing that "at the close of two decades of neoliberal dominance in international finance and development, 1.6 billion people are worse off economically."[7] Indeed, since the end of the 1970's economic benefits had gone to the top quintile of the population in poor countries, together with foreign corporations and banks, while in the United States, the top one percent of the population more than doubled its ownership of private wealth.[8]

Inequality between countries was growing too. By the turn of the millennium, on average, sub-Saharan African governments were transferring four times more in debt repayments to Northern countries than they spent on the health and education of their citizens.[9] Just as in Peru, in many cases this debt was denominated in variable rate instruments, making long-term national development planning virtually impossible. As Sergio Spinaci of the WHO Commission on Macroeconomics and Health noted, it was not easy to invest more in health "if you have a large proportion of the budget invested in debt repayments and a macroeconomic policy focused on containing even minor inflation and setting rigid spending ceilings for social sectors."[10] Further, "financial modernization" had dismantled meaningful regulation against exploiting asymmetries in information, and fluctuations in interest and exchange rates, so destabilizing effects could now spread across countries and regions with alarming speed.[11] Protests such as the one launched against the WTO in 1999—the "tear-gas ministerial meeting"—received spurts of media attention but were largely dismissed by policymakers as radicals out of touch with reality.[12] That is, out of touch with the hegemonic reality that had been so carefully constructed.

Global Economic Governance versus National Politics: The Case of HIV in South Africa

In South Africa the economic strictures imposed on the postapartheid government dramatically clashed with the ability of national politics to address the social and health crisis posed by HIV/AIDS. In addition to its new transformative Constitution, Nelson Mandela's government promised sweeping social and economic reforms to address the structural inequalities built into the society from decades of apartheid—which were acutely reflected in health. Poverty-related diseases and lack of basic care and sanitation were widespread, especially in rural areas. The country also faced a growing HIV epidemic, which by 1999 was estimated to affect 22% of the adult population. By 2000, there were estimates that "up to 70,000 children were being born every year with HIV."[13]

Yet in the late 1990's, the US revoked favorable tariffs to pressure the government into abandoning its efforts to distribute free ARVs. In February 1999, US Vice President Al Gore even visited South Africa to pressure Mandela's government into overturning newly passed legislation on generics.[14] The WTO's TRIPS Agreement, which had gone into effect just a few years earlier, increased the cost of pharmaceuticals and in turn reduced access, making it much harder to distribute generics in poorer countries.[15] It was not until 2001, at the Ministerial Conference in Doha, Qatar, that exceptions were made to TRIPS for public health emergencies, such as HIV/AIDS.

South Africa was "underborrowed" during apartheid because it had been a pariah state, but in short order the World Bank orchestrated huge loans to the new democracy for housing, infrastructure, and other projects. The government was also desperate to join the world economy and secure foreign investment. The first two African National Congress (ANC) governments generally followed international economic prescriptions and, "hoping for redistribution through growth,"[16] slashed tariffs and opened the country to international trade and capital flows, fought inflation, and pursued conservative fiscal policies despite the massive impoverishment left visible in the wake of apartheid. South Africa was facing a volatile situation; conservative political elites had to be pacified, which meant, among other things, subsidized privatization, which scholars later found offered vast opportunities for corruption, including in health.[17]

At the same time, during the administration of the second ANC president, Thabo Mbeki, unemployment (disproportionately young, black, unskilled workers) rose to as high as 40% by some estimates—the highest in the world. By the early 2000's liberalized capital flows precluded trying to boost profitability in manufacturing through devaluation of the currency. Further, greater subsidies to manufacturing industries, which might have created more jobs for unskilled laborers, ran counter to WTO rules—already the source of friction regarding compulsory licensing of medicines.[18]

Social Mobilization in Light of Blocked Political Opportunity Structures

In 1998, the Treatment Action Campaign (TAC) was founded by Zackie Achmat and other activists who were mostly veterans of the antiapartheid movement; it quickly grew into a broad social movement around the HIV crisis. Under social and political pressure from TAC and others, the government had agreed to fund a two-year pilot program of PMTCT (prevention of mother-to-child transmission)—via nevirapine (the drug that Elva had received)—and to scale up from two sites per province after the pilot, if the program proved to be efficacious. By 2001, nevirapine had officially been registered as a PMTCT drug. But Mbeki's government questioned the linkage between HIV and AIDS, as well as the safety and efficacy of nevirapine and the capacity of the health system to administer it, and the ministry of health failed to augment its pilot program. The TAC turned to social and political mobilization and policy proposals, and when political initiatives did not work, they turned to litigation.[19]

The story of South Africa's response to HIV is deeply contested until this day. Thabo Mbeki and then health minister Manto Tshabalala-Msimang, together with provincial health ministers, unquestionably blocked political channels of advancing lifesaving HIV treatment. But some, who are far from apologists, argue that Mbeki has been unduly vilified and caricatured. For example, former Statistician-General Pali Lehohla argued that at the prevailing cost of ARVs in the early 2000's (more than 10,000 USD/year per person), "South Africa would have borrowed itself into bankruptcy from the IMF, World Bank and capital markets with a result of more death." Lehohla asserts that Mbeki's strategy was "first stopping the capitalist feeding frenzy at the door, second mobilizing global solidarity for generics, third conscientizing [*sic*] the world for global resources, and fourth demanding a practical medicine-dispensing regime that would be less complex and not harm those who are less fortunate and illiterate."[20] In the end, though, it was civil society that curbed the price demands of pharmaceutical companies, mobilized global solidarity, and raised the world's consciousness—and in that struggle the judiciary played a critical role.

The TAC PMTCT Judgment: A Watershed for Strategic Litigation on Health Rights

In a now-famous landmark decision, in 2002, South Africa's Constitutional Court held that restricting PMTCT to two sites per province unreasonably restricted access to nevirapine, violating the rights to dignity and life, as well as the rights of adults and children to medical services. The opinion did not dictate to the government exactly what it needed to do but ordered that it develop a national plan of action for PMTCT, which the court would then review to see if it passed constitutional muster in terms of both formulation and implementation.[21] In so doing, the opinion was widely hailed as striking a balance between the kind of robust review consonant with the goals of promoting a just and equitable society, and retaining the constitutional legitimacy of a balance of powers, which had been one of the chief critiques of enforcement of economic, social, and cultural (ESC) rights. Far from usurping powers of the political branches, the court was catalyzing action on their part.[22]

The PMTCT opinion was not uniformly enforced due to federal and provincial government resistance. Further litigation was necessary, including contempt of court orders. But new policies and a national plan of action were adopted. Ole Norheim and Siri Gloppen have estimated that by 2010, the estimated life years saved by women and babies having access to nevirapine at 60% coverage was approximately one million.[23]

Beyond the direct and indirect material impacts, there were enormously consequential symbolic effects, as discussed in Chapter Four. Deaths from HIV were no longer chalked up in public discourse to being unfortunate casualties of this dreaded disease, but were considered legal injustices. Desperately ill, impoverished blacks came to see themselves as equal members of the new South African nation and appropriated the agency to make their nation live up to the promises of the iconic constitution.

The norm diffusion effects were also significant and went far beyond South Africa; the initial success ushered in a tide of other HIV-related litigation in South Africa and elsewhere in Africa, such as HIV in prisons,[24] access to second-line treatment,[25] involuntary sterilization of people living with HIV (PLHIV),[26] violations of privacy of PLHIV,[27] and intellectual property litigation challenging legislation that, under the guise of prohibiting "counterfeit medicines," erected barriers to ARVs and other medicines.[28] And many more.

The groundwork for the TAC PMTCT case had been laid by an earlier case, and access to ARVs was extended greatly by another; these were arguably equally important in the process of effecting change. In 1999—the same year that Gore visited to pressure the government into not producing generics and before Doha exceptions—thirty-nine pharmaceutical companies sued the South African government after it passed legislation allowing for parallel importation and compulsory licensing to distribute affordable ARVs.[29] The Pharmaceutical Manufacturing Association settled, fearing the publicity that would ensue if they were to insist upon enforcing their intellectual property rights when people were dying at such rates. Then TAC undertook a number of legal actions against transnational pharmaceutical companies to reduce prices.

In 2003, after the PMTCT judgment, the *Hazel Tau* case was settled at the South African Competition Commission. TAC had argued that the collusive pricing practices of two foreign pharmaceutical companies, Glaxo SmithKline and Boeringer Ingelheim, violated South Africa's anticompetition laws. The companies agreed to import generic AZT, lamivudine, and nevirapine subject to a maximum 5% royalty, which was a major victory for access to ARVs and precedents against private companies.[30] Today, as a result of relentless lobbying by TAC and other actors in global civil society, the great majority of South Africa's ARVs are generics, largely imported from India. As these cases showed, legal advocacy for health rights requires a broad array of strategies that deploy not just international human rights or constitutional law, but also antitrust law, as well as property, contract, and administrative law, among other things.

In short, the impacts of the PMTCT case cannot be evaluated in isolation from the other cases or from the broader social and political mobilization. At the time, courts enforcing newly expanded constitutional rights seemed to offer a bulwark against neoliberal incursions into democratic politics and gave advocates hope. Mark Heywood, of the AIDS Law Project, expressed what most of us in the ESC rights community felt at the time, that the TAC story demonstrated that "there can be successful campaigns for better health rights . . . that are driven by human rights demands and that take advantage of legal systems and the law."[31] In retrospect the opportunity structures afforded by TAC's politics-centered approach, and the unique circumstances around HIV/AIDS, were essential in allowing "judicial recognition to help bring social rights to earth in the form of actual social provision."[32]

Global Health and Development

To human rights advocates, HIV/AIDS represented a dramatic illustration of the possibility for the enforcement of affirmative entitlements to health as part of health rights; establishing the primacy of rights over intellectual property, a manifestation of economic rules; and the possibilities of global solidarity. To global institutions, HIV/AIDS not only represented a global health security threat but a potentially devastating economic impact for the economies of sub-Saharan Africa, as most people with HIV were in their productive years. As a result, funding for HIV/AIDs increased dramatically, resulting in expanded programming, not just in South Africa or sub-Saharan Africa, but around the world.[33]

Three of the eight MDGs were devoted to health: child health, maternal health, and communicable diseases (HIV/AIDS, tuberculosis, and malaria).

The PLHIV civil society movement, together with institutional leadership at the newly created, multi-institutional Joint United Nations Programme on HIV/AIDS (UNAIDS), successfully campaigned for greatly increased donor funding to fight HIV/AIDS during the MDGs. In 2002, the UN Global Fund to Fight AIDS, Malaria and Tuberculosis (Global Fund) was founded as a partnership between governments, civil society, and private sector actors (including the Gates Foundation), and the funding it raised went overwhelmingly to HIV during the MDGs.[34] In 2003, US President George Bush created the United States President's Emergency Plan for AIDS Relief (PEPFAR) and increased US funding for HIV from 2.7 billion USD to 6.8 billion USD annually during the MDGs.[35]

The exponentially increased funding and institutional attention to HIV/AIDS during the MDGs was no doubt attributable to multiple factors beyond the development framework itself. But HIV programming reflected the shift away from the need for broader transsectoral institutional initiatives that included efforts to transform gender inequities in relation to both HIV/AIDS and sexual and reproductive health issues, as had been called for in the Beijing Platform of Action.[36] The MDG focus was now on technical vertical interventions with quantitative metrics (e.g., ARV coverage) that could be tracked at global levels.

A Shift in Governance and Accountability

In the MDGs, progress in the world was measured through a nested structure of goals, targets, and indicators. The goals were intended as global goals to establish priorities in health and other areas of poverty reduction. But because of donor financing and agendas, these global goals were quickly transformed into national planning goals, using the targets and indicators.[37] This change implied a tremendous shift in power from sovereign governments in resource-poor countries to global bureaucracies and institutions to set (1) priorities through choosing the goals, as the imperatives for national development; (2) the performance targets governments were supposed to meet in exchange for aid; and (3) the metrics through which progress would be measured. Aid-dependent countries were then held accountable not for institutional changes that might be considered necessary to sustain change, or even for rates of change in the outcome indicators chosen, but for meeting specific outcome targets.

Not only does this not make sense—that is, reducing maternal mortality by 75% in Peru is totally different than in Malawi—but, as a result, many national governments became accountable to global institutions and donors more than to their own populations for setting and meeting health priorities. The priorities of national development were ceded to experts at the global level rather than determined by those who made policies or lived by them. In the case of HIV, this greatly expanded HIV testing and treatment; in other areas impacts were far more mixed. By the end of the MDGs, not surprisingly, the majority of off-track countries were in sub-Saharan Africa, because the vertical programs of the MDGs failed to take into account starting places and infrastructure and institution-building, let alone the social determinants of HIV.[38]

The UN was losing core funding in its development agencies, as Gita Sen writes, "pushing the UN ever closer to transnational corporations through the Global Compact [which included private entities] that began in mid-2000."[39] At the same time as the WHO was experiencing shrinking and narrowing of budgets, the private Institute for Health Metrics and Evaluation (IHME), funded by the Bill & Melinda Gates Foundation, was launched in 2007 to be an alternative source of global health data. IHME took over publishing the annual Global Burden of Disease (GBD) survey—which used disability-adjusted life years (DALYs) to measure health. From the beginning, IHME supplemented data from National Statistical Offices (NSOs) with other sources of data and used algorithms to combine sources and produce estimates of progress on MDGs. IHME explicitly argued it was not their job to build capacity in NSOs. Thus the setting of goals, knowledge production, and the measurement of progress moved from national level to governance at a distance, just as the economic adjustment targets had facilitated before. In retrospect, the governance discourse embedded in MDGs—pasted onto the neoliberal architecture of the world—reinforced "the seemingly irresistible fate of assimilation to the institutions of the great powers and the rich countries, institutions made to represent the necessary face of progress."[40]

Human Rights–Based Approaches to Development: Health and Health Systems

By the early 2000's human rights at national level had been effectively separated from macroeconomic development in practice. Against the backdrop of the impact of the IFIs and their powerful member states on the development agenda, the UN attempted to reassert itself and insert human rights back into at least one aspect of development: development assistance. Under the 2003 UN Common Understanding on Development Assistance, assistance programs were to be based upon and promote human rights principles including universality and inalienability; indivisibility; interdependence and interrelatedness; nondiscrimination and equality; participation and inclusion; accountability; and the rule of law.[41]

In 2005, Lynn Freedman and Ronald Waldman co-led the Millennium Task Force on MDG 4 and 5 (Child and Maternal Health) that set out the critical importance of human rights in achieving the MDGs.[42] The task force emphasized the importance of *health systems*, which were widely perceived as being undermined by the vertical programs.[43] For example, with some exceptions, programs for the laboratories and treatment of HIV/AIDS were carried out in isolation from the rest of health systems infrastructure in countries across sub-Saharan Africa.

As discussed in previous chapters, if health is considered a *right*, it requires the just arrangements of a democratic society, including health systems.[44] Thus, a health system should reflect the equal concern and respect owed to each individual, which has implications for everything from financing to the treatment of patients and health workers. Too often health systems do not enshrine principles of equal concern and respect, as we have seen in previous chapters. Thus, the task force's system approach, as shown in Table 5.1, was critically important in advancing this understanding within the MDGs.

The Realities of Maternal Health, Health Systems, and a Right to Health

That this emphasis on health systems came from Lynn Freedman, whose work related to maternal mortality, was no surprise. Just as ARVs were being recognized as a life or death intervention, in 1997 the UN *Guidelines for Monitoring the Availability and Use of Obstetric Services* had been adopted,[45] signaling that the paradigm had finally shifted in maternal health programming from treating women as instrumental to children, to making emergency obstetric care (EmOC) accessible for every pregnant woman. Driven in good measure by the research of Deborah Maine and her network of colleagues in West Africa, the new public health paradigm related to reducing the three delays that cause the deaths of the overwhelming majority of women who die from maternal mortality, including Elva: (1) the delay in recognizing an obstetric emergency and seeking help (in pregnancy, the perinatal period, or postpartum); (2) the delay in arriving at a facility capable of providing EmOC; and (3) the delay in receiving appropriate EmOC once at a health facility.[46] As Elva's death showed, preventing maternal death required SRHR, including comprehensive sexuality education, capacity to negotiate sex and protect herself from sexually transmitted infections, and protections from violence. But it also required a functioning health *system,* including emergency capacity and referrals, as well as access to contraception to prevent unwanted pregnancies. There was no single magic bullet, such as ARVs. And indeed, ARVs did nothing to shift patriarchal and other social norms that placed women like Elva systematically at risk, and created patterns of stigma and exclusion.

Table 5.1. Health Systems Based on a Right to Health (modified from Millennium Project Task Force on Child and Maternal Health, www.unmillenniumproject.org)

ITEM	CONVENTIONAL APPROACH	TASK FORCE APPROACH
Primary unit of analysis	Specific diseases or health conditions, with focus on individual risk factors	Health system as core social institution
Driving rationale in structuring the health system	Commercialization and creation of markets, seeking financial sustainability and efficiency through the private sector	Inclusion and equity, through cross-subsidization and redistribution across the system
Patients/users	Consumers with preferences	Citizens with entitlements and rights
Role of state	Gap-filler where market failure occurs	Duty-bearer obligated to ensure redistribution and social solidarity rather than segmentation that legitimizes exclusion and inequity
Equity strategy	Pro-poor targeting	Structural change to promote inclusion

As discussed in previous chapters, health systems had long been contested in struggles for democratization, and the notion that health systems are political and social institutions has often been noted by sociologists and anthropologists, as well as some leading health systems scholars.[47] Nonetheless, Freedman's work was critical in explicitly identifying health systems *as central to the human right to health*, just as other systems were to other rights.[48] Indeed, just after the 2005 MDG Task Force report, the first UN Special Rapporteur on the Right to Health, Paul Hunt, called for a human rights campaign on maternal mortality in his 2006 report to the UN General Assembly, which explicitly grounded both the right to health and the prevention of maternal mortality in functioning health systems.[49]

In 2005, the year the task force report came out, Lynn Freedman wrote, "The reflection of poverty in health systems is made apparent through analyses of who . . . can access health care, and the conditions upon which that access is contingent. . . . Moreover, the relationships that patients and providers have with each other and with health systems as a whole via payment schemes, the accessibility of information, or human-resource practices emulate societal values and discriminations."[50] However, the concrete groundedness of focusing on the implications of a right to health for specific issues and power relationships in health systems diverged from other approaches to developing a right to health that gained ground during this decade.

International Human Rights: Proliferating Norms, Contestation, and the Growth of a Global Bureaucracy

Despite the connections between HIV/AIDS and national courts, as well as with global health institutions, and despite the centrality of human rights to the MDGs asserted by the MDG Task Force on Child and Maternal Health, the broader human rights community was largely operating in isolation from the development agenda.[51] In the first decade of the millennium, the ever more diverse human rights community was occupied with its own expansion into new domains, and professionalization of human rights as a career increased as a growing body of international and regional human rights hard and soft law instruments, and domestic and supranational judgments could be studied. New treaties and instruments continued to be ratified, including the groundbreaking Convention on the Rights of Persons with Disabilities. Litigation around SRHR produced new jurisprudence, as well as backlash. With proliferating guidance from international experts, this decade further pulled human rights in relation to health away from national politics toward a global-level bureaucracy.

Reframing "Humanness": Disability Rights and Sexual Rights

The landmark Convention on the Rights of Persons with Disabilities (CRPD) was promulgated in 2007 and entered into force in record time in 2008.[52] The CRPD transformed frameworks of disability—physical, intellectual, and psychosocial—as human rights instruments had done for children's and women's rights earlier. The CRPD defined disability as resulting "from the interaction between persons with impairments and attitudinal and environmental barriers that hinders their full and effective participation in society on an equal basis with others."[53] Thus, the CRPD explicitly rejected the prevalent biomedical individualization of disability, recognized the social nature of disability itself as well as the penalty it produced in society, and called for measures to promote full participation in society.

The implications of this understanding of disability were enormous, for health and far beyond. For example, advancing the right to health cannot merely mean recovering the greatest possible degree of "species-normal functioning" for an individual. Rather, it requires doing such things as modifying educational programs to ensure accessibility of access to knowledge for vision- or hearing-impaired persons, as well as the built environment, and changing legal norms and institutional practices so as not to stigmatize bodies and minds that tend to be reflexively *othered*. Building on the CRC, the CRPD further challenged conventional assumptions regarding who possessed legal capacity. Just as with women and children, changing our understanding of persons with disability, including those with intellectual disabilities, as equal subjects of dignity required reinterpreting how we understand what capabilities are essential to being fully human, and how to reflect that in laws and institutional arrangements.[54]

In turn, taking disability rights seriously requires changing how we measure progress in the world. As Sudhir Anand, Fabienne Peter, and Amartya Sen have pointed out, health utility measures, such as DALYs—introduced through IHME's Global Burden of Disease estimates and adopted widely in this decade in mainstream public health planning—impose a double penalty. DALYs and their counterpart, quality-adjusted life years (QALYs), devalue interventions for persons with disabilities, as their underlying life-years are already "discounted."[55] For example, an intervention to prolong the life of a blind person or a person with an intellectual disability would not have the same value as the identical intervention provided to someone of "species-normal functioning."

The nonbinding Yogyakarta Principles in 2006 (revised in 2017) filled a gap left by ICPD and other normative guidance regarding sexual orientation and gender identity (SOGI) rights. In turn, Yogyakarta challenged entrenched stigma relating to gender-nonconforming identities and the idea that with whom people choose to have sex, as long as they are consenting adults, is relevant to them being equal subjects of rights.[56] Since the early 1990's, activists and scholars have gone beyond the recognition of the distinction between biological sex and the cultural construction of gender. Indeed, over the years between the first and revised Yogyakarta Principles, queer theory has increasingly enabled us to see the unfinished and more fluid nature of gender expression and sexuality, which is deeply destabilizing to the traditional patriarchal family. SOGI rights today call not just for emulating heterosexual relations, but of reimagining sexual citizenship and human relations.

The Yogyakarta Principles of 2007 also signaled an imperative to protect LGBTQ populations from widespread stigma, violence, and discrimination in law and practice. Both the aspirational and protective dimensions of the Yogyakarta Principles reflected the vastly differing lived realities of LGBTQ communities across the world at the turn of the century.

In the 1990's, in the middle of the HIV/AIDS pandemic, cases were brought to national and international tribunals to repeal sodomy and other discriminatory laws, such as in the UN Human Rights Committee's landmark decision in *Toonen v. Australia* in 1994.[57] In the 2000's, cases were also brought to enable same-sex couples to form civil unions. But in other countries, during the 2000's, anti-LGBTQ laws and practices increased, and antisodomy laws were strengthened and used for political gains. In highly aid-dependent sub-Saharan African countries, one way to show independence from the colonialist West was to reject their moral values, such as LGBTQ rights, even while accepting donor priorities. President Museveni in Uganda perfected this spectacle in his 2009 "Kill the Gays" bill, which created the new crime of "aggravated homosexuality."[58] But Museveni was egged on by legislators and abetted by a hate and misinformation–spreading media and the global reach of far right anti-SRHR groups, such as the American Center for Law and Justice, Family Watch International, and Human Life International, proponents of the view that AIDS was a punishment for sexual deviance.[59]

Mobilization and Countermobilization on Women's SRHR

The women's SRHR movement placed their time and energy into using the human rights machinery—litigation and shadow reporting—to establish standards on abortion, in vitro fertilization, and access to emergency contraception, among other topics. Progressive advocacy groups, such as CRR, had developed successful strategies, and by the early 2000's global framings of issues such as abortion encouraged national legal mobilization, and regional networks as well.[60]

At the same time, the use of international forums by progressive SRHR advocates drew enormous backlash by conservatives, who had become mobilized after Beijing. During the first decade of the millennium, these conservative groups increasingly deployed human rights language to make their arguments in public policy forums instead of overtly moralistic ones that were still used in other settings, such as talking about rights of the unborn and the rights of the family. At the same time, conservative groups started systematically attacking many of the notions that underpinned advocacy for all people's SRHR, including gender. It was first in deeply Catholic Poland that the notion of so-called gender ideology—which encompasses issues of abortion, gender equality, sexuality education, and occasionally even the right to die (because of its association with abortion)—started to be used by conservative groups and disseminated through school curricula. These groups began to use schools and basic education in their home countries; they also appropriated international forums to advance their views that the social construction of gender was an "ideology" which promoted unnatural ideas, which in turn undermined the traditional and correct view of the family and sex roles.[61]

UN forums were increasingly marked by hostile verbal confrontations as well as contestation in outcome documents between those influenced by feminists and an alliance of politically and religiously conservative countries. In 2004, when then UN Special Rapporteur on the Right to Health Paul Hunt addressed the UN General Assembly with a report on SRHR, one conservative group claimed Hunt's report was "part of a coordinated effort to push for homosexual, transsexual and multi-partner sexual license, and unrestricted, government funded abortion."[62]

Women's health and rights groups had seen international law as outside of domestic power politics and sought to use it to extend equality and combat gender discrimination in health and beyond. Conservative groups brought politics directly to UN forums through legal and political mobilization against SRHR. At the same time, conservatives promoted the view that international law generally was undemocratic and illegitimate.

A Shift toward the Global in International Human Rights

During the decade of the 2000's there was also a proliferation of normative guidance and procedures at international level. Before 2000, a total of eighty-nine General Comments or Recommendations, in which treaty-monitoring bodies

(TMBs) set out general normative interpretive guidance of provisions of treaties, had been issued. Since 2000 almost 200 have been issued, often addressing issues that overlap the jurisdictions of multiple treaty bodies. Further, so called Special Procedures were developed during the decade, which included Special Rapporteurs, Independent Experts, and Working Groups. Paul Hunt, a law professor from the University of Essex in the UK, was named the first Special Rapporteur on the Right to Health in 2001.

By the end of the decade, 39 of these Special Procedures had been created, with 13 new mandate-holders in 2010 alone.[63] During 2010 alone, Special Procedures carried out 67 country visits to 48 countries and territories; submitted 156 reports to the Human Rights Council, including 58 country visit reports, and 26 reports to the UN General Assembly; and issued 232 public statements and 604 separate written communications to 110 different states.[64]

The rapid growth of these procedures and forums required an expanded bureaucracy to support them. The Office of the High Commissioner for Human Rights was underfunded and overstretched. The burgeoning machinery of human rights depended on and encouraged a professionalization of human rights advocates and advocacy organizations. International NGOs opened offices in Geneva and New York to lobby in important UN forums; toward the end of the decade international groups started establishing regional offices, which naturally attracted human and financial resources from local groups.

Professionalization, however, was not merely occurring in the North. A growing group of professionally trained human rights advocates from North and South alike became increasingly focused on digesting the proliferating normative guidance and decisions from supranational and regional tribunals, although in the global South this was more linked to navigating the interactions between international and national developments. While conservative were focusing on changing hearts and minds at primary school level, human rights education in health, and more broadly, grew around teaching *competencies*—from international law to research techniques to growing numbers of graduate students.

The rapid expansion of human rights norms and institutions also had the inevitable effect of creating fragmentation since all of these different groups, commissions, and committees at the UN level needed to be considered along with regional human rights systems. By 2006, the International Law Commission felt the need to publish a report on the "Fragmentation of International Law: Difficulties Arising from Diversification and Expansion of International Law" in which it emphasized "the presumption against normative conflicts" implied that "attempts should be made to read them as compatible" insofar as possible including when they did not specify any relationship. In Latin America, where the incorporation of international law into domestic law had been most prominent, scholarship and courses began more systematically to address the harmonization of constitutional and international treaty regimes.

Health-Related Rights Get Further Defined at UN Level

The Committee on Economic, Social and Cultural Rights' (CESCR) General Comment on the right to health, issued in May of 2000, had been in preparation for some time. In 1996, the UN Committee on the Elimination of Racial Discrimination (CERD) issued a General Recommendation on Article 5 of the Convention on the Elimination of All Forms of Racial Discrimination, which addresses public health and medical care.[65] The Committee on the Rights of the Child had also issued General Comments that touched upon various dimensions of children's health and would issue specific ones in relation to HIV and adolescent health in 2003 and the right to health in 2013.[66]

The Convention on the Elimination of All Forms of Discrimination against Women (CEDAW) Committee had also issued a General Recommendation on "Women and Health" in 1999, which followed other narrower recommendations on aspects of women's health and took up many of the ideas that had been set out in Cairo and Beijing.[67] Importantly, the CEDAW Committee noted both discrimination against women and *among* different women based on class, ethnicity, etc. Recognition of the intersectional forms of discrimination, vulnerability, and disadvantage now extended to disability, displacement, and age. On the other hand, disadvantage was still tethered to factors that kept women (and people) low on the socioeconomic ladder; decidedly absent was *how* the social gradient was being shaped by macroeconomic policy.

General Comment 14 on *The Right to the Highest Attainable Standard of Health* adopted analytical frameworks common in multiple TMBs and demonstrated shifts in international human rights law, which have affected how human rights were able to be deployed in health. First, General Comment 14, as did other rights-specific General Comments, updated important aspects of the International Covenant on Economic, Social and Cultural Rights (ICESCR), as for example, in 1966, reproductive health had not even been mentioned in the treaty.[68] It also included analytical frameworks that had begun to be used across TMBs. For example, the so-called AAAQ framework set out that the right to health required that health facilities, goods, and services be **a**vailable, accessible, acceptable, and of adequate quality.[69] The CEDAW Committee had earlier elaborated AAAQ in the context of women's health, noting just after the eruption of Peru's sterilization scandal that "acceptable services" must be "delivered in a way that ensures that a woman gives her fully informed consent, respects her dignity, guarantees her confidentiality, and is sensitive to her needs and perspectives."[70]

A second framework used in General Comment 14, as well as in other General Comments, was "respect, protect, fulfill" which had originally been elaborated by the Norwegian legal scholar, Asbjorn Eide, in the context of eroding the fallacious negative-versus-positive distinctions between CP and ESC rights, and had been taken up in the nonbinding *Maastricht Guidelines on Violations of Economic, Social and Cultural Rights*.[71] General Comment 14 set out that health, like all rights—CP as well as ESC—entails obligations by states parties to *respect* by refraining from direct infringement (e.g., discrimination); *protect* against third party interference (e.g., domestic violence, pollution); and *fulfill* through positive legislative and other measures (e.g., extending health care or sanitary measures).

The Right to Health and the Legitimacy of International Human Rights Law

General Comment 14 is a document that purports to present quite detailed policy guidance; in some ways it was a triumph of those who saw aspects of human rights as useful in programming over those who saw the theorization of the right to health as essential to further advancing a legal right. This is true for at least three reasons. First, it understates the importance of legal enforceability; although General Comment 14 states that "any person or group victim of a violation of the right to health should have access to effective judicial *or* other appropriate remedies at both national and international levels,"[72] it unduly limits the scope of such remedies: "The right to health includes certain components which are legally enforceable,"[73] and a footnote points to nondiscrimination in health facilities, goods, and services. But this is clearly not the case and undercuts the critical significance of the recognition of respect, protect, fulfill; for example, laws curbing pollution or domestic violence or regulating occupational safety were clearly widely in place and enforceable at the time it was issued. Indeed, by 2000, there was already important jurisprudence from both common law jurisdictions (e.g., India, as well as beginning in South Africa) and civil law or mixed jurisdictions (e.g., Brazil, Argentina, Colombia, Costa Rica) on positive dimensions of fulfilling the right to health.

Second, the CESCR's interpretation of the right to health, by swallowing other rights, made it impossible for a court or other oversight body to assess the reasonableness of measures adopted for the right's progressive realization. General Comment 14 asserted that the right to health was "an inclusive right" comprising not just care but "the underlying determinants of health, such as access to safe and potable water and adequate sanitation, an adequate supply of safe food, nutrition and housing, healthy occupational and environmental conditions, and access to health-related education and information, including on sexual and reproductive health."[74] In previous chapters, we have discussed the importance of recognizing and distinguishing between: (1) the notion that *health* is both inherently tied to dignity, subject to social influence, and susceptible to a broad array of economic and political policies; and (2) the *right to health*, which includes both public health preconditions and care, is interdependent on many other rights. As John Tobin has noted, the wording in General Comment 14 left hazy the boundaries of the right to health vis-à-vis other rights (e.g., food and housing) that are of equal significance to a life of dignity.[75] It also left equally hazy the duty-bearers at national and subnational level for such a varied and expansive list of obligations.

Third, despite the CESCR's statement that incorporation into domestic law would enable courts to adjudicate at least the core obligations relating to the right to health "by direct reference to the Covenant,"[76] the expansive core obligations did just the opposite. In General Comment 14, the CESCR abandoned any approximation of a minimum threshold approach, as it had set out in General Comment 3. Instead, the committee set out an extensive list of core obligations, which included: access to health facilities; goods and services on a nondiscriminatory basis; freedom from hunger for everyone; basic shelter and sanitation; adequate safe and potable water; essential drugs; an equitable distribution of all health facilities, goods, and services; and a "a national public health strategy and plan of action, on the basis of epidemiological evidence, addressing the health concerns of the whole population . . . on the basis of a participatory and transparent process."[77] In the following paragraph, CESCR provided another list of obligations of "comparable priority" including "appropriate training for health personnel, including education on health and human rights."[78]

Multiple scholars have offered critiques of the list of core obligations in General Comment 14, which I generally share. These critiques include: (1) the vagueness inherent in many of the terms; (2) the scope of theoretically "non-derogable" obligations—i.e., those that can never fail to be met—as opposed to the prima facie presumption established in General Comment 3; (3) the unclear relationship between "core obligations" and those set out as of "comparable priority"; and (4) the ill-defined nature of obligations of "international assistance and cooperation." Most importantly, as John Tobin asserts, the list "simply does not offer a principled, practical or coherent rationale."[79]

These ostensibly non-derogable obligations are far from the overlapping consensus or common ground for practical action that had arguably been set out in the Universal Declaration of Human Rights. They are far, too, from the nondependence necessary for dignity enshrined in General Comment 3. We have gone from incompletely theorized agreements to be deliberated and vernacularized, to laundry lists, which are not supported by normative or even empirical rationales. As Norman Daniels has written of health specifically, "Rights are not moral fruits that spring up from bare earth, fully ripened, without cultivation."[80]

To be clear: it is entirely appropriate that General Comment 14 would update the story that General Comment 3 set out regarding significant numbers of people deprived of "essential primary care," among other things, depriving the rights in the ICESCR of their raison d'être. General Comments are supposed to update the terms of treaties as well as earlier statements in light of changing realities, and in other areas, General Comment 14 did indeed do this.

However, with respect to minimum core obligations, CESCR alternatively could have clarified the connection between "essential primary care services" and the primary health-care approach adopted in the Alma-Ata Declaration, which included references to both local empowerment and the effects of the global order. By the year 2000, we also had a much better idea of the intersectional and gendered aspects of health system design, from financing to referral networks, which go beyond "primary health care services." There are a multiplicity of other approaches to updating the list.

The basic obligations list in General Comment 14 did not update a story about what minimum levels are required for the dignity of diverse people and the institutional arrangements in health necessary to support them. On the contrary, the unjustified list undermined the critical normative distinction between core content and progressive realization, which it defined in terms of a "specific and continuing obligation to move as expeditiously and effectively as possible towards the full realization of article 12."[81] In other words, progressive realization is a fixed path to an endpoint that presumably has been or will soon be reached in high-income countries, as opposed to the more dynamic notion of constant evolution linked to deliberative process that we discussed in earlier chapters.[82]

This latter approach does not mean that states can indefinitely postpone taking appropriate measures; nor does it deny dramatic differences in resources between countries or real international obligations to reshape transboundary impacts. As argued in previous chapters, this more dynamic approach does suggest that: (1) health needs, and in turn the contents of the right to health, evolve; (2) even in the wealthiest country, all health needs are not met at any given point; and (3) therefore, we require a choice situation to meet health needs fairly, which we have learned implies controlling factors beyond health systems and borders. As a purely empirical matter, the extensive list of substantive core obligations were not met in high-income countries either. Thus, calling these "non-derogable" (which was not used in subsequent General Comments by CESCR) not only undermined the normative legitimacy of General Comment 14. In blurring the distinction between meaningful progressive realization and a minimum threshold, it fueled the narrative that human rights can be satisfied with subsistence guarantees.

In practice General Comment 14 has produced two general types of reactions. Among many human rights practitioners and academics it has achieved an almost biblical status and is often cited and analyzed in both journal articles and legal briefs; among public health ethicists and health economists the list of core obligations in particular has been widely scorned or disregarded as unhelpful.[83] At national level, in the PMTCT case, South Africa's Constitutional Court rejected the notion of a minimum core in favor of seeing it as an aspect of a reasonableness review. Even those national courts that have adopted a minimum core have done so based on national social insurance schemes and other criteria.

In retrospect, General Comment 14 did not advance a sense of coherence and meaningfulness in relation to health under international law.[84] David Kennedy has been harsher in his appraisal of the broader trend General Comment 14 reflected in human rights law, calling it a "combination of overly formal reliance on textual articulations that are anything but clear or binding and sloppy humanitarian argument."[85] We in human rights would do well to recall that the authority of CESCR and other TMBs with respect to interpretations of treaties is not a given; it is defeasible.

At the same time as international human rights law was being used to "trump" national laws and politics in SRHR and other health issues, it was becoming increasingly fragmented and untethered from normative justification. Arguably, CESCR as well as other TMBs in other interpretive statements of the time, were also stepping well beyond the remit of a TMB, making it harder for those same bodies to provide independent oversight of the degree of cogently reasoned arguments provided by states to justify their actions. The delicate balance between recognizing that health and all policy-making call for trade-offs, and requiring states to justify failures in meeting basic obligations or in progressively realizing the right to health, is essential to maintain the legitimacy of international human rights law.

Further, at the same time as UN TMBs were declaiming what governments had to do to be in compliance with human rights obligations, in health and other ESC rights during the 2000's, the MDGs had far more powerful incentives to determine what governments did in practice. And, finally, increased financialization and other measures of global economic governance structured the shrinking policy space for governments in much of the global South so as to be unable to undertake much more than the technical interventions dictated by donors in the MDGs.

Concluding Reflections

In the spring of 2013, I participated in a session at the UN Palais de Nations in Geneva on the measurement of progress in gender equality and poverty alleviation under the MDGs. Most of the state delegates who spoke chose to highlight the successes of their countries, citing an array of statistical indicators monitored in the MDGs. Reading a transcript of the session could lead one to believe that the blights of both poverty and patriarchal domination were fading away across the globe as a result of the MDGs.

A few weeks later, I was in Neno, Malawi, where I interviewed Pauline about Elva's death. I flew to Blantyre, stopping at the district hospital to which Elva had been taken, and then drove to Neno on the same road Pauline had taken Elva on. The capital of Neno district was essentially one dirt road, dotted with international NGOs, which had set up camp to help Malawi meet the MDGs. Most Malawians in Neno lived in extreme poverty in huts without electricity, water, or even household latrines.

The next morning, I found myself wrapping a *khanga* around my waist as a skirt and crawling on my knees up a reasonably steep gravelly incline to the house of the Paramount Chief—the highest traditional leader of a chiefdom community—in order to obtain approval to conduct interviews. To me it was just a curious ritual because I had not grown up internalizing these particular gender scripts. But to the women who lived in the community, as Elva had, these intricate enactments of traditional tribal, patriarchal and neopatrimonial power, and obeisance, influenced their identities and were passed from generation to generation.

Yet even in this apparently remote area of the world, the real powers that shape the conditions under which we live increasingly flowed in global space, while these social institutions remained tied to the ground. My argument throughout these pages is not that there is *or even that it is possible to imagine* a local "lived reality," as unrelated to the global order—shaped both by human rights and development norms, and economic governance. Rather, it is that to deploy human rights to advance health and social justice, it is imperative to understand, and make visible, the recursive relationships between the global and local, including the epistemic dissonances. These include, for example, the divergent understandings of advancing gender and social justice evinced at the Palais de Nations, those driving the international development NGOs that dotted Neno's main road, and those of Elva and others who are literally forced to embody injustice.

The story of Malawi's neighbor, South Africa, illustrates the challenges in attempting to map and address both the national and the global—but also gives reason for hope. By the mid 2000's South Africa had seen significant economic growth; average household income had tripled between 2000 and 2007.[86] But it had gone to the very wealthiest. A little over a decade after becoming a democracy, South Africa was also the most unequal country in the world. According to the Palma Index, the wealthiest 10% had 7.1 times the wealth of the bottom 40%.[87] Protesters across the country clamored for the ANC to keep its promises. The IMF argued in the mid 2000's that the problems in South Africa and economic crises elsewhere did not imply that its prescriptions should be rethought; rather measures were needed to contain national inefficiency, ineptitude, and corruption.[88] Indeed, politics in South Africa had become performative in public and transactional in private; but it is also true that opportunity structures created by the IFIs' dictates closed space for democratic governance and created incentives for crony capitalism and rent-seeking. In 2009, South Africa had elected Jacob Zuma, who would be forced to resign in 2018 in disgrace after unprecedented corruption scandals.[89] By then, much of society had grown cynical about the democratic institutions in which they had placed such tremendous hope.

Yet as we have seen in previous chapters, the story of human rights advocacy is one of continual adaptation. By the time I participated in an inspiring activist leadership school at Section 27 in 2019, a broad spectrum of civil society groups, including TAC and Section 27, were mobilizing around tax justice; privatization of services, including those for people with mental disabilities; and, importantly, drawing the connections between national economic and health realities and such issues as economic dependence on mining and the global economic order.

Moreover, perhaps more than any other example in global health and rights, twenty years ago the use of human rights strategies in the face of the deadly global HIV pandemic demonstrated that ordinary people could change the narratives they had been told about themselves and act collectively to challenge the power of governments, transnational pharmaceutical companies, and intergovernmental institutions. Just as in the antiapartheid struggle, what once seems impossible, suddenly was not. Today, the most important source of human rights consciousness and energy is still—and always will be—the diverse people who have been affected by, and collectively struggle against "pathologies of power."[90]

CHAPTER 6

Inequality, Democracy, and Health Rights

[M]aternal deaths can no longer be explained away by fate, by divine purpose or as something that is predetermined to happen and beyond human control . . . when governments fail to take the appropriate preventive measures, that failure violates women's human rights.
—*Rebecca Cook*[1]

Social justice is a matter of life and death. It affects the way people live, their consequent chance of illness, and their risk of premature death.
—*WHO Commission on Social Determinants of Health*[2]

Today . . . we can see our political institutions being robbed more and more of their democratic substance during the course of the technocratic adjustment to global market imperatives. Our capitalist democracies are about to shrink to mere façade democracies.
—*Jürgen Habermas*[3]

IN AUGUST OF 2015, the neonatal intensive care unit in the Hospital Géral de Nova Igaçu outside of Rio de Janeiro was filled with incubators, virtually all occupied by babies who had been born prematurely and had neonatal complications. The postpartum wards were lined with women who had just had cesareans. The two are related, as cesarean sections are associated with placental problems that lead to premature labor in future pregnancies. Moreover, cesareans are major abdominal surgery that entails possible complications, including infection, blood loss, hysterectomies, and even death.[4] At the time, Brazil had the highest cesarean rate in the world: 88% in the private sector where 30% of deliveries were performed, and 46% in public facilities.[5] Based on the best evidence at the time, the WHO was calling for C-section rates of 5–15% of deliveries. The extreme overuse of cesarean surgeries revealed systemic problems as well as gender-based discrimination, just as their absence did in Elva's case in Malawi in Chapter Five. As discussed in Chapter Three, in the context of the Symbolic Tribunal in Mexico, by 2015, not just disrespect and abuse but the pathologization of natural reproductive processes and overmedicalization of childbirth had been conceptualized as "obstetric violence."[6]

I was at Nova Igaçu, together with a Brazilian colleague and physician, Sandra Valongueiro, because Alyne da Silva Pimentel had died there, and her death had become a landmark case under international law in 2011, establishing an affirmative right to maternal health care in 2011.[7] Despite the UN Committee on the Elimination of All Forms of Discrimination against Women (CEDAW) calling government "compliance" formally complete, at the invitation of the Brazilian government we went to Brazil to catalyze political engagement around implementation of the structural recommendations. In 2015, CESCR had yet to implement a formal follow-up procedure for its judgments, and those of other treaty-monitoring bodies (TMBs), including CEDAW, had been critiqued for lacking resources and capacity.[8] As Víctor Abramovich had noted, effective implementation of structural remedies by supranational regional tribunals (and similarly TMBs) calls for re-engaging domestic actors, including national agencies, judiciaries, national human rights institutions, and civil society actors.[9] Moving from the global to the national level, from the legal and adversarial realm to the political and deliberative, is exactly what we were attempting to do, in order to encourage local actors to examine how complex health rights can be made to function within a specific context.

Alyne was 28 when she died in her second pregnancy in 2002. She was barely six and a half months pregnant when she went into labor and delivered a stillborn fetus at the private health center in Belford Roxo. But she had to wait until the next day to undergo surgery to remove the retained tissue. Afterward, Alyne's condition deteriorated, though her family's concerns were dismissed, just as Mamérita Mestanza's in Chapter Four had been. A few days later, Alyne needed a blood transfusion; she had been hemorrhaging internally. The only hospital that would accept her refused to use its ambulance for the transfer. Because so many patients are booked in advance for cesareans in Brazil, women who want natural births or need other maternal care routinely encounter long waits to find free beds. In this case, the delay was a death sentence. Alyne's family did not have money for a private ambulance, so they waited eight hours before she was finally taken to a hospital, which turned out not to have any bed space for her. Alyne died at the Hospital Géral de Nova Igaçu five days after she had initially gone to the Belford Roxo health center complaining of nausea and abdominal pain.

In 2007, the Center for Reproductive Rights (CRR) and a Brazilian NGO, Advocacia Cidadã Pelos Direitos Humanos (which subsequently closed), brought Alyne's case to the CEDAW Committee under the Optional Protocol, which had just entered into force. In 2011, the committee's findings established important precedents in international law. For the first time, a supranational "tribunal" (1) enforced a state's obligations to ensure affirmative entitlements to emergency obstetric care, as a matter of nondiscrimination against women; (2) explicated intersectional discrimination on the basis of race, gender, and class in a concrete case; and (3) elaborated on duties to regulate private actors in the health sector, as part of a state's duty to protect women's rights to health and life.[10]

This chapter places the *Alyne* case in context, highlighting the linkages between democratic institutions and processes and the advancement of health rights. By 2011, we had come a long way from when human rights violations relating to reproductive health were confined to the kinds of abuses that had taken place in the ESMA in Argentina, or even the coercive sterilizations in Peru. The *Alyne* case was the result of many years of parallel and synergistic work in human rights and public health. As Rebecca Cook noted, *Alyne* demonstrated that maternal mortality was understood to be a foreseeable result of government actions and inactions; the policies and programs needed to prevent it were understood as enforceable under international law, and the case changed our understanding of "human rights as abstract and aspirational to obligatory and concrete"[11]—which had all been unthinkable just two decades before.

Indeed, by the second decade of the millennium, judicial enforcement of health rights had grown far beyond HIV to include not only many issues of sexual and reproductive health and rights (SRHR) and maternal health, but also access to treatments for a wide variety of conditions. However, in Brazil, and Latin America more broadly, where tens of thousands of protection writs were being brought to courts through individuals, the enforceable right to health was portrayed very differently than it had been in South Africa.

By the end of the 2000's, several apex courts had experimented with structural remedies to address the multivalent policy implications in health. These remedies, as did the one used in TAC PMTCT case discussed in Chapter Five, do not set out black-letter rulings of what the government must do, but rather attempt to catalyze dialogue with the political organs of government. Briefly reviewing a right to food case in India, a case involving pollution in Argentina, and a case calling for significant restructuring of the Colombian health system, I argue that such remedies offer promise of shifting political actions around health, but also face significant challenges.

We had also advanced significantly in terms of defining what governments were required to do to apply human rights obligations in policymaking and programming related to health, and maternal health in particular. In the latter half of the Millennium Development Goals (MDGs), human rights activists developed human rights–based approaches (HRBAs) to health, among other things, as a Trojan horse to insert rights issues into the narrow approaches to reproductive, maternal, newborn, and child health (RMNCH) being promoted in the MDGs. Early HRBAs advanced conceptualization of the contrasts with conventional approaches, but in retrospect revealed ongoing contestation about the purpose of applying human rights frameworks to health. The *Alyne* case was also precedent-setting in the deployment of an HRBA to guide implementation of a supranational decision with the intent of catalyzing local actors to take actions, and Brazil provides an example of what HRBAs can (and cannot) do.

At the same time, we have seen inequalities increase over the decades in which health rights have been increasingly articulated. Beyond damaging population health effects, extreme social inequality erodes possibilities for democracy. Brazil was a perfect example of how in countries with unresponsive health systems, and dysfunctional political institutions, people turned to favorable legal opportunity structures in courts at the national level and to human rights bodies at the supranational level. And in politics, they often turn to populist saviors, such as Luis Inácio Lula da Silva, founder of the Workers Party (PT, with its Portuguese acronym), who was seen as the champion of the working class in Brazil and who was elected president in 2002. "Lula"—as he was universally called—had stated in speeches that watching his wife die during the eighth month of her pregnancy, along with the baby, because they could not afford care, had been what drove him into politics.[12]

Ultimately, this chapter underscores that advancing health rights requires strategies that foster meaningfully democratic processes and institutions, and social accountability to people whose lives are affected. It further requires challenging the global power dynamics that systematically shrink policy space for advancing health rights.

Inequality: Implications for Health and Democracy

Brazil is a sprawling country with huge inequalities based on gender, race, ethnicity, and social class, as well as geographic region. The post-dictatorship transformative Constitution of 1988 exemplifies Gargarella's insight discussed in Chapter Three about the conflicts that arise from maintaining strong centralization of power in the executive, even while adding a robust enumeration of economic, social, and cultural (ESC) rights.[13] At the same time, responsibilities—including for health—are shared between the federal government, the states, and the municipalities, which produces fragmentation and difficulties in governance in health and beyond. The political system adds to governance problems, with a presidential system in the upper house and a proportional representation system that looks more parliamentarian among over twenty parties in the lower house. In this system, where candidates have to promote themselves more than any specific party, the cross-party "caucuses"—evangelical, rural, etc.—have far more power than the political parties. As Ryan Lloyd and Carlos Oliveira write: "Now let's add up all those elements: politicians perpetually searching for funds; parties that lack organization or power; and powerful interests that cut across party lines. Getting a law passed involves forming a voting coalition of hundreds of individuals from more than a dozen parties.... To move the wheels of government, you have to pay individual members of Congress. Without that grease, Congress grinds to a halt."[14] Brazil is a striking case of political dysfunction but is not unique; the notion of liberal power that has been historically embedded in human rights law as discussed in Chapter One—where interests are understood as equivalent to political behavior in overt decision-making and to exercise power is to prevail over the opposing views on key issues—cannot explain the real power that is employed in deal-making behind closed doors to control the political agenda.[15]

Moreover, Brazil's economy had been badly affected by the 1997 Asian financial crisis, which had been driven by capital market volatility and resulted in a decrease in growth, a drop in employment rates, and a rise public debt.[16] With a national government that was seen as indifferent to massive human suffering, dysfunctional and largely captured by elites, the charismatic Lula was overwhelmingly elected in a run-off election in 2002. But before the former socialist was elected, due to the perceived "Lula Risk" affecting foreign investor confidence, he was forced to sign an extraordinary "Carta ao povo brasileiro" (Letter to the Brazilian People), in which he promised not to do anything to upset foreign markets and investments if he won the election.[17]

Poverty, Inequality, and Metrics

In 2002, when Lula was elected president, approximately 22 million Brazilians, over 12% of the population, were living below the World Bank's poverty threshold of $1.90 per day. In 2003 when Lula took office, 25% of the population lived below the national poverty line, but by 2009 this had declined to approximately 11%.[18] Further, Brazil's income inequality, according to the Gini index, which measures the dispersion of income, steadily decreased over Lula's tenure.

Lula implemented immensely popular programs, such as Bolsa Familia, a conditional cash transfer program for poor people such as Alyne da Silva, as well as an ambitious campaign against hunger. He also increased minimum wages in areas such as construction and gave hundreds of thousands of newly formally employed workers (disproportionately men) more power to negotiate. He reduced dependency on international financial institutions by paying off debt, and Brazil even became a creditor nation. It also helped that Brazil's economy recovered during these years and economic growth boomed on global commodity trading, among other things.

Lula stressed the need to establish an international economic order that would be more democratic, sought to strengthen a free trade zone in South America (MercoSur), traded more with Africa, and came to be viewed globally as one of the architects of changing global power dynamics, strengthening the clout of the so-called BRICS countries (Brazil, India, China, and South Africa). In 2010, Lula was named one of most influential leaders in the world by *Time Magazine*.[19] Two years later, in 2012, as a result of planning under Lula and his handpicked PT successor, Dilma Rousseff, the United Nations Conference on Sustainable Development was held in Río, as a follow-up to the 1992 UN conference mentioned in Chapter Three. The so-called Río + 20 Conference would produce a process that led to Agenda 2030 and the Sustainable Development Goals, the successor to the MDGs—and would wrest power over the development agenda from the club of donors to a broader group of countries.

Lula's tenure seemed to illustrate that tolerating poverty was a political choice that could be remedied through elections. And that is no doubt true to some extent. In retrospect, however, much of the Brazilian miracle has come to be questioned, as economists pointed out that social programs and wage increases had shrunk poverty (making more people closer to the middle and reducing the Gini index), but wealth inequality—including investment wealth—between rich and poor grew as well, making the gap between the top 10% and the bottom 90% larger, and the gap between the top 1% and the rest larger. Conditional cash transfers cushioned needs to pay for urgent medical care and allowed the lower-middle class to become consumers driving demand for goods and services. Yet they did not alter the structural inequality in Brazil, in which Afro-descendant women, such as Alyne da Silva, were at the bottom.

Brazil reflected a broader trend in increasing wealth inequality between the top and the bottom. From the early 1980's to 2008, the top 10% of the US population received 100% of benefits from growth, seeing their incomes rise, while the incomes of the bottom 90% fell.[20] The top one percent had increased their share of income by over 60%. Why and how had this happened? It is true that, for example, in 1979, chief executive officers (CEOs) of the US's most successful businesses earned on average 30 times as much as their workers. By 2013, that figure had changed to 300 times as much as their workers.[21] But that is not the whole story; both Brazil and the US, and elsewhere, were also subject to the continuing shift from production to financialization (boosted enormously by digital technology in the 2000's), deregulation, and tax policy.

Decades of financialization and deregulation coupled with tax policy had fundamentally changed the balance of private and public wealth. An ever greater share of national economies and the global economy was driven and controlled by financial sectors, which for decades had been subject to differing tax regimes (and often escaped most taxation in practice) while the public wealth necessary to create fiscal space and in turn invest in social programs had continually shrunk under adjustment prescriptions. The 2008 global financial crisis began with the bursting of the housing bubble in America but quickly spread across the world and caused commodity prices to drop and growth rates to fall precipitously.[22] Brazil weathered the crisis remarkably well for the first few years, but its economy eventually fell too, given other commodity forces.

Inequality and Health

The 2008 global crash occurred just as a groundbreaking report was released by the WHO Commission on Social Determinants of Health, which reframed health equities as the starting place to formulate policy, rather than something to address after aggregate health advances were attained. The report synthesized a multitude of studies using a variety of different methodologies and demonstrated the overwhelming importance of the "conditions in which people are born, grow, live, work, and age" to health—precisely the conditions affected by effective enjoyment of human rights.[23] If human rights work over the last few decades had shown how certain people are kept low on the social ladder as a result of intersectional discrimination, stigma, and other forms of marginalization, the WHO Social Determinants of Health report strongly reinforced earlier reports showing how the social gradient in wealth itself affected health.

The effects of social gradients on health had been systematically documented for decades, as mentioned in Chapter Two. A burgeoning literature in social epidemiology had made it increasingly evident since the 1980's that inequality was bad for our health in a multitude of ways.[24] One highly influential study found that the "pernicious effects that inequality has on societies: eroding trust, increasing anxiety and illness, (and) encouraging excessive consumption" held true not just among those who were deprived but also among the wealthy in such societies.[25] Nonetheless, scholars continued to debate about the appropriate measure of inequality, and in turn *why we should care*—i.e., because it was associated with poverty and social exclusion, or for broader reasons relating to democratic governance. The distinction matters because as Brazil shows, poverty can be reduced without reducing inequality.

Inequality and Democracy

For human rights the distinction in why we care about inequality is critical; it determines whether a right to health is merely a sufficiency guarantee or demands broader measures to address the ordering of institutions in society—and in the global order. Since the philosophers of ancient Greece, scholars have noted that great wealth inequality is fatal to democracy. Wealthy elites interact less with ordinary citizens and begin to believe they are more capable of governing society. The Argentine dictatorship had held this view of the "masses," and apartheid institutionalized separation based on race and class in South Africa; but extreme wealth inequality can achieve the same effect in a democracy. Thus, the epistemic value of democracy lies not in the formal form of government. Mexico under seven plus decades of the PRI in the early 1990's was a "democracy"—as was Fujimori's Peru, Jacob Zuma's South Africa, etc. We value democracy because it allows ordinary people to have a say in governing themselves. Substantive democracy is the political manifestation of understanding members of a polity as subjects of dignity. The Spanish philosopher Maria Zambrano goes even further arguing democracy does not merely permit people to be fully human, it demands that they be so.[26] This more robust understanding of democracy, and its relation to human rights, including health rights, requires not merely keeping people apart through civil liberties protections but bringing diverse people together in mutually humanizing interaction.[27]

However, these conditions cannot be met when there is an increasing gap between the elites and the general public; between those who make laws and policies and those affected by policy decisions. By the second decade of the 2000's, elites in many countries of the North and South alike, including politicians, were largely buying their way out of public education, public health systems, public transport, and the literal public spaces to exercise, socialize, and collectively gather. For example, the renowned Brazilian modernist landscape architect, Roberto Burle Marx, famously preferred to design in public spaces because they were "to provide dignity for the people"; by the time I was there in 2015, stretches of his iconic black and white mosaic sidewalk "painting" along Copacabana Beach were still public spaces for people to promenade. But by 2015 the private corporation Facebook had become the "global public square" in digital reality, and in physical reality Rio, just as the rest of Brazil, was staggeringly segregated by race and class. Wealthy Brazilians, largely of European and Asian descent, lived in posh areas with extremely high security, while the poor—Afro-descendants and others of mixed race—were amassed in favelas (slums) that often lacked even piped water and basic sanitation.

Within months of my visit to Rio, the Zika outbreak occurred. Impoverished women, who lived in favelas and other areas with standing water and had difficulty accessing contraception and negotiating sexual relations with their partners, were told to wear mosquito repellant and, if bitten, to abstain from getting pregnant. If they did get pregnant, at the time they could not obtain abortions under Brazilian law. The initial Zika response from Brazil and other governments, which discursively transformed political failures into personal responsibilities of poor, powerless women, was exactly what HRBAs to health had been designed to combat.[28]

Human Rights–Based Approaches to Health Get Defined

Since the UN outlined the pillars of a human rights–based approach to development in 2003, then High Commissioner for Human Rights Navanethem Pillay had encouraged incorporating rights "into the implementation of programmes as a mechanism for making rights easier to claim and understand, and thereby be more effective."[29] For its part, the objectives of the WHO related to health also included strengthening WHO's capacity to integrate a human rights–based approach in its work.

In women's health, by the mid-point of the MDGs, advocates were increasingly aware of the adverse empirical consequences of depoliticization of SRHR issues in MDG 5, the vertical approaches to delivery care that failed to build health systems or address social determinants of diverse women's risks. Even as many feminist groups distanced themselves from the MDGs, new alliances and coalitions were formed, and maternal health became a space to advance both health as an ESC right as well as SRHR. In 2007, the largest membership human rights NGO in the world, Amnesty International, launched the Demand Dignity campaign, enlarging its traditional mandate from a narrow slice of CP rights to include a set of ESC rights; in health, the campaign focused on maternal health.

In the same year, the International Initiative on Maternal Mortality and Human Rights (IIMMHR) was launched, which brought together groups working on human rights and SRHR advocacy with those implementing health service delivery programs. The mandate of the IIMMHR would have been unimaginable even a decade earlier. Among other things, IIMMHR sought to promote understanding that "maternal death can be as much a human rights violation as extrajudicial executions, torture, and arbitrary detentions."[30]

Moreover, Paul Hunt, the first Special Rapporteur on the Right to Health, played a pivotal role in galvanizing support for action on a human rights–base approach in the context of maternal health at the UN Human Rights Council. The convergence of Hunt's leadership, institutional support, and the fundamental role of civil society, including IIMMHR, led to a series of resolutions from the UN Human Rights Council in 2009, 2010, and 2011, calling for the Office of the High Commissioner for Human Rights (OHCHR) to prepare reports on linkages between maternal mortality and human rights, best practices, and finally "concise technical guidance on the application of a human rights-based approach to the implementation of policies and programmes to reduce preventable maternal mortality and morbidity" (referred to as UN Technical Guidance).[31]

Health Frameworks Define Rights and Rights-Holders in HRBAs: SRHR versus RMNCH

The UN Technical Guidance was the first intergovernmentally approved statement from the UN Human Rights Council setting out an HRBA in relation to any health issue. Thus, it is worth highlighting a few elements regarding the elaboration of a human rights–based approach: (1) placing maternal mortality in the context of SRHR; (2) establishing key definitional issues distinguishing an HRBA from conventional approaches to health; and (3) ensuring an HRBA encouraged local appropriation, vernacularization, and deliberation over how health rights function in practice.

First, the UN Technical Guidance embedded maternal health in a broader SRHR framework, as opposed to the so-called continuum of care approach based on RMNCH (reproductive, maternal, newborn, and child health), which had been institutionalized in the MDGs in the Partnership for Maternal Newborn and Child Health (PMNCH) created as a global umbrella for stakeholders in these issues working under the WHO.³² This is far from a semantic issue; recall how articulating women's health rights required normatively separating them from children and their reproductive roles, as discussed in Chapters Two and Three. Despite highlighting the need for continuity of care within the health system, which is aligned with the need for a referral network, the RMNCH framework was a step backwards in reducing women to their reproductive intentions and capacities, rather than treating them as individuals with agency over their bodies and lives, as had been the aspiration at the International Conference on Population and Development (ICPD).

This was a red line because it would foreseeably trigger a cascade of implications with respect to how women's health and rights got institutionalized. For example in Brazil, the government had taken an extraordinary number of measures regarding maternal mortality to achieve MDG 5, including adopting a National Policy on Sexual Rights and Reproductive Rights. Nevertheless, Brazil's central initiative and strategy for reducing maternal mortality and morbidity was the Rede Cegonha (Stork Network), which adopted an approach based on RMNCH. On our follow-up mission after the *Alyne* decision, we found that the instrumentalization of women in terms of reproductive intentions and capacities generated through a continuum of care approach was greatly exacerbated by the Brazilian health system's highly medicalized approach to reproduction. The untrammelled power of physicians to define women's delivery choices and processes resulted in not just elevated rates of cesarean sections, but other intrusive and abusive interventions in both pregnancy and delivery care (e.g., the overuse of fundal pressure and oxytocin to accelerate contractions).[33]

Clarifying What Applying Human Rights to Health Means, and Why It Matters

More broadly, the UN Technical Guidance had to demonstrate that international legal standards regarding the right to health, and related rights, could be translated into principled policy guidance, while still allowing sufficient room for plural understandings of how to make health rights function in contexts, as well as the inescapable need for trade-offs. This intertwined goal implied four key points.

First, the UN Technical Guidance established *a human rights–based approach to health*, applied *in the context of reducing preventable maternal morbidity and mortality*. That is, in contrast to the biomedical paradigm, applying a human rights framework is *not* disease-specific.[34] Further, if we understand patterns of health and ill-health to be caused by social relations and determinants—as I have argued throughout these pages—an HRBA must seek to transform those drivers of ill-health of different populations.[35] In Brazil, as noted by the CEDAW Committee itself, Alyne's death was emblematic of patterns of exclusion in the Brazilian health system, which in turn reflect intersecting issues of social, racial, and gender inequality in Brazilian society.

Second, as we have discussed, if health is a right, health systems are not merely delivery apparatuses for interventions and commodities, nor marketplaces. They are a reflection of the quality of substantive democracy in any given society. Thus, the UN Technical Guidance asserted that "claims for sexual and reproductive health goods, services, and information should be understood by health system users, providers, and policymakers as fundamental rights, not as commodities to be allocated by the market or matters of charity."[36]

In Brazil, the constitutional recognition of the right to health in the 1988 Constitution, and its institutionalization through the universal health system, or Sistema Único de Saúde (SUS), had over the years given way to marketization of health which undermined the essence of a universal system. Due to the wealthy opting out and shrinking budgets for the rest, the SUS had entered into an increasing number of *convenios* with private providers. By 2009, private health spending accounted for 54% of total health spending.[37] Failure to establish parameters for contracting private health care, together with standards of performance, left a significant legal and regulatory gap, with serious repercussions for the equitable delivery as well as accountability of health care services.[38] Alyne's death had been a consequence of this gap, as noted by the CEDAW Committee in underscoring the failure of effective regulation of private providers.[39]

Further, within the health system understood as a democratic institution, an HRBA seeks to promote, as Lynn Freedman says, "a dynamic of entitlement and obligation between people and their government and within the complex system of relationships that form the wider health system, public and private."[40] This includes every level from frontline providers and patients to policymakers, which requires bringing tensions to the fore and examining obstacles that might not be immediately evident to create constructive accountability within and beyond the health system. In Brazil, we began from the premise that there could be no constructive accountability in the health system if women were disempowered and made to feel like objects and providers, in turn, had no sense of obligations to the female patients they were ostensibly serving.

Third, if health rights are *real* rights, HRBAs should entail multiple forms of accountability, including judicial remedies. Unlike other "accountability frameworks" that had been offered in global health that reduced accountability to monitoring, review, and actions that could be taken without external enforcement,[41] the UN Technical Guidance not only called for the establishment of judicial remedies, it also called for adequate funding and human capacity, together with authority and independence of mandates for judiciaries and other oversight institutions *from the beginning of the policy and budgeting cycle*, not as an afterthought.[42]

In the *Alyne* case, the CEDAW Committee had indeed called for the government to ensure adequate remedies and for training of judiciaries in reproductive rights. In our follow-up mission, we argued compensation for Alyne's mother and daughter should be coupled with systemically transformative remedies, not merely punitive remedies for frontline health workers, who rarely are solely at fault for a maternal death. Although we noted some positive developments from the Brazilian federal prosecutor's office, there was also a notable gap in effective oversight and management in health.

Finally, based upon CESCR's General Comment 14, the *Maastricht Principles on Extraterritorial Obligations of States in the Area of Economic, Social and Cultural Rights*, issued in 2011, and other relevant sources of soft and hard law, the UN Technical Guidance noted that donors also have an obligation not to do harm[43] and to effectively regulate "private actors over which they exercise control. These include pharmaceutical companies, commodities and device manufacturers, and other companies that affect the delivery of sexual and reproductive health services abroad."[44] It was already clear that realizing health rights required curbing the power of transnational corporations and shifts in global dynamics, not merely national regulation within countries.

HRBAs Cannot Dictate How Rights Function in Practice

On the other hand, it is critical that an HRBA not presume to foreclose the local contestation that occurs in the real world. That is, some of the *appropriateness* of measures to address maternal mortality—or any other issue of health-related rights under international law—can be determined by empirical evidence, as in the centrality of emergency obstetric care or the appropriate range for cesarean rates. Some of the *appropriateness* of state actions can be determined by normative premises about diverse women as entitled to substantive as well as formal equality, whose SRHR enable them to be emancipated from morbidity and misery, and to participate fully in society. Similarly, others can be determined by principles on gender-based violence (including obstetric violence) and intersectional discrimination (such as against Afro-descendant, poor women like

Alyne, as the CEDAW Committee had stated). Still others can be grounded in self-governance (e.g., informed consent). Further, health rights should not be overridden by ordinary economic priorities unless they are adequately justified; cuts should not disproportionately affect the disadvantaged; and all people should be given fair chances to enjoy health rights, rather than focusing purely on aggregate outcomes. Of course these principles have effects on the formulation and outcomes of budgets and policies, as well as on implementation, monitoring, and oversight.

However, an HRBA cannot provide a magic formula for how much of a health budget to spend on one condition—or even on health as compared to other aspects of a life of dignity, as some have argued; nor can it specify what to spend on remote areas of the country with marginalized persons in contrast to a populous area even though it can establish those persons deserve fair chances. The MDGs had fostered this undemocratic approach to HIV/AIDS and other communicable diseases, as well as vertical interventions relating to maternal and child health.

Nor can priority-setting be determined by extensive lists of "core obligations" in treaty monitoring body General Comments, as discussed in Chapter Five. As we will discuss further in Chapter Seven, setting priorities in health requires democratically legitimate processes to determine how to meet health needs fairly within the diversity of any context. There is no way to avoid political contestation; so when advocates refuse to engage in persuasive dialogue, whether out of absolutist principles or fear they will lose ground, they limit the impact of health rights in practice. In turn, in accord with human rights, this process requires transparency, and opportunities for affected populations not just to be tokenistically consulted, but to be engaged meaningfully. A democratic health system, based on rights, requires that the affected population's voice matters in diagnosing problems and systemic barriers to improvement, as well as in proposing remedial actions.[45]

Surfacing the complex reasons for cesarean rates in Brazil is a perfect example of a complex structural problem in the health system and the larger societal issues it reflects, which require contextual knowledge as well as collective deliberation on the most effective way to make women's health rights underpin policies, programs, and women's own beliefs. That is, among many other reasons, we found in Brazil that even if they contain unnecessary and potentially increased risk to the mother and the newborn, C-sections have a lower risk for the obstetrician and are convenient if they are scheduled in advance. Second, in private facilities, C-sections had become a money-maker, as the SUS had been increasingly privatized. Third, training of physicians encouraged cesareans, as assisted vaginal delivery was not even taught in most medical schools. Fourth, the entrenched *machismo* in Brazil, coupled with the extreme biomedicalization and unfettered discretion of physicians of the Brazilian health system, encouraged the dehumanization of women and objectification of their bodies.

Moreover, culturally, vaginal deliveries were largely portrayed as messy, ugly, and primitive, and the abusive health system encouraged this; cesareans were "modern" and did not involve pain—except of course in recovering from significant abdominal surgery. Further, in vastly unequal Brazil, the very wealthy often went to "resort clinics" where they could get manicures, facial treatments, and even tummy tucks along with their cesareans. Poor women sought to emulate the wealthy in what they purchased and what they did to their bodies. After all, desire is not an individual phenomenon but is deeply shaped by what others whom we envy want, and this "mimetic desire," as René Girard called it, is ever more prevalent in the social media age that has taken root.[46]

Thus, obstetric violence reflects systemic issues which require more than criminal sanctions against providers and more than abstract statements of human rights principles; they require messier, contextual inquiries and deliberation in order to make health rights function in a complex system and society. Although Brazil is famous for having structures for broad participation in health because the SUS was seen as part of the conquest of democracy, women's rights were often addressed through formalistic consultation, and therefore the report of our visit underscored the nature of meaningful discussions and debates needed.

This is a key point to recognize in deploying human rights for social justice, because too often the rhetoric of "participation" masks an uglier reality. Just as creating social differences based on identity—gender, class, race, caste—represent exercises in power, so too does the erasure of *real* power differences in so-called participatory forums, which are invariably political spaces. As Nancy Fraser writes, for meaningful participation of equals to occur, there first should be rough parity of wealth/class to allow for equal voice and opportunity and second, parity of recognition/social status/culture to allow for equal respect in interaction.[47] So-called multi-stakeholder forums that pretend all stakeholders—government, private sector, health workers, all members of a generic civil society—can act as equals when background conditions are indeed far from equal create a Kabuki theater of democratic decision-making, which does nothing to alter fundamental structures of power.

Evolution of HRBA Initiatives

The follow-up in the *Alyne* case was far from the only example of using the UN Technical Guidance; the OHCHR has filed three follow-up reports with the UN Human Rights Council on activities and potential applications of the UN Technical Guidance. Organic approaches sprang from members of IIMMHR and a constellation of related civil society organizations, from Uganda to Mexico. For example, in Peru, CARE Peru together with ForoSalud, mentioned in Chapter Four, organized community health workers to feed back information into district level policymaking. In India, SAHAYOG used mobile technology to promote social accountability among facilities.[48] Although they remained very small in comparison with the sweeping changes TAC had achieved, they inspired and continue to build subaltern sites of resistance and consciousness, which, as I have argued, are likely one of the most significant effects of deploying rights in health in the long term.

Moreover, as soon as the Human Rights Council passed a resolution welcoming the UN Technical Guidance, another was introduced on child health. HRBAs began to proliferate not just as intergovernmental documents, but as guidelines from UN Special Procedures and even as programming guidance in service-delivery NGOs. Again, organic efforts to address laws, policies, and implementation, as well as symbolic appropriation of rights using different methodologies, provided extremely useful information on barriers to making rights work in practice.[49] But often, these most inspiring and useful examples were (appropriately) contextualized. Too many HRBAs have become disease-specific, setting out abstract lists of principles which are unhelpful in making necessary trade-offs, neglecting the conditions necessary for bottom-up negotiation and participation as equals, and often omitting or underplaying the central role of remedies in a democratic state.

Efforts to measure impacts of HRBAs quickly followed suit as well, which were complicated by widely varying definitions. In 2013, the WHO published a monograph analyzing the evidence of impact of an HRBA on aspects of women's and children's health. That study, the first of its kind, focused on the evidence of impact of governments' human rights–shaped health interventions, with particular attention to the initiatives of ministries of health.[50] By 2014, many of us were concerned about the trend in HRBAs. At the time, I cautioned that although they potentially offer ways to make rights more understandable and claimable, as Navi Pillay had suggested, "it is essential that HRBAs not be converted into technocratic formulas, which . . . gloss over the inherently messy, controversial and political—as well as contextual—issues that keep certain people systematically disempowered and exposed to abuses of sexual and reproductive health and rights, as well as other abuses."[51] Not all, of course, but too many HRBAs were being reduced to "pleas for human rights to be conferred by the state," as Neocosmos has argued,[52] and we were losing the connection between human rights and emancipatory politics that is critical for applying human rights in health to be transformative.

The Role of Courts in Bringing Justice to Health

The frustration with blocked political channels that led to seeking redress for the *Alyne* case, and many others, in supranational forums also led people to turn to courts to champion their rights. The path for right-to-health litigation globally was undoubtedly shaped by early cases on access to antiretroviral therapy (ARVs) to treat HIV/AIDS. However, litigation spread beyond HIV quickly. Maternal mortality cases were litigated in countries from India to Uganda.[53] Litigation covered a multiplicity of issues and populations (e.g., mental health, environmental health); populations (e.g., persons with disabilities, sex workers, drug users); and increasingly included issues of regulating not just public but private actors (e.g., rescission of insurance contracts) as well as public institutions.[54] Health-related rights litigation, sometimes based on expansive interpretations of the right to life (e.g., India), as well as other freedoms, had begun to affect political discourses as well as institutional policies.

The right to health had reached maturity as a real legal right in many of the same countries with transformative constitutions and was being deployed as such to expand formalist readings of other constitutions. Yet, the explosion of health rights litigation using protection writ actions in Latin America—predominantly although not exclusively for individual entitlements—led to polarized views on whether health *rights* improved health equity or exacerbated inequalities in health systems and societies.

Judicialization in Brazil and Latin America: Issues and Controversies

Some of the debates over health rights litigation in Brazil can be generalized to the region. First, despite the broad outlines of the right to health in the 1988 Constitution, the preponderance of the hundreds of thousands of health rights claims since the 1990's have involved the use of provisional protection measures for individual access to health entitlements, such as medications, which has also generally been the case throughout the region.[55] Critics such as Octavio Ferraz and Daniel Wang argue that judicialization has undermined *formal equality*—the need to treat all similarly situated patients equally—by fostering queue jumping whereby those who get access to courts and care are not necessarily treated the same as others who have a certain condition. Second, critics argue expensive and clinically unproven treatments awarded by the courts also undermine *substantive equality*—the need to take measures to address unequal background conditions in the highly unequal societies that make up the region, including Brazil, which prevent people from equal enjoyment of health rights in practice.[56]

However, others scholars, such as João Biehl, Mariana Socal, and Joe Amon, argue that claims that litigation benefit the wealthy in Brazil are unjustified based on empirical evidence.[57] Still others, such as Danielle Borges, argue that individualized litigation, precisely by creating unfairness and inefficiency, spurs action by the government to rationalize decision-making and make it more fair, such as through the creation of a national health technology assessment institution in Brazil in 2012.[58] Mariana Mota Prado notes that the debates over equity impact of litigation obscures another important aspect of judicial enforcement: greater normative accountability and oversight in the complex Brazilian health system.[59]

My own view is that judicial enforcement of health rights in Brazil and across Latin America is a complex phenomenon, and it is important to examine the many forms of impacts—understood broadly as I have outlined in earlier chapters—looking at both the legal and health systems, and beyond. To date, there is scant empirical evidence to suggest that judicial decisions are displacing funding from other programs, or that opaque and fragmented priority-setting processes in affected countries would be done in a more pro-poor manner but for the litigation. Further, the majority of these cases in Colombia and Argentina, if not Brazil, are more properly understood as clusters of compliance and regulatory gap cases—where entitlements guaranteed in social insurance schemes are either not provided in practice or poorly defined (e.g., if an angioplasty includes the stent)—that fuel judicial exasperation more than judicial activism. In functioning governments, such cases should lead to improved regulation and definitions of benefits schemes, but that is often not the case.

Some argue that judicialization of health rights was driven by the gap between supply and demand, which was accentuated in many instances by health reforms that increased coverage of social insurance.[60] If we focus less on individual consumer choice and behavior and more on the functioning of democracy, the turn to courts can be understood as a resort to a favorable opportunity structure when the political venues for both addressing inexorably shifting contours of health rights and regulating actors in the sector were chronically dysfunctional, in Brazil and elsewhere. Litigation in Latin America is inextricably related to gaping (and growing) underlying social inequalities, and deeply fragmented and medicalized health systems, which are poorly regulated and in which priority setting is too often done without coherent rationales or public justification.

It would be misleading not to note the important collective cases that have brought in Latin America, regarding, for example, the manufacture of orphan vaccines in Argentina and the public health conditions of a poor department in Colombia, or that in the absence of appropriate regulation, courts in Latin America as elsewhere have imposed important standards of constitutional justifications on private providers, insurers, and other actors in health systems,[61] and standards of information and other aspects of marketing of products affecting health. Courts have also shifted burdens of proof to mitigate bureaucratic burdens on disadvantaged plaintiffs, whether in showing indigence to receive benefits or in terms of provincial budget allocations for maternal-child health needs. However, it would be equally misleading not to acknowledge that the majority of health rights litigation involving access to entitlements relates to curative treatments, as opposed to preconditions of health or social determinants, which would likely have greater pro-poor impacts.[62] Further, there are transaction costs to this "routinization" of judicialization for the health system, the judicial system, and the functioning of democracy.[63]

In short, broad-brush characterizations of judicial enforcement of health rights are unlikely to hold up over time or across contexts. Thus, answering our original question of whether health rights could be made enforceable was not sufficient; we now had to address the question of under what circumstances judicial enforcement could enhance equity and accountability across health systems, and promote broader social equality.

Reframing Remedies: Using Judgments to Catalyze Political Action

Courts across multiple countries have sought to use remedies to catalyze action by the political organs of government since at least *Brown v. Board of Education*.[64] As early as 1989, the provincial government of Quebec had invoked the "notwithstanding clause" in the Canadian Charter of Rights and Freedoms to "override" a decision by the Canadian Supreme Court regarding signage in French constituting a violation of freedom of expression under the Charter.[65] This decision is usually cited as the starting point for Mark Tushnet's "weak form" of judicial review[66] or what Gargarella calls a "dialogical understanding" of the system of checks and balances.[67]

Due to the inherent "spider web"-like[68] effects of decisions affecting more than a single entitlement to an intervention, to use Lon Fuller's term, and the need to balance public policies and multiple interests in ways that the legislature and executive tend to be better suited to do, this form of remedy seemed particularly apposite to issues regarding public health. And indeed, public health issues have been the subject of different levels and forms of dialogical remedies, including the TAC PMTCT case discussed in Chapter Five, the right to food in India, pollution in Argentina, and the guiding principles of the health system in Colombia.

In India and Argentina, courts used such open-textured processes with respect to issues beyond care. In India, the Supreme Court had read into the constitutional right to life conditions for health care and other issues, such as food. A writ petition alleging a violation of the "right to food" was brought in 2001 under the public interest litigation mechanism at the Indian Supreme Court.[69] The court held that the state violated the right to life (food) and ordered the state to ameliorate the food shortages caused through warehousing and distributional problems, among other things. Thus, just as *Alyne* had done with maternal mortality, the court recognized that hunger was neither natural nor inevitable but clearly the product of policies and government decisions.

The court also kept the case open, issuing interim orders as the case has progressed. And crucially, a civil society Right to Food Campaign was also established in 2001, viewing the court's orders alone as insufficient to bring about lasting social change. Thus, similar to the TAC campaign, this was a politics-centered campaign, using the court as a "hammer" to advance its issues.[70] Most scholars agree that it is the campaign's consistent pressure on connecting issues (corruption, employment, women's empowerment, social security pensions, and integrated child development services) that has achieved significant successes in this case, as opposed to so many other rulings by the court which have languished.[71]

In Argentina, the environmental damage of the Matanza-Riachuelo river basin was having serious effects on the health of nearby residents. The *Mendoza* case involved multiple stages at the Argentine Supreme Court. In 2008, the court found that the fragmented and overlapping responsibilities of government authorities and lack of political will underpinned the problems, and mandated the national, provincial, and local governments to address both past and future harm by cleaning the river basin and making a drainage and sanitation system as well as an emergency plan.[72] But the strategy for implementing cleanup was not dictated by the court.

Ongoing implementation has required several follow-up judgments from the court, but, with significant financial support from international institutions, the case has achieved removal of thousands of tons of waste from the banks and the water, greater regulation and oversight, and measures to relocate citizens living in the contaminated areas. However, the cleanup has been inadequate and slow; further, different municipalities' capacities to use financial resources have generated inequalities among the poor communities where people have been relocated, even as overall poverty has been reduced. Sigal, Rossi, and Morales argue such orders extend compliance phases and surface institutional deficiencies, which then produce responses.[73] In the *Mendoza* case, an "inter-jurisdictional river basin authority" (ACUMAR, for its Spanish acronym) was established to carry out the environmental management plan, and a new body was established to monitor compliance with the court order.[74]

As in India, the involvement of civil society has been critical to keeping the *Mendoza* case on the public agenda. The Argentine Supreme Court held public hearings over years and in 2016 established criteria intended to ensure that the quality of civil society's participation was meaningful as opposed to tokenistic.[75]

Colombia: Applying Rights to Restructure a Health System

Colombia's transformative constitution quickly came into conflict with a 1993 health system designed essentially along neoliberal tenets. Law 100 had many flaws including a two-tiered system that entrenched inequity between the "formally" and "informally" employed, poorly defined and designed benefit packages, and a complex "managed competition" system that required strong regulation and oversight, which was lacking from the outset. As elsewhere in Latin America, health reforms were adopted with little public scrutiny, often by decree, and in a piecemeal manner.[76] Given lack of appropriate oversight or regulation, as well as problems built into the design of the system, the courts increasingly became an escape valve—with tens of thousands of *tutelas* (protection writs) for health rights violations being brought every year to courts under the diffuse constitutional jurisdiction established in the 1991 Constitution.

In 2008, after repeatedly reiterating constitutional criteria for policies to the executive (in terms of eligibility criteria for subsidized regime, the duty to reduce bureaucratic barriers, etc.) and the legislature (funding the unification of the contributory and subsidized regimes, as the law had envisioned), the Constitutional Court issued a sweeping decision that called for restructuring important elements of the health system (T-760/08). The court reiterated that the right to health was a fundamental right in accordance with prior jurisprudence and called for achieving universal coverage, updating and unifying the two-tier system of benefits, and rationalizing reimbursement from the government to private insurers for judicially ordered care outside the obligatory scheme (POS, by its Spanish acronym).[77] As a previous structural judgment by the Justice Manuel José Cepeda had done (T-025/04), the 2008 ruling provided for follow-up by the review chamber and a special unit within the court.[78]

Together with other scholars, I have lauded the ruling for its use of dialogical remedies and "experimentalist regulation" in Charles Sabel and William Simon's term.[79] Nevertheless, the framing is also worth noting for the lack of gender perspective which limited the vision of the health system as space for creating inclusion for *all*. The notion of "health" is a biomedical absence of disease or pathology which is to be remedied by access to medical services determined by the scientific expertise of the clinician.[80] The court adopts the "respect, protect, fulfill" framework from General Comment 14, yet includes zero examples of reproductive health in illustrating how a state can fail to respect or protect the rights to health—which is especially notable as, at the time, *tutelas* were being brought to courts to enforce the court's C-335/2006 ruling permitting therapeutic abortions.[81] Indeed, the court uses fertility treatments for women as an example of what can be excluded a priori from the right to health, without discussions regarding the justification.[82] Third, the decision makes no mention of how the division between the two regimes for formal and nonformal workers disproportionately harmed women, who were either dependent on their husband's status (just as children, whom are specifically mentioned by the court) or because they disproportionately work in the nonformal sector.

The T-760/08 decision produced a broad array of impacts, including a heightened awareness of the right to health arguably triggered by the Uribe administration's initial clumsy response and issuance of autocratic decrees quickly found to be unconstitutional. All of the direct material claims of the twenty-two petitioners were resolved, and over time *tutela* claims have shifted from merely access to ancillary services and quality.[83] There has been increased access to care for the poor due to the unification of the benefits package, although marginalized groups still face substantial barriers to accessing health services. Significant institutional and procedural changes, including the periodic updating of the benefits package, have occurred.[84] Nonetheless, the highly biomedical health system in Colombia remains poorly regulated, subject to powerful corporate interests, corruption and political cronyism, and vast inequities, as well as abuses (perhaps especially in SRHR) that persist, which reflect the social inequalities in Colombian society.

Many in Colombia cast the iconic court in heroic terms as the defender of the people, in contrast to the indifference of the political branches. In this case, as in others, the court held public hearings which Everaldo Lamprea, a former auxiliary magistrate in charge of the follow-up chamber, characterized as spaces of authentic deliberation that have created substantial pressure on the government.[85] Others are less sanguine, noting that court hearings merely allowed for statements of widely divergent political and power positions without meaningful deliberation. Nevertheless, through the follow-up process, civil society was then able to play a central role in a new Statutory Framework Law on Health, which entered into force in 2015.[86] An "organic law" (civil code) for health, to implement the statutory framework, was to be debated as this book went to press.

Since 2008, the dialogue with the executive branch has gone through various phases. Moreover, the court has strayed from the broad orders meant to catalyze political action, into specific orders, which have generally not proven effective.[87] Further, the court has grown increasingly conservative and seems to be losing appetite for structural remedies that require massive follow up. In the wake of the political context, including the election of President Ivan Duque in 2018, the current justices may be seeking to close the T-760/08 judgment.

In short, there is a complex political economy surrounding the judicialization of health-related issues. On the one hand, the insulated and technical nature of health means that policies and priorities are rarely subjected to public scrutiny, and priorities in a sector subject to politicization and rent-seeking interests often are not justified by coherent let alone democratically accepted rationales. As a result, people have turned to courts for remedies, which social constitutions in these countries created.

While individual protection writ actions exploit opportunities in broken systems, these broader judgments, as Keith Syrett argues, potentially offer "an arena in which argumentation, reasoning and explanation for policies and decisions can be publicly advanced and scrutinized . . . and such decisions play an 'educative' role, enabling wider 'political discussion to take a principled form so as to address the constitutional question in line with the political values of justice and public reason.' "[88] This normative role is essential if we construe health systems as social institutions in society. It is also important to note that in these creative remedies the courts are not dictating specific action, as in a liberal understanding of judicial power; rather they are reshaping the political agenda in conjunction with pressure from civil society.

These judgments also belie the dichotomy between legal mobilization and social mobilization. As Colombian legal scholar Rodrigo Uprimny explains: "Judicial intervention, especially when linked to certain kinds of rights struggles, can also operate as a mechanism of social and political mobilization to the extent that it empowers social groups and facilitates their social and political action."[89] In the end, transforming the conditions underlying health depends upon using rights strategies—including courts and supranational forums—to open political opportunity structures around health-related issues—whether reproductive health as in *Alyne*, food, pollution, or the system itself.

Concluding Reflections

Perhaps the greatest irony in Alyne's particular case is that, in effect, Alyne died not because she wanted a child, but because she did not want any more. The health center in Belford Roxo was known for lax compliance with government regulations regarding tubal ligations, which required a woman have two living children. Alyne only had one previous child but did not want any more after that pregnancy. She chose a private facility known for skirting Brazil's ineffective regulation of family planning; she died because of ineffective oversight of obstetric care.

In retrospect, the landmark *Alyne* case was the product of idiosyncratic factors, as much as calculated construction of international human rights law. Doña Lourdes, Alyne's mother, happened to work as a caregiver for the mother of one of Latin America's leading feminists, Sonia Correa. Correa connected Doña Lourdes to CRR precisely at the time CRR was looking for a case to bring on access to maternal health care because the MDGs had shifted the world's attention to maternal health—and the result was a groundbreaking precedent. The positive and negative findings of the Technical Follow-Up Commission were submitted to and discussed with the Brazilian government.[90] It is fair to say that the visit, the extensive conversations with different actors, and the report enabled a reinitiation of local dialogues for a time—before politics intervened.

In 2011 when the CEDAW Committee issued its conclusions in *Alyne*, Brazil had been one of the fastest growing economies in the world. Nevertheless, by 2015, commodity markets had fallen, and there were high unemployment rates, austerity measures, and corruption scandals over government contracts.

The same year the *Alyne* decision was issued, the World Bank had announced that its lending arm would be providing an innovative partial credit guarantee facility under which Construtora Norberto Odebrecht S.A. would be able to obtain surety bonds to support billions of dollars worth of construction contracts in Brazil. Collusion was foreseeable in this financing model from the beginning. Yet, the World Bank implemented the model in Brazil and subsequently throughout Latin America. In August 2016, President Rousseff was impeached by the Congress in relation to corruption stemming from the Odebrecht contracts in a polarized atmosphere that was likened by her allies to a coup.[91] In 2017, Lula—who had been the favorite to win Brazil's 2018 elections—was indicted on corruption charges linked to Odebrecht as well; he was convicted and jailed amid enormous furor in 2018 and reconvicted in 2019, although many claim both trials were plagued with irregularities.

What is incontrovertible is that in December 2016, the conservative-controlled Congress that had ousted Rousseff approved a constitutional amendment to freeze public spending over the next two decades, in violation of obligations under international law.[92] The share of health spending within the federal budget dropped 17% in 2017 alone. The budget for women's social and legal empowerment programs was cut by 52% that year, and the number of services for violence against women was cut by 15%. Cuts to food security programs undid much of Lula's antihunger achievements, with disproportionate impacts on Afro-descendants and other disadvantaged groups. But austerity did not hurt the wealthy; by 2018, Oxfam calculated that that six individual Brazilians had as much wealth as the poorest one half of citizens.[93]

In the midst of this spectacular dysfunction in 2018, the hard-line conservative Jair Bolsonaro was elected president, promising to root out corruption and impose order. Despite having been a senator for years, Bolsonaro portrayed himself as an outsider who would clean up politics and get things done. The conservative populist was openly misogynistic, racist, and homophobic.[94] In the era of "sustainable development," which had been launched out of the process that emerged from Rio in 2012, Bolsonaro was eager to open the Amazon—the "lungs of the world"—to further oil drilling and accelerate deforestation, displacing and destroying indigenous communities in the process.

In sum, by 2015, we had seen, on the one hand, many of the initial aspirations of the SRHR movements and health rights movements come to fruition. Courts at national and supranational level were enforcing rights to affirmative entitlements and treating maternal deaths not as misfortune but injustice, which had been unimaginable not long before. Health rights enforcement had proliferated, and the question was no longer how to add a specific treatment to the accepted formulary but how to meet health needs fairly across health systems. Further, apex courts began using structural remedies to catalyze political action regarding health-related and other issues, including with respect to the health system itself in Colombia.

Similarly, HRBAs had been validated at official UN levels. We had clarified how applying human rights to health could guide policymaking, program implementation, and oversight processes, and how they differed from conventional top-down, technocratic approaches. The question was no longer whether we could identify what it would mean to apply human rights to health. We now had to face the epistemic inconsistencies between different HRBAs. And perhaps even more so, we had to ensure that HRBAs left room for local actors to vernacularize rights understandings and collectively find ways for health rights to function within specific social spaces. In the end, advancing health rights depends upon catalyzing action by democratic institutions and processes whereby people can mobilize to hold their governments to account, whether through HRBAs or through judicially led processes.

We have seen again in this chapter that health systems are themselves democratic institutions, which either function as spaces to create social belonging and equality or replicate systemic discrimination and marginalization. In Brazil, a highly medicalized health system, in synergy with patriarchal attitudes about the purpose of women in society, reduced too many women to objects of obstetric violence. In Colombia, even in the expansive T-760/08 opinion, women's lived realities were largely overlooked. The lack of constructive accountability to women in health systems reflects and refracts the continuing structural injustices that shadow the lives of poor women, such as Alyne da Silva.

Finally, advances in the articulation of health rights as injustices were occurring against a backdrop of ballooning inequality, in which elites captured increasingly greater portions of wealth as well as political processes. In the face of spectacular political dysfunction in Brazil and elsewhere, citizens lost confidence in democratic institutions. Across the globe, people erupted in frustration, including in the Arab Spring, which turned quickly into reconsolidated military or conservative populist power everywhere but Tunisia. Political institutions were depicted as "the problem." And while conservative populists could impose draconian austerity, showing that poverty is produced by political choices, by 2015 its roots were deeply entangled across networks of exchange and norms of economic governance that extended far beyond national borders.

CHAPTER 7

Power, Politics, and Knowledge

The gap between what our economic and political systems are supposed to do—what we were told they did do—and what they actually do became too large to be ignored.

—*Joseph Stiglitz*[1]

Right now we face a manmade disaster of global scale, our greatest threat in thousands of years: climate change. If we don't take action, the collapse of our civilisations and the extinction of much of the natural world is on the horizon.

—*Sir David Attenborough*[2]

[B]ecause human rights compliance indicators threaten to close space for democratic accountability and purport to turn an exercise of judgment into one of technical measurement, advocates of human rights should remain vigilant to effects of the elisions at work in the indicators project.

—*AnnJanette Rosga and Margaret Satterthwaite*[3]

IN APRIL 2018, walking through the newly inaugurated National Library of Qatar in Doha, I came upon one of only ten surviving copies of *The Book of Pleasant Journeys into Faraway Lands* (*Tabula Rogeriana*), a book of medieval geography written by Abu Abdullah Muhammad al-Idrisi. The 12th-century work included detailed descriptions of the geography and culture, as well as political, social, and economic aspects of each region, and seventy distinct maps.[4] It was a landmark in the history of science, changing one way of perceiving and living in the world for another more capacious one that admitted of other worlds within our world.

Of course al-Idrisi's work was based not just on empirical investigation, but on culturally constructed and normative premises about the world, which were likely not evident to the average person of the day. I reflected on al-Idrisi's achievement in light of the emergence of technologies that have recently come to shape our understanding of our own physical world today in ways we have rapidly come to take for granted—and with similarly little sense of the sociopolitical and epistemic implications that are embedded in them.

I was in Qatar to present guidance on researching the health and rights of migrant workers. Over 90% of Qatar's population is migrant workers, who fit into an elaborate taxonomy of entitlements and benefits set by the skill sets they have and nature of the work they do under the current labor/sponsorship law. Employers have unilateral power to cancel workers' residency permits, deny workers' ability to change employers, report a worker as "absconded" to police authorities, and deny permission to leave the country.[5] Strikingly, there was a virtually complete absence of reliable empirical information about migrant health status. Indeed, there appeared to be a deliberate strategy of the so-called Supreme Committee on Deliverance and Legacy to censor information about migrant health conditions in the approach to the upcoming 2022 World Cup Qatar was set to host, and for which migrants were building stadiums. An all-day seminar dedicated to the topic in Education City developed proposals to address *their* health problems, when none of *them* participated, or had even been consulted.

In many ways the contract labor has not changed workers' conditions of life since the days of legal slavery, which was only banned in Qatar in 1952.[6] Slaves were shipped from areas in East Africa, which I knew well from having lived there for years: they were taken from around Lake Nyasa, and then sent to Kilwa on the Indian Ocean coast just north of Dar es Salaam, then to the nearby island of Zanzibar, where they were held in the slave caves described in the Introduction, before being sent either directly to Qatar, or to Oman and then onward to Qatar and elsewhere. Lives uprooted and interrupted, these people were denied basic dignity in their home countries and in the countries they made such great efforts to reach. Indeed, generations later descendants of former slaves were still living with social and embodied consequences of both the Arab and Atlantic slave trades.

In the era of "sustainable development," which according to the UN comprises three pillars—environmental, economic, and social—Qatar stands out for the absence of all of the above. Although ostensibly a constitutional monarchy, an emir from the ruling al-Thani family, whose ten-meter tall portrait is on the sides of many buildings in downtown Doha, rules without any meaningful institutional controls in practice. Qatar's economy is based overwhelmingly on extractive industries; it has an intensely hot subtropical climate where giant new building complexes, immense shopping malls with rivers running through them, and even footpaths in some outdoor areas are profligately air-conditioned to make life comfortable for wealthy Qataris, while unskilled single male laborers (SMLs, as they are called) live amassed in squalid tenements and face dehydration on a daily basis. The far fewer female migrant domestic workers have no rights, nor remedy for abuse from their employers.

Qatari society is not only divided based on strict gender roles and family or tribal identity among nationals; it has the highest Palma Index in the world at 9.2, meaning that the top 10% of the population control close to ten times as much wealth as the bottom 40%—a figure which is calculated based on contribution to gross national income.[7] But in 2018 Qatar was an extreme example of what had been happening all over the world. In 2015, Oxfam reported that the wealthiest 1% had accumulated more wealth than the entire rest of the world population.[8] By 2016, in the face of both genuine grievances regarding unabating income concentration and institutional indifference, and manipulated ethnonationalist fears, citizens who had become generally passive exercised their only remaining right of participation—to "withhold acclamation," as Habermas says, from the traditional political elites.[9] Thus in 2016 we saw Brexit pass in a referendum and a wave of populists who billed themselves as anti–political establishment come to power across a wide swath of countries, including the election that brought Donald Trump to power, showing once and for all that the US was not immune to history.

In this chapter, we examine events that have occurred around and since 2016 to highlight the connections between politics, knowledge, and democratic institutions, including health systems. Rather than using one place to illustrate themes in our current reality, the chapter discusses various significant political and economic trends affecting health, together with different analytical frameworks for understanding and in turn addressing them through human rights. First, I set out the sociopolitical context in which global and regional politics seemed to be as ineffectual in stopping the carnage in foreign conflicts as domestic politics had become in solving national sociopolitical problems. Further, climate change had become too urgent for rational politicians to ignore. The lofty postwar aspirations of a world order based upon peace and security were eviscerated as television and the internet allowed billions to become witnesses, as the Tracy Chapman song goes, to "the rape of the world."[10]

Second, we turn to the Sustainable Development Goals (SDGs), which were the successor goals to the MDGs and were meant to be a blueprint for progress in the world of the second decade of the 21st century. Agenda 2030 and the SDGs apply to wealthy and poor countries alike and centrally set out the notion of balancing economic growth with environmental and social sustainability. After briefly setting out the political process for arriving at Agenda 2030, I discuss the technical process for arriving at targets and indicators to measure the transformative agenda, arguing that in selecting the indicators, the nature of the political goals was redefined in practice. Using both the inequality measure selected in the SDGs and indicators to measure "access to universal sexual and reproductive health and reproductive rights,"[11] The chapter illustrates different aspects of how technocratic knowledge and methodologies can change our understanding of key issues in the quest for greater social justice in health and beyond.

Measurement always embeds premises about what matters and how we know what we claim to know. Thus, to place the SDGs in context, I look back through the evolution of efforts to enhance measurement of economic, social, and cultural (ESC) rights violations, as well as the progressive realization of these rights, which are critical in assessing progress in the struggle for health rights. Significant advances have been made since the 1990's, yet measurement using abstracted metrics to define rights, as opposed to supplement other forms of knowledge, has also changed in ways that may obscure more than they reveal about the political economy of effective enjoyment of sexual and reproductive health rights (SRHR) and other rights. In health in particular, we may now have slid into measuring rights bureaucratically and instrumentally to provide value added to conventional health programs in ways that do not challenge pathologies of power.

I then turn more specifically to Universal Health Coverage (UHC), which was the centerpiece of the health goal in the SDGs. UHC presents opportunities for health systems to be organized as core social institutions in synergy with the right to health, but UHC is not synonymous with a right to health and is limited by a continuing background of untrammeled privatization in health and beyond. Thus, this chapter deepens the theoretical exploration of the implications of treating health as a right for a health system, such as including migrants, the democratization of decision-making in health, and the need for normative oversight.

Finally, in the midst of gaping inequalities within and between countries with rising private power with enormous implications for health, together with a virulent backlash against SRHR, I consider responses from the human rights community (official and civil society), noting positive developments and continuing challenges. With respect to divergent strategies for pursuing global health justice through human rights, I argue for instruments and mobilization around extraterritorial obligations (ETOs). Recognizing ETOs constitutes a justified extension of the social contract to transboundary obligations of states, directly and through multilateral institutions, as well as transnational corporations (TNCs), in today's globalized world.

A New World Disorder

By 2016, multiple interrelated trends had occurred to shape the period of upheaval and transition in which we now live, including austerity as a response to the global recession; growing private finance and transnational corporate power; the irrefutability of impending climate cataclysm without remedial action being urgently taken; conflict and massive displacement; and a wave of pronationalist votes in referenda and elections.

Global Inequality, State Capacity, and Gendered Impacts of Austerity

As a result of the policies over the decades we have discussed in previous chapters, the financial economy had exceeded the productive economy in many countries, and private wealth exceeded public wealth, both of which extended inequality and fueled what Jean Drèze has referred to in India particularly as a "vicious cycle of elitism and exclusion"[12] In the United States in 2017, the top 10% owned 77% of the nation's wealth—a greater income inequality than in the so-called Gilded Age.[13] Globally, the world's richest 1% owned as much as the rest of the world population combined.

As noted in Chapter Six, poverty is a political choice, but there was a difference in states' capacities to respond to crisis. After the 2008 crash that became a global recession, the US used both fiscal and monetary policy to restore the economy; however, indebted countries, primarily in the global South, were largely unable to use monetary policy to address their national economic collapses because of strictures on containing inflation, which had been imposed by the international financial institutions (IFIs) over years. Thus across the global South, governments were left with expanding national debts and what was euphemistically called "fiscal consolidation." As Juan Pablo Bohoslavsky, the UN Independent Expert on the Effects of Foreign Debt and Other Related International Financial Obligations of States noted, this cluster of policies amounts to *austeridad machista* (sexist austerity), as women are disproportionately affected by spending cuts to social protection and health systems, as well as shrinking in the economy and layoffs (including those women who make up the majority of the health workforce)—as we have seen over and over again since the end of the 1970's.[14] The dominant economic paradigm, which treats the household as a single unit, makes invisible the intrafamily power dynamics, and, in turn, diverse women's unremunerated care work, reduced agency in paying for school or health-associated costs of the children, and lack of control over their life plans wrought by austerity.

Transnational Actors: Political Determinants of Health

By the second decade of the century, it had become impossible to ignore the impacts of transnational actions and actors on health. The 2014 report from the Lancet–University of Oslo Commission on Global Governance for Health coined the term *political determinants of health* for the "norms, policies, and practices that arise from transnational interaction."[15] The commission particularly underscored the role of TNCs in shaping the global governance rules regarding trade, tax policy, and regulation, and in turn global markets: "These [tobacco, beverage, and pharmaceutical] industries dwarf most national economies."[16] And, in turn, their power to capture the political processes in relation to legislation and regulation overwhelmed many governments.[17] Only 0.1% of world firms are TNCs, but they account for 50% of global trade and 10% of world's GDP.[18]

Climate Change and Political Will

In 2005, the Kyoto Protocol to the 1992 UN Framework Convention on Climate Change had entered into force, which committed states parties to reduce greenhouse gas emissions to "a level that would prevent dangerous anthropogenic interference with the climate system" and set those targets for different countries.[19] In 2013 the Intergovernmental Panel on Climate Change asserted conclusively that there was no doubt that human activities were the principal cause of climate change.[20] The 2015 Paris Agreement added new frameworks for monitoring and capacity-building for vulnerable countries to the Kyoto framework, but the targets for reducing carbon emission were set in terms of countries' "best efforts."[21]

In 2017 Trump abruptly pulled the US out of the Paris Agreement and signaled to other governments that natural resources—from the Arctic to the Amazon—were there to be exploited. Mbeki's administration had been vilified for denying a connection between HIV and AIDS; conservatives had cavalierly ignored scientific data about gestational development and distorted data on health effects in abortion debates around the world for decades.[22] But now, the leader of the most powerful country in the world—and the one that contributed most to greenhouse gas emissions—together with his supporters and cronies around the world, were denying the empirical evidence upon which the continued existence of the world as we know it depended.

Conflict, Humanitarian Crises, and Migration

Inequality and instability—exacerbated by climate change in many countries—coupled with tyranny and conflict, had created the largest migration crisis since the Second World War. In 2016 Syria's war topped the world in producing internal displacement and refugees. But at least fifteen conflicts had erupted or reignited since 2010—including the brutal conflict in Yemen in which Qatar had supported rebels against the Saudi-backed regime—few of which have been resolved as of this writing.

By the end of 2016, worldwide there were almost 23 million refugees,[23] a population larger than that of three-quarters of the countries on the planet. Further, despite the attention given to Europe and the "caravan of migrants" arriving on the US border in 2018, almost nine out of every ten refugees were in low-resource countries.

Digital Realities, Democracy, and Truth Claims

By 2018 we knew that the internet, which had promised democratization of information and power, had a dark side too; it had also become a site for weaponizing misinformation, and tracking and repressing dissidents. In this new alternative to the physical world, the public and private domains had become confounded as the majority surrendered their most intimate details while believing they were doing so freely. Rather than a broader global public square, platforms such as Facebook—the main entry point to the internet in many countries—lent themselves to tribalistic interactions controlled by private TNCs with virtually no accountability.

The digital world had become another site for social action, which required a new social contract, yet institutions and regulations lagged behind the breathtaking pace of progress in technology. In 2018, a data and privacy law in the European Union—the General Data Protection Regulation (GDPR)—was passed creating a right to "be forgotten" as well as "a right to explanations,"[24] but we have yet to see the cascade of effects of this law in many domains in which data regularly crosses borders, including health.

In short, these and other factors created opportunity structures for exploitation of a wave of ethnonationalism and populism that expressed itself in "anti-establishment" elections and referenda. None of these events was inevitable; nor was it just that these outcomes were based on internet trolls spreading disinformation. We have seen throughout these pages that, in Habermas' words, "the arrangement of formal democratic institutions and procedures [had long permitted] administrative decisions to be made largely independently of specific motives of the citizens."[25] The lack of transparency and unfairness of both national decision-making and global economic arrangements, coupled with the apparent impotence of ordinary citizens to create substantive change through politics, tapped into a justified rage at the administrative state, and in turn the political classes representing it.

These votes, of course, did not produce the magical solutions that many sought. A slim majority of yes votes in the Brexit referendum cannot simply divorce the UK from the European Union after decades of integration in every domain of activity. Similarly, in a now inexorably interconnected world, Trump's capricious imposition of tariffs—sometimes in relation to issues wholly unrelated to trade—could not possibly equalize benefits to populations left out of decades of trade liberalization zeal.

Moreover, elections of populists surfaced a wave in xenophobia, misogyny, and racial and other discrimination that we had believed to be safeguarded by advances in human rights and constitutional law. It turned out that our ever-thinning democracies—based on keeping people apart through formal institutional safeguards—did not protect against polarization and populist fearmongering as much as we would have liked. In this climate of polarization, reasoned debate based on shared empirical premises cannot be sustained. A significant number of people had grown so cynical about politics that they came to "believe everything and nothing, think that everything was possible and that nothing was true."[26] Many, encouraged by new technologies that promoted individualized consumerism and that offered whole new dimensions of digital reality, retreated to what Habermas terms "civic privatism"—which further undermines our ability to build collective political endeavors.

It was amidst this new world disorder that the United Nations set out a transformative Agenda 2030 for "The World We Want."

The Sustainable Development Goals: "The World We Want"?

The SDGs were meant to provide a blueprint for the way forward, taking stock of the achievements of the MDGs and building on those efforts. Among the women's movement, organized discussions began to take place about strategies for reclaiming a broader SRHR and gender equality agenda, and these would bear fruit in the groundbreaking Montevideo Consensus in 2013, which specifically mentioned "sexual rights" in addition to reproductive rights as essential for development.[27] The Montevideo regional meeting was held as part of a broader process on ICPD + 20. But the power dynamics in and beyond the United Nations made clear that ICPD + 20 was not going to have the same influence that other processes would have.

The process that resulted in the SDGs was also not driven by UN insiders and a small clique of donor countries that had designed the MDGs. Rather, at Rio + 20 in 2012, the Open Working Group of the General Assembly on SDGs (OWG) was created, which was led by a group of thirty member states (with rotating memberships to break up voting blocs). The OWG allowed for an innovative dynamic of negotiations and far greater input from middle- and lower-income countries, which ultimately led to a transformative declaration on development for Agenda 2030.

Civil Society Mobilization and Important Gains from MDGs

Just as it had been in the UN conferences of the 1990's, the participation of civil society, including women's and human rights groups, through the OWG, was critical to the final outcome document, which set out a vision of "universal respect for human rights and human dignity."[28] The architecture of the SDGs was a universal framework—like human rights—not one that applied to poor countries alone. The agenda was explicitly "integrated and indivisible," as the Vienna Conference and other documents had reaffirmed with respect to human rights. "Sustainable development" explicitly encompassed economic sustainability, environmental sustainability, and social sustainability. Thus, economic growth was not unfettered but tied to environmental and social goals. And unlike the sidelining of SRHR in the MDGs, in the SDGs, SRHR was included across health and gender equality goals, among others.

How Indicators Reshape Meaning: From Inequality to SRHR

The transformative political narrative in the SDGs, achieved in large measure through the active participation of civil society, was, however, undermined by the indicators chosen to measure progress. Let's take just two examples to show that indicators change meaning in different ways, which require different strategies by health and other ESC rights activists. First, as noted in Chapter Six, there are different measures of inequality depending on what we care about. In light of the egregious wealth inequalities between top and bottom we have been discussing in these pages, prominent figures such as former Assistant UN Secretary-General Michael Doyle and Economics Nobel Laureate Joseph Stiglitz weighed in on the measure of inequality to be used in the SDGs, arguing for the Palma Index.[29] Nonetheless, that was not the measure that was adopted.

Instead the World Bank early on preempted open debate and ensured that the measure would be given the euphemistic title of "shared prosperity"—measured by the by "growth rates of household expenditure or income per capita among the bottom 40 percent of the population and the total population," with the target being the bottom 40 percent exceeding the average.[30] Shared prosperity is one measure of social exclusion—which is critical for achieving the possibility of basic dignity and creating incentives for pro-poor growth. Moreover, multiple inequality measures must be used to create a full picture of any given economy and society. Nonetheless, as Sakiko Fukuda-Parr has asserted, shared prosperity does not change the antidemocratic extremes of wealth; it does nothing to redistribute ballooning private wealth at the top for the common good.[31]

This seemingly technical question matters a great deal from a human rights perspective as the selection of the indicator shapes understanding of where the solution to inequality lies. Using the Palma Index would have pointed to an array of policies aimed at redistribution of wealth, including through regulation and taxation. However, by preempting open debate on the inequality measure, the World Bank and other powerful players in development redefined the overall transformative political aims of the SDGs into the more modest goal of mitigating exclusion. The selection of this inequality metric aligned well with the use of private investment and so-called blended finance to implement the SDGs,[32] which calls for making countries more investor-friendly, not imposing greater regulation and taxes— which foreseeably will, if anything, exacerbate extreme inequality in health and beyond. The story of what happened to SRHR is no less revealing of the way power shapes knowledge claims.[33] At a time when understanding of the world had been reduced to *what got counted*, some believed that the marginalization of SRHR in the MDGs could be remedied by including rights indicators. Under Target 5.6.2, "ensuring universal access to SRHR" was to be measured by laws and regulations relating to SRHR in five areas. These areas were evaluated as yes/no on fulfilling certain criteria, and they were then tallied and put through a statistical program to rank countries.

There is no question that the SDGs reflected hard-fought progress over the

MDGs in SRHR aspirations. However, reducing "universal access to SRHR" to checklists of criteria abstracted from context, cultural significance, and sociological and normative legitimacy is deeply problematic if rights are understood as contested bundles of relationships negotiated within social spaces. As each example of the book has shown, much of advancing SRHR requires identifying the barriers to effective enjoyment in specific contexts—from Peru to Malawi to Brazil—and the role laws can play in addressing them.

When SRHR and health rights are reduced to an abstracted set of rules, components of which are then isolated as yes/no indicators, we lose the dimensions of vernacularization and contestation over the grounds of arguments for interpreting them that we have discussed throughout these pages. For example, one of the five components of Target 5.6.2 relates to abortion. We saw in Chapter One how if a constitutional right to abortion is based on privacy, as it is in the United States, it has very different ramifications than if it is based on the intensity of the burden pregnancy entails, as it is in Germany. The laws reflect different understandings of women's relationships with their own bodies and the fetus, as well as the nature of sexuality and reproduction as purely private or social; the grounds for rights also reflect different understandings of social contracts and the responsibilities of the state in relation to women's health.

In short, how laws function to (dis)allow women control over their bodies and lives cannot be synthesized into tallied indicators, which pretend to be neutral and unchallengeable. This "indicatorization" exacerbates a tendency to fetishize specific rights, including health and SRHR, and isolate them from the need for robust democratic institutional arrangements. For example, as of this writing, since 2012, almost 100 countries have enacted laws restricting civil society activities, including freedoms of expression and association, and foreign funding—a significant percentage of which relates to SRHR—and that does not include the effects of the "Global Gag Rule," which restricts US funding to foreign groups that provide information relating to abortion, even if they provide many other services as well.[34] Moreover, globally, SRHR had become a political crucible, a moral distraction from economic realities, where conjured fears of gender ideology were used to manipulate voters, including in Colombia's peace referendum in 2016. Decontextualized indicators can make attempts to reprivatize women's life plans, populist nationalism, and socioeconomic inequality exacerbated by austerity appear to be distinct from the realization of SRHR and other rights. It is crucial for advancing health and social equality to understand that they are not.

The Evolution of Health and ESC Rights Indicators and What Can Be Done

Since the 1990's it was evident that in ESC rights, and health perhaps in particular, it would be inadequate to use paradigmatic illustrations or inductively argue that there were systematic violations, without broader information. Thus, for example, as discussed in Chapter Four, in Peru it was essential to collect as many cases as possible and to locate policy documents that revealed a systematic pattern of violations to go beyond fighting individualized impunity, which Giulia and others realized at the time was not the whole issue. It was clear early on that not just more but different kinds of information would be necessary to measure violations, as well as the progressive realization of the right to health.

By the time the SDGs were launched, an array of efforts within the United Nations and regional bodies, as well as by NGOs, had been dedicated to capture distinct dimensions of ESC rights compliance. For example, the Committee on Economic, Social and Cultural Rights (CESCR) devised the OPERA framework to measure **o**utcomes, **p**olicies, **e**conomic **r**esources, and **a**ssessment.[35] The Office of the High Commissioner for Human Rights (OHCHR) developed indicators related to structure (laws), processes (policy inputs), and outcomes.[36] Indicators were also developed in the Inter-American System to measure progress on ESC rights under the Protocol of San Salvador.[37] Further, human rights advocates called for disaggregation of data already collected to be able to discern patterns of discrimination. These initiatives all recognize that quantitative indicators are useful tools to enhance the picture of state compliance by going beyond the adoption of laws and policies to assess the effective enjoyment of rights in practice; but they are not stand-alone measures.

To give a concrete example, in the late 1990's Deborah Maine and I argued that emergency obstetric care indicators could help to measure compliance with international human rights obligations relating to women being free of avoidable mortality in pregnancy and childbirth, asserting that these measures helped define "appropriate measures" under international law.[38] The idea was simple: if states were taking *inappropriate measures*—as many were, based on outdated ideas of maternal health as opposed to the best public health evidence at the time—their actions could not be deemed *reasonable*. The argument was parallel in some ways to that used by TAC in Chapter Five to argue for ARVs, but the emergency obstetric indicators were designed to measure multiple aspects of health systems. Thus, for example, these indicators were highlighted in the UN

Technical Guidance and examined in the context of Brazil in Chapter Six. But it was always clear that they alone do not provide the whole story about maternal health–related rights; they literally *indicate* issues that need to be further explored in that messy, contextual, bottom-up inquiry into what is happening and why— which in human rights must include the populations who are affected. Twenty years later, despite all of the efforts mentioned above and countless others, SDG indicators had "ceased to be supplemental tools to measure reflections of the freedoms that we value in objective ways—i.e., staying alive through pregnancy—and instead had too often come to define the freedoms themselves."[39]

The indicatorization of the world matters very much for rights advocacy, as rights are tools for the regulation of power, including the power to define what we know and how we think.[40] Just as indicators could be used by international financial institutions, so too do rights indicators lend themselves to global governance from afar. As Sally Merry notes, numerical indicators are seductive as tools to understand the world precisely because of their reductionism and simplicity; yet these same qualities blunt the capacity of civil society to understand their theoretical origins and demand justification for policy outcomes and the reasoning behind policies.[41] Neither the selection of one indicator nor the use of numerical or ranked indicators to measure rights is inevitable. Indeed, as we have seen in this narrative, the representation of reality that indicators encode in global development, and economic governance, is relatively recent. When we recognize that indicators are mere techniques of representation, we see them differently. Further, the devices that we choose (e.g., inequality measure) and how we use them (e.g., adding qualitative information to place an SRHR tallied indicator in context) are subject to change through concerted advocacy.

Universal Health Care, the Right to Health, and Health Systems

The advent of UHC as a centerpiece in the SDGs came to be referred to as the "materialization of the right to health,"[42] which is simply not true. The right to health includes freedoms as well as entitlements; the right to health is not synonymous with packages of goods and services, set without regard for social and political determinants of health or arrangement of social institutions necessary to realize them. Yet, as we have seen in each chapter, patterns of social exclusion, often enshrined in legal norms, are reflected in the treatment of marginalized populations and women within the health system. In short, the health system itself is a social determinant. Thus, without setting aside questions of the social construction of health, many of the issues that arise regarding horizontal equity (equal public health as well as care for similarly situated people) and vertical equity (added public health protections and care when needed to mitigate background inequalities) can be analogized to questions of formal and substantive equality in human rights.[43]

In Chapters Five and Six, we noted how conceptualizing health systems as social institutions would entail changing relationships to foster dynamics of entitlement and obligation within and beyond the system, and reflecting normative principles, such as equality and dignity at every level within the system. Here, I suggest that approaching UHC consistent with the notion of a health system as a social institution requires three broad elements: fair financing, fair priority-setting, and effective regulation and oversight, including of private actors.

Fair Financing: The Challenge of Including Everyone

Accepting the reality of limited resources does not mean we need to accept that the government's health budget is prima facie reasonable, nor that the global rules of intellectual property or conditions for international investment are reasonable. In South Africa, we saw the challenge to intellectual property rules on access to medicines and how they would have affected the available resources for antiretroviral therapy.

A health system based on the right to health calls for fair financing that requires pooling of resources to contain out-of pocket costs so that people are not driven to bankruptcy by catastrophic health expenditures, and takes into account the denominator of who gets access to public health measures as well as care. Schemes based on cross-subsidies from those formally employed to others have significant gendered impacts and have grown increasingly less viable, as flexibilization of labor and the "gig economy" have increased the so-called informal sector compared with the formal sector. This has exacerbated fragmentation and inequities in systems, more reliance on private care for the wealthy, and public systems that provide poor care for the poor. The T-760/08 decision discussed in Chapter Six called for the equalization of the contributory and subsidized regimes in Colombia, but the fundamental issue of financing that relies on expectations of employment formality remains a major barrier to sustaining Colombia's health system. In many sub-Saharan African countries, where formal employment is even thinner and national budgets are tighter, Attiya Waris and Laila Latif argue for setting aside a percentage of value-added taxes (VAT) and corporate tax to go toward the health budget, in addition to other measures.[44]

If fair financing requires extending access to care to those not formally employed, it also requires extending access to migrants both under human rights law and as a matter of sustainable development, as noted by the 2018 report of the University College of London–Lancet Commission on Migration and Health.[45] What does this mean? Arguably, social—and not just legal—citizens should be entitled to the benefits of the social contract. But at a minimum, human rights law requires migrants to have essential health care regardless of status.[46] Second, migrants are entitled to emergency care, as the UN Human Rights Committee, which monitors the International Covenant on Civil and Political Rights, ruled in *Toussaint v. Canada*.[47] Similarly, in Colombia, the Constitutional Court has held that in situations of emergency or where delay would produce irreparable harm, irregular migrants can access care without awaiting the time-consuming bureaucracy required to obtain registration in the social protection system.[48] Finally, under international law and much domestic law, when babies are born in countries of destination, they are entitled to receive care, regardless of their parents' irregular status.[49]

In short, under human rights law, health systems should include estimates for such costs in their financing.

Fair Priority-Setting: Accountability for Reasonableness

A second critical aspect of fairness in a health system involves procedural justice—*who* decides *how* to meet health needs fairly when not all can be met? Because of the bottomless need, there is *no* society—no matter how wealthy—in which all health needs can be met at any given time.[50] Therefore, to deny the need for explicit, transparent rationing is to surrender to the market mechanism (and implicit, opaque rationing) in practice, which is highly arbitrary, and which in practice means the wealthy get more. Advancing health rights requires grappling with how to ration *fairly and democratically*, not facile sloganeering.

Democratic priority-setting calls for the process whereby the contours of an enforceable right are defined not taken behind closed doors by "experts." That is, in a democracy, outcomes of elections must be justified (as free and fair), but we also care about evaluating the rules for determining the outcome, such as the electoral college in the US, the effects of drawing districts through gerrymandering, and restrictions on voter registration. In the area of health rights, reasonable people can disagree about what priorities should be, and these change over time; thus, the rules governing how we decide health priorities and policies become ever more important to justify.

Norman Daniels has set out procedural justice requirements for setting fair priorities in line with procedural justice, which he calls "accountability for reasonableness" (A4R).[51] First, rationales for decision-making must be public and transparent. In human rights, criteria used must be visible to the people who will be affected by them, especially those who are marginalized and excluded generally. This applies to marginalized populations due to socioeconomic reasons, and stigma such as issues of mental health, but it also applies to those with costly diseases, which will likely not be covered in a mandatory scheme. Just as a defendant in a trial or the loser in an electoral process needs to accept the result as fair *because of the process*, so too does someone who is being deprived of a critical treatment have that entiutlement, if health is taken seriously as a right.

Second, the reasons for setting priorities must be based upon arguments that would be accepted by "fair-minded" people as advancing population health. For example, cost-effectiveness permits a broader coverage of interventions and is therefore a matter of equity as well as efficiency; without cost-effectiveness health systems could provide expensive curative treatment to the privileged few without providing basic preventive care for the many. Nevertheless, cost-effectiveness alone cannot automatically dictate what treatments are included in any particular context or with respect to a particular population, such as persons with disabilities; both normative deliberation and criteria such as clinical effectiveness and the gravity of the condition, and strength of evidence, are also critical. And as we have seen, struggles for SRHR illustrate that *which* health goods and services are included in discussions cannot be fairly determined by personal religious or ideological views.

Third, decisions should be subject to review or appeal based upon new information. As I have argued throughout these pages, both UHC and the right to health should not be thought of as endpoints but rather as entailing dynamic renegotiation in light of emerging epidemiologic, demographic, and other information. Thus, priority-setting in health cannot be a one-off event; it calls for institutionalizing health technology assessments (HTAs) and legitimate processes to evaluate constantly evolving technologies,[52] as well as changing conditions regarding social determinants. Finally, both the process and decisions should be subject to regulation and enforcement.

Democratizing Health Decision-Making

Human rights is consistent with but goes beyond accountability for reasonableness. In both frameworks, it is not sufficient to rely on broad principles to sort out whether priorities in meeting health needs are *reasonable*. Rather, it requires something much closer to what Habermas refers to as "active will-formation" regarding our specific motives and reasons, such as how much we value aggregation of small benefits versus concern for the worst-off (in health terms—sickest—not just socioeconomic terms). Human rights and constitutional commitments to formal and substantive equality, nondiscrimination, and concern for the vulnerable and marginalized, unintended stigma, and so on impose substantive restrictions and protective guardrails on what priorities will be enforceable and how criteria will be applied that could inadvertently or deliberately marginalize certain populations. Moreover, as we have discussed, if health is a right, participation should be open to those who are affected by the policies (including *social* citizens); deliberation should be undertaken on conditions of background equality of status, gender, class, and accessible information; and rent-seeking interests should be excluded.

I am often told that health is too technically complex for ordinary people to take part in deliberations and that we should leave priority-setting to "experts." I disagree. It is ultimately the government's responsibility to set priorities. However, this reflexive resort to technocratic expertise (1) masks the normative judgments inherent in ranking criteria; and, in turn, (2) systematically de-democratizes health systems by reinforcing that only biomedical or econometric knowledge is of value. Nevertheless, just as in the discussion of indicators, taking the idea of self-governance and dignity underlying health and other rights seriously requires us to be able to understand the uses of distinct forms of knowledge and practices to arrive at that knowledge.

Experience with James Fishkin and Robert Luskin's "deliberative polling" in health reveals positive impacts on weighting criteria after ordinary lay participants are educated about what is at stake.[53] In a deliberative poll in Italy, for example, participants notably changed their minds as to the need to allocate financing away from hospital beds to making the health system structures more efficient.[54] Deliberative polling is costly and sacrifices widespread participation for greater representativeness, equality, and reflection. However, as Jane Mansbridge points out, it also has indirect positive effects on citizen participation in other electoral and consultative processes, which is invaluable if we want to promote robust deliberative democracy more broadly.[55]

Further, multiple efforts to promote citizen deliberation are already being used successfully in national and local health priority-setting. For example, Christopher Newdick describes how for almost twenty years in the Thames

Valley in England, National Health Service (NHS) commissioners have balanced different claims within a nonstatutory Priorities Committee made of ordinary local residents, which makes recommendations to local health-care commissioners: "[Each] committee of 30 [is] composed of a lay chair, NHS clinicians, managers, a legal and an ethical advisor (who are also lay)."[56] The decisions of the committee on specific cases are subject to appeal to courts. One such appeal involved a trans woman seeking cosmetic breast enhancement surgery because she was left unsatisfied with hormonal treatments she received as part of her sex change (which was covered by NHS). The committee realized that whether equal treatment in such a case required comparing the plaintiff with the population of trans women, or to all "natalist" women, there were reasoned arguments on both sides. After denial of treatment, the committee's decision was appealed to a court, which in the end ratified it.[57]

Independent Review, Regulation and Oversight, Including Judicial Review

The final criterion of accountability for reasonableness is regulation and enforceability of the contours of a legal entitlement. As discussed in Chapter Six, national courts and supranational tribunals have found that regulation must include public and private actors within the health system, as well as those beyond the health system that affect pricing, quality, and access to health goods and services—including relevant information. For example, Uruguay was challenged by Philip Morris for putting plain packaging on all cigarettes, and in 2016 won a ruling in which the International Centre for Settlement of Investment Disputes explicitly noted the state's "margin of appreciation" in making public policies that protected the right to health—and in turn save medical costs associated with smoking.[58]

More generally, explicitly considering the manner in which priority-setting and health systems in general encode norms enables an understanding of the role courts can play in health systems and beyond, in legitimating and regulating the exercise of public *and private* power in relation to health. Roberto Gargarella argues, "Judges can . . . ensure that the process through which norms have been enacted has fulfilled its basic deliberative requirements and that the norms are applied in a manner compatible with our equal moral status."[59]

Historically, courts have often played reactionary roles regarding health, perhaps especially the use of criminal law regarding SRHR. However, if health systems are core social institutions, the question is not *whether* courts have a role to play, but, as discussed in Chapter Six, *how* judicial enforcement can foster systemic inclusion, equity, and accountability, including through catalyzing social and political action.

Human Rights and Global Justice: Responses to the Current Context

At every stage of this history, human rights NGOs and social movements have responded with new strategies and involved new configurations of actors. In the second decade of the millennium, both the official organs of human rights and diverse civil society organizations were responding to the glaring threats to equal dignity arising not just within states, such as growing attacks on SRHR, but also stemming from the international economic order.

Special Procedures and Treaty Monitoring Bodies

The UN created or filled an array of Special Procedures in the second decade of the millennium. Despite the ever-growing problems of fragmentation and incoherence, some new mandates explicitly addressed structural economic dimensions of human rights, such as the "Independent Expert on the Effects of Foreign Debt and Other Related International Financial Obligations of States on the Full Enjoyment of All Human Rights, Particularly Economic, Social and Cultural Rights."[60] As UN Special Rapporteur on Extreme Poverty and Human Rights, Philip Alston used the platform to explicate the application of human rights principles in the context of both national and global economic realities, including the role of IFIs.[61]

Further, as noted in Chapter Five, by the early 2000's advocates recognized that sexual and reproductive rights norms in particular, given their instability and political contestation, would benefit greatly from consistent frameworks for interpretation. As early as 2006–2007 there were discussions about a general comment on sexual and reproductive rights that would be jointly issued by the CEDAW Committee, the Human Rights Committee, and the CESCR. However, after a contentious process, the three TMBs issued separate and overlapping statements regarding issues relating in part to SRHR.

CESCR issued a General Comment on the *Right to Sexual and Reproductive Health* in 2016. General Comment 22 adopted the same structure as General Comment 14 in terms of legal obligations—specific legal obligations and a list of core obligations. Nonetheless, the CESCR updated and responded partially to the critiques of General Comment 14. For example, the shorter list of core obligations is more coherently justified, both normatively and empirically, and does not claim to be non-derogable. General Comment 22 included a far greater emphasis on access to effective and transparent remedies, enshrined a more updated view of health systems, emphasized international obligations, and asserted that the right to sexual and reproductive health is "interdependent" on a number of other CP and ESC rights and that it is affected by "intersectional discrimination."[62]

In 2017, the CEDAW Committee adopted General Recommendation No. 35, updating its General Recommendation No. 19 on violence against women,[63] which asserted that *opinio juris* reflects that the prohibition of gender-based violence against women has become a peremptory norm of international customary law (*jus cogens*)—akin to norms against torture, slavery, and piracy. Despite continuing flagrant violation of this norm, as the CEDAW committee noted, we have come a long way since the early 1990's, when most countries did not even recognize violence against women as an issue of human rights, and that progress has been driven largely by civil society and its use of human rights standards.[64]

In 2018, the Human Rights Committee issued General Comment 36, updating its earlier General Comment on the right to life, and extending the right to a right to life with dignity, illustrating the dialectical and recursive relationship between national, regional, and international law. The Human Rights Committee called on states to provide the necessary conditions for a life with dignity, including health, and in particular, significant protections for women to seek abortions.[65]

Despite approaching safe abortion from distinct perspectives—as an obligation not to jeopardize the right to life with dignity, as strict criminalization being a form of structural violence, and the equal enjoyment of the right to sexual and reproductive health—the collective conclusions of these three TMBs provide a plurality of normative grounds for arriving at an overlapping consensus on this most controversial of aspects of women's health rights.

Civil Society Advocacy Turns toward the Global Order

As argued throughout these pages, human rights has and will always depend on civil society for its creative normative development and political energy. In recent years, civil society has turned increasingly to advocacy around global as well as national drivers of social inequalities, including in health. For example, cross-border tax evasion far exceeded the amount of overseas development assistance in 2014.[66] Cross-border tax evasion is one form of "illicit financial flow," which includes other forms of "transfer pricing." For instance, mispricing of US pharmaceutical patents using so-called intangible capital (i.e., patents) created a 140 billion USD tax vacuum in 2016 by transferring the patents to subsidiaries in tax havens, where the parent company was then charged a high price to use its own intangible asset.[67] NGOs rightly argue these losses directly affect countries' abilities to realize health and other social rights; further they point not just to the need to redistribute unequal wealth within countries through progressive taxation, but to the need to change the global rules of the game that enable illicit transfers and tax evasion by transnational corporations.

Global Health Justice: Issues and Proposals

There is significant debate among scholars and activists as to how to address global health (in)justice specifically and the role of rights in doing so. Space precludes considering all proposals, but two highlight a significant difference in approach.

First, Lawrence Gostin and Eric Friedman, among others, have spearheaded proposals for a Framework Convention on Global Health (FCGH), which has no draft but is meant to be modeled on the Framework Convention on Tobacco Control (FCTC),[68] which calls for legislation and regulation of tobacco. A far broader treaty on "global health," however, raises entirely different questions regarding the scope of action. As most transnational determinants of health—unlike tobacco—cannot be controlled by national governments, proposals for an FCGH tend to focus on obligations of international assistance to address these dimensions. However, as Leigh Haynes et al. argue: "Limiting the project to questions of inter-governmental financial transfers [creates] the risk of neglecting the underlying structural determinants of health injustice. Such neglect would help to legitimize an unjust and unsustainable global economic regime."[69]

A distinct but closely related proposal to the Framework Convention comes from Gorik Ooms, Rachel Hammonds, and others, who have argued that "obligations of international assistance and cooperation" should require wealthy states to be "sufficient to enable countries to fulfill at the very least the minimum core obligations" under General Comment 14 relating to health.[70] There is no doubt that economic assistance and cooperation are required.

However, along with others, I believe there are more fruitful approaches to promoting global health justice than focusing on inter-state funding transfers. First, as a matter of law, even if it were binding—which it is not—as I argued in Chapter Five, the "minimum core" set out in General Comment 14 is not justified by any coherent rationale and therefore provides a poor normative grounding for imposing international obligations of economic assistance. Second, as an empirical matter, stopping even a fraction of illicit financial flows would be a more effective way to address global inequalities due to resources in health and beyond. If these measures were coupled with curtailing the harmful impacts of trade and intellectual property, as well as debt agreements and the like, the benefits for countries in the global South would dwarf any possible financial aid. Third, as a matter of doctrine, calling for such a global funding obligation reinforces that ESC rights as opposed to CP rights require such "assistance," which is empirically not true. Finally, as a matter of political economy, as Haynes argues with respect to the FCGH, focusing on intergovernmental transfers reinforces a neocolonialist charity relationship between the economic North and global South, which does not address the structural injustice in the global economy we have discussed throughout these pages.

What is a plausible alternative to such proposals? First, countries in the economic North do have obligations of international assistance and cooperation, which are not just financial but also imply technical and institution-building assistance. Second, countries in the economic North also have the obligation to do no harm—which is well established in international law beyond human rights, as a matter of extraterritorial obligations (ETOs). Imposing ETOs on states more systematically to capture illicit financial flows and prevent other harms (to health and beyond) offers a potential conceptual expansion of the social contract to include the transboundary effects of states and transnational corporations (TNCs) in this globalized world.

The 2011 *Maastricht Principles on the Extraterritorial Obligations of States in the Area of Economic, Social and Cultural Rights* (Maastricht Principles), on which parts of a zero draft of a binding treaty on TNCs and Other Business Entities with Respect to Human Rights is based, illuminate what efforts to curb ETOs entail.[71] The Maastricht Principles clarified ETOs as "obligations relating to the acts and omissions of a State, within or beyond its territory, that have effects on the enjoyment of human rights outside of that State's territory; and obligations of a global character that are set out in the Charter of the United Nations and human rights instruments."[72] A state has such ETOs in situations "over which it exercises authority or effective control"; in which its "acts or omissions bring about foreseeable effects" on the enjoyment of ESC rights, whether within or outside its territory; and in which "the State, acting separately or jointly, whether through its executive, legislative or judicial branches, is in a position to exercise decisive influence or to take measures to realize" ESC rights.[73]

The need to recognize and enforce ETOs is no magic bullet and alone is radically insufficient to redress global health and social inequalities that stem from the international economic order. However, addressing ETOs is an important extension of state obligations with respect to political determinants of health, which overcomes some of the inherent tensions that have divided initiatives for more egalitarian development and human rights. The idea of states controlling TNCs and other business entities is spreading rapidly in social mobilization by advocacy organizations and networks, and creating both explicit and intrinsic norms.[74] For example, cases have been brought to domestic courts, including in Holland where a Hague district court extended ETOs to greenhouse gas emissions.[75] Almost all of the TMBs have begun to regularly refer to states parties' obligations to control the impacts on rights of business enterprises within and beyond their borders. The OECD even rates its wealthy club of members on being good global citizens and examines transboundary, as well as intergenerational, effects of policies aimed at achieving the SDGs.[76]

In short, these are still nascent efforts. Nonetheless, even in this hostile global environment—perhaps particularly because of the obvious transnational health issues from climate health to mass migration to health security, and the equally obvious inadequacy of national responses—there are reasons to advance social and legal mobilization around ETOs.

We have seen repeatedly that it is possible in the course of a few decades to shift public discourses and doctrinal understandings of the responsibilities of states, together with institutional arrangements for enforcing such obligations. Social mobilization around transboundary health and other rights effects reinforces our webs of mutuality, exposing patterns of exploitation that benefit corporations, not the tax-paying populations in countries of the global North. Thus, mobilizing around ETOs has the potential to energize domestic political deliberations with respect to what sort of global citizen ordinary people want their country to be in a way that insisting on foreign aid simply does not.

Concluding Reflections

In February 2019, I was in Costa Rica, a small middle-income country in Central America known for eliminating its armed forces in 1948. Costa Rica has set aside approximately a quarter of its territory under some level of protection for rain forest, undeveloped lands, marine reserves, etc., has abolished all extraction industry, and is allegedly on target to be the first country in the world to be carbon neutral by 2022—the same year Qatar is to hold the World Cup.

I was in San José for the first-of-its kind transdisciplinary symposium on a rare disease, Hereditary Angioedema (HAE), which is estimated to affect approximately 1 in 50,000 to 1 in 250,000 people worldwide.[77] I met with patients the day before the forum. Leticia, a strikingly lovely young woman, showed me photos on her cell phone of when she had experienced an attack—with facial swelling making her entirely unrecognizable. She told me how hard it was for her to see herself that way and teared up as, recently married, she wanted to have children but wasn't sure about the effects of hormones in pregnancy. Even seemingly gender-neutral diseases have deeply gendered effects.

HAE is difficult to diagnose and therefore the reported prevalence likely represents an underestimate. Caused by several genetic mutations affecting C1 protein, HAE expresses itself in uncontrolled inflammation, which can be caused by physical pressure or stress, or seemingly nothing at all. Wherever it manifests, physicians tend to treat it as an isolated inflammation—appendicitis in the abdomen, an anaphylactic reaction to food, an insect bite on the arm or leg, etc. When it affects the larynx people can asphyxiate. Patients lose days of work and school, and are often subjected to unnecessary and damaging treatments (such as removal of parts of the intestine or appendectomies) as a result of inaccurate diagnoses. And outside of a handful of wealthy countries, the standard effective treatment (not the latest) is unavailable. In Costa Rica, per capita health spending is approximately 1,200 USD per year; a single dose of the recommended medication costs over 3,000 USD, and patients may have need for five or ten, or even more, doses per year. Thus, patients such as Leticia find themselves repeatedly in the emergency room, subjected to intrusive procedures, living in terror of each attack—i.e., with a dramatically limited quality of life for themselves and their families. International assistance to meet subsistence needs would not help HAE patients in Costa Rica, but adjusting intellectual property rules to encompass the harms of pharmaceutical pricing for such rare diseases potentially could.

Litigation was not the answer either. An *amparo* (protection writ) action was brought in 2018 on behalf of a young girl under Costa Rica's easy access to courts and expansive interpretation of the right to life with dignity. The constitutional chamber of the Supreme Court (*Sala Cuarta*) ratified the rejection of the highly expensive treatment but asked the government to explain the reasoning for denial to the patient, which it failed to do.

The precedent-setting forum at the University of Costa Rica was attended by people engaged in setting Costa Rica's formulary, the vice-minister of health, physicians and academics from the entire region, as well as patients with the disease. The health authorities appeared indifferent to the patients' suffering; one even telling the HAE patients that the collective good trumped their costly needs. A human rights lawyer argued the HAE patients should take the case to the Inter-American system to force the government to pay for the medications. I disagreed with both sides. Arguing for the highly costly treatments to be included in the formulary as a matter of health rights would be inconsistent with the ideas espoused in these pages; however, the health system was currently doing harm to these patients and thereby disregarding their equal moral value. Thus, among other things, I argued for a diagnostic test to be made available so that patients would not be subjected to iatrogenic harm, and patients in turn could take more control over their bodies and lives. Further, there was a clear imperative to democratize the way priorities were set, including transparently explaining the reasoning used by the health system to HAE patients.

Within days of this symposium, I was told there were signs that the government would consider making the diagnostic test available in Costa Rica for the first time. As of the time this book went to press, that had not occurred, but doing so would permit an accurate registry of patients, reduce enormous amounts of suffering due to medical error, and potentially save lives. My presence may have catalyzed the intersectoral meeting and discussion, just as our presence in communities in Peru had done so many years ago. However, the key is that, unlike Qatar, the HAE patients were speaking for themselves, meeting with policymakers, and making their voices and interests known.

The HAE patients I met were inspiring not just in their daily struggles to live with the disease, but because they were seeking structural change. As I have argued throughout these pages, the idea that they had dignity enabled these individuals with HAE to situate their personal struggles in relation to broader institutional questions. When deploying rights opens spaces for such dialogues about complicated health justice issues, with themselves, with fellow patients, and with policymakers, it is invaluable in connecting health equity to human dignity and meaningful democracy.

In short, the snapshot of today's reality in this chapter will inexorably change. However, I have argued throughout this book our current situation is only understandable in light of how we got here. In the second decade of the millennium, we have seen the explosive effects of increasing inequality within and between countries, and ever-growing illegitimacy of both democratic institutions in liberal democracies and the postwar multilateral order—coupled with the global threat posed by climate cataclysm.

Further, despite the exciting allusions to dignity and concern for the least advantaged in the SDGs, the reductionism of the indicators redefines the transformative aspirations, whether of reducing egregious inequalities or of the very understanding we have of rights, and SRHR in particular. It may seem inconsistent to argue that more data is not the answer in a world where autocratic leaders deny scientific facts, but the two are not unrelated, in that the recourse to technical measurement can close the space for democratic struggle. We need not ignore the importance of empirical facts to recognize that the knowledge structures we use to construct our world today are invariably political, just as in Al-Idrisi's time. We have seen throughout this book that creating a narrative about what knowledge counts, and whose expertise decodes it, does not just happen; it requires institutions and internalized norms that support that authority, whether in law, medicine, or governance. Further, they interact; the knowledge structures (re)produced through the SDGs indicators must be seen against the backdrop of the neoliberal architecture of the global economy onto which the SDGs are pasted.

We have also seen what would be required to implement UHC consistently with the right to health. A health system built around a right to health requires fair financing (including migrants and non-legal citizens), fair priority setting (including evidence-based interventions, but also the meaningful participation of affected groups), and effective regulation and oversight of private and public actors in line with normative commitments. Health systems can provide spaces to enhance democratic practices and accountability in the broader government—as suggested by possibilities in Costa Rica—but they can also easily reflect and refract patterns of exclusion and invisibilization, as in Qatar.

Finally, global health justice requires addressing the political determinants of health and the rules of economic governance that underpin many of the egregious imbalances of unnecessary suffering across the globe. Throughout these pages I have discouraged the idea of easy fixes; conquering health rights for diverse groups of people is a continual and messy challenge, and we have seen that the goal posts constantly change. At the same time, I have also underscored that acknowledging that truth in no way reduces the imperative of continuing the struggle for health and social equality. Apathy and cynicism are our worst enemies.

No doubt we live in unsettling times, with chaotic and disconcerting shifts wreaking upheavals around the world in virtually every domain. Further the threats that challenge health rights today are often not the intimate forms of domination we saw in the ESMA; they are the result of complex interactions between social, political, and economic—and environmental—realities that operate on multiple levels simultaneously. Nonetheless, this period of massive transition may shatter some of the false inevitability of neoliberal tenets, which have exercised an ever-greater grip on our collective imaginations since the 1980's—with the cascade of effects on health rights and social justice recounted in these pages. As the French critical theorist Jean Baudrillard notes, domination is overthrown from without, but hegemony is only inverted or reversed from the inside.[78] Trump and company have—in addition to everything else—pulled away the curtain on the masquerade performance of "the way things need to be done" in the post-World War II order, which the US played a fundamental role in designing. In sum, the sheer outrageousness of our current political spectacles in the US and elsewhere ironically has opened the door to new possibilities for progressive transformation—which we must now seize.

CONCLUSIONS

Turning Toward the World We Want

> We have not overcome our condition, and yet we know it better.... Our task as [human beings] is to find the few principles that will calm the infinite anguish of free souls. We must ... make justice imaginable again in a world so obviously unjust.... Naturally, it is a superhuman task. But superhuman is the term for tasks [we humans] take a long time to accomplish, that's all.
> —*Albert Camus*[1]

ON A STEAMY DAY IN OCTOBER OF 2017, I found myself looking out at part of the Panama Canal in Panama City. I was there to present expert testimony on behalf of the Inter-American Commission of Human Rights in a Special Session of the Inter-American Court the next day.[2] It was potentially a momentous case in which the court definitively would establish its willingness to enforce the right to health as an autonomous right under Article 26 of the Protocol of San Salvador to the American Convention on Human Rights.[3] The court had been taking steps toward such a move for a number of years, but there was internal contestation. In 2017, it signaled its willingness to go beyond previous jurisprudence and enforce economic, social, and cultural (ESC) rights directly in a labor rights case involving Fujimori's Peru, as well as a consultative opinion requested by the government of Colombia in an environmental dispute with Nicaragua. However, this case, *Poblete Vilches v. Chile*,[4] would be the most significant to date because it was in a contentious case about the right to health, which was likely to be heavily litigated and had been excluded from direct enforcement multiple times in previous Inter-American Court of Human Rights (Inter-American Court) jurisprudence. The protocol itself does not explicitly make the right to health justiciable and the court had previously opted to interpret it in light of connections to other rights. Thus, while the CESCR (Committee on Economic, Social and Cultural Rights) had moved in the direction of the right to health swallowing other rights, in its General Comment 14, the Inter-American Court's approach had led, as Judge Ferrer MacGregor noted in a concurrence, "to interpreting overlapping contents and to not enabling the evaluation of the implications of obligations to respect, protect and fulfill each right for its effective implementation."[5]

As Oscar Parra wrote about the 2017 *Lagos del Campo v. Perú* decision (establishing the independent enforceability of Article 26 of the Protocol in relation to a right to stability of employment conditions),[6] the opinion was, in keeping with Ronald Dworkin's hermeneutic way of seeing jurisprudence as literature,[7] a fitting episode in a long story. The attempt to break with formalistic interpretations of the law and make ESC rights independently justiciable had been occurring since the adoption of the Protocol of San Salvador in 1999, as discussed in Chapter Four, and had been a long struggle played out not just in activism but in footnotes within cases, as well as debates between scholars.[8] Although not a contentious case, the Colombian environmental case was conceptually important because the court had found that a comprehensive understanding of the right to a healthy environment—as could be argued about health—was too complex in its implications to be analyzed through a nexus with a plethora of other rights.[9]

I had often thought of the Panama Canal in terms of the geopolitical power grab by the United States that it was, including from Colombia. But that afternoon as I stood on the viewing platform and looked at the historical photographs, it was impossible not to marvel at the feat of engineering undertaken over 100 years ago. The canal connects the Atlantic and Pacific oceans through the Isthmus of Panama, using a series of locks. Not only did it greatly reduce travel time around the bottom of South America, and thereby facilitate commerce, but in the process of building it, major public health advances were made relating to malaria, yellow fever, and other mosquito-borne diseases.[10] Indeed, at a time when we face grave new public health threats from climate change, the construction of the canal shows the extraordinary capacity of human beings to collectively innovate practical progress and overcome enormous obstacles to human flourishing.

The next day I presented my testimony in *Poblete Vilches v. Chile*. In 2001, Vinicio Poblete Vilches had died in the Hospital Sotero del Río on the outskirts of Santiago, Chile, after being admitted for a respiratory emergency. After surgery, he was prematurely sent home but then presented complications, which made him return to the hospital. At that point, both parties agreed that he should have been placed in intensive care but was not; he died later of infections contracted at the hospital. The family alleged a series of violations of informed consent and bodily integrity, rights to information and life, and the right to health, as well as due process rights. The family had attempted to exhaust domestic remedies—administrative, civil, and criminal—but had obtained no redress, and they then brought a case to the Inter-American Commission on Human Rights, which later referred the case to the Inter-American Court of Human Rights.[11]

The background of the case reflects many of the themes in this book. Chile under the Pinochet dictatorship was an early adopter of structural adjustment in the 1980's, with the health effects discussed in earlier chapters. By 2001, the health system in post-dictatorship Chile reflected the reforms pushed by the international financial institutions (IFIs), divided between private health care and a residual, underfunded public health system for low-income populations. In addition to background social inequality, there had been minimal investment in preventive measures and health promotion, and the health care system had become highly medicalized.[12] In the early 2000's, President Ricardo Lagos, of a center-left coalition, and his minister of health, Dr. Hernán Sandoval, designed and implemented the Plan AUGE (Acceso Universal a Garantías Explícitas). Together with greater investment in the health system and reducing inequities, the so-called Universal Access to Explicit Guarantees reform was an imperfect but systematic attempt at setting priorities in the system fairly, transparently, and explicitly; guaranteeing timely access (i.e., setting maximum wait times); implementing quality standards and financial risk coverage; and eventually incorporating a fund for costly diseases, as well as citizen participation into the setting of priorities and oversight of the system (e.g., dental coverage was decided through citizen consultation).[13] The Chilean constitutional court, not known as an activist court, had also exercised a normative function in the health system when in 2010 it declared the private insurance system's premium adjustments for health risk by age and gender to be unconstitutional discrimination.[14]

The morning after the hearing, both Vinicio Marco Poblete Tapia, the son of the deceased man, and I were up early, and we chatted as I had coffee in the hotel. Vinicio said he didn't drink coffee anymore because of his blood pressure. At 56, he was a heavy-set man with the dark leathery hands that revealed a life of little comfort and an expressive face with dark sad eyes. Those eyes filled with tears when speaking of his father and his family. He had been pursuing this case for seventeen years of his life and had given up steady employment to do so. His mother had died after his father's death "of grief"; his sister had attempted suicide and later died; his disabled brother had also died. He had faced his own struggles with cancer and heart disease, had lost one kidney, and walked with a cane. We talked about his family, about Chile—about the food dishes I had tried and the ones he recommended, about how in spring in Santiago snow can still be visible on the tops of the surrounding Andes mountains, even when the jacarandás are in bloom. We watched together as the dawn spread its rosy fingers across the horizon, and then I left to catch my flight. "May God bless you," he said as we hugged tightly goodbye, and I held back tears myself, repeating "que Dios te bendiga."

In contemplating the complex sorrows this man had experienced in his life, I couldn't help but think that even after decades of talking to people on the wrong end of pathologies of power about their most profound suffering, to paraphrase Rilke: I was still just a novice in the realm of pain. Vinicio had stated in the hearing, "My family was destroyed by injustice, we were discriminated against, humiliated for being poor. . . . The state never investigated. . . . For them [my father] was just another poor man who died in a public hospital . . . we have suffered too much."[15] He repeated the same sentiments to me, with the same sense of indignation as a victim of rights abuses by the military in Chile or Argentina might have said decades ago with respect to the abuse they had suffered—and with the same hope in the supranational human rights system.

In the Introduction, I noted that this has been a personal journey, and in many ways a critical reflection on my own professional career. When I began my human rights career and, together with many others around the world, set out to advocate for ESC rights in the early 1990's, I argued that we faced three challenges. First, we had to establish that health and other ESC rights were real, legal rights and not mere programmatic aspirations. This required drawing conceptual connections between health and human dignity, as well as changing legal norms to reflect state responsibility for meeting material conditions across public and private spheres; this evolution is incomplete but is far more widely recognized at national and international levels, as the *Poblete Vilches* case and the many others cited in these pages show. More broadly, the question is no longer whether health rights are legal rights that can be judicially enforced, although they still are not recognized in the majority of countries. The most challenging question now is how courts, in contexts of differing legal and health systems, can best enforce health-related rights to promote greater equity, open social and political opportunity structures, and improve diverse people's lives in practice—and what institutional changes are required in mandates, capacity, and authority for them to best do so.

Second, we had to demonstrate what it would mean to apply human rights to health, not just in laws and policies, but also in terms of institutionalization in health systems and beyond. We now have far greater clarity on many aspects of HRBAs (human rights–based approaches) to health. Even as there continues to be contestation regarding what principles such as participation and accountability call for in practice, we have diverse case studies of implementation, and the barriers faced, from regions around the world.[16] The challenge going forward has become ensuring that HRBAs do not devolve into hollow prescriptions that reinforce preexisting power relations by governments and private actors, rather than challenging the dominant understandings of global health and health systems that perpetuate systemic inequities.

Finally, in the early 1990's we believed that using ESC rights could be used to promote norms of greater egalitarianism, as civil and political rights had promoted norms of democratic pluralism and protections of individual liberties. At the time, we hoped that highlighting issues of health and water and the like, as rights, would not only affect national government policies but also diffuse norms regarding actions across borders, such as US-wrought destruction in the first Gulf War or transnational oil companies in the Ecuadoran Amazon. Here I have suggested that we in the human rights community, including myself, have been less successful. Perhaps we hoped for too much and settled for too little. Social inequalities within countries have exponentially increased over these years, and without relinquishing the central idea of *diverse human beings as subjects of claims against states*, it is clear that the decisions affecting patterns of global health justice require new tools and theorization to address transnational forces, as well as those located in national space.

Nevertheless, while Stephen Hopgood, Samuel Moyn, and other critics, argue that it is the "endtimes of human rights," that human rights has been "a powerless companion" in the steady march of Croesus,[17] or even that human rights has been complicit in the advance of neoliberalism.[18] I have argued that it is inaccurate to portray the human rights ecosystem as monolithic or unchanging over these years. It is indeed now common for scholars and activists from within human rights to note the contradictions between neoliberalism and human rights, including in relation to health in particular.[19] But equally importantly, as I have argued throughout, neither the official "Human Rights System" nor large northern international NGOs should be taken to represent a diverse set of actors, perspectives, and practices in human rights. Indeed, the power of applying human rights to health derives precisely from those processes of vernacularization that are necessary to make health and other rights function and meaningful in diverse lived realities. The unifying thread in this tapestry is a narrative of what it means to be human, which has enabled impoverished and marginalized people—from persons with disabilities to sex workers to impoverished indigenous women to people living with HIV—whose lives had been deemed expendable, to appropriate a sense of their own agency and collectively change their well-being and lives, and their societies for future generations.

I have developed a particular account here, from the perspective of the struggle for health rights, about how we came to be in the position in which we find ourselves, which in my view calls for disrupting cherished certainties in the collected fields of "health and human rights."[20] That is, even as formal enshrinement of ESC rights, including health, has progressed rapidly at both domestic constitutional and international levels, as has the normative understanding of the effective enjoyment of rights by diverse populations, there was an unfortunate synergy created between autocratic governments and increasing restrictions imposed upon fiscal and policy space by macroeconomic policies. The multilateral political order that had endorsed aspirations of international human rights gave way in importance to an evolving multilateral economic order, which began propagating a contradictory set of norms about the role of governments, including in health systems.[21] As the possibilities for progressive intentional transformation through politics became ever smaller over these decades, the more a self-fulfilling narrative of the need for the private sector to step in and for market-based solutions came to seem like the only way toward modernity.

Throughout these pages, I have rejected the inexorability of specific developments, as well as fatalism about the paths that certain constructions of international law have taken us on. Further, I have noted the iterative nature of using rights for social change and argued against dismissing the tremendous progress we have made in both normative conceptualization and practical progress in health rights, and social rights more broadly. To do so discounts the dignity of real human beings for whom those advances have literally changed their lives. I believe the way forward calls neither for business as usual nor abandoning the aspirations of the Universal Declaration of Human Rights of a "social and international order in which the rights and freedoms" therein can be realized.[22] It is now our task to challenge ourselves and to change some of the ways in which human rights have come to be applied in health and beyond, in order to, as Camus asserted in the aftermath of the cataclysmic World War II, "make justice imaginable again in a world so obviously unjust."[23]

An Evolving (and Continual) Struggle

By placing this struggle in a historical narrative, it becomes clearer how incremental progress is, the extent of recursivity between global and national developments, and the contingency of normative evolution. Rather than set out an a priori theory I have examined a consistent set of factors—ranging from empirical knowledge and technological developments to social and legal mobilization, and from institutional leadership and funding to economic and development paradigms—that have all shaped the path we in health and ESC rights took, and the challenges we have faced. In examining these shifting opportunities and barriers, I have taken pains to be transparent about the limitations of my own knowledge and my narrowly subjective perspective on the evolution of health rights described in these pages, as well as about when I mistook a partial story of what was going on for what was really going on.

Further, I have focused on women's health in many cases, in part because that is the path I have walked, and some of the most interesting normative developments in deploying rights for health have been advanced in relation to women's health and sexual and reproductive health rights (SRHR). However, that is no coincidence, as the challenges faced in women's health and SRHR required creative paradigm change in both health and rights, and still do. Indeed, as set forth in the Introduction, insofar as rights scholarship and advocacy default to (heterosexual) male perspectives as to what constitutes human existence, relegating the majority of the world to being departures from this carefully scrubbed version of reality, it will ineluctably continue to reinforce our *otherness* as *particularity*. We need to question why we think the way we do about *humanness* if we seek to use human rights to meaningfully challenge the interlocking systems of power that perpetuate gender, racial, and other forms of social inequality in practice.

In these conclusions, I make explicit some of the implications of the starting points I set out at the beginning regarding human rights, law, and democracy, as well as health and health systems. In particular, I emphasize four themes that have been central to this narrative, which engage these implications in intertwined ways: (1) the multiplying dimensions of power that we must use rights to regulate in relation to health, as well as new openings to do so in our current reality; (2) the evolving challenges of addressing women's SRHR in particular across the public and private domains, including in light of digital realities; (3) the continuous expansions of the social contract and the need to extend it beyond borders now in ways that promote democratic engagement; and (4) the imperative for democracy, not just health outcomes, of treating health systems as social institutions. Finally, based on the arguments throughout the book, I call for more critical praxis and transdisciplinary perspectives in relation to human rights and global health.

The Many and Changing Faces of Power

In Chapter One, I noted the almost surreal intimacy of the ESMA in the 1970's and the unmistakable domination of state agents acting on individual human bodies. I argued that a limiting factor in human rights has been that they were largely based upon regulating this liberal understanding of power: as "power over" or power as a control of overt behavior.[24] The protections offered by civil rights, such as freedom from torture, freedom from arbitrary detention, freedom of speech, and the like, emerged from this classical liberal understanding of rights as curbs on the power of the state to override the sphere of liberty of an autonomous subject. Further, this vision assumes a masculinist view of persons, as well as ignoring the economic and social conditions that affect freedoms in practice.

This one-dimensional understanding of power produces a thin conception of political rights and democracy, focused on overt conflicts in traditionally conceived political forums connected to the state. To be clear: this curb on state abuses has been extraordinarily important in deploying rights for health. For example, we have seen how nondiscrimination under international and much constitutional law has evolved from proscribing formal de jure discrimination to substantive de facto discrimination and disproportionate impacts of laws that are neutral on their face. Further, constitutional and human rights jurisprudence and guidance have evolved to address the construction of social vulnerability through harmful gender and other stereotypes that are enshrined in law.

Yet, over these years, we have seen that if rights are meant to meaningfully regulate power that shape people's life chances and well-being, they must address dimensions beyond this narrow liberal understanding of power which focuses on overt conflict.[25] Beginning in the 1980's, IFIs, in complicity with many governments, began controlling the policy and legislative agenda, determining which issues could come up for decision and excluding others that would contravene their goals of structural adjustment and trade liberalization. In the 1990's decisions regarding what could be decided began to be taken largely behind closed doors by technocrats at IFIs, and their definition and adjudication was exiled from democratic space to specialized tribunals or forums, from the WTO to investment dispute resolution panels. This agenda-shaping power—by the IFIs as well as private lobbyists and corporate interests—was a more significant form of power than the liberal, plural power exercised openly by public officials in national legislatures, and it could not be contested or curbed in the same manner. Over these decades, as the agenda-shaping power of these global economic architects became increasingly intrusive—with structural adjustment, trade, investment, intellectual property, flexibilization of labor, and the like—the sphere of open debate and policy space to make decisions promoting and institutionalizing health and ESC rights shrank. Therefore, rights strategies based upon premises that what was required was to bolster arguments in overt disputes between traditional political actors based on HRBA priciples could not address the ways in which hidden agenda-setting power precluded democratic debates to implement health rights.

On the other hand, it was never—and is not—inevitable that human rights strategies be confined to this narrow notion of rights as shields from openly exercised domination in a narrow political realm. For example, we saw innovative strategies devised by apex courts in multiple countries, which, rather than issuing black-letter rulings—to dictate certain specific behaviors or outcomes—used dialogical remedies to set agendas for the implementation of health-related rights in ways that had much broader material and symbolic impacts. Moreover, in Chapter Five, we saw that the "rules of the game" with respect to intellectual property and pharmaceutical policy can be successfully challenged at global levels as well as national levels. The breathtaking success of mobilization around HIV drugs led not only to greater access but to the creation of new institutions and new norms at national and global levels when poor people refused to accept that saving their lives was not cost-effective.

Throughout this account, I have argued for the importance of redefining political arenas as well as "the political" in a robust understanding of rights and democracy.[26] For example, with respect to the hidden exercise of power, many of the advances in women's and children's health we have discussed have been forged by contesting the boundaries of the political and the agendas that get set. Further, informal deliberative arenas beyond traditional state assemblies are critical both for advancing health rights and substantive democracy, which are inextricably connected. These include plural spaces in which subaltern groups relate themselves and their histories to larger societal realities, such as the Zapatistas in Mexico or campesinas in Peru.

At the international level in recent years, I noted in Chapter Seven that there has been increasing human rights pushback on the hidden, agenda-setting power exercised by the IFIs and in the context of economic governance. For example, the UN Special Rapporteur on Extreme Poverty and Human Rights, has called out the World Bank and the International Monetary Fund in particular, challenging long-standing pretensions that their policies and lending do not affect "political questions."[27] The UN Independent Expert on the Effects of Foreign Debt and Other Related International Financial Obligations has noted the inappropriateness of subjecting sovereign debt disputes to technical tribunals, when debt issues are fundamentally political and affect the rights of vast swaths of people across the global South.[28] And the advocacy of civil society has always been a driver of this increasing recognition by official representatives and institutions. For instance, a recent US Supreme Court case brought by Indian advocacy groups may even restrict the IFIs' near complete immunity from prosecution for environmental and human rights impacts.[29] Rejecting that economic issues are taken off the table in democratic debates and the role of IFIs, private banks, and technocrats in doing so is essential to beginning to redemocratize decision-making that affects people's health and ability to live with dignity.

Finally, throughout this account we have seen a third kind of power, which entails the internalization of norms and values. In Chapter Two, we discussed how children internalize senses of themselves and their place in society as they grow up. Too often, for girls, persons with disabilities, and other disadvantaged racial, ethnic, caste, or other groups, a violation of health rights does not mean life will not be the way they had planned. Rather, they come to accept this order of things as being natural and inalterable, sometimes even as divinely ordained.

Likewise, in Chapter Two we also saw that the biomedical paradigm, which also has particular impacts on SRHR, has become so widely accepted in the West as to seem beyond question, which in turn makes the specialized expertise of biomedical researchers and clinicians difficult to challenge. Further, I noted the deep linkage between the individualism of biomedicine and the marketization of health, which aligned with the neoliberalism sweeping the US and, through structural adjustment, much of the world.

This neoliberal view of the world was actively constructed and systematically legitimized by the IMF and other global institutions. However, over time, financial markets became increasingly all-encompassing, and governments across the global South became increasingly dependent on them as everything from sovereign debt to critical food commodities were securitized and traded. By the second decade of the 2000's, if not before, it had become difficult to locate any overarching relationship of domination. Rather, neoliberal hegemony came to be sustained through a vast netlike organization of exchange, of information as well as capital, facilitated by the diffusion of a market fundamentalist ideology. Over these years this hegemony has taken on enormous implications for planetary health and the environment, as well as the organization of economies and expanding inequalities, with gendered impacts in health and beyond. For human rights to be used effectively against this third form of power, we should first recall that these neoliberal ideas only recently conquered our collective imaginations and became so entrenched against challenge—which is the lynchpin of hegemony.[30]

Further, we need not be Pollyanna-ish to see that the events of these past few years have changed opportunity structures with respect to the hegemonic acceptance of neoliberal tenets. Not just national but global politics has become a repugnant "game of idolatry and marketing."[31] The open flouting of all kinds of norms, including those regarding classic CP rights, by Trump and his cronies around the world has awakened a much wider group of people not just to the dangers of populism and ethnonationalism, but also to the false inevitability of these global economic arrangements that have only been in place a matter of decades.

The events of recent years may well provide an opportunity to break with rigid adherence to market principles tempered only by palliative tax-and-transfer schemes. If trade regimes are not immutable, they can be modified not simply to capture profits in specific industries but to allow for greater pluralism in markets and more carve-outs for public health, the environment, and other public goods—as once was hoped and expected. If world leaders not only hide their tax evasion but dismiss paying taxes as being for "chumps," the need to reform this pillar of the social contract in order to reform that antidemocratic sense of plutocratic entitlement to private wealth—which we have seen growing over decades—suddenly can be made a pressing political imperative. The hard-fought and comparative knowledge we have gained in public health and ESC rights over these years about neoliberalism's impacts, including their gendered effects, should inform emerging legal, political, and societal debates about economic policy.

The Evolving Challenges of the Public/Private

I began the book by noting that diverse women's realities did not neatly fit into classical definitions either of subjects of rights or the application of rights. In the 1970's (and to a great extent still) women's health rights were doubly marginalized by an understanding of the liberal state that viewed the purview of rights as extending only to a narrowly defined public realm, while many abuses faced by women occurred in the domestic realm, and many of the issues that were central to their life plans, such as control over their bodies, were considered private matters. Thus, I argued that reconceptualizing both the subjects of rights protection and the responsibilities of the state were inherently part of expanding *human* rights, to include half of humanity's lived realities, in terms of health and beyond. As noted in Chapter One, many of the issues faced in SRHR blurred the lines between public policy and private activity from the beginning. Sexual pleasure for women requires knowledge of one's sexuality, access to contraception and/or barriers to potential infection, access to abortion or to obstetric care, freedom from violence, and the ability to choose one's partner(s) and the time/place of having relations. Thus, this intimate private activity depends upon laws and public institutions—from education to justice to health—to make rights real in the lives of diverse women. And importantly, these issues require affirmative entitlements as well as protections for decisional autonomy.

In the 1970's and 1980's women began to demand more empirical data in order to systematically bring what had been private issues into the public policy domain—from contraception and abortion, to freedom from violence. But women also assembled their physical bodies to literally occupy and resignify public space and the ways in which their societies had represented them—from marches, to "take back the night" and confrontations over abortion rights in legislatures and courts, to protests for democratization elsewhere. To be clear: there was no single women's movement; women of different races, classes, and sexual orientations, among other things, faced (and continue to face) distinct struggles in their local contexts. But women across these manifold divides began to exercise their voices in public spaces, not as victims or martyrs, but as citizens demanding their rights, including SRHR.

In the 1990's, as we saw in Chapters Three and Four, violence against women became recognized as a human rights issue requiring states to prevent, sanction, and eradicate violence in the private as well as the as public spheres. This major breakthrough was followed by the establishment of institutions and enactment of laws at national level. By 2017, violence against women had been declared an issue of *jus cogens* by the Committee on the Elimination of Discrimination against Women, despite continuing flagrant violations across the world, from Me Too to femicide to obstetric violence.

From the beginning of this account I have highlighted how we have had to face traditional forms of patriarchy that interfere with agency and health, including SRHR, and we still do. In Chapter Five, we saw how conservative movements had begun appropriating rights arguments and forums in the 2000's, while seeking to delegitimate international law and institutions. The wave of populism that emerged in recent years has exploited the moral arguments around SRHR, including abortion, and the fabricated threat of "gender ideology." I have also suggested that we have had to continuously navigate the alignments and disjunctures between the moral economy of SRHR and the political economy of global health.

Throughout these chapters we have witnessed how the neoliberal organization of our economies, at the micro-, meso- and macrolevels intersects with women's health rights across the public and private spheres. Thus, we noted that the sexual division of power is inextricably intertwined with the sexual division of labor, which means that, for example, access to household resources affects protection from domestic violence.[32] Likewise, we have seen how premises built into health insurance based on formal versus nonformal employment in systems such as in Colombia, or into the overall dominant economic model, systematically disadvantage women and their health.

On the other hand, over these years—in large measure as a result of rights struggles—gender norms and family forms have become more diverse, suggesting different kinds of arrangements necessary to protect equality of women and LGBTQ persons across the private and public spheres, including but not limited to caregiving. Thus, we can no longer even pretend it is sufficient to seek caregiver parity between the sexes to address austerity in a world of nontraditional family configurations and flexibilized labor. Diane Elson, Radhika Balakrishnan, and others have argued that ever-growing unremunerated care work needs to be *recognized* (made visible in its scope and impact); *reduced* (through institutional change); and *redistributed* (not just within families but through broader societal change).[33] Nancy Fraser proposes a "universal care-giver model," where all people share breadwinner and caregiving responsibilities, but the strain of doing so is eased by public institutional arrangements.[34] Some countries are far ahead of others in addressing the privatization of these caregiving burdens and offer comparative models of how to restructure our institutional arrangements in line with gender equality and social justice.

Finally, we have also seen the public and private spheres changed fundamentally with the advent of the internet and social media. Even though the internet can be critical to mobilizing awareness and protests in such moments, it has also become clear that in the age of social media we face other battles which affect women disproportionately. Private transnational corporations (TNCs), such as Facebook, now offer simulacra of the global public square in the digital age. The gaping digital divide remains a concern globally, but the advent of new digital worlds is also changing our relationship to our physical reality, and to one another other within it. With the incredibly rapid onset and development of these technologies, young people especially began sharing their most intimate details—voluntarily, even if unwittingly as to all the implications.

For girls and young women, the miasma of mediated desire effected by all these social media platforms[35] has had particular effects as they package and represent themselves at a time when it is also ever-easier in much, but not all, of the world to medically alter one's physical self. If the principal challenge had previously been to transform masculinist public space, and the contours of public debate in our physical world, digital reality proposed a narrative of changing our digitally mediated individual selves. On the one hand, the diversity of sexual orientation and gender identity, as well as differently-abled and physical diversity, can flourish in more fluid connections made across platforms. On the other hand, there is little opportunity for exploring one's evolving and ambivalent relationships to multiple identities, much less what Rilke called the unfolding of our damaged selves to another three-dimensional human being. Its worst effects include making pornography far more readily accessible, which changes relationships with real women and girls. And social anxiety, depression, and suicide have skyrocketed, in particular among young women and girls.[36]

As noted in Chapter Seven, it is early days yet in thinking through the kinds of regulations and social contract that could or should govern the digital world, and throughout these pages we have seen how laws and institutions lag behind technological and commercial innovation. Nevertheless, human rights scholars and activists, and women's health advocates, must be vigilant that the arrangements that are arrived at promote rather than undermine equality and dignity across the blurred "public" and "private" realms in what are now multiple realities, which affect real human lives. More broadly, over these years we've seen that advancing gender equality through rights, in health and beyond, calls for complicated navigation across these porous divides, and these navigations shift with new technologies as well as geopolitical configurations. It has always been essential, but moving forward it is increasingly so, to collectively think through the distinctions between bringing deliberations on issues to public arenas, calling for regulatory oversight by the state of given activities, and making markets, including labor markets, function for diverse women's lived realities.[37]

The Expanding Social Contract and Global Governance for Health

In Chapter One, I began by noting the restriction of human rights to the nation-state and the separation of human rights from global development. That was not coincidental, but shaped by both geopolitical power dynamics and also conceptual genealogies. Modern human rights are based largely on liberal social contractarian theories, as discussed throughout these pages. As we have seen, the struggle to use rights for advancing health has been one of constantly tinkering with the definition of that social contract, as well as who is included within it. As noted above, women, children with evolving capacities, LGBTQ persons, persons with disabilities, people employed in nonformal sectors, and irregular migrants are all subjects who have been progressively (and continue to be) incorporated into the social contract.

Moreover, the emergence of social constitutionalism enshrined notions of nondependence as necessary to live with dignity, and enumerations of ESC rights, in the social contract from Colombia to South Africa. General Comment 3 from the CESCR followed this tradition and established a minimum essential level of ESC rights without which these rights would not have meaning. Throughout these chapters, we have seen that re-envisioning the social contract in a democratic state of law has been essential to making health-related rights justiciable.

Today, in the face of obvious limitations of being bounded by the nation-state in terms of ethical responsibilities and legal accountability of states and nonstate actors that operate across the globe, and the potentially existential threats to the planet posed in some cases, it is empirically more urgent than ever to address political determinants of health. Philosophically, there is no reason we cannot move beyond what Sen calls "the tyranny of ideas" posed by limiting our conceptual frameworks to the nation-state.[38] Some alternatives to address global justice that have been suggested both in human rights and economics focus on strengthening a supranational global government.[39] By contrast, Jennifer Prah Ruger proposes a "provincial globalism" to signal the necessary recognition of the dual dimensions of and shared responsibilities for global health justice.[40]

In Chapter Seven I argued for the strengthening of norms around extraterritorial obligations (ETOs), as a variant of provincial globalism that could help stem threats to global health justice including but beyond those that arise from differences in national income. For example, think of carbon emissions in the US and elsewhere that affect planetary health and drive migration and conflict, or modifications to the human genome by scientists working with biotech corporations in one country that will invariably affect generations of human beings in many others.

The drafting of a treaty on Human Rights and TNCs and Other Business Enterprises is a step in the right direction. Moreover, this is the key: polycentric forms of governance that regulate TNCs and other ETO issues more broadly need not depend primarily on global institutions, nor on the hope that wealthy states will commit themselves to giving poor states minimal assistance and cooperation. As Benedicte Bull and Desmond McNeill point out, TNCs "are increasingly dependent on other transnational actors, including the media and civil society organizations. Their long-term survival may therefore be dependent on concern with issues other than profit, including maintaining a good image, and securing markets and work forces," which may well require attention to broader social goals.[41] The transnational advocacy networks that Margaret Keck and Kathryn Sikkink defined twenty years ago—networks "bound together by shared values, a common discourse, and dense exchange of information and services"—have proliferated exponentially and are well positioned to leverage influence over TNCs, and governments' other ETOs, in ways that were far harder to imagine when global networks mobilized around HIV and SRHR.[42] Keck and Sikkink noted that "where governments are unresponsive to groups whose claims may nonetheless resonate elsewhere, international contacts can 'amplify' the demands of domestic groups, pry open space for new issues, and then echo these demands back into the domestic arena."[43] Today, the objective of transnational networks, which include transdisciplinary scholarship as well as advocacy, must be to continue to influence the behavior of states and other powerful actors. However, what Keck and Sikkink call a "boomerang effect" does not just apply to states where the effects of transboundary activities are being experienced in health, but also to mobilize groups politically and legally in states which are directly or indirectly profiting from those activities.

Take for example the impoverished Wayúu indigenous community in La Guajira, Colombia, which, due in large measure to mining, has seen their water poisoned and exhausted, their crops and livelihoods destroyed, and their community's health decimated, including most acutely in children. The Glencore, Anglo-American, and Billiton-BHP companies jointly control the Cerrejón mine,[44] one of the largest coal mines in the world. Both a judgment from the Colombian Constitutional Court, which established a process not unlike T-760/08 but one outside of the court itself, and the precautionary measures that the Inter-American Commission on Human Rights issued in 2015 have not produced accountability or catalyzed political action.[45] In this and other cases, a horizontal strategy for promoting health rights across borders that focuses on enhancing relational networks and politics-centered mobilization in national spaces—where the mining companies are headquartered as well as in Colombia—could complement, and potentially make more effective, traditional human rights strategies.

Seeding norms and mobilizing actions around ETOs will require trial and error. However, even if we do not yet know what forms it will take, what is clear is that human rights advocacy around TNCs and other political determinants of health will demand new forms of institutions and sustainable networks of advocacy and information, as well as social, political, and legal mobilization. Such an experimentalist and networked model of health and ESC rights advocacy in turn calls for different funding, different institutional mandates, and different power relationships between advocates and scholars and between North and South.

The Imperative of Democratizing Health Systems

Strengthening democratic control over social policy in general is an imperative for advancing health and social equality, as we have seen throughout these pages. But it is also specifically true for health systems. As Lynn Freedman writes, "Human rights activists have long understood the political arms of the state—prisons, judicial systems, and police forces—to have the power to exclude, abuse and silence. But rarely are . . . the social institutions on which [ESC rights including health] depend approached with the same understanding."[46] Indeed, advancing health rights is deeply linked to creating more robust democracies in today's world, and both depend upon re-envisioning health systems.

Throughout this account, I have argued that poor and marginalized people experience much of their inclusion or exclusion from society through their repeated contacts with health systems, and that due to their socially constructed caretaking roles as well as reproductive needs, women are especially affected. We need only look to young African-American males' treatment in the US justice system and the grievous disparities in maternal deaths between whites and women of color in the health system, which we discussed in the Introduction.

We have seen this around the world. In Mexico, first the EZLN revolted in part for lack of access to basic services, and then the government used the health system as part of the counterinsurgency to gather information about the Zapatistas. In Peru, the health system was oppressively colonialist, and the punitive treatment of health workers on flexible contracts contributed to its structural abuse against indigenous women. In South Africa, the public health system that was supposed to be a site of reconciliation in postapartheid South Africa had to be legally forced to address the needs of poor, overwhelmingly black people. In Brazil, the health system reflected the dehumanization of Afro-descendant women in the overall society in its provision of obstetric care. In Qatar, migrants were invisibilized and excluded in the health system, and too often undocumented migrants have been excluded from care in Western democracies—from Europe to the United States. People with rare diseases can all too often be disregarded and even subjected to iatrogenic abuse, as we saw in Costa Rica. And in Chile, and everywhere—poor people are all too often degraded and denied dignity in health systems that allocate quality and content of care according to ability to pay rather than criteria of justice.

We have also seen that the model we use to understand *health* has enormous impacts for how health systems are organized and how people, including women, are treated. For example, in those systems in which providers are given unfettered power to define conditions such as pregnancy in biomedical terms—as in Brazil—the possibilities of combatting the patriarchal values those same providers may hold (such as through conscientious objection to abortion) are far more difficult. Similarly, in Peru under Fujimori involuntary sterilization in the family planning program was facilitated both by the biomedical objectification of women's bodies and by their instrumentalization for a neoliberal idea of modernization. More broadly, throughout this history, we have seen how the biomedical paradigm systematically depoliticizes health issues, in removing decisions to the realm of medical expertise, and functions in synergy with the commodification and marketization of care in health systems to displace attention from the broader conditions of people's lives. Indeed, the increasingly rapid pace of biotechnological and genetic innovation may well exacerbate not just commercialization of health care but other health and individual hierarchies in the future.

Throughout this history, and in depth in Chapter Seven, I argued that structuring the health system as a social institution in a democracy—as a space for weaving together polarized populations, constructing social inclusion, and reinforcing normative commitments to equality and dignity—requires fair financing, fair and democratically legitimate priority-setting, as well as normative oversight by courts. Moreover, the constantly evolving nature of the right to health due to epidemiologic, demographic, and technological changes requires an ongoing institutionalized priority-setting process. Such a process must take account of differential impacts of social determinants, but also affords meaningful participation of people who will be affected by policies. When criminal justice or electoral decisions are taken with the lack of transparency that characterizes most health priority-setting, as well as much decision-making in health, we decry them as violating basic democratic principles; the same should be true in health systems.

I have pointed out an array of examples of positive citizen engagement, from judicially initiated processes to institutionalized citizen panels to experimental polling techniques to various civil society campaigns and efforts. As we saw in examples from South Africa to Latin America, the role of courts is not to second-guess legitimate priority-setting, but to ensure that processes meet standards for procedural fairness and adequately consider the *reasonableness* of arguments and actions, beyond cursory administrative review. As we seek to spread and deepen engagement of social citizens in health systems, as well as effective normative oversight, it will always be a challenge to break down epistemic barriers that insulate health as "technical" and to devise appropriate institutional forms.

The SDGs may not offer "the world we want" in practice. Nonetheless, given the prominence afforded to Universal Health Coverage in the SDG agenda, the intensive work being done regarding legitimate priority-setting, and the rhetorical acceptance of a right to health,[47] there are opportunities to advance the rhetoric of rights into meaningful claims and institutional proposals for democratizing health systems. Moreover, epidemiologic and demographic transitions, coupled with rising costs of new therapies and technologies, lend urgency to including health and health systems in discussions about strengthening equality and democracy across the globe.

In sum, we require broader and deeper dialogue about these four themes, as well as many others relating to the future of global health and human rights, where promises and proposals are debated among a wider circle of people. In our interdependent and simultaneously fragmented world, the issues that deeply affect democracy, health, and rights—from climate change to financial hyperglobalization—are simultaneously too complex to be explained by the tools of one discipline and not susceptible to actions in one country alone. Moreover, throughout this account, I have stressed the need for critical praxis, which calls for learning from our own and others' engagement in messy real-world struggles. Those who have seen the distinct importance of their lives discarded on the neoliberal march of progress, or by arbitrary discrimination and dehumanizing abuse, including individuals mentioned in these pages, are the true experts in why deploying rights in health matters.

It is youth—for whom a new phenomenology of agency is still conceivable—who will undoubtedly be the architects of future political transformation. Yet all of us—young and old, activists and scholars, economic North and global South—should be inspired to bold action to, as Roberto Unger suggests, "find the ideas our efforts and commitments require."[48]

Concluding Reflections

In March 2018, the Inter-American Court of Human Rights handed down its opinion in *Poblete Vilches*, in which they found for the first time that the right to health was independently justiciable under Article 26 of the Protocol of San Salvador.[49] The court noted that the case offered the opportunity to analyze the right to health in the context of the structural aspects of the health system, and rights of nondiscrimination and the conditions of people in poverty. On a personal level, I sighed with relief for Vinicio and his family. On a professional level, along with many colleagues, I had worked toward this ruling for decades. Nonetheless, this victory also showed how inexorably iterative progress is and how much work still lies ahead.[50]

In addition to the reparations Vinicio and his family would receive, the Inter-American Court ordered structural remedies, including training of health providers and medical students on the rights of patients and in particular elderly patients. It also called for Chile to invest in refurbishing the Hospital Sotero del Río and in upgrading its capacity to address the health needs of elderly patients, and to report back annually on such progress.[51] But as noted in Chapter Six, singling out one place, such as the Hospital Sotero del Río, may undermine formal equality with respect to all of the anonymous patients going to other institutions in the health system. Further, calling for the government to spend more on specialized care for elderly persons in hospital formats arguably undermines substantive equality as well, given the array of health needs in Chile.

In the Inter-American Court hearing, both plaintiffs and defense seemed to accept that the progressive realization of the right to health included making more care units available, more gerontologists, more dialysis, and the like. I had argued the contrary: while it is true that emergency care is a fundamental aspect of a health system, which was sorely missing in the Hospital Sotero del Río, and for which the state of Chile should have been held responsible, *progressive realization* would require examining the entire health system as well as political and social determinants that lead to chronic health conditions in old age.[52] For example, Chile has the highest percentage of obesity in Latin America; 60% of its population is overweight or suffering from related health problems. A 2012 law required warning signs on the front of packaged foods that are high in sugar, calories, sodium, or saturated fat and prohibited such products from being sold or advertised in schools.[53] A subsequent law, passed in 2016, prohibited advertising such products to children under 14.[54] These laws are not only far more likely to prevent children from developing chronic diseases when they become adults, and prevent much greater suffering than investments in curative care; they are also more equitable, as the poor are the most afflicted by the advertising and pricing of fast food.

I had further argued that it would be appropriate to think about redesigning the *health-care* system to provide community-based care for the elderly and those with noncommunicable diseases—such as those Vinicio Poblete Vilches had suffered—as opposed to further medicalization, which would inevitably lead to greater inequities.[55] Indeed, just a year earlier, in 2016, I had spoken at a conference in Santiago on the contours of a right to health in the context of the proposals to draft a new constitution for Chile—a country that has not thoroughly reformed its constitution since the Pinochet dictatorship.[56] At that time, Dr. Hernán Sandoval himself—the architect of AUGE—had made precisely this point about the Chilean health-care system and had later argued that determining care for the elderly should be done through a legitimate priority-setting process.[57]

Dr. Sandoval struck me as an extraordinary man who "had lived his life well"—with profound regard for the inextricable relation between his dignity and that of others.[58] He had dedicated his life to advancing the health of the poor in Chile and around the world, not as charity but as a matter of entitlement.[59] Sandoval had been a former militant in the MIR, a revolutionary movement in

Chile in the late 1960's and early 1970's. But in the early 1970's, Sandoval joined President Salvador Allende, a doctor himself and a famous proponent of social medicine, who argued for a "revolution in stages," respectful of the Constitution, the rule of law, and the institutions of the state. Allende was overthrown in a military coup in 1973, which ushered in a brutal dictatorship, at around the time of the one in Argentina described in Chapter One. Not surprisingly, given ballooning economic inequality and the ravages of neoliberalism, there has been a recent surge in Marxist-inspired laments that an anemic human rights framework had replaced the grand hopes of socialism in Latin America (and elsewhere). Despite acute awareness of national and global inequalities, Sandoval—and many other former combatants I have met over these years around the world—did not share that nostalgia. The ineluctable truth is that the social and mental structures needed to sustain armed conflict, revolution, class warfare, and the like, change a person's humanity. The "other" necessarily becomes a less than entirely human enemy in order to achieve greater objectives, and in turn, you yourself necessarily become less than fully human. Above all, as I have argued throughout, human rights is a story about what it means to be human, in which recognizing the dignity in ourselves—in all our diversity—is inextricably done in relation to others and their equal dignity. We can and we must make that story one which accords sufficient importance to addressing the grotesque inequalities and misery that stain our world, while, to paraphrase former ANC militant and later South African Constitutional Court justice, Albie Sachs, promising not a hard vengeance but pluralism and justice.[60]

Even in this era of radical transition—indeed *because* we live in such an era—the way diverse people cooperate in this complicated and fractured world can be changed when we decide to tell different stories, stories based upon the twin importance of robust democratic discourse to realizing our collective humanity and universal aspirations of equality and dignity in health and beyond. The importance of engaging in political deliberation and shaping our relation to the world is an old story. Yet it is one which we are continually being tempted to dismiss by conservative elites—who claim that ordinary people lack the necessary depths of individuality and therefore can only seek to attach themselves to a preformed religious/nationalistic/class identity, or their own narrow interests (as in health)—and by other "revolutionary elites" who think they understand best the deep structures of history.[61] The latter is a newer narrative, which emerged most fully out of the horrific cataclysm of World War II, and has faced constantly evolving challenges, and which no doubt can never be made believable to everyone. As

Philip Alston has argued about human rights in general, "dejection and despair are pointless and self-defeating. It's assuredly not a lost cause, but we should not be fooled into thinking that it's ever going to be a winning cause; it's an ongoing struggle."[62] If we believe in the story of why it matters, we cannot abandon the collective struggle for human dignity; but we urgently need creative critical praxis to help us advance health and social equality, and turn toward constructing the world we want.

Notes

Introduction

1. Amartya Sen, *Development as Freedom* (Oxford: Oxford University Press, 1999), 282–83.

2. Manny Fernandez, Richard Pérez-Peña, and Jonah Engel Bromwich, "Five Dallas Officers Were Killed as Payback, Police Chief Says," *New York Times*, July 8, 2016, https://www.nytimes.com/2016/07/09/us/dallas-police-shooting.html.

3. Katie Reilly, "Read President Obama's Speech from the Dallas Memorial Service," *Time*, July 12, 2016, http://time.com/4403543/president-obama-dallas-shooting-memorial-service-speech-transcript/.

4. Jason Horowitz, Nick Corasaniti, and Ashley Southall, "Nine Killed in Shooting at Black Church in Charleston," *New York Times*, June 17, 2015, https://www.nytimes.com/2015/06/18/us/church-attacked-in-charleston-south-carolina.html?_r=0.

5. Duncan Kennedy, "Are Lawyers Really Necessary?" interview by Vicki Quade, *Barrister* 14, no. 4 (1987): 36.

6. For example, the *Harvard Human Rights Journal* (first called *Harvard Human Rights Yearbook*) was formed in 1988, precisely with the idea of creating a scholarly field.

7. There were of course well-known CLS scholars who were deeply skeptical of international law, but at the time such critiques seemed to unduly discount the possibilities for taking advantage of shifting global dynamics. For example, see David Kennedy, "A New Stream of International Law Scholarship," *Wisconsin International Law Journal* 7 (1988).

8. International Study Team on the Gulf Crisis, *Health and Welfare in Iraq after the Gulf Crisis: An In-Depth Assessment* (Cambridge, MA: Harvard Center for Public Health, 1991), http://archive.cesr.org/downloads/Health%20and%20Welfare%20in%20Iraq%20after%20the%20Gulf%20Crisis%201991.pdf.

9. Center for Economic and Social Rights (CESR), *Twenty Years of Economic and Social Rights Advocacy* (Brooklyn, NY: Center for Economic and Social Rights, 2015).

10. The UN Special Rapporteur on Extreme Poverty and Human Rights, Philip Alston, sets out a similar framework: *Report of the Special Rapporteur on Extreme Poverty and Human Rights*, UN Doc. A/HRC/32/31 ¶ 21 (April 28, 2016).

11. *S. v. Baloyi and Others* 1999 (1) BCLR 86 (CC) 29/99 ¶ 12 (Sachs, J.) (S. Afr.).

12. Kathryn Sikkink, *Evidence for Hope: Making Human Rights Work in the 21st Century* (Princeton, NJ: Princeton University Press, 2017); Samuel Moyn, *Not Enough: Human Rights in an Unequal World* (Cambridge, MA: Harvard University Press, 2018).

13. Alicia Ely Yamin. *Power, Suffering, and the Struggle for Dignity: Human Rights Frameworks for Health and Why They Matter* (Philadelphia: University of Pennsylvania Press, 2016).

14. Simone de Beauvoir, *The Second Sex*, trans. H. M. Parshley (New York: Vintage Books, 1972), 161.

15. James Ron, "Survey: Most Believe Women's Rights Are Human Rights," *Open Global Rights*, November 23, 2017, https://www.openglobalrights.org/survey-many-believe-human-rights-are-womens-rights/.

16. Kwame Anthony Appiah, *The Lies That Bind: Rethinking Identity* (New York: Liveright, 2018).

17. Jürgen Habermas, *Legitimation Crisis* (Boston: Beacon Press, 1975).

18. For example, see Audrey R. Chapman, *Global Health, Human Rights and the Challenge of Neoliberal Policies* (Cambridge, UK: Cambridge University Press, 2016); Paul O'Connell, "On Reconciling Irreconcilables: Neo-Liberal Globalisation and Human Rights," *Human Rights Law Review* 7, no. 3 (2007): 483–509; Samuel Moyn, *Not Enough: Human Rights in an Unequal World* (Cambridge, MA: Harvard University Press, 2018).

19. For example, see David Collier, "Understanding Process Tracing," *Political Science and Politics* 44, no. 4 (2011): 823–30.

20. Pierre Bourdieu, *Outline of a Theory of Practice*, trans. Richard Nice (New York: Cambridge University Press, 1977), 2.

21. For example, see Mark Heywood, *Get Up! Stand Up!: Personal Journeys towards Social Justice* (Capetown, SA: Tafelberg, 2017).

22. Personal stories are based on journal and fieldwork notes taken contemporaneously and supplemented by research conducted during the writing of the book. All names of individuals that are not in the public domain have been changed to protect privacy. All public health studies referred to in the book obtained informed consent in accordance with ethical protocols at Harvard University and within the respective countries. Additionally, I have obtained written consent to use all quotations from key informants and others.

23. For example, see, Ruth Fletcher, "Feminist Legal Theory," in *An Introduction to Law and Social Theory*, ed. Max Travers and Reza Banakar (Portland, OR: Hart Publishing, 2002), 137.

24. Daniel Kahneman, *Thinking, Fast and Slow* (New York: Farrar, Straus and Giroux, 2011).

25. Audre Lorde, "The Master's Tools Will Never Dismantle the Master's House," in *Sister Outsider: Essays and Speeches* (Berkeley, CA: Crossing Press, 2007), 110–14.

26. Bourdieu, *Theory of Practice*, 22.

27. UN General Assembly, Resolution 217 A (III), Universal Declaration of Human Rights, A/RES/3/217 A (Dec. 10, 1948), art. 1.

28. For example, see John Rawls, *A Theory of Justice* (Cambridge, MA: Harvard University Press, 1971).

29. For an in-depth discussion of the concepts of dignity in different traditions, see Alicia Ely Yamin, "Dignity and Suffering: Why Human Rights Matter" in *Power, Suffering, and the Struggle for Dignity: Human Rights Frameworks for Health and Why They Matter* (Philadelphia: University of Pennsylvania Press, 2016), 25–48.

30. Roberto Unger, *False Necessity: Anti-Necessitarian Social Theory in the Service of Radical Democracy (Politics, Volume 1)* (Brooklyn, NY: Verso Books, 2004).

31. In *The Law of Peoples*, John Rawls extends his ideas of justice as fairness to international politics but espoused a thinner conception of global justice. See John Rawls, *The Law of Peoples* (Cambridge, MA: Harvard University Press, 2002), 3.

32. Amartya Sen, "Adam Smith and the Contemporary World," *Erasmus Journal for Philosophy and Economics* 3 (2010): 50–67.

33. For example, see Unger, *False Necessity*.

34. Kwame Anthony Appiah, *The Ethics of Identity* (Princeton, NJ: Princeton University Press, 2010), 260.

35. Alicia Ely Yamin, "Will We Take Suffering Seriously? Reflections on What Applying a Human Rights Framework to Health Means and Why We Should Care," *Health and Human Rights* 10 (2008): 50.

36. Norman Daniels, *Just Health: Meeting Health Needs Fairly* (Cambridge, UK: Cambridge University Press, 2007).

37. Seyla Benhabib, "Toward a Deliberative Model of Democratic Legitimacy," in *Democracy and Difference: Contesting the Boundaries of the Political* (Princeton, NJ: Princeton University Press, 1996), 68.

38. Roberto Mangabeira Unger, *Democracy Realized: The Progressive Alternative* (Brooklyn, NY: Verso, 1998), 5.

39. Max Roser, "The Short History of Global Living Conditions and Why It Matters That We Know It," Our World in Data, accessed March 7, 2019, https://ourworldindata.org/a-history-of-global-living-conditions-in-5-charts.

40. Roser, "Global Living Conditions."

41. Stephen Pinker, *Enlightenment Now: The Case for Reason, Science, Humanism, and Progress* (New York: Viking, 2018).

42. Gregg Easterbrook, *It's Better Than It Looks: Reasons for Optimism in an Age of Fear* (New York: Public Affairs, 2018).

43. Dean T. Jamison et al., "Global Health 2035: A World Converging within a Generation," *The Lancet* 382, no. 9908 (2013): 1898–955.

44. Linda Villarosa, "Why America's Black Mothers and Babies Are in a Life-or-Death Crisis," *New York Times*, April 11, 2018, https://www.nytimes.com/2018/04/11/magazine/black-mothers-babies-death-maternal-mortality.html.

45. Jamison et al., "Global Health 2035."

46. "Life Expectancy at Birth, Total (Years)," The World Bank, accessed March 7, 2019, http://data.worldbank.org/indicator/SP.DYN.LE00.IN?order=wbapi_data_value_2014+wbapi_data_value+wbapi_data_value-last&sort=asc.

47. UN Development Programme (UNDP), *Human Development Report 2016: Human Development for Everyone* (New York: UN Development Program, 2016).

48. "Working with Police in South Sudan to Assist Survivors of Gender-Based Violence," *United Nations Population Fund (UNFPA) News*, January 20, 2011, http://www.unfpa.org/public /home/news/pid/7156.

49. Jamison et al., "Global Health 2035," 1898–955.

50. Daniels, *Just Health*; Amartya Sen, "Elements of a Theory of Human Rights," *Philosophy and Public Affairs* 32, no. 4 (2004): 315–56.

51. Jo C. Phelan, Bruce G. Link, and Parisa Tehranifar, "Social Conditions as Fundamental Causes of Health Inequalities: Theory, Evidence, and Policy Implications," *Journal of Health and Social Behavior* 51 (2010): S28–S40.

52. Phelan, Link, and Tehranifar, "Social Conditions."

53. For example, see *Report from Maternal Mortality Review Committees: A View into Their Critical Role: Building U.S. Capacity to Review and Prevent Maternal Deaths* (Atlanta: Centers for Disease Control and Prevention Foundation, 2017), https://www.cdcfoundation.org /sites/default/files/upload/pdf/MMRIAReport.pdf.

54. World Health Organization (WHO), *Trends in Maternal Mortality: 1990–2015: Estimates from WHO, UNICEF, UNFPA, World Bank Group and the United Nations Population Division* (Geneva: World Health Organization, 2015).

55. Paul Farmer, *Pathologies of Power: Health, Human Rights, and the New War on the Poor* (Berkeley, CA: University of California Press, 2003).

56. Sen, *Development as Freedom*, 15; Farmer, *Pathologies of Power*.

57. Carmel Shalev, "Rights to Sexual and Reproductive Health: The ICPD and the Convention on the Elimination of All Forms of Discrimination Against Women," *Health and Human Rights* 4, no. 2 (2000): 39.

58. Nancy Fraser, "Rethinking the Public Sphere: A Contribution to the Critique of Actually Existing Democracy," *Social Text* 25/26 (1990): 67.

59. UN Human Rights Council, *Technical Guidance on the Application of a Human Rights–Based Approach to the Implementation of Policies and Programmes to Reduce Preventable Maternal Mortality and Morbidity*, UN Doc. A/HRC/21/22 (2012).

60. In relation to this point, see Unger, *Democracy Realized*, 14.

61. Jan Knappert, "A Short History of Zanzibar," *Annales Aequatoria* 13 (1992): 15–37.

62. Leda Farrant, *Tippu Tip and the East African Slave Trade* (London: Hamilton, 1975).

Chapter 1

1. Carlos Santiago Nino, *Radical Evil on Trial* (New Haven, CT: Yale University Press, 1996), vii.

2. Gloria Steinem, "10th Anniversary Convention of the National Women's Political Caucus" (speech, National Women's Political Caucus, Albuquerque, NM, July 1981).

3. "Espacio memoria y derechos humanos [ex ESMA]," Espacio memoria y derechos humanos, accessed January 13, 2019, http://www.espaciomemoria.ar/.

4. Díaz Bessone and Ramon Genaro, *Guerra revolucionaria en la Argentina (1959–1978)* (Buenos Aires: Editorial Fraterna, 1986), 13–18.

5. Lucía Luna, "Un actor de 'la guerra sucia' revela los crímenes de los militares," *Proceso*, January 14, 1984, https://www.proceso.com.mx/137811/un-actor-de-la-guerra-sucia-revela-los-crimenes-de-los-militares.

6. "Lista de víctimas de desaparición forzada y ejecución sumaria por la secretaría de derechos humanos," El proyecto desaparecidos, accessed January 13, 2019, https://www.desaparecidos.org/arg/victimas/listas/.

7. Simone de Beauvoir, *The Second Sex*, trans. H. M. Parshley (New York: Vintage Books, 1949/1972), xviii.

8. Ngaire Woods, "Bretton Woods Institutions," in *The Oxford Handbook on the United Nations*, ed. Sam Daws and Thomas G. Weiss (Oxford: Oxford University Press, 2008), 235.

9. "Fiftieth Anniversary of the Multilateral Trading System," World Trade Organization, accessed January 13, 2019, https://www.wto.org/english/thewto_e/minist_e/min96_e/chrono.htm.

10. Immanuel Kant, *Grounding for the Metaphysics of Morals*, trans. James W. Ellington (Cambridge, MA: Hackett Publishing, 1981), 434.

11. Audre Lorde, "The Uses of Anger: Women Responding to Racism," in *Sister Outsider: Essays & Speeches by Audre Lorde* (Trumansburg, NY: Crossing Press, 1984), 132–33.

12. Ronald Dworkin, *Life's Dominion: An Argument about Abortion, Euthanasia, and Individual Freedom* (New York: Vintage, 1994), 239.

13. Carlos Santiago Nino, *Derecho, moral y política: Una revisión de la teoría general del derecho* (Barcelona: Editorial Ariel, 1994), 11–12, 17.

14. Amartya Sen, "Adam Smith and the Contemporary World," *Erasmus Journal for Philosophy and Economics* 3 (2010): 50.

15. Alasdair MacIntyre, "The Privatization of the Good," *Review of Politics* 52, no. 3 (1990): 344–77.

16. Jacques Maritain, *Man and the State* (Chicago: University of Chicago Press, 1951), 77.

17. Maritain, *Man and the State*, 77.

18. John Rawls, *Political Liberalism* (New York: Columbia University Press, 1993), 134.

19. Cass R. Sunstein, "Incompletely Theorized Agreements in Constitutional Law," *Social Research* 74 (2007), 1–24; Cass R. Sunstein, "Incompletely Theorized Agreements," *Harvard Law Review* 108, no. 7 (1995): 1733–72.

20. Sunstein, "Incompletely Theorized Agreements," 1739–42.

21. John Tobin, *The Right to Health in International Law* (Oxford: Oxford University Press, 2012); Jennifer Prah Ruger, "Toward a Theory of a Right to Health: Capability and Incompletely Theorized Agreements," *Yale Journal of Law & the Humanities* 18, no. 2 (2006): 273–327.

22. Ruger, "Toward a Theory," 309.

23. Amartya Sen, "Elements of a Theory of Human Rights," *Philosophy and Public Affairs* 32, no. 4 (2004): 320–24.

24. UN Human Rights Council, *Report of the Special Rapporteur on Extreme Poverty and Human Rights*, UN Doc. A/HRC/32/31 ¶ 12 (Apr. 28, 2016).

25. Samuel Moyn, *The Last Utopia: Human Rights in History* (Cambridge, MA: The Belknap Press of Harvard University Press, 2010), 8.

26. Joseph L. Love, "Raúl Prebisch and the Origins of the Doctrine of Unequal Exchange," *Latin American Research Review* 15, no. 3 (1980): 45–72.

27. UN General Assembly, *Proclamation of Teheran, Final Act of the International Conference on Human Rights, Teheran, 22 April to 13 May 1968*, UN Doc. A/CONF. 32/41 ¶ 13 (New York: UN, 1968).

28. Raúl Prebisch, UN Department of Economic Affairs, *The Economic Development of Latin America and Its Principal Problems*, UN Sales No. 50 II.G. 2 (1950); Charles R. Beitz, "Justice and International Relations," *Philosophy and Public Affairs* 4, no. 4 (1975): 360–89.

29. UN General Assembly, Resolution 3201 (S-VI), Declaration of the Establishment of a New International Economic Order, A/RES/S-6/3201 (May 1, 1974); UN General Assembly, Resolution 3281 (XXIX), Charter on the Economic Rights and Duties of States, A/RES/29/3281 (Dec. 12, 1974). For more detailed discussion, see Samuel Moyn, *Not Enough: Human Rights in an Unequal World* (Cambridge, MA: Harvard/Belknap Press, 2018), 68–145.

30. UN Commission on Human Rights, *Further Promotion and Encouragement of Human Rights and Fundamental Freedoms, Including the Question of the Programme and Methods of Work of the Commission*, UN Doc. E/CN.4/RES/4 (XXXIII) (Feb. 21, 1977).

31. UN General Assembly, Resolution 41/128, Declaration on the Right to Development, A/RES/41/128 (Dec. 4, 1986).

32. Moyn, *Last Utopia*, 9.

33. Daniel Zamora, "Foucault, the Excluded, and Neoliberal Erosion of the State," in *Foucault and Neoliberalism*, ed. Daniel Zamora and Michael Behrent (Cambridge, UK: Polity Press, 2016), 63–85.

34. Dani Rodrik, *The Globalization Paradox: Why Global Markets, States, and Democracy Can't Coexist* (Oxford: Oxford University Press, 2011), 110.

35. "USA," World Inequality Database, accessed January 16, 2019, https://wid.world/country/usa/.

36. For example, see Shoshanna Ehrlich, *Regulating Desire: From the Virtuous Maiden to the Purity Princess* (Albany, NY: SUNY Press, 2014).

37. For example, see James Perloff, "Iran and the Shah: What Really Happened," *The New American*, May 12, 2009, https://www.thenewamerican.com/culture/history/item/4690-iran-and-the-shah-what-really-happened.

38. For a discussion of these elements, see Philip Alston and Ryan Goodman, *International Human Rights*, an updated edition of *International Human Rights in Context: Law, Politics, Morals* (Oxford: Oxford University Press, 2012), 160.

39. Steven Lukes, *Power: A Radical View* (London and New York: Macmillan, 1974), 11–15.

40. Benjamin Barber, "Foundationalism and Democracy," in *Democracy and Difference: Contesting the Boundaries of the Political*, ed. Seyla Benhabib (Princeton, NJ: Princeton University Press, 1996), 354.

41. Jürgen Habermas utilizes the term *will-formation* as a description for citizen's political participation in "Three Normative Models of Democracy," in *Democracy and Difference: Contesting the Boundaries of the Political*, ed. Seyla Benhabib (Princeton, NJ: Princeton University Press, 1996), 21–31.

42. Norman Daniels, *Just Health: Meeting Health Needs Fairly* (Cambridge, UK: Cambridge University Press, 2007).

43. UN General Assembly, Resolution 2200A (XXI), International Covenant on Economic, Social and Cultural Rights (ICESCR), A/RES/21/2200A (Dec. 16, 1966), art. 12.

44. World Health Organization (WHO), Constitution of the World Health Organization, Off. Rec. (July 22, 1946), 2, 100.

45. A/RES/21/2200A, art. 12.

46. A/RES/21/2200A, art. 2.

47. U.N. ESCOR C.4 (236th mtg.), U.N. Doc. E/CN.4/SR.236 (1951) at 20–21 (Mr. Sorenson, Denmark).

48. For example, see Rachel Hammonds and Gorik Ooms, "National Foreign Assistance Programs: Advancing Health-Related Human Rights through Shared Obligations for Global Health," in *Human Rights in Global Health: Rights-Based Governance for a Globalizing World*, ed. Benjamin Mason Meier and Lawrence Gostin (Oxford: Oxford University Press, 2018), 397–421.

49. Aryeh Neier, "Social and Economic Rights: A Critique," *Human Rights Brief* 13, no. 2 (2006): 2.

50. *Minister of Health & Others v. Treatment Action Campaign & Others* 2002 (5) SA 721 (CC) (S. Afr.).

51. For example, see Naomi Klein, *The Shock Doctrine: The Rise of Disaster Capitalism* (Toronto, Canada: Knopf Canada, 2007), 147.

52. Beauvoir, *Second Sex*, 161.

53. For example, see Judith Butler, *Gender Trouble: Feminism and the Subversion of Identity* (New York: Routledge, 1990); Kate Millett, *Sexual Politics* (New York: Columbia University Press, 1970).

54. Jane Mansbridge, "Using Power/Fighting Power: The Polity," in *Democracy and Difference: Contesting the Boundaries of the Political*, ed. Seyla Benhabib (Princeton, NJ: Princeton University Press, 1996), 46–66.

55. Jean-Jacques Rousseau, *The Social Contract and the First and Second Discourses* (New Haven, CT: Yale University Press, 2002), 189.

56. For example, see Hilary Charlesworth and Christine Chinkin, "The Gender of Jus Cogens," *Human Rights Quarterly* 15 (1993): 63–76.

57. UN General Assembly, Resolution 3520 (XXX), World Conference of the International Women's Year, A/RES/30/3520 (Dec. 15, 1975).

58. UN General Assembly, Resolution 34/180, Convention on the Elimination of All Forms of Discrimination against Women (CEDAW), A/RES/34/180 (Dec. 18, 1979), art. 5.

59. Karen Engle, "International Human Rights and Feminisms: When Discourses Keep Meeting," in *International Law: Modern Feminist Approaches*, ed. Doris Buss and Ambreena Manji (Oxford: Hart Publishing, 2005), 61.

60. Nancy Fraser, "Rethinking the Public Sphere: A Contribution to the Critique of Actually Existing Democracy," *Social Text* 25/26 (1990): 57.

61. Holly J. McCammon et al., "Becoming Full Citizens: The U.S. Women's Jury Rights Campaigns, the Pace of Reform, and Strategic Adaptation," *American Journal of Sociology* 113, no. 4 (2008): 1104–47.

62. A/RES/34/180, art. 12.

63. Committee on Economic, Social and Cultural Rights (CESCR), *General Comment No. 20: Non-discrimination in Economic, Social and Cultural Rights (Art. 2, Para. 2, of the International Covenant on Economic, Social and Cultural Rights)*, UN Doc. E/C.12/GC/20 (2009).

64. UN Department of International Economic and Social Affairs, *The World's Women 1970–1990: Trends and Statistics*, UN Sales No. E.90.XVII.3 (1991), 4.

65. *Violence Against Women Act of 1994 (VAWA)*, U.S. Code 42 (1994), § 13701–14040.

66. Bernard Asbell, *The Pill: A Biography of the Drug That Changed the World* (New York: Random House, 1995).

67. John Cleland, "Contraception in Historical and Global Perspective," *Best Practice & Research Clinical Obstetrics & Gynaecology* 23, no. 2 (2009): 168.

68. For example, see Nancy Krieger, *Epidemiology and the People's Health: Theory and Context* (Oxford: Oxford University Press, 2011); Michel Foucault, *Discipline and Punish: The Birth of the Prison* (New York: Vintage Books, 1979).

69. Heather Stephenson and Kiki Zeldes, "'Write a Chapter and Change the World': How the Boston Women's Health Book Collective Transformed Women's Health Then—and Now," *American Journal of Public Health* 98, no. 10 (2008): 1741–42.

70. For example, see Sonia E. Alvarez, *Engendering Democracy in Brazil: Women's Movements in Transition Politics* (Princeton, NJ: Princeton University Press, 1990).

71. For example, see Catherine MacKinnon, "Reflections on Sex Equality under the Law," *Yale Law Journal* 100, no. 5 (1991): 1308.

72. For example, see Judith Jarvis Thomson, "A Defense of Abortion," in *Biomedical Ethics and the Law*, ed. James Humber and Robert Almeder (Boston: Springer, 1976), 39–54.

73. Dworkin, *Life's Dominion*, 103.

74. Robin West, "Taking Freedom Seriously," *Harvard Law Review* 104 (1990): 84.

75. *Roe v. Wade*, 410 U.S. 113 (1973).

76. Dworkin, *Life's Dominion*, 25.

77. For example, see Carol Sanger, *About Abortion: Terminating Pregnancy in Twenty-First-Century America* (Cambridge, MA: Harvard University Press, 2017).

78. Thomas M. Keck, *Judicial Politics in Polarized Times* (Chicago: University of Chicago Press, 2014).

79. *Griswold v. Connecticut*, 381 US 479, 483 (1965).

80. West, "Taking Freedom Seriously," 84.

81. West, "Taking Freedom Seriously," 85.

82. *Whole Women's Health v. Hellerstedt*, 579 US (2016); *Planned Parenthood of Southeastern Pennsylvania v. Casey*, 505 US 833, 874 (1992); *Harris v. McRae*, 448 US 297, 314 (1980).

83. That undue burden test, which had been applied with great variation by circuit courts, was unified, if temporarily, in *Whole Women's Health*.

84. Bundesverfassungsgericht [BVerfG] [Federal Constitutional Court] Feb. 25, 1975, 39 *Entscheidungen des Bundesverfassungsgerichts* [BVerfGE] 1 (2–3), 1975 (Ger.).

85. 39 BVerfGE 1, (48–49) (Ger.).

86. 39 BVerfGE 1, (13–14) (Ger.).

87. 39 BVerfGE 1, (36) (Ger.).

88. Tribunal Constitucional [T.C.], 23 de fevereiro de 2010, Acórdão nº 75/2010 (Port.) http://www.tribunalconstitucional.pt/tc/acordaos/20100075.html.

89. Tribunal Constitucional [T.C.], 28 agosto 2017, "Requerimientos de inconstitucionalidad presentados por un grupo de Senadores y Diputados, respecto de normas del proyecto de ley que regula la despenalización de la interrupción voluntaria del embarazo en tres causales, correspondiente al boletín N° 9895–11," Rol de la causa: 3729(3751)-17 CPT (Chile), http://www.tribunalconstitucional.cl/expediente?rol =3729wsdefrtg.

90. For example, see Rachel Rebouché, "A Functionalist Approach to Comparative Abortion Law," in *Abortion Law in Transnational Perspective: Cases and Controversies*, ed. Rebecca J. Cook, Joanna N. Erdman, and Bernard M. Dickens (Philadelphia: University of Pennsylvania Press, 2014), 98–118; Reva B. Siegel, "The Right's Reasons: Constitutional Conflict and the Spread of Woman-Protective Antiabortion Argument," *Duke Law Journal* 57, no. 6 (2008): 1641–92.

91. Bundesverfassungsgericht [BVerfG] [Federal Constitutional Court] May 28, 1993, 88 *Entscheidungen des Bundesverfassungsgerichts* [BVerfGE] 203, 1993 (Ger.); see also for example, Rebouché, "A Functionalist Approach," 99, 102–3.

92. La comisión nacional sobre la desaparición de personas, *Nunca más* (Buenos Aires: Editorial Universitaria de Buenos Aires, 1984), 131–32.

93. Tina Rosenberg, *Children of Cain: Violence and the Violent in Latin America* (New York: Penguin Books, 1991), 92.

94. "Murió José Alfredo Martínez de Hoz," *Página 12*, March 16, 2013, http://www.pagina12.com.ar/diario/ultimas/20-215954-2013-03-16.html.

95. *Alfajores* are a typical kind of small pastries, in this case made with corn flour as well as *dulce de leche*.

96. Paul Lewis, *The Crisis of Argentine Capitalism* (Chapel Hill, NC: University of North Carolina Press, 1990).

97. Law 23.492, Extinción de la acción penal, December 26, 1986, Diario Oficial [D.O.] (Argentina).

98. Nino, *Radical Evil*; Carlos Santiago Nino, "The Human Rights Policy of the Argentine Constitutional Government: A Reply," *Yale Journal of International Law* 11 (1985): 217–30.

99. Carlos Forment, "Peripheral Peoples and Narrative Identities: Arendtian Reflections on Late Modernity," in *Democracy and Difference: Contesting the Boundaries of the Political*, ed. Seyla Benhabib (Princeton, NJ: Princeton University Press, 1996), 322.

Chapter 2

1. Eduardo Galeano, *Upside Down: A Primer for the Looking-Glass World*, trans. Mark Fried (New York: Picador, 1998), 34.

2. Susan Sontag, *Illness as Metaphor and AIDS and Its Metaphors* (New York: Macmillan Publishers, 2001), 133.

3. Mahmoud Fathalla, *On Safe Motherhood at 25 Years: Looking Back, Moving Forward* (Dorchester, UK: Hands On for Mothers and Babies, 2012), 10, https://www.birmingham.ac.uk/Documents/heroes/on-safe-motherhood-fathalla.pdf.

4. *Brown v. Board of Education of Topeka*, 347 U.S. 483 (1954); *Brown v. Board of Education of Topeka*, 349 U.S. 294 (1955); *Morgan v. Hennigan*, 379 F. Supp. 410 (D. Mass. 1974).

5. Boston Public Health Commission, *Place Matters* (Boston: Boston Public Health Commission, 2013), http://www.bphc.org/whatwedo/health-equity-social-justice/tools-and-resources/Documents/PlaceMatters-Update-04-13.pdf.

6. Franklin Roosevelt, "Radio Address on Unemployment and Social Welfare" (speech, Albany, NY, October 13, 1932).

7. The Personal Responsibility and Work Opportunity Reconciliation Act of 1996, Pub. L. No. 104-193, 110 Stat. 2105 (1996).

8. William J. Clinton, "Remarks on Welfare Reform Legislation and an Exchange with Reporters" (speech, Washington, DC, July 31, 1996), The American Presidency Project, https://www.presidency.ucsb.edu/node/223295.

9. Charles Murray and Richard Herrnstein, *The Bell Curve: Intelligence and Class Structure in American Life* (New York: A Free Press Paperbacks Book, 1996), 186–201.

10. The Economic Recovery Tax Act of 1981, Pub. L. No. 97-34, § 95 Stat. 172 (1981) and Tax Reform Act of 1986, Pub. L. 99-514, 100 Stat. 2085 (1986) (Together these are referred to as the Reagan Tax Cuts); Office of Management and Budget, "Historical Tables," The White House, accessed January 28, 2019, https://www.whitehouse.gov/omb/budget/Historicals.

11. Kent Matthews et al., "Mrs. Thatcher's Economic Policies 1979–1987" *Economic Policy* 2, no. 5 (1987): 59–101.

12. John Williamson, "A Short History of the Washington Consensus," *Law and Business Review of the Americas* 15 (2009): 7–23.

13. Amartya Sen, *Development as Freedom* (Oxford: Oxford University Press, 2001).

14. Shahid Yusuf et al., *Development Economics through the Decades: A Critical Look at 30 Years of the World Development Report* (Washington, DC: World Bank, 2009), 134.

15. Joseph E. Stiglitz, *Globalization and Its Discontents* (New York: W. W. Norton & Company, 2002).

16. For example, see Audrey R. Chapman, *Global Health, Human Rights and the Challenge of Neoliberal Policies* (Cambridge, UK: Cambridge University Press, 2016).

17. Adam Smith, *The Theory of Moral Sentiments* (New York: Penguin Classics, 1759/2009)

18. Sen, *Development as Freedom*, 87.

19. Jean Drèze and Amartya Sen, *Hunger and Public Action* (Oxford: Oxford University Press, 1989), 42.

20. Amartya Sen, *Inequality Reexamined* (Cambridge, MA: Harvard University Press, 1992).

21. Sen, *Development as Freedom*, 88.

22. "Human Development Index (HDI)," United Nations Development Programme (UNDP), accessed January 29, 2019, http://hdr.undp.org/en/content/human-development-index-hdi.

23. United Nations Development Programme (UNDP), *Human Development Report of 2000* (Oxford: Oxford University Press, 2000).

24. John Peabody, "Economic Reform and Health Sector Policy: Lessons from Structural Adjustment Programs," *Social Science & Medicine* 43, no. 5 (1996): 823–35.

25. John Gershman and Alec Irwin, "Getting a Grip on the Global Economy," in *Dying for Growth: Global Inequality and the Health of the Poor*, ed. Jim Yong Kim et al. (Monroe, ME: Common Courage Press, 2000), 20.

26. John Williamson, "What Washington Means by Policy Reform," in *Latin American Adjustment: How Much Has Happened?* (Washington, DC: Institute for International Economics, 1990), 5–21.

27. John Williamson, "The Washington Consensus as Policy Prescription for Development," in *Development Challenges in the 1990s: Leading Policymakers Speak from Experience*, eds. Timothy Besley and Roberto Zagha (Washington, DC: World Bank Publications, 2005), 33–53.

28. Christina Ewig, *Second-Wave Neoliberalism: Gender, Race, and Health Sector Reform in Peru* (University Park, PA: The Pennsylvania State University Press, 2010), 11–12.

29. Brooke G. Schoepf, Claude Schoepf, and Joyce V. Millen, "Theoretical Therapies, Remote Remedies: SAPs and the Political Ecology of Poverty and Health in Africa," in *Dying for Growth: Global Inequality and the Health of the Poor*, ed. Jim Yong Kim et al. (Monroe, ME: Common Courage Press, 2000), 109.

30. Peabody, "Economic Reform and Health," 823; also, for example, see Chapman, *Global Health, Human Rights*, 171–73.

31. Schoepf, Schoepf, and Millen, "Theoretical Therapies," 108–9.

32. Schoepf, Schoepf, and Millen, "Theoretical Therapies," 113.

33. UNICEF, *Adjustment with a Human Face: Protecting the Vulnerable and Promoting Growth*, ed. Giovanni Andrea Cornia et al. (New York: Clarendon Press, 1987).

34. Schoepf, Schoepf, and Millen, "Theoretical Therapies," 123.

35. Philip Alston, UN Commission on Human Rights, *The International Dimensions of the Right to Development as a Human Right in Relation with Other Human Rights Based on International Cooperation, Including the Right to Peace, Taking into Account the Requirement of the New International Economic Order and the Fundamental Human Needs: Report of the Secretary-General*, UN Doc E.CN.4/1334 ¶315 (Jan. 2, 1979).

36. UN General Assembly, Resolution 41/128, Declaration on the Right to Development, A/RES/41/128 (Dec. 4, 1986), art. 1.

37. Peter A. Hall and David W. Soskice, eds., *Varieties of Capitalism: The Institutional Foundations of Comparative Advantage* (Oxford: Oxford University Press, 2001).

38. Dani Rodrik, *The Globalization Paradox: Why Global Markets, States, and Democracy Can't Coexist* (Oxford: Oxford University Press, 2011), 75.

39. Smoot-Hawley Tariff Act of 1930, Pub. L. No. 71-361, 46 Stat. 590 (1930).

40. Stiglitz, *Discontents*.

41. John Ruggie, "Globalization and the Embedded Liberalism Compromise: The End of an Era?" (working paper, Max Planck Institute for the Study of Societies, Cologne, 1997), 52.

42. Ruggie, "Globalization," 52.

43. Amartya Sen, "Elements of a Theory of Human Rights," *Philosophy and Public Affairs* 32, no. 4 (2004): 315.

44. Sir Douglas Black, Department of Health and Social Security, *Inequalities in Health: Report of a Research Working Group (Black Report)* (Great Britain: Department of Health and Social Security, 1980).

45. World Health Organization (WHO) and United Nations Children's Fund (UNICEF), "Declaration of Alma-Ata," in *Primary Health Care: Report of the International Conference on Primary Health Care, Alma-Ata, USSR, Sept. 6–12, 1978* (Geneva: World Health Organization, 1978), 2–6; World Health Organization (WHO), *Global Strategy for Health for All by the Year 2000* (Geneva: World Health Organization, 1981).

46. WHO and UNICEF, Declaration of Alma-Ata, art. 1.

47. World Health Organization (WHO), *The Ottawa Charter for Health Promotion* (Geneva: World Health Organization, 1986).

48. Arthur Kleinman, *The Illness Narratives: Suffering, Healing, and the Human Condition* (New York: Basic Books, 1988).

49. Nancy Krieger, *Epidemiology and the People's Health: Theory and Context* (Oxford: Oxford University Press, 2011).

50. Michel Foucault, *Discipline and Punish: The Birth of the Prison* (New York: Vintage Books, 1979).

51. Sontag, *Illness as Metaphor*, 113.

52. Elizabeth Fee and Nancy Krieger, "Understanding AIDS: Historical Interpretations and the Limits of Biomedical Individualism," *American Journal of Public Health* 83, no. 10 (1993): 1477–86.

53. For example, see Jonathan Mann and Daniel Tarantola, Responding to HIV/AIDS: A Historical Perspective, *Health and Human Rights Journal* 2, no. 4 (1998): 5–8.

54. George Orwell, "How the Poor Die," in *Shooting an Elephant and Other Essays* (London: Secker and Warburg, 1950).

55. For example, see María Emma Mannarelli, *Limpias y modernas: género, higiene y cultura en la Lima del novecientos* (Lima: Ediciones Flora Tristán, 1999).

56. Kenneth Arrow, "Uncertainty and the Welfare Economics of Medical Care," *American Economic Review* 53, no. 5 (1963): 941–67.

57. Paul Starr, *The Social Transformation of American Medicine: The Rise of a Sovereign Profession and the Making of a Vast Industry* (New York: Basic Books, 2008).

58. Marsha Gold, "HMOs and Managed Care," *Health Affairs* 10, no. 4 (1991): 189–205.

59. Richard Epstein, *Mortal Peril: Our Inalienable Right to Health Care?* (New York: Addison-Wesley, 1997).

60. Today a small percentage of trans persons are also at risk of dying in pregnancy, but that was not the case at the time.

61. Vicente Navarro, "Production and the Welfare State: The Political Context of Reforms," *International Journal of Health Services* 21, no. 4 (1991): 585–614.

62. Anne-Emanuelle Birn, Laura Nervi, and Eduardo Siqueira, "Neoliberalism Redux: The Global Health Policy Agenda and the Politics of Cooptation in Latin America and Beyond," *Development and Change* 47, no. 4 (2016): 734–59.

63. James Cockcroft and Jane Canning, eds., *Salvador Allende Reader: Chile's Voice of Democracy* (Melbourne: Ocean Press, 2000), 36–42.

64. Constituição Federal de 1988 [C.F.] [Constitution], artigo 1 (Braz.).

65. United Nations Children's Fund (UNICEF), *State of the World's Children Report 1982–1983* (New York: Oxford University Press, 1982), 25.

66. Helen Epstein, "The Strange Politics of Saving the Children," review of *A Mighty Purpose: How Jim Grant Sold the World on Saving Its Children*, by Adam Fifield, *New York Review of Books*, November 5, 2015, https://www.nybooks.com/articles/2015/11/05/strange-politics-saving-children/.

67. Peter Adamson et al., *Jim Grant—UNICEF Visionary*, ed. Richard Jolly (Florence, Italy: UNICEF Innocenti Research Centre, 2001).

68. UNICEF, *Children Report*, 4.

69. Lucia Hug, David Sharrow, and Danzhen You, UN Inter-agency Group for Child Mortality Estimation, *Levels and Trends in Child Mortality: Report* 2017 (New York: UNICEF, 2017), 4.

70. The Convention on the Rights of the Child came into force on September 2, 1990. UN General Assembly, Resolution 44/25, Convention on the Rights of the Child, A/RES/44/25 (Nov. 20, 1989).

71. UN Committee on the Rights of the Child, *General Comment No. 14 (2013) on the Right of the Child to Have His or Her Best Interests Taken as a Primary Consideration (Art. 3, Para. 1)*, UN Doc. CRC/C/GC/14 (2013).

72. Lynda Lange, "Woman Is Not a Rational Animal: On Aristotle's Biology of Reproduction," in *Discovering Reality: Feminist Perspectives on Epistemology, Metaphysics, Methodology, and Philosophy of Science*, ed. Sandra Harding and Merrill B. Hintikka (Dordrecht, Netherlands: Kluwer Academic Publishers, 1983), 1–16.

73. For example, see Jean Piaget, *Behavior and Evolution* (New York: Pantheon Books, 1978).

74. Raewyn Connell, *Gender and Power: Society, the Person, and Sexual Politics* (Cambridge, UK: Polity Press, 1987).

75. Suruchi Thapar-Björkert, Lotta Samelius, and Gurchathen S. Sanghera, "Exploring Symbolic Violence in the Everyday: Misrecognition, Condescension, Consent and Complicity," *Feminist Review* 112 (2016): 148.

76. The WFS was administered between 1972 and 1987. "World Fertility Survey," Global Health Data Exchange (GHDx), last modified September 1, 2014, http://ghdx.healthdata.org/series/world-fertility-survey-wfs.

77. World Health Organization (WHO), *Maternal Mortality Rates* (unpublished report, World Health Organization, Geneva, 1985).

78. Allan Rosenfield and Deborah Maine, "Maternal Mortality—A Neglected Tragedy: Where is the M in MCH?," *Lancet* 326, no. 8446 (1985): 83.

79. Irvine Loudon, "Maternal Mortality in the Past and Its Relevance to Developing Countries Today," *American Journal of Clinical Nutrition* 72 (2000): 241S–46S.

80. Deborah Maine, personal communication with author, June 15, 2017.

81. Rosenfield and Maine, "Maternal Mortality," 84.

82. Rosenfield and Maine, "Maternal Mortality," 83.

83. Deborah Maine, interview by author and Emily Maistrellis, February 18, 2016.

84. Ann Starrs, World Bank, World Health Organization (WHO), and United Nations Fund for Population Activities (UNFPA), *Preventing the Tragedy of Maternal Deaths: A Report on the International Safe Motherhood Conference, Nairobi, Kenya, February 1987* (Washington, DC: World Bank Publications, 1987), 5–8.

85. Jeremy Shiffman and Stephanie Smith, *A Protracted Launch: The First Two Decades of the Safe Motherhood Initiative* (Chicago: MacArthur Foundation, 2006).

86. Martha C. Nussbaum, "Emotions and Women's Capabilities," in *Women, Culture, and Development: A Study of Human Capabilities,* ed. Martha Nussbaum and Jonathan Glover (Oxford: Oxford University Press, 1995), 360–96.

87. John Rawls, "The Independence of Moral Theory," *Proceedings and Addresses of the American Philosophical Association*, 48 (1974): 20.

88. Galeano, *Upside Down*, 32.

Chapter 3

1. Jonathan Mann et al., "Health and Human Rights," *Health and Human Rights* 1 (1994): 19.

2. Subcomandante Marcos, "The Fourth World War Has Begun," trans. Nathalie de Broglio, *Nepantla: Views from the South* 2, no. 3 (2001): 560–61.

3. Ejército Zapatista de Liberación Nacional (EZLN) Command, "First Declaration from the Lacandón Jungle, Today We Say 'Enough is Enough!' (Ya Basta!)"

Brown University Library, accessed February 8, 2019, https://library.brown.edu/create/modernlatinamerica/chapters/chapter-3-mexico/primary-documents-with-accompanying-discussion-questions/document-9-first-declaration-from-the-lacandon-jungle-today-we-say-enough-is-enough-ya-basta-ezln-command-1993/.

4. "Acerca de la Red TDT," Red Nacional de Organismos Civiles de Derechos Humanos: Todos los Derechos Para Todas y Todos, accessed February 8, 2019, https://redtdt.org.mx/?page_id=13.

5. Cited in Jane Mansbridge, "Using Power/Fighting Power: The Polity," in *Democracy and Difference: Contesting the Boundaries of the Political*, ed. Seyla Benhabib (Princeton, NJ: Princeton University Press, 1996), 58.

6. Physicians for Human Rights, El Colegio de la Frontera Sur, Centro de Capacitación en Ecología y Salud para Campesinos-Defensoría del Derecho a la Salud, *Excluded People, Eroded Communities: Realizing the Right to Health in Chiapas, Mexico* (Somerville, MA: Physicians for Human Rights, 2006).

7. Alicia Yamin, V. Penchaszadeh, and T. Crane, *Health Care Held Hostage: Violations of Medical Neutrality and Human Rights in Chiapas, Mexico* (Boston, MA: Physicians for Human Rights, 1999).

8. Yamin, Penchaszadeh, and Crane, *Held Hostage*.

9. Physicians for Human Rights, *Excluded People*, 27–34.

10. "Meet the World's Newest Billionaires," *Forbes Magazine*, July 5, 1993, 87.

11. Robert Howse, "From Politics to Technocracy—And Back Again: The Fate of the Multilateral Trading Regime," *American Journal of International Law* 96 (2002): 94–117.

12. Roger Normand and Sarah Zaidi, *Human Rights at the UN: The Political History of Universal Justice* (Bloomington, IN: Indiana University Press, 2008), 319.

13. UN Office of the High Commissioner for Human Rights, *Vienna Declaration and Programme of Action: Adopted by the World Conference on Human Rights in Vienna on 25 June 1993*, A/CONF/157/23, ¶ 5 (June 25, 1993).

14. *World Conference on Human Rights: The Vienna Declaration and Programme of Action June 1993 with the Opening Statement of United Nations Secretary-General Boutros Boutros-Ghali* (Vienna: UN, 1993), 1.

15. A/CONF/157/23, ¶ 25.

16. A/CONF/157/23, ¶ 1.

17. A/CONF/157/23, ¶ 2.

18. A/CONF/157/23, ¶ 1.

19. "About Us: World Conference on Human Rights, June 14–25, 1993, Vienna, Austria," United Nations Human Rights Office of the High Commissioner, accessed February 8, 2019, https://www.ohchr.org/en/aboutus/pages/viennawc.aspx.

20. UN Population Information Network (POPIN), "Highlights of NGO Forum '94," *ICPD 94 Newsletter* 19 (1994), http://www.un.org/popin/icpd/newslett/94_19/icpd9419.eng/4ngos.html.

21. Phumzile Mlambo-Ngcuka, "The Beijing Platform for Action Turns 20," *UN Women News*, May 22, 2014, http://beijing20.unwomen.org/en/news-and-events/stories/2014/5/phumzile-mlambo-ngcuka-un-women.

22. Elisabeth Reichert, "'Keep on Moving Forward': NGO Forum on Women, Beijing, China," *Social Development Issues* 18 (1996): 89–97.

23. For example, see Philip Alston, *The United Nations and Human Rights: A Critical Appraisal* (Oxford: Oxford University Press, 1995).

24. UN General Assembly, Resolution 48/141, High Commissioner for the Promotion and Protection of All Human Rights, A/RES/48/141 (Dec. 20, 1993).

25. UN Office of the High Commissioner for Human Rights (OHCHR), Resolution 1994/45, Question of Integrating the Rights of Women into the Human Rights Mechanisms of the United Nations and the Elimination of Violence against Women, E/CN.4/RES/1994/45 (March 4, 1994).

26. A/CONF.157/23 ¶ 100.

27. For example, see Ryan Goodman and Thomas Pegram eds., *Human Rights, State Compliance, and Social Change: Assessing National Human Rights Institutions* (Cambridge, UK: Cambridge University Press, 2011).

28. Naila Kabeer, "Tracking the Gender Politics of the Millennium Development Goals: Struggles for Interpretive Power in the International Development Agenda," *Third World Quarterly* 36, no. 2 (2015): 379.

29. Charlotte Bunch and Niamh Reilly, *Demanding Accountability: The Global Campaign and Vienna Tribunal for Women's Human Rights* (Newark, NJ: Rutger's University Center for Women's Global Leadership, United Nations Development Fund for Women, 1994), 15–16.

30. Mark Osiel, *Mass Atrocity, Collective Memory, and the Law* (New Brunswick, NJ: Transaction Publishers, 1997), 7.

31. UN General Assembly, Resolution 48/104, Declaration on the Elimination of Violence against Women, A/RES/48/104 (Dec. 20, 1993).

32. The Convention entered into force March 5, 1995. Organization of American States (OAS), Inter-American Convention on the Prevention, Punishment and Eradication of Violence against Women (Convention of Belém do Pará), 33 ILM 1534 (June 9, 1994).

33. Amartya Sen, *Development as Freedom* (Oxford: Oxford University Press, 2001), 213–16.

34. Sen, *Development as Freedom*, 213–16.

35. Marie Jean Antoine Nicholas de Caritat, Marquis de Condorcet, *Esquisse d'un Tableau Historique des Progrès de l'Esprit Humain*, Xe Epoque (1795), cited in Sen, *Development as Freedom*, 214.

36. Thomas Robert Malthus, *Essay on the Principle of Population, as It Affects the Future Improvement of Society, with Remarks on the Speculation of Mr. Godwin, M. Condorcet, and Other Writers* (London: J. Johnson, 1798), cited in Sen, *Development as Freedom*, 214.

37. *Report of the International Conference on Population and Development* (Cairo, 5-13 September 1994), A/CONF.171113/Rev.1 ¶ 1.8 (New York: UN, 1995).

38. A/CONF.171/13/Rev.1, ¶ 7.2.

39. Mindy Roseman, speech at Bergen Exchanges 2016 (Bergen Resource Center for National Development, Bergen, Norway, August 23, 2016).

40. Kabeer, "Tracking," 377–95.
41. A/CONF.171/13/Rev.1, ¶ 8.25.
42. Mindy Roseman and Laura Reichenbach, "Global Reproductive Health and Rights: Reflecting on ICPD," in *Reproductive Health and Human Rights: The Way Forward* (Philadelphia: University of Pennsylvania Press, 2011), 9.
43. UN Entity for Gender Equality and the Empowerment of Women, *Beijing Declaration and Platform of Action*, A/CONF.177/20/Rev.1 ¶ 113 (New York: United Nations, 1995).
44. A/CONF.177/20, ¶ 90.
45. Judith Butler, *Gender Trouble: Feminism and the Subversion of Identity* (New York: Routledge, 1990).
46. Kabeer, "Tracking," 380–81.
47. Mann et al., "Health and Human Rights," 20–21.
48. Mann et al., "Health and Human Rights," 6–22.
49. For example, see American Public Health Association, *Control of Communicable Disease in Man,* 15th ed. (Washington, DC: American Public Health Association, 1990).
50. Committee on Economic, Social and Cultural Rights (CESCR), *General Comment No. 3: The Nature of States Parties' Obligations (Art. 2, Para. 1, of the Covenant)*, U.N. Doc. E/1991/23 ¶ 10 (1990).
51. U.N. Doc. E/1991/23, ¶ 10.
52. Katherine Young, "The Minimum Core of Economics and Social Rights: A Concept in Search of Content," *Yale Journal of International Law* 33 (2008).
53. U.N. Doc. E/1991/23, ¶ 9.
54. Claudia Bittner, "Human Dignity as a Matter of Legislative Consistency in an Ideal World: The Fundamental Right to Guarantee a Subsistence Minimum in the German Federal Constitutional Court's Judgment of 9 February 2010," in "Special Section on The Hartz IV Case and the German *Sozialstaat*," *German Law Journal* 12, no. 11 (2011*)*: 1941–60, http://www.germanlawjournal.com/volume-12-no-11/.
55. Karl Klare, "Legal Culture and Transformative Constitutionalism," *South African Journal on Human Rights* 14 (1998): 150.
56. Judgment C-1064, Corte Constitucional [C.C.] [Constitutional Court], octubre 10, 2001, Sentencia C-1064/01 (Colom.).
57. Roberto Gargarella, *Latin American Constitutionalism, 1810–2010: The Engine Room of the Constitution* (Oxford: Oxford University Press, 2013).
58. Judgment T-406, Corte Constitucional [C.C.] [Constitutional Court], junio 5, 1992, Sentencia T-406 (Colom.).
59. Bruce Wilson, "Costa Rica: Health Rights Litigation: Causes and Consequences," in *Litigating Health Rights: Can Courts Bring More Justice to Health?*, ed. Alicia Ely Yamin and Siri Gloppen (Cambridge, MA: Harvard Human Rights Series, Harvard University Press, 2011).
60. Terence Halliday and Bruce Carruthers, "The Recursivity of Law: Global Norm Making and National Lawmaking in the Globalization of Corporate Insolvency Regimes," *American Journal of Sociology* 112, no. 4 (2007): 1135–202.

61. Sally Engle Merry, "Transnational Rights and Local Activism: Mapping the Middle," *American Anthropologist* 108 (2006): 39.

62. Daniel M. Brinks, Varun Gauri, and Kyle Shen, "Social Rights Constitutionalism: Negotiating the Tension between the Universal and the Particular," *Annual Review of Law and Social Science* 11 (2015): 290–91.

63. Brinks, Gauri, and Shen, "Social Rights Constitutionalism," 290.

64. Jean Drèze, "Democracy and the Right to Food," in *Human Rights and Development: Towards Mutual Reinforcement*, ed. Philip Alston and Mary Robinson (New York: Oxford University Press, 2005), 54.

65. Gargarella, *Latin American Constitutionalism*, 139.

66. UN Security Council, Resolution 955, Establishment of an International Tribunal and Adoption of the Statute of the Tribunal, S/RES/955 (Nov. 8, 1994); "The ICTR in Brief," United Nations International Residual Mechanism for Criminal Tribunals, accessed February 8, 2019, http://unictr.irmct.org/en/tribunal; UN Security Council, Resolution 827, International Criminal Tribunal for the Former Yugoslavia (ICTY), S/RES/827 (May 25, 1993); "International Criminal Tribunal for the Former Yugoslavia: 1993–2017," United Nations International Residual Mechanism for Criminal Tribunals, accessed February 8, 2019, http://www.icty.org/.

67. UN, Rome Statute of the International Criminal Court, A/CONF.183/9 (July 17, 1998); "About," International Criminal Court, accessed February 8, 2019, https://www.icc-cpi.int/about.

68. "About CEJIL," Center for Justice and International Law, accessed February 8, 2018, *https://cejil.org/en*.

69. UN Committee against Torture, *Concluding Observations: Mexico*, UN Doc. A/48/44(SUPP) ¶¶ 208–229 (Jan. 1, 1993).

70. For example, see *Anti-Impunity and the Human Rights Agenda*, ed. Karen Engle, Zinaida Miller, and D. M. Davis (Cambridge, UK: Cambridge University Press, 2016).

71. Asa Cristina Laurell, "La Política Social en el Proyecto Neoliberal. Necesidades Económicas y Realidades Sociopolíticas." *Cuadernos Médico Sociales* 60 (1992): 3–8.

72. Janet Halley, "Rape at Rome: Feminist Interventions in the Criminalization of Sex-Related Violence in Positive International Criminal Law," *Michigan Journal of International Law* 30, no. 1 (2009): 4–5.

73. Martha Finnemore and Kathryn Sikkink, "International Norm Dynamics and Political Change," *International Organization* 52, no. 4 (1998): 896.

74. Luisa Cabal, Mónica Roa, and Lilian Sepúlveda-Oliva, "What Role Can International Litigation Play in the Promotion and Advancement of Reproductive Rights in Latin America?" *Health and Human Rights* 7 (2003): 52.

75. Finnemore and Sikkink, "International Norm Dynamics."

76. Jorge A. Vargas, "Mexico's Legal Revolution: An Appraisal of Recent Constitutional Changes: 1988–1995," *Georgia Journal of International and Comparative Law* 25, no. 3 (1996): 497–559.

77. Alexander E. Kentikelenis and Sarah Babb, "The Making of Neoliberal Globalization: Norm Substitution and the Politics of Clandestine Institutional Change," *American Journal of Sociology* 124, no. 6 (2019): 1721.

78. Kentikelenis and Babb, "Neoliberal Globalization," 1721.
79. Kentikelenis and Babb, "Neoliberal Globalization," 1724.
80. John Gershman and Alec Irwin, "Getting a Grip on the Global Economy," in *Dying for Growth: Global Inequality and the Health of the Poor*, ed. Jim Yong Kim et al. (Monroe, ME: Common Courage Press, 2000), 23.
81. Don A. Schanche, "Venezuela Riots Not Political, Perez Says: President Blames Unrest on Foreign Debt, Confirms 300 Killed," *Los Angeles Times*, March 4, 1989, http://articles.latimes.com/1989-03-04/news/mn-19_1_foreign-debt.
82. Ross P. Buckley, "The Facilitation of the Brady Plan: Emerging Markets Debt Trading From 1989 to 1993," *Fordham International Law Journal* 21, no. 5 (1998): 1802–89.
83. Terence Halliday, "Legal Yardsticks: International Financial Institutions as Diagnosticians and Designers of the Laws of Nations," Center on Law and Globalization Research Paper No. 11-08 (2011).
84. TRIPS: Agreement on Trade-Related Aspects of Intellectual Property Rights, Marrakesh Agreement Establishing the World Trade Organization, Annex 1C, 1869 U.N.T.S. 299, 33 I.L.M. 1197 (Apr. 15, 1994).
85. Laurence R. Helfer, "Regime Shifting: The TRIPs Agreement and New Dynamics of International Intellectual Property Lawmaking," *Yale Journal of International Law* 29 (2004): 1–83.
86. Halliday, "Legal Yardsticks," 33.
87. Suerie Moon and Thirukumaran Balasubramaniam, "The World Trade Organization: Carving Out the Right to Health for Access to Medicines and Tobacco Control," in *Rights-Based Governance for a Globalizing World*, ed., Benjamin Mason Meier and Lawrence O. Gostin (Oxford: Oxford University Press, 2018), 375–96.
88. Dani Rodrik, *The Globalization Paradox: Why Global Markets, States, and Democracy Can't Coexist* (Oxford: Oxford University Press, 2011), 198.
89. Halliday, "Legal Yardsticks."
90. Halliday, "Legal Yardsticks."
91. Morten Bøås and Desmond McNeill, eds., *Global Institutions and Development: Framing the World?* (London: Routledge, 2004), 220.
92. Carlos Salinas de Gortari, "Discurso de Toma de Posesión de Carlos Salinas de Gortari como Presidente Constitucional de los Estados Unidos Mexicanos" (speech, Mexico, Dec. 1, 1988).
93. Juan Arroyo, *Salud: La reforma silenciosa* (Lima: Universidad Peruana Cayetano Heredia, 2000).
94. Thomas L. Friedman, *The Lexus and the Olive Tree* (New York: Farrar, Straus and Giroux, 1999); Rodrik, *Globalization Paradox*, 189.
95. Olinka Valdez Morales, "Presentan 27 casos de Violencia Obstétrica ante Tribunal Simbólico," *Milenio*, May 9, 2016, http://www.milenio.com/df/Violencia_Obstetrica_GIRE_0_734326864.htmll; GIRE: Grupo de Información en Reproducción Elegida, "Childbirth: A Violent Experience for Women in Mexico," *Pronunciamientos*, May 11, 2016, https://gire.org.mx/en/childbirth-a-violent-experience-for-women-in-mexico/.
96. James Ron, "Survey: Most Believe Women's Rights Are Human Rights," *Open Global*

Rights, November 23, 2017, https://www.openglobalrights.org/survey-many-believe-human-rights-are-womens-rights/.

97. Oscar Lopez and Andrew Jacobs, "In Town with Little Water, Coca-Cola is Everywhere. So is Diabetes," *New York Times*, July 14, 2018, https://www.nytimes.com/2018/07/14/world/americas/mexico-coca-cola-diabetes.html.

98. Bruce Link and Jo Phelan, "Social Conditions as Fundamental Causes of Disease," special issue, *Journal of Health and Social Behavior* 35 (1995): 80–94; Bruce Link and Jo Phelan, "Social Conditions as Fundamental Causes of Health Inequalities," in *Handbook of Medical Sociology*, 6th ed. (Nashville: Vanderbilt University Press, 2000), 3–17.

Chapter 4

1. Carlos Iván Degregori, "La posibilidad de la memoria," in *Verdad, memoria, justicia y reconciliación: Sociedad y comisiones de la verdad* (Lima: Asociación Pro Derechos Humanos-Aprodeh, 2002), 22 (translated by the author).

2. Giulia Tamayo, *Bajo la piel: Derechos sexuales, derechos reproductivos* (Lima: Centro de la Mujer Peruana Flora Tristán, 2001), 15 (translated by the author).

3. Dr. Juan Succar Rahme et al., "No. 5: Oficio SA-DM-N° 0818/97, August 6, 1997, Dirigido por el ex Ministro de Salud Marino Costa Bauer al Presidente de la República Alberto Fujimori" in *Comisión especial sobre actividades de Anticoncepción Quirúrgica Voluntaria (AQV): Informe Final* (Lima: Ministerio de Salud, 2002), 101.

4. "Committee for Latin America and the Caribbean for the Defense of Women's Rights" in English. See "Visión y misión," Mujeres usando el derecho como una herramienta de cambio, accessed February 10, 2019, https://cladem.org/nosotras/#vision-mision.

5. *María Mamérita Mestanza Chávez v. Perú*, Inter-Am. Cmm'n. H.R., Report No. 71/03 (Oct. 22, 2003).

6. "Law Firm for the Defense of Women's Rights" in English.

7. *María Mamérita Mestanza Chávez*, ¶ 350.

8. *María Mamérita Mestanza Chávez*, ¶ 668.

9. Karl Polanyi, *The Great Transformation: The Political and Economic Origins of Our Time*, 2nd ed. (Boston: Beacon Press, 2001), 3.

10. Thomas L. Friedman, *The Lexus and the Olive Tree* (New York: Farrar, Straus and Giroux, 1999), 102–3.

11. Stephanie McNulty, *Voice and Vote: Decentralization and Participation in Post-Fujimori Peru* (Stanford, CA: Stanford University Press, 2011), 20.

12. Jim Yong Kim et al., "Sickness Amid Recovery: Public Debt and Private Suffering in Peru," in *Dying for Growth: Global Inequality and the Health of the Poor*, ed. Jim Yong Kim et al. (Monroe, ME: Common Courage Press, 2002), 127–54.

13. Friedman, *The Lexus and the Olive Tree*, 102–3.

14. "Contexto demográfico, sociopolítico y de salud" in Alicia Ely Yamin, *Castillos de arena en el camino hacia la modernidad: Una perspectiva desde los derechos humanos*

sobre el proceso de reforma del sector salud en el Perú (1990–2000) y sus implicancias en la muerte materna (Lima: Centro de la Mujer Peruana Flora Tristán, 2003), 93.

15. Oracio Potestá, "Información para la verdad" in *Verdad, memoria, justicia y reconciliación: Sociedad y comisiones de la verdad* (Lima: Asociación Pro Derechos Humanos-Aprodeh, 2002), 53–56.

16. *Barrios Altos v. Perú*, Inter-Am. Ct. H.R. (ser. C) No. 75 (Mar. 14, 2001); *Barrios Altos v. Perú*, Inter-Am Ct. H.R. (ser. C) No. 83 (Sept. 3, 2001); *Barrios Altos v. Perú*, Inter-Am. Ct. H.R. (ser. C) No. 87 (Nov. 30, 2001).

17. Maruja Barrig, "La persistencia de la memoria: Feminismo y estado en el Perú de los 90," in *Sociedad civil, esfera pública y democratización en América Latina: Andes y Cono Sur*, ed. Aldo Panfichi (Lima: Pontificia Universidad Católica del Perú, Fondo de Cultura Económica, 2002), 578–610.

18. Cited in Giulia Tamayo, *Nada personal: Reporte de derechos humanos sobre la aplicación de la anticoncepción quirúrgica en el Perú* (Lima: CLADEM, 1999), 15.

19. C. Pen., Decreto Legislativo No. 635 (1991), art. 170–178 (Peru).

20. Bonnie Shepard, Delicia Ferrando, and Arlette Beltran, *Evaluación de medio término del Proyecto REPROSALUD* (Lima: Project Monitoring, Evaluation and Design Support, 2002).

21. Rahme et al., "No. 5: Oficio SA-DM-N° 0818/97," 101.

22. Xavier Bosch, "Former Peruvian Government Censured over Sterilisations," *British Medical Journal* 325, no. 7358 (2002), 236.

23. Christina Ewig, *Second-Wave Neoliberalism: Gender, Race, and Health Sector Reform in Peru* (University Park, PA: The Pennsylvania State University Press, 2010).

24. Ministerio de Salud del Perú, *Un sector salud con equidad, eficiencia y calidad: Lineamientos de políticas en salud 1995–2000* (Lima: Ministerio de Salud del Perú, 1998) (translated by the author).

25. La Oficina del Primer Ministro, "Lineamientos básicos de la política social," (Lima: Primer Ministro, 1993) (translated by the author).

26. Yamin, *Castillos de arena en el camino hacia la modernidad*, 150.

27. Tamayo, *Nada personal*, 50–67.

28. Tamayo, *Nada personal*, 50–67.

29. For example, see Nazmul Chaudhury et al., "Missing in Action: Teacher and Health Worker Absence in Developing Countries," *Journal of Economic Perspectives* 20 (2006): 91–116.

30. Yamin, *Castillos de arena en el camino hacia la modernidad*.

31. Jo-Marie Burt, "Fujimori vs. the Inter-American Court," *NACLA*, September 25, 2007, https://nacla.org/article/fujimori-vs-inter-american-court.

32. *Five Pensioners v. Perú*, Inter-Am. Ct. H.R. (ser. C) No. 98 (Feb. 28, 2003); *Lagos del Campos v. Perú*, Inter-Am. Ct. H.R. (ser. C) No. 340 (Aug. 31, 2017) ¶¶ 142–145.

33. Organization of American States (OAS), Additional Protocol to the American Convention on Human Rights in the Area of Economic, Social and Cultural Rights ("Protocol of San Salvador"), A-52 (Nov. 16, 1999).

34. Pascha Bueno-Hansen, *Feminist and Human Rights Struggles in Peru: Decolonizing Transitional Justice* (Champaign, IL: University of Illinois Press, 2015).

35. Adriana Ortiz-Ortega, "Law and the Politics of Abortion," in *Decoding Gender: Law and Practice in Contemporary Mexico*, ed. Helga Baitenmann, Victoria Chenaut, and Ann Varley (New Brunswick, NJ: Rutgers University Press, 2007), 206.

36. Tamayo, *Nada personal*, 50–67.

37. The concept of intersectional discrimination was first set out by Kimberlé Crenshaw. For example, see "Demarginalizing the Intersection of Race and Sex: A Black Feminist Critique of Antidiscrimination Doctrine, Feminist Theory and Antiracist Politics," in "Feminism in the Law: Theory, Practice, and Criticism," special issue, *The University of Chicago Legal Forum* (1989): 139–67.

38. María Esther Mogollón, "Cuerpos diferentes: Sexualidad y reproducción en mujeres con discapacidad," in *Ciudadanía sexual en América Latina: Abriendo el debate*, ed. Carlos F. Cáceres et al. (Lima: Universidad Peruana Cayetano Heredia, 2005), 153–64.

39. "Hilaria Supa Huamán," Congreso de La República del Perú, accessed February 11, 2019, http://www4.congreso.gob.pe/congresista/2006/hsupa/_hoja-vida.htm.

40. The Peruvian Congress rejected Fujimori's resignation and instead impeached him on the grounds that he was morally unfit. See Sebastian Rotella, "Peruvian Congress Rejects Fujimori's Resignation and Fires Him Instead," *Los Angeles Times*, November 22, 2000, http://articles.latimes.com/2000/nov/22/news/mn-55679.

41. Sally E. Merry, *Human Rights and Gender Violence: Translating International Law into Local Justice* (Chicago: University of Chicago Press, 2006), 180.

42. "The ICTR in Brief," United Nations International Criminal Tribunal for Rwanda, accessed February 11, 2019, http://unictr.unmict.org/en/tribunal; "Crimes of Sexual Violence," International Criminal Tribunal for the former Yugoslavia," accessed February 11, 2019, http://www.icty.org/en/in-focus/crimes-sexual-violence.

43. *M.M. v. Peru*, Inter-Am. Ct. H.R., (ser. L) No. 69/14, OEA/Ser.L/V/II.151, doc. 34 (Jul 25, 2014).

44. Rebecca J. Cook, "Gender, Health and Human Rights," *Health and Human Rights* 1, no. 4 (1995): 362.

45. Karen Engle, Zinaida Miller, and D. M. Davis, eds., *Anti-Impunity and the Human Rights Agenda* (Cambridge, UK: Cambridge University Press, 2016).

46. *Gelman v. Uruguay*, Inter-Am. Ct. H.R. (ser. C) No. 221 (Feb. 24, 2011).

47. Roberto Gargarella, "No Place for Popular Sovereignty? Democracy, Rights, and Punishment in Gelman v. Uruguay," (seminar paper, Seminario Latinoamericano de Teoría Constitucional y Política, Yale University, New Haven, CT, 2013).

48. Samuel Moyn, "Human Rights and the Crisis of Liberalism," in *Human Rights Futures*, eds. Stephen Hopgood, Jack Snyder, and Leslie Vinjamuri (Cambridge, UK: Cambridge University Press, 2017): 261–282.

49. UN Human Rights Committee, Communication No. 1153/2003, *Views of the Human Rights Committee Under Article 5, Paragraph 4, of the Optional Protocol to the International Covenant on Civil and Political Rights (Karen Noelia Llantoy Huamán v.*

Peru), U.N. Doc. CCPR/C/85/D/1153/2003 (Nov. 22, 2005); UN Committee on the Elimination of Discrimination Against Women, Communication No. 22/2009, *Views Adopted by the Committee at its Fiftieth Session, 3 to 21 October 2011 (L.C. v. Peru)*, U.N. Doc. CEDAW/C/50/D/22/2009 (Nov. 25, 2011).

50. Omnibus Consolidated and Emergency Supplemental Appropriations Act 1999, Pub. L. No. 105-277, § 101, 112 Stat. 2681-154 (1998).

51. David Hulme, "Reproductive Health and the Millennium Development Goals: Politics, Ethics, Evidence and an 'Unholy Alliance'" (working paper, *Brooks World Poverty Institute*, University of Manchester, Manchester, UK, 2009), 26.

52. Naila Kabeer, "Tracking the Gender Politics of the Millennium Development Goals: Struggles for Interpretive Power in the International Development Agenda," *Third World Quarterly* 36, no. 2 (2015): 377–95.

53. Hulme, "'Unholy Alliance,'" 16.

54. UN General Assembly, Resolution 55/2, United Nations Millennium Declaration, A/RES/55/2 (2000).

55. Sakiko Fukuda-Parr and Joshua Greenstein, "Monitoring MDGs: A Human Rights Critique and Alternative," in *The Millennium Development Goals and Human Rights: Past, Present, and Future*, ed. Malcolm Langford, Andy Sumner, and Alicia Ely Yamin (New York: Cambridge University Press, 2013), 450.

56. Barbara Crossette, "Reproductive Health and the Millennium Development Goals: The Missing Link," *Studies in Family Planning* 36 (2005): 71–79.

57. Marge Berer, "Images, Reproductive Health and the Collateral Damage to Women of Fundamentalism and War," *Reproductive Health Matters* 9, no. 18 (2001): 6.

58. Defensoría del Pueblo, *Informe defensorial nº. 69: La aplicación de la anticoncepción quirúrgica y los derechos reproductivos III* (Lima: Defensoría del Pueblo, 2002).

59. Yamin, *Castillos de arena en el camino hacia la modernidad*, 153.

60. Mark Malloch Brown, "Foreword," in *Targeting Development: Critical Perspectives on the Millennium Development Goals*, ed. Richard Black and Howard White (London: Routledge, 2004), xviii–xix.

61. Marge Berer, "Repoliticising Sexual and Reproductive Health and Rights," *Reproductive Health Matters* 19, no. 38 (2011): 8.

62. Sofia Gruskin, Dina Bogecho, and Laura Ferguson, "'Rights-Based Approaches' to Health Policies and Programs: Articulations, Ambiguities, and Assessment," *Journal of Public Health Policy* 31, no. 2 (2010): 131; Sofia Gruskin, "Rights-Based Approaches to Health: Something for Everyone," *Health and Human Rights* 9, no. 2 (2006): 5.

63. Audrey R. Chapman, "A 'Violations Approach' to Monitoring the International Covenant on Economic, Social and Cultural Rights," *Human Rights Dialogue* 1, no. 10 (1997), https://www.carnegiecouncil.org/publications/archive/dialogue/1_10/articles/580.html.

64. UN Committee on Economic, Social and Cultural Rights, *The Maastricht Guidelines on Violations of Economic, Social and Cultural Rights*, U.N. Doc. E/C.12/2000/13 (Oct. 2, 2000).

65. Alicia Ely Yamin, "The Future in the Mirror: Incorporating Strategies for the

Defense and Promotion of Economic, Social and Cultural Rights into the Mainstream Human Rights Agenda," *Human Rights Quarterly* 27, no. 4 (2005): 1200–44; Alicia Ely Yamin and Deborah P. Maine, "Maternal Mortality as a Human Rights Issue: Measuring Compliance with International Treaty Obligations," *Human Rights Quarterly* 21, no. 3 (1999): 563.

66. Cesar Rodríguez Garavito and Diana Rodríguez Franco, *Cortes y cambio social: Cómo la Corte Constitucional transformó el desplazamiento forzado en Colombia* (Bogotá: DeJusticia, 2010); Cesar Rodríguez Garavito, "Beyond the Courtroom: The Impact of Judicial Activism on Socioeconomic Rights in Latin America," *Texas Law Review* 89, no. 7 (2011): 1669–98.

67. Rodríguez Garavito and Rodríguez Franco, *Cortes y cambio social*.

68. Health Services User's Rights, Law No. 29414 (2009) (Peru) (translated by the author).

69. UN Commission on Human Rights, *Report of the Special Rapporteur on Violence against Women, Its Causes and Consequences, Ms. Radhika Coomaraswamy, in Accordance with Commission on Human Rights Resolution 1997/44, Addendum: Policies and Practices That Impact Women's Reproductive Rights and Contribute to, Cause, or Constitute Violence against Women*, U.N. Doc. E/CN.4/1998/68/Add.4 (Jan. 21, 1999): ¶¶ 44–45.

70. *V. C. v. Slovakia*, No. 18968/07, 2011–V Eur. Ct. H. R. (Nov. 8, 2011); *N. B. v. Slovakia*, No. 29518/10, Eur. Ct. H. R. (June 12, 2012); *I.G. and others v. Slovakia*, No. 15966/04 Eur. Ct. H. R. (Nov. 13, 2012).

71. *I. V. v. Bolivia*, Inter-Am. Ct. H. R., (ser. C) No. 336 (Nov. 30, 2016).

72. *S.W.K. and Others v. Attorney General and Others* (2014) High Court of Kenya (H.C.K.); *Government of the Republic of Namibia v. LM and Others* (2014), 2014 NASC 19, SA 49/2012 Supreme Court [SC] (Namib.).

73. Giulia Tamayo, "Presentación" in Alicia Ely Yamin, *Castillos de arena en el camino hacia la modernidad: una perspectiva desde los derechos humanos sobre el proceso de reforma del sector salud en el Perú, 1990–2000 y sus implicancias en la muerte materna* (Lima: Centro de la Mujer Peruana Flora Tristán, 2003), 18.

74. Alice M. Miller, "Sexual Orientation as a Human Rights Issue," in *Learning to Dance: Case Studies on Advancing Women's Reproductive Health and Well-Being from the Perspectives of Public Health and Human Rights*, ed. Alicia Ely Yamin (Cambridge, MA: François-Xavier Bagnoud Center for Health and Human Rights Series, Harvard University Press, 2005), 159.

75. *Hacia el cumplimiento de los objetivos de desarrollo del milenio en el Perú: Un compromiso para acabar con la probreza, la desigualdad y la exclusion* (Lima: Organización de las Naciones Unidas, 2004).

76. Camila Gianella and Alicia Ely Yamin, "Struggle and Resistance: Using International Bodies to Advance Sexual and Reproductive Rights in Peru," *Berkeley Journal of Gender Law and Justice* (2018): 101–33.

77. Eleanor Roosevelt, "The Great Question," (speech, UN, New York, March 27, 1958).

78. Lucie White and Jeremy Perelman, eds., *Stones of Hope: How African Activists Reclaim Human Rights to Challenge Global Poverty* (Stanford, CA: Stanford University Press, 2010).

Chapter 5

1. World Health Organization Commission on Macroeconomics and Health, *Macroeconomics and Health: Investing in Health for Economic Development* (Geneva: World Health Organization, 2001), 1.

2. Philip Alston, "Ships Passing in the Night: The Current State of Human Rights and Development," *Human Rights Quarterly* 27, no. 3 (2005): 756.

3. Kofi A. Annan, *We the Peoples: The Role of the United Nations in the 21st Century*, Sales. No. E. 00.1.16 (New York: UN Department of Public Information), 11.

4. Diana Cammack, *Poorly Performing Countries: Malawi, 1980–2002* (background paper for study, Overseas Development Institute, London, UK, 2004), 5.

5. Thomas L. Friedman, *The World Is Flat* (New York: Farrar, Straus and Giroux, 2005), 176.

6. João Guilherme Biehl, "Pharmaceuticalization: AIDS Treatment and Global Health Politics," *Anthropological Quarterly* 80, no. 4 (2007): 1083–126.

7. Jim Yong Kim, Joyce V. Millen, and Alex Irwin, "Introduction: What is Growing? Who is Dying?," in *Dying for Growth: Global Inequality and the Health of the Poor*, ed. Jim Yong Kim et al. (Monroe, ME: Common Courage Press, 2000), 7.

8. Jim Yong Kim, "Introduction," 7.

9. Oxfam, *Making Debt Relief Work: A Test of Political Will* (Oxford: Oxfam International, 1998), 1.

10. Clare Nullis Kapp, "Macroeconomics and Health Commission Findings Become Reality," *Bulletin of the World Health Organization* 82, no. 12 (2004): 957.

11. Joseph E. Stiglitz, *Globalization and Its Discontents* (New York: W.W. Norton & Company, 2002).

12. Alex Tizon, "Monday, Nov. 29," *The Seattle Times*, Dec. 5, 1999, http://community.seattletimes.nwsource.com/archive/?date=19991205&slug=2999667.

13. Mark Heywood, "Preventing Mother-to-Child HIV Transmission in South Africa: Background, Strategies and Outcomes of the Treatment Action Campaign Case against the Minister of Health," *South African Journal on Human Rights* 19, no. 2 (2003): 280.

14. Ellen F. M. 't Hoen, *The Global Politics of Pharmaceutical Monopoly Power: Drug Patents, Access, Innovation and the Application of the WTO Doha Declaration on TRIPS and Public Health* (Netherlands: AMB, 2009), 20; Linsey McGoey, *No Such Thing as a Free Gift: The Gates Foundation and the Price of Philanthropy* (Brooklyn, NY: Verso, 2016), 188–89.

15. Lisa Forman, "Trade Rules, Intellectual Property, and the Right to Health," *Ethics & International Affairs* 21, no. 3 (2007): 337–57.

16. William Forbath et al., "Cultural Transformation, Deep Institutional Reform, and ESR Practice: South Africa's Treatment Action Campaign," in *Stones of Hope: How*

African Activists Reclaim Human Rights to Challenge Global Poverty, ed. Lucie White and Jeremy Perelman (Stanford, CA: Stanford University Press, 2010), 56.

17. For example, see Laetitia Rispel, Pieter de Jager, and Sharon Fonn, "Exploring Corruption in the South African Health Sector," *Health Policy and Planning* 31, no. 2 (2016): 239–49.

18. Dani Rodrik, *The Globalization Paradox: Why Global Markets, States, and Democracy Can't Coexist* (Oxford: Oxford University Press, 2011), 180.

19. Forbath, "Cultural Transformation," 56.

20. Pali Lehohla, personal communication with author, February 10, 2018.

21. *Minister of Health v. Treatment Action Campaign (TAC)* 2002 (5) SA 721 (CC) (S.Afr.).

22. Theunis Roux, "Democracy," in *Constitutional Law of South Africa*, ed. S. Woolman and M. Bishop (Cape Town: Juta, 2006).

23. Ole Frithjof Norheim and Siri Gloppen, "Litigating for Medicines: How Can We Assess Impact on Health Outcomes?," in *Litigating Health Rights: Can Courts Bring More Justice to Health?*, ed. Alicia Ely Yamin and Siri Gloppen (Cambridge, MA: Harvard Human Rights Series, Harvard University Press, 2011), 320.

24. *N and Others v. Government of South Africa and Others (No. 1)* 2006 (6) SA 543 (D); *N and Others v. Government of South Africa and Others (No. 2)* 2006 (6) SA 568 (D); *N and Others v. Government of South Africa and Others (No. 3)* 2006 (6) 575 (D) (S. Afr.).

25. *Common Cause v. Union of India*, W.P. (C) No. 61/2003 (2003) (India).

26. *Government of the Republic of Namibia v. LM and Others* (2014), 2014 NASC 19, SA 49/2012 Supreme Court [SC] (Namib.).

27. *Kenya Legal and Ethical Network on HIV & AIDS (KELIN) and Others v. Cabinet Secretary-Ministry of Health and Others*, Petition No. 250 of 2015 (2016) High Court of Kenya (H.C.K.).

28. *Patricia Asero Ochieng & Others. v. Attorney General*, Petition No. 409 of 2009 (2012) High Court of Kenya (H.C.K.).

29. *Pharmaceutical Manufacturers Association of South Africa and Another: In re Ex Parte President of the Republic of South Africa and Others* 2000 (2) SA 674 (CC) (S. Afr.).

30. "Glaxo Responds to Aids Drugs Call," *BBC News*, December 10, 2003, http://news.bbc.co.uk/2/hi/business/3306079.stm; Mark Heywood, "South Africa's Treatment Action Campaign: Combining Law and Social Mobilization to Realize the Right to Health," *Journal of Human Rights Practice* (2009): 14–36.

31. Mark Heywood, "Preventing Mother-to-Child HIV Transmission," 15.

32. Forbath, "Cultural Transformation," 52.

33. Nicoli Nattrass, "Millennium Development Goal 6: AIDS and the International Health Agenda," in "Special Issue on Millennium Development Goals," *Journal of Human Development and Capabilities* 15, no. 2–3 (2014): 232–46.

34. "Global Fund Overview," The Global Fund for AIDS, Malaria and Tuberculosis, accessed February 14, 2019, *https://www.theglobalfund.org/en/overview/*.

35. United States President's Emergency Plan for AIDS Relief (PEPFAR), "PEPFAR

Funding," (Washington, DC: Office of the U.S. Global AIDS Coordinator and Health Diplomacy, 2016), https://www.pepfar.gov/documents/organization/252516.pdf.

36. UN Entity for Gender Equality and the Empowerment of Women, *Beijing Declaration and Platform of Action*, A/CONF.177/20/Rev.1 ¶ 107 (New York: United Nations, 1995).

37. Sakiko Fukuda-Parr, *Millennium Development Goals: Ideas, Interests and Influence* (New York: Routledge, 2017).

38. For example, see Rafael Lozano et al., "Progress towards Millennium Development Goals 4 and 5 on Maternal and Child Mortality: An Updated Systematic Analysis," *The Lancet* 378, no. 9797 (2011): 1139–65.

39. Gita Sen, "Gender Equality and Women's Empowerment: Feminist Mobilization for the SDGs," *Global Policy* 10 (2019), 30.

40. Roberto Mangabeira Unger, *Democracy Realized: The Progressive Alternative* (Brooklyn, NY: Verso, 1998), 58.

41. United Nations Development Group, *The Human Rights Based Approach to Development Cooperation: Towards a Common Understanding Among UN Agencies* (2003), https://undg.org/wp-content/uploads/2016/09/6959-The_Human_Rights_Based _Approach_to_Development_Cooperation_Towards_a_Common_Understanding _among_UN.pdf.

42. Task Force on Child Health and Maternal Health, *Who's Got the Power? Transforming Health Systems for Women and Children* (London: UN Millennium Project and Earthscan, 2005), 29.

43. For example, see Charles Chikodili Chima and Nuria Homedes, "Impact of Global Health Governance on Country Health Systems: The Case of HIV Initiatives in Nigeria," *Journal of Global Health* 5 (2015).

44. John Rawls, *Political Liberalism* (New York: Columbia University Press, 1993).

45. UNICEF, WHO and UNFPA, *Guidelines on Monitoring the Availability and Use of Obstetric Services* (New York: UNICEF, 1997).

46. Sereen Thaddeus and Deborah Maine, "Too Far to Walk: Maternal Mortality in Context," *Social Science and Medicine* 38, no. 8 (1994): 1091–110.

47. For example, see Lucy Gilson, "Trust and the Development of Health Care as a Social Institution," *Social Science and Medicine* 56, no. 7 (2003): 1453–68; Norman Daniels, "Health Care Needs and Distributive Justice," in *In Search of Equity: Health Needs and the Health System,* ed. Ronald Bayer, Arthur Caplan, and Norman Daniels (Boston: Springer, 1983).

48. Lynn P. Freedman, "Achieving the MDGs: Health Systems as Core Social Institutions," *Development* 48 (2005): 20.

49. UN Economic and Social Council, *Report of the Special Rapporteur on the Right of Everyone to the Enjoyment of the Highest Attainable Standard of Physical and Mental Health, Paul Hunt*, UN Doc. E/CN.4/2006/48 ¶ 4 (2006); UN General Assembly, *Report of the Special Rapporteur on the Right of Everyone to Enjoy the Highest Attainable Standard of Physical and Mental Health*, UN Doc. A/61/338 ¶ 34 (2006).

50. Freedman, "Achieving the MDGs," 19–24.

51. Philip Alston, "Ships Passing," 755–829.

52. UN General Assembly, Resolution 61/106, Convention on the Rights of Persons with Disabilities (CRPD), A/RES/61/106 (Dec. 13, 2006).

53. A/RES/61/106, "Preamble."

54. For example, see Michael Ashley Stein, "Disability Human Rights," *California Law Review* 95 (2007): 75–121; Anita Silvers and Michael Ashley Stein, "Disability and the Social Contract," review of Martha Nussbaum, *Disability, Nationality, Species Membership, University of Chicago Law Review* 74, no. 4 (2007): 1615–40.

55. Sudhir Anand, Fabienne Peter, and Amartya Sen, eds., *Public Health, Ethics, and Equity* (Oxford: Oxford University Press, 2006).

56. Conference of International Legal Scholars, *Yogyakarta Principles: Principles on the Application of Human Rights Law in Relation to Sexual Orientation and Gender Identity (Yogyakarta, Indonesia, Nov. 6-9, 2006)* (March 2007).

57. UN Human Rights Committee, Communication No. 488/1992, *Views of the Human Rights Committee Under Article 5, Paragraph 4, of the Optional Protocol to the International Covenant on Civil and Political Rights (Toonen v. Australia)*, U.N. Doc. CCPR/C/50/D/488/1992 (Mar. 31, 1994).

58. Abby Ohlheiser, "Uganda's New Anti-Homosexuality Law Was Inspired by American Activists," *The Atlantic*, December 20, 2013, https://www.theatlantic.com /international/ archive/2013/12/uganda-passes-law-punishes-homosexuality-life -imprisonment/356365/.

59. Kapya John Kaoma, *Colonizing African Values: How the U.S. Christian Right Is Transforming Sexual Politics in Africa* (Somerville, MA: Political Research Associates, 2012).

60. For example, see Consorcio Latinoamericano Contra el Aborto Inseguro (CLACAI), accessed February 15, 2019, *http://clacai.org/*; Red Latinoamericana de Académicas/os del Derechos (RED ALAS), accessed February 15, 2019, https://www.redalas .net/.

61. For example, see Gabriele Kuby, *Global Sexual Revolution: Destruction of Freedom in the Name of Freedom* (Brooklyn, NY: Angelico Press, 2016).

62. Cynthia Rothschild, *Written Out: How Sexuality Is Used to Attack Women's Organizing* (New York: International Gay and Lesbian Human Rights Commission and the Center for Women's Global Leadership, 2005), 118–19.

63. Office of the High Commissioner for Human Rights (OHCHR), *United Nations Special Procedures: Facts and Figures 2010* (Geneva: OHCHR, 2011), http://www.ohchr. org/Documents/HRBodies/SP/Facts_Figures2010.pdf.

64. OHCHR, *Facts and Figures* 2010.

65. UN Committee on the Elimination of Racial Discrimination, *General Recommendation 20, the Guarantee of Human Rights Free from Racial Discrimination*, UN Doc. A/51/18, annex VIII (Mar. 14, 1996).

66. UN Committee on the Rights of the Child, *General Comment No. 15 (2013) on the Right of the Child to the Enjoyment of the Highest Attainable Standard of Health (Art. 24)*, UN Doc. CRC/C/GC/15 (Apr. 17, 2013); UN Committee on the Rights of the

Child, *General Comment No. 3 (2003): HIV/AIDS and the Rights of the Child,* UN Doc. CRC/GC/2003/3 (Mar. 17, 2003); UN Committee on the Rights of the Child, *General Comment No. 4 (2003): Adolescent Health and Development in the Context of the Convention on the Rights of the Child,* UN Doc. CRC/GC/2003/4 (Jul. 1, 2003).

67. UN Committee on the Elimination of All Forms of Discrimination Against Women (CEDAW), *General Recommendation No. 24: Article 12 of the Convention (Women and Health),* UN Doc. A/54/38/Rev.1 ¶ 3 (1999).

68. Committee on Economic, Social and Cultural Rights (CESCR), *General Comment No. 14: The Right to the Highest Attainable Standard of Health (Article 12 of the Covenant),* UN Doc. E/C.12/2000/4 ¶ 12 (Aug. 11, 2000).

69. UN Doc. E/C.12/2000/4, ¶ 12.

70. UN Doc. A/54/38/Rev.1, ¶ 22.

71. UN Committee on Economic, Social and Cultural Rights, *The Maastricht Guidelines on Violations of Economic, Social and Cultural Rights,* UN Doc. E/C.12/2000/13 (Apr. 3, 1997).

72. UN Doc. E/C.12/2000/4, ¶ 39.

73. UN Doc. E/C.12/2000/4, ¶ 1.

74. UN Doc. E/C.12/2000/4, ¶ 11.

75. John Tobin, *The Right to Health in International Law* (Oxford, UK: Oxford University Press, 2012), 56.

76. UN Doc. E/C.12/2000/4, ¶ 60.

77. UN Doc. E/C.12/2000/4, ¶¶ 43–45.

78. UN Doc. E/C.12/2000/4, ¶ 44(a–e).

79. John Tobin, *Right to Health,* 240.

80. Norman Daniels, *Just Health: Meeting Health Needs Fairly* (Cambridge, UK: Cambridge University Press, 2008), 15.

81. UN Doc. E/C.12/2000/4, ¶ 31.

82. Philip Alston and Gerard Quinn, "The Nature and Scope of States Parties' Obligations under the International Covenant on Economic, Social and Cultural Rights," *Human Rights Quarterly* 9, no. 2 (1987): 222.

83. John Tasioulas, "Minimum Core Obligations: Human Rights in the Here and Now" (working paper, Nordic Trust Fund, World Bank, Washington, DC, 2017).

84. UN Doc. A/CN.4/L.682, ¶ 419.

85. David Kennedy, "The International Human Rights Movement: Part of the Problem?," *Harvard Human Rights Journal* 15 (2002): 120.

86. *Global Wealth Report* 2013 (Zurich: Credit Suisse Research Institute, 2013).

87. Alex Cobham and Andy Sumner, "Is It All about the Tails? The Palma Measure of Income Inequality" (working paper, Center for Global Development, Washington, DC, 2013), 7.

88. Rodrik, *The Globalization Paradox,* 185–89.

89. "The Disastrous Legacy of South Africa's President Jacob Zuma: South Africa's Lost Decade," *The Economist,* February 15, 2018, https://www.economist.com

/middle-east-and-africa/2018/02/15/the-disastrous-legacy-of-south-africas-president-jacob-zuma.

90. Paul Farmer, *Pathologies of Power: Health, Human Rights, and the New War on the Poor* (Oakland, CA: University of California Press, 2004).

Chapter 6

1. Rebecca J. Cook, "Human Rights and Maternal Health: Exploring the Effectiveness of the Alyne Decision," *Journal of Law, Medicine and Ethics* 41 (2013): 109.

2. WHO Commission on the Social Determinants of Health, *Closing the Gap in a Generation: Health Equity through Action on the Social Determinants of Health Executive Summary* (Geneva: World Health Organization, 2008), 3.

3. Jürgen Habermas, "Critique and Communication: Philosophy's Missions: A Conversation with Jürgen Habermas," interview by Michaël Foessel, *Eurozine*, October 16, 2015, https://www.eurozine.com/critique-and-communication-philosophys-missions/.

4. FIGO Safe Motherhood and Newborn Health (SMNH) Committee, "FIGO Guidelines: Management of the Second Stage of Labor," *International Journal of Gynecology and Obstetrics* 119, no. 3 (2012): 111–16; FIGO Safe Motherhood and Newborn Health (SMNH) Committee, "Prevention and Treatment of Postpartum Hemorrhage in Low-Resource Settings," *International Journal of Gynecology and Obstetrics* 117, no. 2 (2012): 108–18.

5. Rosa Domingues et al., "Process of Decision-Making Regarding the Mode of Birth in Brazil: From the Initial Preference of Women to the Final Mode of Birth," *Reports in Public Health* 30 (2014): S101–16.

6. For example, see Law no. 26.485, article 6(e), 11 de marzo, 2009 [31.632] B.O. 1 (Arg.).

7. UN Committee on the Elimination of All Forms of Discrimination against Women (CEDAW), *Views of the Committee on the Elimination of Discrimination against Women Concerning Communication No. 17/2008 (Alyne da Silva Pimentel v. Brazil)*, UN Doc CEDAW/C/49/D/17/2008 (2011).

8. UN Committee on Economic, Social and Cultural Rights, *Working Methods Concerning the Committee's Follow-up to Views under the Optional Protocol to the International Covenant on Economic, Social and Cultural Rights*, UN Doc. E/C.12/62/4 (2017).

9. Víctor Abramovich, "From Massive Violations to Structural Patterns: New Approaches and Classic Tensions in the Inter-American Human Rights System," *Sur: International Journal on Human Rights* 6, no. 11 (2009): 6–39.

10. UN Doc CEDAW/C/49/D/17/2008.

11. Cook, "Human Rights and Maternal Health," 106.

12. Michael Moore, "Luiz Inácio Lula da Silva," *Time Magazine*, April 29, 2010, http://content.time.com/time/specials/packages/article/0,28804,1984685_1984864,00.html.

13. Roberto Gargarella, *Latin American Constitutionalism, 1810–2010: The Engine Room of the Constitution* (Oxford: Oxford University Press, 2013).

14. Ryan Lloyd and Carlos Oliveira, "How Brazil's Electoral System Led to the Country into Political Crisis," *Washington Post*, May 25, 2016.

15. Jürgen Habermas, "Hannah Arendt's Communications Concept of Power," in *Power*, ed. Steven Lukes (New York: New York University Press, 1986), 75–94; Steven Lukes, "Introduction," *Power*, ed. Steven Lukes (New York: New York University Press, 1986), 1–18.

16. Joseph Stiglitz, *Freefall: America, Free Markets, and the Sinking of the World Economy* (New York: W. W. Norton & Company, 2010).

17. Leia íntegra da carta de Lula para calmar o mercado financeiro, *Folha Online*, June 24, 2002, https://www1.folha.uol.com.br/folha/brasil/ult96u33908.shtml.

18. "Brazil—Poverty Headcount Ratio at National Poverty Line," Knoema, accessed February 19, 2019, https://knoema.com/atlas/Brazil/Poverty-rate-at-national-poverty-line.

19. Moore, "Lula da Silva."

20. For example, see Lawrence Mishel and Jessica Schieder, "As Union Membership Has Fallen, the Top 10 Percent Have Been Getting a Larger Share of the Income," Economic Policy Institute, May 24, 2016, https://www.epi.org/publication/as-union-membership-has-fallen-the-top-10-percent-have-been-getting-a-larger-share-of-income/.

21. For example, see Alyssa Davis and Lawrence Mishel, "CEO Pay Continues to Rise as Typical Workers are Paid Less," Economic Policy Institute, June 12, 2014, https://www.epi.org/publication/ceo-pay-continues-to-rise/.

22. Stiglitz, *Freefall*.

23. WHO Commission on Social Determinants of Health, *Closing the Gap in a Generation: Health Equity through Action on the Social Determinants of Health* (Geneva: World Health Organization, 2008), 26.

24. Norman Daniels, Bruce Kennedy, and Ichirō Kawachi, *Is Inequality Bad for Our Health?* (Boston: Beacon Press, 2000).

25. Richard Wilkinson and Kate Pickett, *The Spirit Level: Why More Equal Societies Almost Always Do Better* (London: Allen Lane, 2009).

26. Maria Zambrano, *Persona y Democracia*, 2nd ed. (Madrid: Ediciones Siruela, 1987).

27. Benjamin Barber, *Strong Democracy: Participatory Politics for a New Age*, 20th anniversary ed. (Oakland, CA: University of California Press, 2003).

28. *Unheard Voices: Women's Experiences with Zika: Brazil* (New York: Center for Reproductive Rights, Harvard T. H. Chan School of Public Health, Women and Health Initiative, 2018) https://www.reproductiverights.org/sites/crr.civicactions.net/files/documents/CRR-Zika-Brazil.pdf.

29. Office of the United Nations High Commissioner for Human Rights, *Scenario and Talking Points for High Commissioner on Human Rights Event to Launch the Technical Guidance on the Application of a Human Rights Based Approach to the Implementation of Policies* (Geneva: OHCHR 2012); Navanethem Pillay, *Human Rights in the Post-2015 Agenda* (Geneva: OHCHR 2013), http://www.ohchr.org/Documents/Issues/MDGs/HCOpenLetterPost2015.pdf

30. "Maternal Mortality Initiative," The Center for Reproductive Rights, accessed February 19, 2019, http://www.reproductiverights.org/initiatives.

31. UN Human Rights Council, *Technical Guidance on the Application of a Human-Rights Based Approach to the Implementation of Policies and Programmes to Reduce Preventable Maternal Morbidity and Mortality*, UN Doc. A/HRC/21/22 ¶ 1 (2012).

32. For example, see The Partnership for Maternal, Newborn and Child Health (PMNCH), *A Global Review of the Key Interventions Related to Reproductive, Maternal, Newborn and Child Health (RMNCH)* (Geneva: PMNCH, 2011).

33. Sônia Lansky et al., "Birth in Brazil Survey: Neonatal Mortality, Pregnancy and Childbirth Quality of Care," *Reports in Public Health* 30 (2014): S1–15.

34. UN Doc. A/HRC/21/22, ¶ 12.

35. UN Doc. A/HRC/21/22, ¶ 13.

36. UN Doc. A/HRC/21/22, ¶ 16.

37. Michele Gragnolati, Magnus Lindelow, and Bernard Couttolenc, *Twenty Years of Health System Reform in Brazil: An Assessment of the Sistema Único de Saúde* (Washington DC: World Bank Publications, 2013).

38. Maria Inês Souza Bravo et al., *A mercantilizaçao da saúde em debate: As organizações sociais no Rio de Janeiro* (Rio de Janeiro: Cadernos de Saúde Pública, FAPERJ, 2015).

39. UN Doc. CEDAW/C/49/D/17/2008, ¶ 7.5, 8.

40. Lynn P. Freedman, "Human Rights, Constructive Accountability and Maternal Mortality in the Dominican Republic: A Commentary," *International Journal of Gynecology and Obstetrics* 82 (2003): 111.

41. Commission on Information and Accountability for Women's and Children's Health, *Keeping Promises, Measuring Results: Final Report of the Commission* (Geneva: World Health Organization, 2011), 8, 19.

42. UN Doc. A/HRC/21/22, ¶¶ 74–98.

43. UN Doc. A/HRC/21/22, ¶ 85.

44. UN Doc. A/HRC/21/22, ¶ 87; International Commission of Jurists, *Maastricht Principles on Extraterritorial Obligations of States in the Area of Economic, Social and Cultural Rights* (Sept. 28, 2011).

45. UN Doc. A/HRC/21/22, ¶¶ 62–63.

46. Cynthia L. Haven, *Evolution of Desire: A Life of René Girard* (East Lansing, MI: Michigan State University Press, 2018), 3.

47. Nancy Fraser, "From Redistribution to Recognition? Dilemmas of Justice in a 'Post-Socialist' Age," *New Left Review* 0, no. 212 (1995): 68–93; Nancy Fraser and Axel Honneth, *Redistribution or Recognition? A Political-Philosophical Exchange* (New York: Verso, 2003), 117.

48. Jashodhara Dasgupta et al., "Using Technology to Claim Rights to Free Maternal Health Care: Lessons about Impact from the My Health, My Voice Pilot Project in India," *Health & Human Rights* 17, no. 2 (2015): 135–47.

49. Brigit Toebes, Rhonda Ferguson, Milan Markovic, Obiajulu Nnamuchi, eds.,

The Rights to Health: A Multi-Country Study of Law, Policy and Practice (The Hague: Springer, 2014).

50. Flavia Bustreo et al., *Women's and Children's Health: Evidence of Impact of Human Rights* (Geneva: World Health Organization, 2013), 19.

51. Alicia Ely Yamin and Rebecca Cantor, "Between Insurrectional Discourse and Operational Guidance: Challenges and Dilemmas in Implementing Human Rights-Based Approaches to Health," *Journal of Human Rights Practice* 6, no. 3 (2014): 479.

52. Michael Neocosmos, "Civil Society, Citizenship and the Politics of the (Im)possible: Rethinking Militancy in Africa Today," *Interface: A Journal for and about Social Movements* no. 2 (2009): 278.

53. *Laxmi Mandal v. Deen Dayal Harinagar Hospital & Others*, W.P. (C) Nos. 8853 of 2008 High Court of Delhi (2010) (India); *Centre for Health, Human Rights and Development (CEHURD) & 3 Others v. Attorney General*, Constitutional Petition No. 16 of 2011 [2012] UGCC 4 (Uganda); *Centre for Health, Human Rights and Development (CEHURD) & 3 Others v. Attorney General*, UGSC Constitutional Appeal No. 1 of 2013 [2015] (Uganda).

54. For discussions of some prominent cases, see Colleen Flood and Aeyal Gross, eds., *The Right to Health at the Public/Private Divide: Global Comparative Study* (New York: Cambridge University Press, 2016); *Litigating Health Rights: Can Courts Bring More Justice to Health?*, ed. Alicia Ely Yamin and Siri Gloppen (Cambridge, MA: Harvard Human Rights Series, Harvard University Press, 2011).

55. For example, see Daniel Wang and Octavio Luiz Motta Ferraz, "Reaching Out to the Needy? Access to Justice and Public Attorneys' Role in Right to Health Litigation in the City of São Paulo," *Sur: International Journal on Human Rights* 10, no. 18 (2013): 158–79.

56. Wang and Ferraz, "Reaching Out," 158–79.

57. *João Biehl, Mariana P. Socal, and Joseph J. Amon*, "The Judicialization of Health and the Quest for State Accountability: Evidence from 1,262 Lawsuits for Access to Medicines in Southern Brazil," *Health and Human Rights* 18 (2016): 209–20.

58. Danielle Borges, "Individual Health Care Litigation in Brazil through a Different Lens: Strengthening Health Technology Assessment and New Models of Health Care Governance," *Health and Human Rights* 20 (2018): 147–62.

59. Mariana Mota Prado, "The Debatable Role of Courts in Brazil's Health-Care System: Does Litigation Harm or Help?" *Journal of Law, Medicine, and Ethics* 41(2013): 124–37.

60. Everaldo Lamprea, *Derechos en la práctica: Jueces, litigantes y operadores de políticas de salud en Colombia (1991–2014)* (Bogotá; Educiones Uniandes, 2015).

61. Laura Pautassi and Víctor Abramovich, "El derecho a la salud en los tribunales: Algunos efectos del activismo judicial sobre el sistema de salud en Argentina," *Salud colectiva* 4, no. 3 (2008): 261–82.

62. For example, see Octavio Luiz Motta Ferraz et al., "Judging the Price of Life: Cost Considerations in Right to Health Litigation," in *Juridification and Social Citizenship in the Welfare State*, ed. Henriette Sinding Aasen et al. (Cheltenham, UK: Edward Elgar, 2014), 121–45.

63. Paola Bergallo, "Courts and the Right to Health: Achieving Fairness Despite 'Routinization' in Individual Coverage Cases?" in *Litigating Health Rights: Can Courts Bring More Justice to Health?*, ed. Alicia Ely Yamin and Siri Gloppen (Cambridge, MA: Harvard Human Rights Series, Harvard University Press, 2011), 43–75.

64. *Brown v. Board of Education of Topeka*, 347 U.S. 483 (1954).

65. *Ford v. Quebec (Attorney General)*, [1988] 2 SCR 712 (Can.). Bruce Porter notes, "After the UN Human Rights Committee considered the same issue . . . and concluded that the provisions also contravened the ICCPR, a subsequent Quebec government amended the legislation." See Bruce Porter, "Canada: Systemic Claims and Remedial Diversity," in *Compliance with Social Rights Judgments and the Politics of Compliance: Making It Stick*, ed. Malcolm Langford, César Rodríguez-Garavito, and Julieta Rossi (Cambridge, UK: Cambridge University Press, 2017), 202.

66. Mark Tushnet, *Weak Courts, Strong Rights: Judicial Review and Social Welfare Rights in Comparative Constitutional Law* (Princeton, NJ: Princeton University Press, 2008).

67. Roberto Gargarella, *Latin American Constitutionalism, 1810–2010: The Engine Room of the Constitution* (Oxford: Oxford University Press, 2013), 199–200.

68. Lon L. Fuller and Kenneth I. Winston, "The Forms and Limits of Adjudication," *Harvard Law Review* 92, no. 2 (1978): 395.

69. *People's Union for Civil Liberties v. Union of India and Others*, Writ Petition (Civil) No. 196 of 2001, Supreme Court (2001) (India).

70. Right to Food Campaign, accessed February 22, 2019, http://www.righttofoodcampaign.in/.

71. For example, see Sanjay Ruparelia, *A Progressive Juristocracy? The Unexpected Social Activism of India's Supreme Court* (working paper, Kellogg Institute for International Studies, Notre Dame, IL, 2013), https://ndigd.nd.edu/assets/172934/a_progressive_juristocracy.pdf.

72. Corte Suprema de Justicia de la Nación [CSJN] [National Supreme Court of Justice], 07/08/2008, "Mendoza Beatriz Silvia y otros c/estado nacional y otros s/daños y perjuicios," ¶ 20.V, Fallos (2008-331-1622) (Arg.).

73. Martín Sigal, Julieta Rossi, and Diego Morales, "Argentina: Implementation of Collective Cases," in *Compliance with Social Rights Judgments and the Politics of Compliance: Making It Stick*, ed. Malcolm Langford, César Rodríguez-Garavito, and Julieta Rossi (Cambridge, UK: Cambridge University Press, 2017), 140–76.

74. "ACUMAR: Autoridad de cuenca matanza riachuelo," accessed February 23, 2019, http://www.acumar.gob.ar/.

75. Sigal, Rossi, and Morales, "Argentina," 160.

76. Jorge Jimenez de la Jara and Thomas Bossert, "Chile's Health Sector Reform: Lessons from Four Reform Periods," *Health Policy* 32 (1995): 162.

77. Corte Constitucional [C.C.] [Constitutional Court], 31 de julio, 2008, Sentencia T-760/08 (Colom.).

78. Lamprea, *Derechos en la práctica*.

79. Charles F. Sabel and William H. Simon, "Destabilization Rights: How Public Law Litigation Succeeds," *Harvard Law Review* 117, no. 4 (2004): 1019.

80. Sentencia T-760/08, ¶ 3.2.2.
81. Corte Constitucional [C.C.] [Constitutional Court], 10 de mayo, 2006, Sentencia C-355/06 (Colom.).
82. Sentencia T-760/08, ¶ 3.5.1.
83. For example, see Rodrigo Uprimny Yepes and Juanita Durán, *Equidad y protección judicial del derecho a la salud en Colombi* (Santiago: Naciones Unidas, CEPAL - Serie Políticas, 2014), 22–23.
84. Oscar Parra Vera, "La protección del derecho a la salud: Algunas notas sobre retos y lecciones de la T-760 de 2008 a sus ocho años de implementacióon," in *Los desafíos del litigio en materia de derechos económicos, sociales y culturales* (Buenos Aires: Ministerio Público de la Defensa Argentina, 2017), 51–70.
85. Lamprea, *Derechos en la práctica*, 121–22.
86. L. 1751/2015, 16 de febrero, 2015, Diario Oficial [D.O.] (Colom.).
87. Corte Constitucional [C.C.] [Constitutional Court], 16 de septiembre, 2015, Auto 413/15 (Colom.).
88. Keith Syrett, "Evolving the Right to Health: Rethinking the Normative Response to Problems of Judicialization," *Health and Human Rights* 20 (2018): 129.
89. Rodrigo Uprimny has discussed the intensification of the judicialization in Colombia. See Rodrigo Uprimny, "La judicialización de la política en Colombia: Casos, potencialidades y riesgos," *Sur: Revista Internacional de Derechos Humanos* 4, no. 6 (2007): 52–69.
90. Alicia Ely Yamin, Beatriz Galli, and Sandra Valongueiro, "Implementing International Human Rights Recommendations to Improve Obstetric Care in Brazil," *International Journal of Gynecology and Obstetrics* 143 (2018): 114–20.
91. For example, see Simon Romero, "Dilma Rousseff Is Ousted as Brazil's President in Impeachment Vote," *New York Times*, August 31, 2016, https://www.nytimes.com/2016/09/01/world/americas/brazil-dilma-rousseff-impeached-removed-president.html.
92. "Brazil 20-year Public Expenditure Cap Will Breach Human Rights, UN Expert Warns," *Office of the High Commissioner for Human Rights News*, December 9, 2016, https://www.ohchr.org/EN/NewsEvents/Pages/DisplayNews.aspx?NewsID=21006.
93. "Brazil: Extreme Inequality in Numbers," Oxfam International, accessed February 23, 2019,
   https://www.oxfam.org/en/even-it-brazil/brazil-extreme-inequality-numbers.
94. Travis Waldron, "Brazil Is about to Show the World How a Modern Democracy Collapses," *Huffpost U.S.* January 1, 2019, https://www.huffingtonpost.com/entry/brazil-jair-bolsonaro-democracy-threat_us_5c2a30c5e4b08aaf7a929cbb.

Chapter 7

1. Joseph E. Stiglitz, *The Price of Inequality: How Today's Divided Society Endangers Our Future* (New York: W.W. Norton & Company, 2012), i.
2. Damian Carrington, "David Attenborough: Collapse of Civilisation Is on the Horizon," *The Guardian*, December 3, 2018, https://www.theguardian.com/environment/2018

/dec/03/david-attenborough-collapse-civilisation-on-horizon-un-climate-summit; David Attenborough, "The People's Address" (speech, 2018 United Nations Climate Change Conference, Katowice, Poland, December 3, 2018).

3. AnnJanette Rosga and Margaret Satterthwaie, "The Trust in Indicators: Measuring Human Rights," *Berkeley Journal of International Law* 27, no. 2 (2009): 258.

4. For example, see Joseph W. Meri and Jere L. Bacharach, *Medieval Islamic Civilization: An Encyclopedia* (New York: Routledge, 2006).

5. For example, see Ravinder Mamtani and Albert B. Lowenfels, eds., *Critical Issues in Healthcare Policy and Politics in the Gulf Cooperation Council States* (Washington DC: Georgetown University Press, 2018).

6. Mariam Ibrahim Al-Mulla, "History of Slaves in Qatar: Social Reality and Contemporary Political Vision," *Journal of History Culture and Art Research* 6, no. 4 (2017): 89, 104.

7. "Palma Index of the Most Recent Year by Country (%)," in *Global Monitoring Report* 2014–2015 (Washington, DC: World Bank, 2015), http://datatopics.worldbank.org/gmr/palma-index.html.

8. Deborah Hardoon, Ricardo Fuentes-Nieva, and Sophia Ayela, *An Economy for the 1%: How Privilege and Power in the Economy Drive Extreme Inequality and How This Can Be Stopped* (OXFAM, 2016).

9. Jürgen Habermas, *Legitimation Crisis* (Boston: Beacon Press, 1975), 32–41.

10. "The Rape of the World," Spotify, track 7 on Tracy Chapman, *New Beginning*, Elektra Records, 1995.

11. UN General Assembly, Resolution 70/1, *Transforming Our World: The 2030 Agenda for Sustainable Development*, A/Res/70/1, Goal 5.6.2 (Oct. 21, 2015).

12. Jean Drèze, "Democracy and the Right to Food," in *Human Rights and Development: Towards Mutual Reinforcement*, ed. Philip Alston and Mary Robinson (New York: Oxford University Press, 2005), 45.

13. Matt Bruenig, "New Fed Data: Top 10% Now Own 77% of the Wealth," *People's Policy Project*, September 27, 2017, https://www.peoplespolicyproject.org/2017/09/27/new-fed-data-the-top-10-now-own-77-of-the-wealth/; Renae Merie, "Wall Street's Average Bonus in 2017? Three Times What Most U.S. Households Made All Year," *Washington Post*, March 26, 2018, https://www.washingtonpost.com/news/business/wp/2018/03/26/wall-streets-average-bonus-in-2017-three-times-what-most-u-s-households-made-all-year/?noredirect=on&utm_term=.c1f626aa2973.

14. Juan Pablo Bohoslavsky, *Consecuencias de la deuda externa y las obligaciones financieras internacionales conexas de los Estados para el pleno goce de todos los derechos humanos, sobre todo los derechos económicos, sociales y culturales*, UN Doc. A/73/179 (Jul. 18, 2018).

15. Ole Petter Ottersen et al., "The Political Origins of Health Inequity: Prospects for Change," *The Lancet* 383, no. 9917 (2014): 630–67.

16. Ole Petter Ottersen, et al., "Political Origins," 634.

17. Øystein Bakke and Dag Endal, "Vested Interests in Addiction Research and

Policy: Alcohol Policies Out of Context: Drinks Industry Supplanting Government Role in Alcohol Policies in sub-Saharan Africa," *Addiction* 105 (2010).

18. Pankaj Ghemawat, "Globalization in the Age of Trump: Protectionism Will Change How Companies Do Business—But Not in the Ways You Think," *Harvard Business Review* 95, no. 4 (2017): 119.

19. UN Framework Convention on Climate Change, *Kyoto Protocol to the United Nations Framework Convention on Climate Change*, Dec. 10, 1997, UN Doc. FCCC/CP/1997/7/Add.1, 37 I.L.M. 22 (1998), art. 2.

20. Intergovernmental Panel on Climate Change (IPCC), *The Fifth Assessment Report* (Geneva: World Meteorological Organization and UN, 2014).

21. UN Framework Convention on Climate Change, *Paris Agreement to the United Nations Framework Convention on Climate Change*, Dec. 12, 2015, T.I.A.S. No. 16-1104 (2015).

22. For example, see Linda Greenhouse and Reva B. Siegel, "*Casey* and the Clinic Closings: When 'Protecting Health' Obstructs Choice," *Yale Law Journal* 125, no. 5 (2015).

23. UN High Commissioner for Refugees (UNHCR), *Global Trends: Forced Displacement in* 2016 (Geneva: UNHCR, 2017), 3.

24. Regulation (EU) 2016/679 of the European Parliament and of the Council of 27 April 2016 on the Protection of Natural Persons with Regard to the Processing of Personal Data and on the Free Movement of Such Data, and Repealing Directive 95/46/EC (General Data Protection Regulation), OJ 2016 L 119/1 (2016).

25. Habermas, *Legitimation Crisis*, 36.

26. Hannah Arendt, *The Origins of Totalitarianism* (New York: Harcourt, 1973), 382.

27. UN Economic Commission for Latin America and the Caribbean, *Montevideo Consensus on Population and Development, First Session of the Regional Conference on Population and Development in Latin America and the Caribbean: Full Integration of Population Dynamics into Rights-Based Sustainable Development with Equality: Key to the Cairo Programme of Action Beyond* 2014, Montevideo, 12–15 August 2013, UN Doc. LC/L.3697 (New York: UN, 2013).

28. UN General Assembly, Resolution 70/1, Transforming Our World: The 2030 Agenda for Sustainable Development, A/RES/70/1 ¶ 8 (Oct. 21, 2015).

29. Michael Doyle and Joseph Stiglitz, "Eliminating Extreme Inequality: A Sustainable Development Goal, 2015–2030," *Ethics & International Affairs* 28 (2014): 5–13.

30. UN Development Programme (UNDP), "Sustainable Development Goal 10: Reduce Inequality Within and Among Countries," *UN Sustainable Development Goals Knowledge Platform*, https://sustainabledevelopment.un.org/sdg10.

31. Sakiko Fukuda-Parr, "Keeping Out Extreme Inequality from the SDG Agenda—The Politics of Indicators," special issue, *Global Policy* 10 (2019): 61–69.

32. Organisation for Economic Co-operation and Development (OECD), *Blended Finance: Mobilising Resources for Sustainable Development and Climate Action in Developing Countries* (Paris: OECD, 2017), 3.

33. For a more in-depth discussion of these points, see Alicia Ely Yamin, "Power, Politics and Knowledge Claims: Sexual and Reproductive Health and Rights in the SDG Era," *Global Policy* 10, no. 8 (2019): 52–60.

34. David Kode, "As NGOs Speak Out, Expect Clampdowns to Grow," *Open Global Rights*, December 6, 2017, https://www.openglobalrights.org/as-ngos-speak-out-expect-clampdowns-to-grow.

35. Allison Corkery, Sally-Anne Way, and Victoria Wisniewski Otero, *The OPERA Framework: Assessing Compliance with the Obligation to Fulfill Economic, Social and Cultural Rights* (Brooklyn, NY: Center for Economic and Social Rights, 2012).

36. UN Office of the High Commissioner for Human Rights (OHCHR), *Report on Indicators for Promoting and Monitoring the Implementation of Human Rights*, UN Doc. HRI/MC/2008/3 (New York: UN, 2008).

37. Working Group of the Protocol of San Salvador, *Progress Indicators for Measuring Rights under the Protocol of San Salvador*, 2nd ed. (Washington, DC: Organization of American States, 2015).

38. Alicia Ely Yamin and Deborah P. Maine, "Maternal Mortality as a Human Rights Issue: Measuring Compliance with International Treaty Obligations," *Human Rights Quarterly* 21, no. 3 (1999): 563–607.

39. Alicia Ely Yamin, "The Politics of Knowledge Claims: Sexual and Reproductive Rights in the SDG Era," *Global Policy* 9 (2019): 52–60.

40. Yamin, "The Politics of Knowledge Claims," 52–60.

41. Sally Engle Merry, *The Seductions of Quantification: Measuring Human Rights, Gender Violence, and Sex Trafficking* (Chicago: University of Chicago Press, 2016).

42. For example, see Maria Nazareth Farani Azevêdo, "Statement by Permanent Representative of Brazil, Co-Chairperson-Rapporteur of the Social Forum" (Closure of the 2017 Human Rights Council Social Forum, *Palais des Nations*, Geneva, Switzerland October 3, 2017), which references Dr. Tedros Adhanom Ghebreyesus's Inaugural Address as Director-General of the World Health Organization (Speech, Geneva, Switzerland, July 3, 2017).

43. A/RES/70/1, Goal 3.8.

44. Attiya Waris and Laila Latif, "Towards Establishing Fiscal Legitimacy Through Settled Fiscal Principles in Global Health Financing," *Health Care Analysis* 23, no. 4 (2015): 376–90.

45. The UCL–Lancet Commission on Migration and Health, "The Health of the World on the Move," *Lancet Commissions* 392, no. 10164 (2018), 2644.

46. For example, see UN Committee on Economic, Social and Cultural Rights (CESCR), *Concluding Observations of the Committee on Economic, Social and Cultural Rights: Spain*, UN Doc. E/C.12/ESP/CO/5 (Jun. 6, 2012); UN Committee on the Elimination of All Forms of Discrimination Against Women (CEDAW), *Concluding Observations on the Combined Seventh and Eighth Periodic Reports of Spain*, UN Doc. CEDAW/C/ESP/CO/7–8 (Jul. 29, 2015); Corte Constitucional [C.C.] [Constitutional Court], 1 de junio, 2018, Sentencia T-210/18 (Colom.).

47. UN Human Rights Committee, Communication No. 2348/2014, *Views of the Human Rights Committee Under Article 5, Paragraph 4, of the Optional Protocol to the International Covenant on Civil and Political Rights (Nell Toussaint v. Canada)*, U.N. Doc. CCPR/C/123/D/2348/2014 (Aug. 7, 2018).

48. Corte Constitucional, Sentencia T-210/18 (Colom.).

49. Corte Constitucional, Sentencia T-210/18 (Colom.).

50. For example, see WHO Consultative Group on Equity and Universal Health Coverage, *Making Fair Choices on the Path to Universal Health Coverage* (Geneva: World Health Organization, 2014).

51. Norman Daniels, "Accountability for Reasonableness in Developing Countries," in *Just Health: Meeting Health Needs Fairly* (Cambridge, UK: Cambridge University Press, 2007), 274–96; Norman Daniels, *Just Health Care* (Cambridge, UK: Cambridge University Press, 1985).

52. See R. Baltussen et al., "Progressive Realisation of Universal Health Coverage: What Are the Required Processes and Evidence?" *BMJ Global Health* 2, no. 3 (2017): 1–7.

53. James Fishkin, *When the People Speak: Deliberative Democracy and Public Consultation* (Oxford: Oxford University Press, 2009).

54. Regione Lazio, *Italy's First Deliberative Poll Shows Informed Views of Citizens on Health Care and on Investment Priorities* (Palo Alto, CA: Center for Deliberative Democracy, Stanford University, 2007).

55. Jane Mansbridge, "Deliberative Polling as the Gold Standard," *The Good Society* 19 (2010): 55–62.

56. Christopher Newdick, "Can Judges Ration with Compassion?—A Priority Setting Matrix," *Health and Human Rights Journal* 20 (2018): 107–20.

57. *AC v. Berkshire West PCT and the EHRC* [2011] 119 BMLR 135 Civ 247 (UK); *AC v. Berkshire West PCT* [2010] EWHC 1162 (Admin) (UK).

58. *Philip Morris Brands Sàrl, Philip Morris Products S.A. and Abal Hermanos S.A. v. Oriental Republic of Uruguay*, ICSID Case No. ARB/10/7 (Jul. 8, 2016), ¶¶ 9–18.

59. Roberto Gargarella, "Dialogic Justice in the Enforcement of Social Rights: Some Initial Arguments," in *Litigating Health Rights: Can Courts Bring More Justice to Health?*, ed. Alicia Ely Yamin and Siri Gloppen (Cambridge, MA: Harvard Human Right Series, Harvard University Press, 2011), 237–38.

60. "Independent Expert on the Effects of Foreign Debt and Other Related International Financial Obligations of States on the Full Enjoyment of All Human Rights, Particularly Economic, Social and Cultural Rights," UN Human Rights Office of the High Commissioner (OHCHR), accessed March 2, 2019, https://www.ohchr.org/en/issues/development/iedebt/pages/iedebtindex.aspx

61. "UN Expert on Extreme Poverty and Human Rights to Visit USA, One of the Wealthiest Countries in the World," UN Human Rights Office of the High Commissioner (OHCHR), accessed March 2, 2019, https://www.ohchr.org/en/NewsEvents/Pages/DisplayNews.aspx?NewsID=22465&LangID=E; "UN Human Rights Expert to Visit UK

to Assess Poverty," UN Human Rights Office of the High Commissioner (OHCHR), accessed March 2, 2019, https://www.ohchr.org/en/NewsEvents/Pages/DisplayNews.aspx?NewsID=23808&LangID=E.

62. UN Committee on Economic, Social and Cultural Rights (CESCR), *General Comment No. 22 (2016) on the Right to Sexual and Reproductive Health (Article 12 of the International Covenant on Economic, Social and Cultural Rights)*, UN Doc. E/C.12/GC/22 (2016).

63. UN Committee on the Elimination of Discrimination against Women (CEDAW), *General Recommendation No. 35 on Gender-Based Violence Against Women, Updating General Recommendation No. 19*, UN Doc. CEDAW/C/GC/35 (2017).

64. For example, see Hilary Charlesworth and Christine Chinkin, "The Gender of Jus Cogens," *Human Rights Quarterly* 15 (1993): 63–76.

65. Office of the United Nations High Commissioner for Human Rights (OHCHR), *General Comment No. 36 on Article 6 of the International Covenant on Civil and Political Rights, on the Right to Life, Revised Draft Prepared by the Rapporteur*, UN Doc. CCPR/C/GC/R.36/Rev.7 ¶ 26 (2017).

66. "Development Aid Stable in 2014 but Flows to Poorest Countries Still Falling," Organisation for Economic Co-operation and Development (OECD), accessed March 2, 2019, http://www.oecd.org/dac/stats/development-aid-stable-in-2014-but-flows-to-poorest-countries-still-falling.htm.

67. Khadija Sharife, "Big Pharma's Taxing Situation," *World Policy Journal* 33 (2016): 88–95.

68. Lawrence O. Gostin, *Global Health Law* (Cambridge, MA: Harvard University Press, 2014); Lawrence O. Gostin et al., "Towards a Framework Convention on Global Health," *World Health Organization Bulletin* 91 (2013): 790–93.

69. Leigh Haynes et al., "Will the Struggle for Health Equity and Social Justice Be Best Served by a Framework Convention on Global Health?" *Harvard Health and Human Rights* (2015): 111.

70. Gorik Ooms and Rachel Hammonds, "The Future of Multilateral Funding to Realize the Right to Health, in *Rights-Based Governance for a Globalizing World*, ed., Benjamin Mason Meier and Lawrence O. Gostin (Oxford: Oxford University Press, 2018), 454.

71. UN Human Rights Council, Resolution 35/17, Business and Human Rights: Mandate of the Working Group on the Issue of Human Rights and Transnational Corporations and Other Business Enterprises, A/HRC/RES/35/7 (Jul. 14, 2017); UN Human Rights Council, Resolution 38/13, Business and Human Rights: Improving Accountability and Access to Remedy, A/HRC/RES/38/13 (Jul. 18, 2018).

72. ETO Consortium, *Maastricht Principles on the Extraterritorial Obligations of States in the Area of Economic, Social and Cultural Rights* (Sep. 28, 2011), ¶ 8.

73. *Maastricht Principles*, ¶ 9.

74. For example, see Malcolm Langford et al., eds., *Global Justice, State Duties: The Extraterritorial Scope of Economic, Social, and Cultural Rights in International Law* (Cambridge, UK: Cambridge University Press, 2013).

75. *Urgenda Foundation v. The State of the Netherlands,* Hague District Court, C/09/456689/HA ZA 13-1396 (June 24, 2015).

76. OECD, *Policy Coherence for Sustainable Development* 2018: *Towards Sustainable and Resilient Societies* (Paris: OECD Publishing, 2018).

77. Timothy Craig et al., "WAO Guideline for the Management of Hereditary Angioedema," *World Allergy Organization Journal* 5, no. 12 (2012): 182–99.

78. Jean Baudrillard, *The Agony of Power* (Cambridge, MA: MIT Press, 2010).

Conclusions

1. Albert Camus, "The Almond Trees" in *Lyrical and Critical Essays* (New York: Vintage Books, 1970), 135.

2. Inter-Am. Ct. H.R., 58th Special Session, Panama City from October 16 to 20, 2017; see Inter-American Court of Human Rights, *Annual Report* 2017 (Washington DC: Organization of American States, 2017), 37, 42.

3. Organization of American States (OAS), Additional Protocol to the American Convention on Human Rights in the Area of Economic, Social and Cultural Rights ("Protocol of San Salvador"), A-52 (Nov. 16, 1999).

4. *Poblete Vilches y Otros v. Chile,* Inter-Am. Ct. H.R. (ser. C) No. 349 (March 8, 2018).

5. *Suárez Peralta v. Ecuador,* Inter-Am. Ct. H.R. (ser. C) No. 261 (May 21, 2013).

6. *Lagos del Campo v. Perú,* Inter-Am. Ct. H.R. (ser. C) No. 340 ¶¶ 142–145 (August 31, 2017).

7. Ronald Dworkin, "Cómo el derecho se parece a la literatura," in *La decisión judicial: El debate Hart-Dworkin,* cited in "La justiciabilidad de los derechos econónomicos, sociales y culturales en el Sistema Interamericano a la luz del artículo 26 de la Convención Americana: El sentido y la promes del caso Lagos del Campo," in *Inclusión, Ius Commune y justiciabilidad de los DESCA en la jurisprudencia interamericana. El caso Lagos del Campo y los nuevos desafíos. Colección Constitución y Derechos,* ed. Eduardo Ferrer Mac-Gregor, Mariela Morales Antoniazzi, and Rogelio Flores Pantoja (Mexico City: Instituto de Estudios Constitucionales, 2018).

8. For example, see Tara J. Melish, "Rethinking the 'Less as More' Thesis: Supranational Litigation of Economic, Social, and Cultural Rights in the Americas," *New York University Journal of International Law and Policy* 39 (2006): 171–343; James L. Cavallaro and Emily J. Schaffer, "Less as More: Rethinking Supernational Litigation of Economic and Social Rights in the Americas," *Hastings Law Journal* 56, no. 2 (2004): 217–82.

9. *Medio ambiente y derechos humanos,* Inter-Am. Ct. H.R., Opinión Consultiva Oc-23/17, Solicitada Por La República De Colombia (Nov. 15, 2017).

10. Logan Marshall, *The Story of the Panama Canal* (Philadelphia: John C. Winston Company, 1913).

11. *Poblete Vilches,* ¶¶ 14–24; *Vinicio Antonio Poblete Tapia and Family v. Chile,* Inter-Am. Cmm'n. H.R., Report No. 1/16 CASE 12,695, OEA/Ser.L/V/II.157 Doc. 5 (April 13, 2016).

12. Gabriel Bastías et al., "Health Care Reform in Chile," *Canadian Medical Association Journal* 179, no. 12 (2008): 1289–92.

13. Thomas J. Bossert and Thomas Leisewitz, "Innovation and Change in the Chilean Health System," *New England Journal of Medicine* 374 (2016): 1–5.

14. Tribunal Constitucional [T.C.] [Constitutional Court], 6 agosto 2010, Rol de la causa: 1710-2010 (Chile).

15. *Poblete Vilches*, ¶ 209.

16. For example, see Brigit Toebes, Rhonda Ferguson, Milan Markovic, and Obiajulu Nnamuchi, eds., *The Rights to Health: A Multi-Country Study of Law, Policy and Practice* (The Hague: Springer, 2014).

17. Samuel Moyn, *Not Enough: Human Rights in an Unequal World* (Cambridge, MA: Harvard University Press, 2018); Stephen Hopgood, *The Endtimes of Human Rights* (Ithaca: Cornell University Press, 2015).

18. For example, see Naomi Klein, *The Shock Doctrine: The Rise of Disaster Capitalism* (Toronto, Canada: Knopf Canada, 2007); Naomi Klein, *No Logo*, 10th anniversary ed. (Toronto: Vintage Canada, 2009).

19. For example, see Margaret R. Somers, *Genealogies of Citizenship: Markets, Statelessness and the Right to Have Rights* (Cambridge, UK: Cambridge University Press, 2008); Paul O'Connell, "On Reconciling Irreconcilables: Neo-Liberal Globalisation and Human Rights," *Human Rights Law Review* 7, no. 3 (2007): 483–509; Audrey R. Chapman, *Global Health, Human Rights and the Challenge of Neoliberal Policies* (Cambridge, UK: Cambridge University Press, 2016).

20. For example, compare Benjamin Mason Meier and Lawrence O. Gostin, "Framing Human Rights in Global Governance," in *Human Rights in Global Health: Rights-Based Governance in a Globalized World* (Oxford: Oxford University Press, 2018), 63-86; Benjamin Meier and William Onzivu, "The Evolution of Human Rights in World Health Organization Policy and the Future of Human Rights through Global Health Governance," *Public Health* 128, no. 2 (2014): 179–87.

21. Benedicte Bull and Desmond McNeill, eds., *Development Issues in Global Governance: Public-Private Partnerships and Market Multilateralism* (New York: Routledge, 2007), 60.

22. UN General Assembly, Resolution 217 A (III), Universal Declaration of Human Rights, A/RES/217A(III), Art. 28 (Dec. 10, 1948).

23. Camus, "The Almond Trees," 135.

24. Steven Lukes, ed., *Power: Readings in Social and Political Theory* (New York: New York University Press, 1986).

25. Much of the analysis of dimensions of power in this section, and in this book, is drawn from the following two works: Steven Lukes' *Power* (New York: New York University Press, 1986), and John Gaventa's works on the "power cube" including "Finding the Spaces for Change: A Power Analysis," *IDS Bulletin* 37, no. 6 (2006): 23–33.

26. Bruce Ackerman, *We the People, Volume 1: Foundations* (Cambridge, MA: Harvard University Press, 1991), 12.

27. Philip Alston, "The World Bank as a Human Rights-Free Zone," in *Doing Peace the Rights Way: Essays in International Law and Relations in Honour of Louise Arbour*, ed. Fannie LaFontaine and François Larocque (Forthcoming).

28. Juan Pablo Bohoslavsky and Edward Guntrip, "Unanticipated Consequences: The Human Rights Implications of Bringing Sovereign Debt Disputes within Investment Treaty Arbitration," in *Yearbook on International Investment Law & Policy* 2017, ed. Lisa Sachs, Lise Johnson, and Jesse Coleman (Oxford: Oxford University Press, 2017).

29. *Jam et al. v. International Finance Corp, slip opinion* 17-1011, US S Ct (2019).

30. Roberto Mangabeira Unger, *Democracy Realized: The Progressive Alternative* (Brooklyn, NY: Verso, 1998), 92.

31. Jean Baudrillard, *The Agony of Power* (Cambridge, MA: MIT Press, 2010), 63.

32. Anita Raj et al., "Longitudinal Analysis of the Impact of Economic Empowerment on Risk for Intimate Partner Violence among Married Women in Rural Maharashtra, India," *Social Science & Medicine* 196 (2018): 197–203.

33. For example, see Radhika Balakrishnan, James Heintz, and Diane Elson, *Rethinking Economic Policy for Social Justice: The Radical Potential of Human Rights* (New York: Routledge, 2016).

34. Nancy Fraser, "Gender Equity and the Welfare State—A Postindustrial Thought Experiment," in *Democracy and Difference: Contesting the Boundaries of the Political*, ed. Seyla Benhabib (Princeton, NJ: Princeton University Press, 1996), 235.

35. For example, see René Girard, *Battling to the End: Conversations with Benoît Chantre* (East Lansing, MI: Michigan State University Press, 2010).

36. Yvonne Kelly et al., "Social Media Use and Adolescent Mental Health: Findings from the UK Millennium Cohort Study," *EClinical Medicine* 6 (2018): 59–68.

37. Nancy Fraser, "Rethinking the Public Sphere: A Contribution to the Critique of Actually Existing Democracy," *Social Text* 25/26 (1990): 56–80.

38. Amartya Sen, *The Idea of Justice* (Cambridge, MA: Harvard University Press, 2009), 143.

39. Dani Rodrik, *The Globalization Paradox: Why Global Markets, States, and Democracy Can't Coexist* (Oxford: Oxford University Press, 2011), 129; Ben Mason Meier and Lawrence O. Gostin, "Introduction: Responding to the Public Health Harms of a Globalized World through Human Rights in Global Governance," in *Human Rights in Global Health: Rights-Based Governance for a Globalizing World*, ed. Lawrence O. Gostin and Ben Mason Meier (Oxford: Oxford University Press, 2018), 1–20.

40. Jennifer Prah Ruger, "Chapter 4: An Alternative Account: Provincial Globalism," in *Global Health Justice and Governance* (Oxford: Oxford University Press, 2018), 81.

41. Bull and McNeill, *Development Issues*, 43.

42. Margaret E. Keck and Kathryn Sikkink, "Transnational Advocacy Networks in International and Regional Politics," *International Social Science Journal* 51, no. 159 (1999): 89.

43. Keck and Sikkink, "Transnational Advocacy Networks," 93.

44. Ynske Boersma, "Living in the Shadow of Colombia's Largest Coal Mine," *Earth Island Journal*, January 30, 2018, http://www.earthisland.org/journal/index.php/articles/entry/shardow_colombia_Coal_Mine_Carrejon/.

45. *Children and Adolescents of the Communities of Uribía, Manaure, Riohacha and Maicao of the Wayúu People, in the Department of the Guajira, Colombia*, Inter-Am. Cmm'n. H.R., PM 51/15 (January 26, 2018).

46. Lynn P. Freedman, "Achieving the MDGs: Health Systems as Core Social Institutions," *Development* 48 (2005): 20.

47. For example, see Jeanette Vega, "Universal Health Coverage: The Post-2015 Development Agenda," *The Lancet* 381, no. 9862 (2013): 179–80.

48. Unger, *Democracy Realized*, 15.

49. *Poblete Vilches*.

50. Later in 2018, the court reaffirmed the fundamental nature and direct justiciability of the right to health in a case involving HIV/AIDS in Guatemala, which reveals some of the same tendencies as the *Poblete Vilches* case. See *Caso Cuscul Pivaral y Otros v. Guatemala*, Inter-Am. Ct. H.R. (ser. C) No. 359 (August 23, 2018).

51. *Poblete Vilches*, ¶¶ 238–239.

52. Alicia Ely Yamin, Documento complementario a prueba pericial, 24 octubre, 2017, incorporado a expediente de fondo, *Poblete Vilches y Otros v. Chile*, Inter-Am. Ct. H.R. (ser. C) No. 349 (March 8, 2018).

53. Law No. 20.606, Junio 6, 2012, DIARIO OFICIAL [D.O.] (Chile).

54. Law No. 20.869, Junio 11, 2015, DIARIO OFICIAL [D.O.] (Chile).

55. Alicia Ely Yamin, Documento complementario.

56. Hernán Sandoval, "Derecho a la salud, ¿Derecho garantizado?," (lecture, Universidad de las Américas, Santiago de Chile, November 22–23, 2016).

57. Oscar Galaz, "Hernán Sandoval: 'Sería interesante establecer un Auge para la tercera edad, sobre todo concebido desde las necesidades sociales,'" Instituto de Políticas Públicas en Salud, Mar 30, 2017, http://www.ipsuss.cl/ipsuss/actualidad/hernan-sandoval-seria-interesante-establecer-un-auge-para-la-tercera/2017-03-30/161659.html.

58. Ronald Dworkin, *Justice for Hedgehogs* (Cambridge, MA: Harvard University Press, 2011), 418–20.

59. "Entrevista a Dr. Hernán Sandoval," *Foro Universitario*, Radio U de Santiago 94.5, November 10, 2018, *https://www.youtube.com/watch?v=bSRFYFgqwZ8*.

60. Albie Sachs, *The Soft Vengeance of a Freedom Fighter* (Oakland, CA: University of California Press, 2014).

61. Francis Fukuyama, *Identity: The Demand for Dignity and the Politics of Resentment* (New York: Farrar, Straus, and Giroux, 2018).

62. Philip Alston, "The Populist Challenge to Human Rights," *Journal of Human Rights Practice* 9 (2017): 15.

Index

Note: page numbers followed by t refer to tables.

AAAQ framework, 140–41
abortion: Argentine law on, 50; arguments for considering as a right, 45; basis of right to under international law, importance of, 185; Catholic Church opposition to, 111; conservative strategies in relation to, 180–81; European law on, 47; SRHR rights and, 83–84; unsafe, and maternal mortality rates, 16; UN statements on, 194; US debate on, 18, 45–47; US law on, 45–46
Abramovich, Victor, 149
Achmat, Zachie, 127
Additional Protocol to the American Convention on Human Rights on ESC Rights (Protocol of San Salvador) [1999], 111, 186, 203, 221
Adjustment with a Human Face (UNICEF), 60
Advocacia Cidadã Pelos Direitos Humanos, 150
advocacy networks, transnational, 217–18
AFDC. *See* Aid to Families with Dependent Children
Africa: southern, prevalence of HIV/AIDS in, 125; sub-Saharan, debt loads of countries in, 126
African American men: and US justice system, 219; killings by police, 2
Agenda 2030: civil society input into, 183; development of, 153, 183; goals of, 178; and measurement indicators' redefining of goals, 178, 183–85. *See also* Sustainable Development Goals (SDGs)
AIDS. *See* HIV/AIDS
AIDS Law Project, 130

Aid to Families with Dependent Children (AFDC): criticisms of, 54; maternal fitness requirements in, 19, 53, 54
Allende, Salvador, 67, 223
Alma-Ata, Declaration of 1978, 63–64, 68, 143
Alston, Philip, 4, 34, 60–61, 122, 193, 223–24
Alyne da Silva Pimentel case (Brazil): and accountability measures, 160, 163; circumstances of, 149–50; and enforceable legal health rights, expansion of, 22, 150; and failures in Brazilian health care system, 159; idiosyncratic factors in, 171; inadequate obstetric care as cause of death in, 171; on intersectional discrimination, 150; and legal right to maternal health care, 150; and state responsibility to regulate private health providers, 150, 160; use of HRBAs in implementation of, 151
Amazon rainforest: Bolsonaro government policies on, 172; transnational oil companies in, 206
American Convention on Human Rights, 110
Amnesty International: Demand Dignity campaign, 156–57; and ESC rights, support for, 156–57
Amon, Joseph, 165
Anand, Sudhir, 136
Angarita, Ciro, 88
Annan, Kofi, 122
antiretroviral therapy (ARVs), development of, 124–25
antiretroviral therapy (ARVs), as human/constitutional right: countries establishing, 125;

269

court rulings on, 129–30; South African struggle for, 21, 125, 126–30
APRODEH. *See* Asociación Pro Derechos Humanos
Arab Spring, 173–74
Argentina: abortion law in, 50; and access to ARVs as human right, 125; constitution of 1994, 89; introduction of ESC rights in Constitution, 49, 78; *Mendoza* case relating to environmental damage in, 167–68; structural adjustment program in, 55, 59–60
Argentina's military dictatorship (1976–83): atrocities of, 47–48; as claimed "defenders of tradition", 28, 36; clandestine detention and torture centers, 27–30; economic policies of, 49, 50; Martínez de Hoz and, 48–49; and rise of international human rights movement, 29; trials of leaders of, 49; violent extremism of, 28; women's protests against, 50–51
Arrow, Kenneth, 66
Arroyo, Juan, 98
Asociación Pro Derechos Humanos (APRODEH), 103–4, 111, 121–22
Association for Human Rights. *See* Asociación Pro Derechos Humanos (APRODEH)
Attenborough, David, 175
austerity programs, disproportional effect on women, 179–80

Babb, Sarah, 94
Baker, James, 95
Balakrishnan, Radhika, 214
Barrios Altos case, 107, 120
Baudrillard, Jean, 201
Bazán, Coca, 48
Beauvoir, Simone de, 5, 29, 40
Beijing Conference. *See* World Conference on Women (Beijing, 1995)
Belém do Pará Convention. *See* Inter-American Convention on the Prevention, Punishment and Eradication of Violence Against Women
Benhabib, Seyla, 13
Berer, Marge, 115, 116
Biehl, João, 165
Bill & Melinda Gates Foundation, 131, 132
biomedical paradigm: as commodifying, 191, 211; dissonances with indigenous Peruvian culture, 108–9; HIV/AIDS and, 19; as inconsistent with health as human right, 17, 56, 64–65, 74, 158–59, 219; involuntary sterilization in Peruvian family planning program and, 219; as powerful internalized norm, 211; rights persons with disabilities and, 136; and women's health rights, 162, 169, 211
birth control. *See* contraception
Black Lives Matter, 2
Black Report, 63
Bøås, Morten, 98
Bohoslavsky, Juan Pablo, 179–80
Bolsonaro, Jair, 172
The Book of Pleasant Journeys into Faraway Lands (*Tabula Rogeriana*, al-Idrisi), 175–76
Borges, Danielle, 165
Bosnian genocide, and international criminal liability, 92, 112
Bourdieu, Pierre, 9, 11
Boutros-Ghali, Boutros, 79
Brady Bonds (Brady Plan), 95
Brady, Nicholas, 95
Brazil: and access to ARVs as human right, 125; Bolsonaro government in, 172; corruption scandals of 2016–17, 172; and courts' role in implementing health as human rights, 23, 164–66; economic downturn, and cuts in health spending, 172; government fragmentation and dysfunction in, 152, 166; health rights activists, use of courts, 151; inequality in, 151, 153–54, 156, 162, 166, 172, 219; Lula's economic policies in, 152–54; and maternal mortality reduction, 158; poverty in, 152–53; segregation by race and class in, 156
Brazil, C-section overuse, 148–49; as obstetric violence, 149; reasons for, 161–62, 219
Brazil, health care for women, inadequacy of, 173; intersectional discrimination and, 159; and need for human rights-based approach to health care, 159; RMNCH approach and, 158; Zika outbreak and, 156. *See also Alyne da Silva Pimentel* case (Brazil)
Brazil, health care in: as human right, 67, 159; inadequacy of, 166; and racial discrimination, 153, 219
Brazilian Constitution of 1988: health as human right in, 67, 159; as transformative Constitution, 151–52
Brazilian Sistema Único de Saúde (SUS) [unified health system]: gradual marketization of health care in, 159, 162; women's rights and, 162

Bretton Woods institutions: as product of postwar multilateralism, 29, 30; and structural adjustment programs, 59–60. *See also* General Agreement on Tariffs and Trade (GATT); International Monetary Fund (IMF); World Bank
Brexit: origins of unrest leading to, 177, 182; unrealistic expectations for, 182
Brinks, Daniel, 90
Brown v. Board of Education case (US, 1954–55), 53
Bulger, Billy, 54
Bull, Benedicte, 217
Bush, George W., 131
busing, court-ordered, 53
Butler, Judith, 84
BVerfGE 39,1 - Abortion I case (Germany, 1975), 47

Cabal, Luisa, 93–94
Cairo Conference. *See* International Conference on Population and Development (Cairo, 1994)
Camus, Alert, 202
capabilities theory of Amartya Sen, 58–59, 78–79
care work, restructuring around gender equality, 214–15
Carruthers, Bruce, 90
Catholic Church, and SRHR, 104, 107–8, 111, 115, 138
CEDAL. *See* Centro de Asesoría Laboral
CEDAW. *See* Convention on the Elimination of All Forms of Discrimination against Women
CEJIL. *See* Center for Justice and International Law
center and periphery, efforts toward more egalitarian development of, 34–35
Center for Economic and Social Rights (CESR), 4
Center for Justice and International Law (CEJIL), 92, 103
Center for Reproductive Law and Policy (now Center for Reproductive Rights), 93
Center for Reproductive Rights (CRR): and abortion rights, 113, 121; and *Alyne da Silva Pimentel* case, 150, 171; founding of, 93; and international litigation, 93, 99–100; and Peru's sterilization program, 103; and SRHR, advancement of, 138

Centro de Asesoría Laboral (CEDAL), 111
Cepeda, Manuel José, 169
CERD. *See* Committee on the Elimination of Racial Discrimination
Cerrejón mine (Colombia), 218
CESCR. *See* Committee on Economic, Social and Cultural Rights
CESCR General Comment 3 (*The Nature of State Parties' Obligations*), 86, 142–43, 216
CESCR General Comment 14 (*The Right to the Highest Attainable Standard of Health*), 140–45; analytical frameworks used in, 140–41; critiques of, 22, 142–44; and human rights as tool for advancing health rights, 140; and ICESCR, updating of, 140–41; range of reactions to, 144; on required minimum level of ESC rights, 142, 195; "respect, protect, fulfill" framework from, 169; and right to health *vs.* other rights, 202–3; as triumph of programming focus over legal enforceability, 141–42
CESCR General Comment 20 (*Non-discrimination in Economic, Social and Cultural Rights*) 43
CESCR General Comment 22 (*The Right to Sexual and Reproductive Health*), 193–94
CESR. *See* Center for Economic and Social Rights
Chamorro, Rubén Jacinto, 48
Chapman, Audrey, 116
Charleston, church massacre in (2015), 2
Chávez, Martha, 110
child mortality rates: large disparity in, 15; UNICEF's "child survival revolution" and, 19, 68
child rights: and erosion of public-private distinction, 68–69; social science justifications for, 69; UN programs on, 19, 68–70. *See also* Convention on the Rights of the Child (CRC), 1989
Chile: abortion law in, 47; Allende government in, 223; health care activism in, 222–23; health care in, 67, 204; obesity in, 222; proposals for new constitution for, 222; structural adjustment in, 204; universal health coverage, adoption of, 204. *See also Poblete Vilches v. Chile* case (2018)
China, and Tiananmen Square protests, 3
civil and political rights (CP): as early focus of rights advocacy, 4, 29, 209; fall of barriers between ESC rights and, in 1990's, 19, 77; importance in battle for health rights, 209;

inadequacy for ensuring health as human right, 37–38, 210; inadequacy for ensuring social justice, 102, 209; as negative rights, 37, 209; remedies in, as return to *status quo ante*, 38; in Universal Declaration of Human Rights, 32, 34; West's privileging of, 29, 34, 36–37
civil society actors: as driver of human rights, 194; empowerment by human rights narrative, 206–7; globalization of activism, 194; transnational advocacy networks and, 217–18; at Vienna Conference, 80
Civil Society Forum on Health (FOROSALUD), 118, 163
CLADEM, 103, 112
climate change: Kyoto Protocol and, 180; and legitimation crisis in democratic institutions, 7; and migration crises, 181; US and, 180–81
Clinton, Bill, 54
CLS. *See* critical legal studies
Cold War: marginalizing of ESC rights in, 38, 50; and Soviet bloc privileging of ESC rights, 34, 36; and West's privileging of CP rights, 29, 34, 36–37
collective deliberation: about health, as necessary, 13; as basis of democracy, 13–14. *See also* democracy
Colombia, Wayúu indigenous community in, 218
Colombian Constitution of 1991: guarantees of ESC rights in, 87–88; judiciary's policy-setting power in, 88; as transformative constitution, 168
Colombian health care system, judicially-led reform of (T-760/08), 168–71, 188; critiques of, 170; inadequate attention to women's health in, 169, 173; ongoing problems unresolved by, 169–70
colonialism: Bretton Woods institutions in relation to, 30; justifications for, 26
commercial actors, and health care, 90. *See also* international financial institutions (IFIs); transnational corporations (TNCs)
Commission on Global Governance for Health (Lancet–University of Oslo), 180
Committee on Economic, Social and Cultural Rights (CESCR): and ESC rights, 77; follow-up on legal judgments by, 149; General Comment on right to health (2000), 140; and OPERA framework, 186; development of, in 2000's, 144–45; on required minimum level of ESC rights, 86–87; on right to health, 202–3; statements on SRHR, 193–94. *See also* CESCR General Comment entries
Committee on the Elimination of Discrimination Against Women, 214
Committee on the Elimination of Racial Discrimination (CERD), 140, 149
Committee on the Rights of the Child, 140
common humanity: as basis of all human rights, 3; and complex identities, dialectic interaction of, 6; necessity of recognizing, 10; Obama on, 2; as potential source of unity, 2–3. *See also* dignity, focus on economic, social and cultural (ESC) rights in, 34, 36
community-based care, benefits of, 222
Condorcet, Nicolas de, 83
consent, informed, as necessary feature of health services, 106, 117, 118, 141, 161
constitutional blocs, 89–90
constitutions of 1990's, recognition of ESC rights in, 78. *See also* social (transformative) constitutionalism
Construtora Norberto Odebrecht S.A., 172
contraception: beginnings of widespread use, 29; and colonialist control of women, 44; Peru's restrictions on, under Toledo, 115; and separation of gender and sex, 29; and women's rights, 18, 44–45
Convention of Belém do Pará. *See* Inter-American Convention on the Prevention, Punishment and Eradication of Violence Against Women
Convention on the Elimination of All Forms of Discrimination against Women (CEDAW), 29–30; and abortion rights, 121; and *Alyne da Silva Pimentel* case, 171–72; and bridging of public-private divide, 42, 69; criticisms of, 42; passage of, 18, 36, 42; and women's health initiatives, 71–72; and women's substantive equality, 43
Convention on the Elimination of All Forms of Discrimination against Women (CEDAW) Committee: and *Alyne da Silva Pimentel* case, 150; on discrimination against women, 140; General Recommendation on Women and Health (1999), 140; statement on SRHR, 193, 194
Convention on the Elimination of All Forms of Racial Discrimination, 140
Convention on the Rights of Persons with Disabilities (CRPD), 136–37

Convention on the Rights of the Child (CRC), 1989, 19, 68–70, 72
conversion gaps in health, 58
Cook, Rebecca, 112, 148, 150
Copenhagen Conference on Social Development, and people-centered development, 79
Correa, Sonia, 171
Costa, Celia, 115–16
Costa Rica: and cost of expensive medications, 198–99, 219; environmental policy in, 197; symposium on Hereditary Angioedema, 197–99
counterpublics: as effect of rights activism, 21; Zapatista autonomous communities as, 76
court rulings as catalyst for political action, 166–71; in Argentine environment damage case, 167–68; in Colombian health care system, 168–71; in Indian "right to food" case, 167
courts: in regulating Universal Health Coverage systems, 192–93, 220; and social constitutionalism, enforcement of, 130. *See also* international and regional legal forums, rights activists turn to
courts' policy-setting role: and balance of powers, 129; importance in advancing ESC rights, 88–89; in transformative constitutionalism, 88–89
courts' role in implementing health as human right, 22–23, 164–71, 220; as catalyst for political action, 167, 168–71, 173; complex impacts of, 165, 170; critiques of, 164–65; and dialogic remedies, 23, 167, 169, 210; educative role, 170–71; expansion of, 150–51, 164, 173; impact on political discourse, 164; important collective cases in Latin America, 166; latitude for governments' implementation of, 150; limited number of cases addressing social determinants of health, 166; origin in HIV/AIDS cases, 164; *Poblete Vilches v. Chile* case and, 221–22; reasons for turn to, 165–66; and regulation of private actors, 150, 164; and space for democratic deliberation, 171, 220; transactional costs of, 166. *See also Alyne da Silva Pimentel* case (Brazil)
CP. *See* civil and political rights
CRC. *See* Convention on the Rights of the Child (CRC), 1989
criminal law in enforcement of women's rights, unintended consequences of, 93

crisis response, variation in state capacities for, 179
critical legal studies (CLS), 3
critical praxis, need for, 221, 224
cross-border actions, ESC rights as tool in fight against, 206
Crossette, Barbara, 115
CRPD. *See* Convention on the Rights of Persons with Disabilities
CRR. *See* Center for Reproductive Rights
C-sections: problems associated with, 148; WHO recommendations on target rates for, 148. *See also* Brazil, C-section overuse

DALYs. *See* disability-adjusted life years
Daniels, Norman, 15, 38, 39, 143, 190
da Silva Pimentel, Alyne, 149–50, 171. *See also Alyne da Silva Pimentel* case (Brazil)
debate on social change, democratization of knowledge required for, 9
debt burdens: in global South, 179; human rights pushback against, 211; and neoliberal structural adjustment programs, 55; as political issue, developing recognition of, 211; in Sub-Saharan Africa, 126; vulnerability created by, 120
Declaration of the Rights of Man and Citizen (France), 32
Declaration on the Elimination of Violence Against Women (1993), 82
Declaration on the Right to Development (1986), 61
Degregori, Carlos Iván, 102
deliberative polling, 191
democracy: collective deliberation as basis of, 13–14; and health systems as social institutions, 209; inequality's undermining of, 7, 22, 151, 155–56; as key component in productive cooperation, 223; as political manifestation of universal dignity, 155
democratic institutions: growing restrictions on, 185; legitimation crisis in, 7
democratized decision-making, in Universal Health Coverage, 190–92, 200; deliberative polling and, 191
Demographic and Health Survey (DHS), 70
DEMUS, 103–4, 112
dependent development theory, 34
depoliticizing of law, origin of concept, 32
deregulation: destabilizing effects of, 126; and expansion of capital markets, 124;

and market fluctuation, impact on debtor countries, 120
desire, as culturally determined, 162
development: economic growth as goal of, in mainstream economics, 57; effect of perceived purpose on goals in, 56; global, and pathologies of power, 17; human *vs.* economic forms of, 19, 20, 57–59, 125, 125, 129; neoliberal economic paradigm of, 55–56; sustainable, UN on three pillars of, 176; UN assertion of right to, 61. *See also* economic growth; human development; Millennium Development Goals (MDGs); neoliberalism; neoliberal reforms
developmental psychology, and child rights, 69
DHS. *See* Demographic and Health Survey
dignity: array of CP and ESC rights required for, 63; dependence on mutual recognition of others' dignity, 31; health and, 15; Kant on, 31
dignity, universal: as basis of health as human right, 62; as basis of human rights law, 26; as core notion of international human rights, 30, 31; democracy as political manifestation of, 155; meaning of, 12; narrative technique and, 9–10; traditional political structures and, 8; transformative potential of belief in, 3; in Universal Declaration of Human Rights, 12, 33; Vienna Conference on, 79
disability-adjusted life years (DALYs): Convention on the Rights of Persons with Disabilities and, 136; as health measurement, 132
disability rights, advancement of, 136–37
disease: biomedical understanding of, as inconsistent with health as human right, 17, 56, 64–65, 74, 158–59; preventive approaches, need for, 222; as social phenomenon, 56, 65, 72, 73–74, 158–59
diversity: and respect for human dignity, 223; value of, 3
Doña Lourdes, 171
Doyle, Michael, 184
Drèze, Jean, 91, 179
Duque, Ivan, 170
Dworkin, Ronald, 31, 45, 203

Easterbrook, Gregg, 14
Echoing Green Foundation, 92
economic, social and cultural (ESC) rights: advocacy for, in Peru, 111; Amnesty International's support for, 156–57; as aspirations in human rights law, 38–39; challenges of advancing, 4; and change of narrative from "misfortune" to "injustice," 4–5; as communist bloc approach to rights, 34, 36–37; courts' policy-setting power as key to, 88–89; data needed to advance, 186; early dismissal of, 4; enforcement of, as current most-pressing issue, 205; growing recognition of, in 1990s, 19, 77–78, 79; indicators to measure, development of, 186–87; and international assistance obligations, 40; marginalization in Cold War, 38, 50; metrics for assessing progress in, 105; necessity of, for establishing health as human right, 210; political contestation in implementation of, 32; progress on, 6–7; resource limitations and, 40; shrinking of, under neoliberal reforms, 210; and social (transformative) constitutionalism, 216; states' postponement of implementation, 39; as tool for promoting greater equality, 206; in Universal Declaration of Human Rights, 32, 34
economic, social and cultural (ESC) rights, as real rights: growing acceptance of, in 1990's, 86; skepticism about, 4, 29, 40, 50; struggle for, 203, 205
economic, social and cultural (ESC) rights, required minimum level of: CESCR establishment of, 86–87; General Comment 14 and, 142, 195; in state constitutions, 87–89
economic dimensions of human rights, UN efforts to address, 193
economic growth: as goal in itself, in mainstream economics, 57; as means of increasing human freedom, in human rights perspective, 57–59; sustainable, benefits of, 57; value of, as contingent on social benefits and costs, 57, 62. *See also* development
economic integration, global. *See* globalization
economic justice, program for achievement of, 8
economic policy, changes of 1980's, 55
ECtHR. *See* European Court of Human Rights
Ecuador, transnational oil companies in, 206
education, large disparity in, 15
Eide, Asbjorn, 141
Ejército Zapatista de Liberación Nacional (EZLN). *See* Zapatista National Liberation Army

Index   275

elites, belief in ability to rule ordinary people, 26
Elson, Diane, 214
Elva (Malawian AIDS patient), 123–24, 133–34, 145
embodies social beings, humans as, 6
empathy, limitations of, 3
equality, social, of 1950's–1980's, progressive income taxes and, 36, 55
equality in health: international law required to achieve, 40; judicialization of health rights and, 165; necessity of transforming existing political system to achieve, 38; principles for, 199; in realization of health as human right, 221–22. *See also* health as human right; health justice, global
ESC rights. *See* economic, social and cultural (ESC) rights
ESMA. *See* Naval Mechanics School, Buenos Aires
ethnonationalism, 26
ETOs. *See* extraterritorial obligations
Europe, universal health care in, 67
European Court of Human Rights (ECtHR), 118
evil, radical, Kant on, 27
evolution, normative, contingency of, 208
extraterritorial obligations (ETOs): as extension of social contract, 24, 179, 217–18; and global health justice, 196–97
EZLN. *See* Zapatista National Liberation Army

Facebook, 181, 215
facts, individual variations in processing of, 26
Farmer, Paul, 17
Fathalla, Mahmoud, 52
FCGH. *See* Framework Convention on Global Health
Federación de Mujeres de Anta, 112
federalist systems, divided responsibility for health care in, 90
feminists: challenges to liberal philosophical tradition by, 40–41; Latin America activism of, 82; on programs to reduce maternal mortality levels, 71. *See also* women's movements
Ferraz, Octavio, 165
financial crisis of 2008: Brazil and, 154; disproportional effect on women, 179–80; impact on global South, 179; and rapid spread of crises in globalized world, 21

financial sector, increased influence under neoliberalism, 154
financing, fair, in Universal Health Coverage, 188–89, 200, 220
Finnemore, Martha, 93–94
First International Conference on Health Promotion (Ottawa, 1986), 64
Fishkin, James, 191
Flora Tristán. *See* Movimiento de la Mujer Flora Tristán
formalism, origin of, 32
Forment, Carlos, 50
Foro Ciudadano en Salud, (FOROSALUD, Peru), 118, 163
Foucault, Michel, 35, 64
Framework Convention on Climate Change (1992), 180
Framework Convention on Global Health (FCGH), 195
framing of issues: neoliberal success in, 98–99; power of, 98
François-Xavier Bagnoud (FXB) Center for Health and Human Rights, founding of, 85
Fraser, Nancy, 21, 76, 162, 214–15
Freedman, Lynn, 133, 135, 159, 218
Friedman, Eric, 195
Friedman, Thomas, 99, 105, 106
Fujimori, Alberto: authoritarian rule of, 20, 106–7; and Catholic Church, 107–8; extradition of, 107; flight to Japan, 104, 107, 112; human rights community's opposition to, 110–12; indictment of, 120–21; neoliberal reforms by, 104, 105–6, 121; pardoning by President Pedro Pabalo Kuczynski, 120; and Peru's use of sterilization in family planning program, 102, 104, 107, 120–21; rooting out of suspected terrorists, 104; UN rights resolutions and, 107–8
Fukuda-Parr, Sakiko, 184

Galeano, Eduardo, 52, 74
Gargarella, Roberto, 91, 113, 151–52, 167, 192
Gates Foundation. *See* Bill & Melinda Gates Foundation
GATT. *See* General Agreement on Tariffs and Trade
Gauri, Varun, 90
Gelman v. Uruguay case (2011), 113
gender as social construct: CEDAW and, 42; conservative backlash against concept, 85; critics of concept, 138; development of

concept, 29, 84–85; as tool for challenging gender roles, 84
gender bias, Beijing Conference on, 84
gender diversity, increase in, 137, 214
gender equality, shifting technologies and geopolitical configurations and, 216
"gender ideology," 138, 214
gender justice, program for achievement of, 8
gender-nonconforming identities, Yogyakarta Principles and, 136–37
gender stereotypes, Beijing Conference on, 84
General Agreement on Tariffs and Trade (GATT): and neoliberal economic integration, 20, 61, 62; and postwar multilateralism, 30; replacement by WTO, 95–96
General Comment 14. *See* CESR General Comment 14
General Data Protection Regulation (DGPR) [EU], 181
generic drugs, and Trade-Related Aspects of Intellectual Property (TRIPS) Agreement, 127
gene therapies, 14, 15
Germany, abortion law in, 47
Gianella, Camila, 102
Girard, René, 162
girls, identity construction in, 69–70
Global Alliance of National Human Rights Institutions, 80
Global Burden of Disease (GDB) survey, 132
Global Fund. *See* United Nations Global Fund to Fight AIDS, Malaria and Tuberculosis
Global Gag Rule, 185
global governance, conflict with national political imperatives, in South African AIDS crisis, 21, 124–25, 126–27, 131–32
globalism, provincial, 217
globalization: and exclusion of unproductive groups, 78; and global impact of economic crises, 21, 124, 126; growth of inequality under, 126; neoliberalism and, 60–61, 78, 98–99
global order, local realities' recursive relationship to, 146, 208
global South: debt burdens in, 55, 179, 211; economic policies, loss of control over, 124; financial crisis of 2008 and, 179; structural adjustment programs in, 55, 59–60, 105
Global Tribunal on Violations of Women's Human Rights, 81–82, 99–100
Gloppen, Siri, 129
Gore, Albert, 127

Gostin, Lawrence, 195
Grant, James, 67, 72
Griswold v. Connecticut case (US, 1965), 46
Gruskin, Sofia, 116
Guidelines for Monitoring the Availability and Use of Obstetric Services (UN, 1997), 133
Gulf War, 4, 206

Habermas, Jürgen, 7, 38, 148, 182, 191
HAE. *See* Hereditary Angioedema
Hall, Peter, 61
Halley, Janet, 93
Halliday, Terence, 90, 96, 97
Hammonds, Rachel, 195
Haq, Mahbub ul, 58
Harvard Law School: disputes over CLS at, 3
Haynes, Leigh, 195, 196
Hazel Tau case (South Africa, 2003), 130
HDI. *See* Human Development Index
health: collective deliberation about, as necessary, 13; dependence on enjoyment of human rights, 154; and dignity, 15; effect of social conditions on, 56, 62, 63, 74, 154–55; human rights violations and, 85; neoliberal privatization of responsibility for, 56; state obligations across boundaries, 16; understanding of, effect on health policies, 63, 65, 74, 219
health and human rights movement, origins of, 65, 85–86
health as human right: Alma-Ata Declaration on, 63–64, 68, 143; as bounded by rights of others, 31; and change in response to new information, 190; complexity of current challenges to, 200–201; constant evolution of healthcare and, 13; and contesting boundaries of political, 210–11; and Convention on the Rights of Persons with Disabilities, 136; and conversion gaps, 58; and critical praxis, need for, 221, 224; definition in ICESCR, 90; and democratization of health systems, as imperative, 218–20; democratization of knowledge required for debate on, 9; equality as principle in, 221–22; as ESC right, 38; focus on, in 1990's, 85–86; and friction between different fields, 5; health impact of social conditions as basis of, 56, 62, 63, 74; and health systems, importance of, 133, 134–35, 134t; HIV/AIDS crisis as opportunity to assert, 85, 130, 147; horizontal and vertical equity and, 187–88; importance

Index   277

jurisprudence on, 141; inadequacy of CP regime to ensure, 37–38; as indivisible from array of other CP and ESC rights, 63; and inextricable link to broader social policy, 31; ITA approach to, 33–34; need to challenge economic, political, and scientific paradigms to implement, 55; and need to rethink conventional approaches, 5; as not synonymous with package of services, 22, 187; Ottawa Charter on, 64; and *Poblete Vilches v. Chile* case, 202–5, 221–22; political contestation in implementation of, 32; and priority setting in health systems, 31; as real rights, 159–60, 164, 173; vs. right to be healthy, 62; and social contract, expansion of, 216; and state's obligation, 133, 134t; and struggle for democratization, 135; universal dignity as basis of, 62; UN statements and conventions on, 140–41. *See also* courts' role in implementing health as human right; human rights-based approaches (HRBAs) to health; political space for advancing egalitarian health rights; Special Rapporteur on the Right to Health; Universal Health Coverage (UHC)

health as human right, progressive realization of: CESCR General Comment 14 and, 142–44; measurement of, 23, 186; vs. minimum thresholds, 22, 87; need for broad reviews of health systems in, 24, 222; need for clear judicable standard for, 142; *Poblete Vilches v. Chile* ruling and, 221

health as human right, progress toward: challenges faced in, 205–6; lives saved by, 7; in specific areas, 5; successes of twenty-first century, 173

health budgets of states: and fair financing of health care, 188–89, 200, 220; resource limitations and, 188

health care: ballooning costs in 1980's, 66; complexity of issue, and viability of democratic deliberation, 191; in Malawi, as rudimentary, 124; managed care, introduction of, 66; and moral hazard, 66, 67; neoliberal commodification of, 19, 56, 60, 66–67, 74; as part of social contract in inclusive democracy, in Europe, 67; as personal responsibility in neoliberal conception, 66–67; for women, *Alyne da Silva Pimentel* case and, 149–50. *See also* Universal Health Coverage (UHC)

health care access: market as inadequate regulator of, 15; state role in assuring, 15–16

health inequalities, unjust: current high levels of, 15; as especially concerning, 16–18; importance of, 15; pathologies of power and, 17

health justice, global: extraterritorial obligations (ETOs) and, 196–97; and global economic regime, need for restructuring of, 195, 200; new tools needed in fight for, 206; proposals for, 195–97; and transnational obligations of wealthy nations, 195–97; WHO Commission on Social Determinants of Health report and, 154. *See also* equality in health

health maintenance organizations (HMOs), 66

health policies: effect of concept of health on, 63, 65, 74, 219; rights infringements by, 85

health rights activism: factors shaping progress in, 208; importance of SRHR in, 208

health rights implementation by governments: complexity of, 90–91; and health rights as incompletely theorized, 91; and state bureaucracies, intransigence of, 91

health systems: broad reviews necessary for, 222; democratization of, as imperative, 209, 218–20; factors affecting access to, 135; in health rights-based approaches (HRBAs) to health, 159; importance to health as human right, 133, 134–35, 134t; in Latin America, contestation over, 67; as marketplaces, neoliberal reforms and, 56, 60, 66–67; model of health, effect of, 63, 65, 74, 219; priority setting in, and health as human right, 31; as reflection of substantive democracy, 159, 173; as social determinant, 187; as social institutions, 209, 218–22; undermining of, by MDGs, 133, 156. *See also* Peru, health system in

health technology assessments (HTAs), 190

Hereditary Angioedema (HAE), 197–99

Heywood, Mark, 130

history, importance of narrative of, 14, 15

HIV/AIDS: activism demanding research on, 65; discrimination against persons with, 65; economic impact of, 130; and health and human rights movement, 85; initial moralizing response to, 64–65; in Malawi, 122–23, 145–46; orphans, protections in South Africa for, 124; plague model and, 19, 52; prevalence in southern Africa, 125; as social phenomenon, 65, 72, 73–74

HIV/AIDS prevention and treatment: effects of South African PMTCT program on, 129; and efficacy of health rights activism, 85, 130, 147, 210; global institutions funding, 130–31; Millennium Development Goals and, 125; mother-to-child transmission, prevention of, 124, 128; reduction to chronic disease, 65, 72; and shift of power from sovereign governments to global bureaucracies, 21, 124–25, 126–27, 131–32; in sub-Saharan Africa, MDGs and, 132; in Tanzania, 72–74

holistic view of human rights: growing recognition of, in 1990's, 79; and human development vs. economic development, 58; as tool for regulating economic abuses, 4

Hopgood, Stephen, 206

hospitals, origin as charitable institutions, 65–66

housing projects, bleakness of, 53–54

HRBAs. *See* human rights-based approaches (HRBAs) to health

human development: as alternative to neoliberal model, 55, 58–59; as expansion of substantive freedoms, 55

Human Development Index (HDI), 55–56

Human Development Report, 58–59, 78–79

human dignity, conservative dismissal of, 223

humanness, reframing of, in Convention on the Rights of Persons with Disabilities, 136

human rights: common humanity as basis of, 3; concept of, before 1990's, 3; dependence of health on enjoyment of, 154; dignity as core principle of, 31; evolution of contexts for, 13; heterosexual male as default holder of, 6, 208; multiple elements within, 11; and neoliberalism, success against, 206, 207, 212; as ongoing struggle, 224; as tool for achieving gender and social justice, 8; as tool for challenging existing systems of power, 208; transition to international focus, 3. *See also* international human rights; Universal Declaration of Human Rights

human rights activism: advocacy networks, transnational, 217–18; author's turn to, 28; continual adaptation required for, 146; courts as tool for, 130; factors shaping progress in, 208; range of causes of, 146–47; SRHR and, 93–94; tapestry of entities involved in, 206–7; turn to regional and international legal forums in 1990's, 78, 113. *See also* human rights community

human rights as tool for establishing women's health rights, 103, 104–5; in 2000's, advances and missteps, 125; General Comment 14 and, 140; measurement of, 116–17; types of effects, 117–20, 119t, 122

human rights as tool for progressive social change: as iterative, nonlinear process, 11, 101, 207, 221; ongoing potential for, 24, 207; successes in, 24, 101

human rights-based approaches (HRBAs) to health: and accountability, 159–60; *Alyne da Silva Pimentel* case and, 22, 151; Brazil's Zika virus response and, 156; critical features in, 157; dependence on political mobilization, 23; dynamic of entitlement and obligation in, 159; epistemic inconsistencies between, 173; focus on social determinants of health, 158–59; and health as human right, 159; and health systems as reflection of substantive democracy, 159; measuring impact of, 163; Millennium Development Goals and, 151; as ongoing struggle, 207; and participation, real vs. illusory, 162; and practical function of rights, inability to dictate, 160–62; progress in understanding practicalities of, 206; proliferation of, 163; and room for democratic deliberation on implementation, 158, 160–62, 173; and subaltern sites of resistance, creation of, 21, 163; and systemic inequalities, necessity of challenging, 206; unhelpful versions of, 163–64; UN implementation of, 156–57, 173; UN Technical guidance on, 22, 157–60, 163

human rights-based approach to development, tensions with neoliberal development goals, 19, 20, 57–59, 125, 129. *See also* human development

human rights community: and aspiration for equivalence of law and justice, 11; expansion of, and fragmentation, 22, 139–40; isolation from development agenda, in 2000's, 135; professionalization of, in twenty-first century, 125, 135, 139. *See also* human rights activism

human rights law: equal dignity of all as basis of, 26; and (de)legitimation of power, 12

human rights violations: designation of domestic abuse as, 29; health effects of, 85

Human Rights Watch, 40

Hunt, Paul, 135, 138, 139, 157

IACHR. *See* Inter-American Commission on Human Rights
ICCPR. *See* International Covenant on Civil and Political Rights
ICESCR. *See* International Covenant on Economic, Social and Cultural Rights
ICPD. *See* International Conference on Population and Development (Cairo, 1994) [ICPD]
IDB. *See* Inter-American Development Bank
identity construction, factors in, and rights of child, 69–70
al-Idrisi, Abdullah Muhammad, 175–76
IHME. *See* Institute for Health Metrics and Evaluation
IIMMHR. *See* International Initiative on Maternal Mortality and Human Rights
illicit financial flows, need for crackdown on, 194–96
IMF. *See* International Monetary Fund
income tax, US: neoliberal reforms and, 55; progressive rates of 1950's–1980's, 36, 55
incompletely theorized agreement (ITA): and health rights, 33–34; Universal Declaration of Human Rights as, 33
Independent Expert on the Effects of Foreign Debt and Other Related International Financial Obligations, 193, 211
India: and access to ARVs as human right, 125; human rights-based approaches (HRBAs) to health in, 163; "right to food" case, 167
inequality: effect on health, 151, 154–55; erosion of democracy by, 7, 22, 151, 155–56; ESC rights as tool in fight against, 206; global increase in, 151, 173, 177, 179, 206; human dignity as necessary principle in fight against, 223; measure of, as issue, 23, 155, 183–85; perceived solutions to, impact of measurement indicators on, 184; and political unrest, 177; in Qatar, 177; in US, 154, 179
Institute for Health Metrics and Evaluation (IHME), 132
institutional order, current: as contingent, 12–13; human rights as tool for dismantling of, 12
intellectual property (IP) protections: as barrier to health justice, 196, 210; new institutions to facilitate, in 1990's, 20, 96–97. *See also* Trade-Related Aspects of Intellectual Property (TRIPS) Agreement

Inter-American Commission on Human Rights (IACHR): and *Barrios Altos* case, 107; Cerrejón mine and, 218; and Peru's sterilization program, 103–4; and *Poblete Vilches v. Chile* case, 202, 204
Inter-American Convention on the Prevention, Punishment and Eradication of Violence Against Women (Belém do Pará Convention), 82, 103, 112
Inter-American Court of Human Rights: and *Barrios Altos* case, 107; and Chilean terrorism trials, 110; Fujimori pardon and, 120; and *Poblete Vilches v. Chile* case, 202–3, 221–22; and SRHR advocacy, 113–14
Inter-American Development Bank (IDB), and Peru's structural adjustment, 106
Inter-American System, 186
Intergovernmental Panel on Climate Change, 180
international and regional legal forums, need for national and local actions, 149
international and regional legal forums, rights activists turn to: in 1990's, 78, 113; and balance of democratic process *vs.* higher "pure" law, 113–14; as means of circumventing country-level political debate, 138. *See also entries under* courts
International Conference on Population and Development (Cairo, 1994) [ICPD]: conservative backlash against, 85, 114; focus on people-centered development, 79; NGOs at, 80; Peru and, 104; Programme of Action from, 82; SRHR rights and, 19–20, 82–84; turn from state-centered to women-centered population debates, 82–83; and women's rights, 19, 77
International Covenant on Civil and Political Rights (ICCPR), 36–37; differences in treatment in comparison to ICESCR, 38–39; on required minimum level of ESC rights, 86
International Covenant on Economic, Social and Cultural Rights (ICESCR), 36–37; commitment to progressive improvement of ESC rights under, 39, 87; differences from ICCPR, 38–39; and ESC rights as aspirations, 38–39; General Comment 14 updates on, 140–41; resource limitations and, 40; on right to health, definition of, 38, 90. *See also* CESCR General Comment entries
international financial institutions (IFIs): human rights pushback against, 193, 211;

immunity for environmental and human rights liabilities, 126; neoliberal reforms and, 7, 19, 96, 98, 105; power of, 209–11
international human rights: anti-impunity turn in, 91–94; basis in CP rights conception, 18, 37; claims to universality, 32; and distinction between CP and ESC rights, 40; and egalitarian global order, efforts to connect, 34–35; *vs.* states' right to self-determination, 35; as touchstone for evaluating national laws, 32; universal dignity as core principle of, 30, 31; and US law, sharp contrast between, 3
international human rights, rise of, 3–4, 18, 29, 30–34; 1970's political change and, 34–36; and acceptance of liberal state legal regimes, 50; legal trends in, 50; and marginalization of ESC rights, 38, 50; postwar multilateralism and, 29, 30; and separation of economic and political domains, 50; and Universal Declaration of Human Rights, 30–31
international human rights law: adaptation of, in social constitutionalism (vernacularization), 89–91; fragmentation of, 144; as intertwined with politics, 11–12; normative development in 2000's, 144–45; recognition of necessary trade-offs, as necessary for legitimacy, 145
International Initiative on Maternal Mortality and Human Rights (IIMMHR), 156–57, 163
international law: conservative characterization as undemocratic and illegitimate, 138, 214; incorporation into domestic law, in Latin America, 140
International Law Commission, 139–40
International Monetary Fund (IMF): human rights pushback against, 211; and postwar multilateralism, 30; on South African inequality, 146; and structural adjustment programs, 59, 94–95
International Study Team on the Gulf Crisis, 4
internet: and changes to public-private distinction, 215; and digital divide, 215; and digital reality, fluidity of, 215; need for regulation of, 181–82, 215–16; and rise of ethnonationalism and populism, 182
IP. *See* intellectual property
Iran, Islamist revolution in, 36
issues faced by global society, as too complex for single actors, 221

Janet (Tanzanian orphan), 73–74
Joint United Nations Programme on HIV/AIDS (UNAIDS), 131
Jomtien Conference on Education, and people-centered development, 79
judicial review, weak form of (Mark Tushnet), 167
justice in health care, procedural fairness and, 38

Kagan, Elena, 1
Kant, Immanuel, 27, 31
Keck, Margaret, 217
Keck, Thomas, 46
Kennedy, David, 144
Kentikelenis, Alexander E., 94
Kim, Jim Yong, 126
knowledge: democratization of, as prerequisite for public debate on social change, 9; structures of, as political, 200. *See also* measurement
Kuczynski, Pedro Pablo, 120
Kurasini Children's Home (Tanzania), 72–74
Kyoto Protocol, 180–81

labor, women's informal, need for recognition of, 214–15
labor unions, and universal health care in Europe, 67
Lagos, Ricardo, 204
Lagos del Campo v. Perú case (2017), 203
Lamprea, Everaldo, 170
Latif, Laila, 188
Latin America: and courts' role in implementing health as human right, 164–66; feminist activism in, 82; health systems in, contestation over, 67; incorporation of international law into domestic law in, 140; Marxist influence in, 223; SAPs in, 98; social constitutionalism in, 87–88, 89, 91
Latonya (poor single mother), 19, 52–54, 72
Laurell, Asa, 92
law: depoliticizing of, origin of concept, 32; as embedded in social-legal narrative, 10; legal rationales of, and legitimacy, 10; and (de)legitimation of power, 12; as necessary venue for social change, 11–12; as representation of world, 10; rights as inexorably tied to, 11; tools for social change within, 11
L.C. v. Peru case, 121
legal progress: dialogic relationship with past events, 10–11; extralegal origins of, 11; and selection of challengeable law, 10

Lehohla, Pali, 128
LGBTQ movements: and HIV/AIDS research, 65; and increasing diversity of family structures, 214; rise of, 36
LGBTQ persons, UN measures to protect, 137; backlash against, 137
liberal philosophical tradition: as basis of traditional CP human rights regimes, 18, 50, 216; feminist challenges to, 40–41; privileging of CP rights, 29, 34, 36–37; and Universal Declaration of Human Rights, 30–31
life expectancy, large disparity in, 15
Link, Bruce, 16
Lloyd, Ryan, 152
local realities, recursive relationship to global order, 146, 208
Lorde, Audre, 11, 31
Lula da Silva, Luis Inácio: corruption scandal of 2017, 172; election of, 152; and inequality, 153; on international economic order, 153; populism of, 151; poverty, reduction of, 152–53; and women's health care, support for, 151
Luskin, Robert, 191

Maastricht Guidelines on Violations of Economic, Social and Cultural Rights, 116–17, 141
Maastricht Principles on the Extraterritorial Obligations of States, 160, 196
MacIntyre, Alasdair, 33
Mahler, Halfdan, 67
Maine, Deborah, 70–71, 133, 186
Malawi: AIDS epidemic in, 122–23, 145–46; and MDGs, 145; rudimentary health care in, 124; traditional cultural practices in, 145–46
Malthus, Thomas R., 83
Mandela, Nelson, 3–4, 126, 127
Mangapwani slave caves, 24–25, 176
Mann, Jonathan, 65, 75, 85–86
Mansbridge, Jane, 191
Manuela Ramos. *See* Movimiento de la Mujer Manuela Ramos
Marcos, Subcomandante, 75
Maritain, Jacques, 33
markets, self-regulating, as illusion, 105
Martínez de Hoz, José, 48–49
Marx, Roberto Burle, 156
Marxism: disillusionment of 1970's with, 35; revolutionaries and, impacts on seeing humanity in other through, 223

maternal health care: continuum of care approach based on RMNCH, 157–58; court-enforceable rights, expansion of, 150–51; distinct needs of pregnant women, 72; as element of sexual and reproductive health and rights, 157–58; as human right, development in 1990's, 77; right to, *Alyne da Silva Pimentel* case and, 149–50; shift to focus on obstetric care, 133
maternal mortality: prevention of, 133–34; Symbolic Tribunal on (2016), 99–100, 149; three delays responsible for, 133, 149
"Maternal Mortality—A Neglected Tragedy" (Rosenfield and Maine), 70–71
maternal mortality rates: abortion and, 16; efforts to reduce, 19, 70–72, 100; feminist views on programs to reduce, 71; large disparity in, 15, 16; and reproductive rights movement, 72; societies' unwillingness to address, 52; women's lack of agency and, 16–17
Mbeki, Thabo, 127, 128
McNeill, Desmond, 98, 217
MDGs. *See* Millennium Development Goals
measurement: of ESC rights, development of indicators for, 186–87; of health rights progress, bureaucratization of, 178; indicators, changing through advocacy, 187; of inequality, as issue, 23, 155, 183–85; overreliance on, and closing of democratic space, 200; premises embedded in, 178; reductionism of, and blunting of civil society's understanding, 187; of SRHR progress, limitations of, 23, 178, 184–85; of Sustainable Development Goals, redefining of goals by indicators used in, 178, 183–85, 199–200
Meloni, Augusto, 102–3, 121
Merry, Sally Engle, 90, 112, 187
Mestanza, Maria Mamérita, case of, 103–4, 111, 112, 117, 118
methodology: narrative techniques, 9–11; process-tracing, 8
Mexico: and Brady Bonds, 95; default of, 59; election of center-left government in 2018, 99; and global economic integration, 78; human rights violations by, accountability in supranational forums, 92–93; SRHR in, Catholic Church and, 111. *See also* Zapatista National Liberation Army (EZLN)
Mexico, neoliberal restructuring in: *ejido* system and, 94; health effects of, 100; opposition to, 92–93; privatizations in, 95, 98

migrants: and global migration crises, 181; rights to health care, 189; and workers' rights, in Qatar, 176–77
Millennium Declaration (2000), 115
Millennium Development Goals (MDGs): and assimilation to institutions of rich countries, 132; and health systems, undermining of, 133, 156; and HIV/AIDS prevention and treatment, 125, 131, 132; and human rights, importance of, 133, 134t; and human rights-based approaches (HRBAs) to health, 151; lack of transparency in setting, 115; Malawi and, 145; measurement of progress, 132; number devoted to health, 130; partnerships with private companies in, 132; practical bent of, 145; RMNCH approach to maternal health and, 157–58; and shift of power from sovereign governments to global bureaucracies, 131–32; and SRHR, 21, 104, 115–16; states' touting of successes of, 145; Taskforce on Child and Maternal Health, 125; turn from broad agenda to siloed interventions, 21–22, 125, 131, 156; *vs.* UN human rights-based approached to development, 125
Millennium Task Force on MDG 4 and 5, 133, 134t
Miller, Alice, 118
Mogollón, María Esther, 111–12
Montesinos, Valdimiro, 104, 106–7
Montevideo Consensus (2013), 183
moral economies, SRHR and, 7, 213
Morales, Diego, 168
Movimiento de la Mujer Flora Tristán (Flora Tristan), 112
Movimiento de la Mujer Manuela Ramos, 108
Movimiento Revolucionario Tupac Amuru, 104
Moyn, Samuel, 34, 206
Msimang, Manto Tshabalala, 128
multilateralism, postwar: and Bretton Woods institutions, 29, 30; rationale for, 31; and rise of international human rights, 29, 30; tension between economic and political versions of, 30, 50; and United Nations, 30

NAFTA. *See* North American Free Trade Agreement
narratives we choose to believe, as scaffolding underlying conception of reality, 26
narrative techniques: as method, 9–11; and politics of power and representation, 10

National Health Service (Britain), priority-setting in, 191–92
National Human Rights Institutions (NHRIs), 80–81
national political imperatives, conflicts with global governance, in South Africa, 21, 124–25, 126–27, 131–32
nation-state concept, need to move beyond, 216–17
The Nature of State Parties' Obligations. *See* CESCR General Comment 3
Naval Mechanics School, Buenos Aires (ESMA), 27–30, 47–48
Nazi ideology, justifications for, 26
Neier, Aryeh, 40
Neocosmos, Michael, 163–64
neoliberalism: current upheaval as opening for breaking hold of, 200–201, 212; and debt, vulnerability created by, 120; derailing of women's movement by, 116; economic development paradigm of, 55–56; and economic policies of 1980's, 55, 59–60; false assumptions of, 57; growing public disgust with, 212; growth of inequality under, 126; and health as personal responsibility, 19, 66–67; hegemony of, as netlike structure, 211–12; human rights' success against, 206, 207, 212; and moral conceptions on role of state, 74; ongoing influence in 2000's, 124; principles of, 56–57; and SRHR, effect on, 100, 120, 121; and UN, conflict between goals of, 19, 20, 125
neoliberal reforms: and changed balance of public and private wealth, 154; and ESC rights, shrinking of, 210; focus on economic *vs.* human development, 96, 97; framing as "best practices," 105; framing as "modernization," 20, 98, 106; and global economic integration, 60–61, 78, 98–99; health effects of, 100; human rights pushback against, 193, 211; IFIs' control of, 96, 98, 105; inadequate distribution of economic benefits under, 62; and power of IFIs, 209–10; and privatization of state functions, 55; and shrinking of political space, 7–8, 20, 105–6, 121, 145, 146, 148, 154; social constitutionalism as force opposing, 96, 97; social justice activists' limited tools against, in 1990's, 100–101; and structural adjustment programs in global South, 55. *See also* structural adjustment programs (SAPs)
Newdick, Christopher, 191–92

New International Economic Order (NIEO), 35, 61; decolonized states' hopes for, 18; replacement with rights-focused agenda in 1990's, 79, 80; WHO's call for, 64
NHRIs. *See* National Human Rights Institutions
NIEO. *See* New International Economic Order
Nino, Carlos Santiago, 27, 32
nondependence as basis of dignity: General Comment 3 and 14 and, 143–44; and required minimum level of ESC rights, 86, 143–44, 216; women's rights and, 41
nongovernmental organizations (NGOs): acceptance of distinction between CP and ESC rights, 40; advocacy for ESC rights, in Peru, 111; expansion of right to bring suit, under transformative constitutionalism, 89; growth of, in 1990's, 80; international *vs.* local, 92–93
nonstate actors, and health care, 90
Norheim, Ole, 129
Normand, Roger, 77, 79
normative arguments, contested construction of, 10
norms, internalized, power of, 211
norm substitution, 94, 97
North American Free Trade Agreement (NAFTA): health effects of, 100; and overriding of local control, 20, 97; and Zapatista Revolution, 75, 94, 95
Nussbaum, Martha, 74

Obama, Barack, 1–2, 25
obstetric care: CEDAW ruling requiring, 150; inadequate, as cause of death in *Alyne da Silva Pimentel* case, 171; as measure of compliance with international human rights, 186; shift to focus on, 133
obstetric violence: in Brazil, 149, 173; institutionalization of delivery and, 100; Symbolic Tribunal on (Mexico, 2016), 99–100, 149; systemic issues in, 162
Office of the High Commissioner for Human Rights (OHCHR): creation of, 19, 80; and ESC rights, measures of, 186; and human rights-based approaches (HRBAs) to health, 157; limited resources of, 139
OHCHR. *See* Office of the High Commissioner for Human Rights
Oliveira, Carlos, 152
Ooms, Gorik, 195
Open Society Foundation, 40
Open Working Group of the General Assembly of SDGs (OWG), 183
OPERA framework, 186
Organisation for Economic Co-operation and Development (OECD), 105, 196
Orwell, George, 65
Osiel, Mark, 81
Other, persons perceived as, and Convention on the Rights of Persons with Disabilities, 136
Ottawa Charter of 1986, 64
Our Bodies, Ourselves (Boston Women's Health Book Collective), 44
outrage at injustice, factors necessary for, 28

Panama Canal, as symbol, 203
parent-child relationship, UN-recognized child rights and, 69
Paris Agreement of 2015, 180
Parra, Oscar, 203
Partnership for Maternal Newborn and Child Health (PMNCH), 157–58
patriarchal family, fluid gender expression and, 137
patriarchal societies, HIV/AIDS and, 134
Personal Responsibility and Work Opportunity Reconciliation Act of 1996 (Welfare to Work Act, United States), 54
Peru: amnesty law, 107; and *Barrios Altos* case, 107; death squads in, 107; debt burden in, 120; discrimination against indigenous women in, struggle against, 111–12; health rights, civil activism for, 118, 121–22; human rights-based approaches (HRBAs) to health in, 163; human rights community in, 110–12; and therapeutic abortion, 113, 121. *See also* Fujimori, Alberto
Peru, health system in, 108–10; decentralization in, 110; decline in services under neoliberal reforms, 108–10, 121; discounting of indigenous needs, 109, 219; lack of funding, 109; rising costs under neoliberal reforms, 106
Peru, neoliberal reforms in, 104; and decline in wages and benefits, 106, 109–10; and inflation, 106; and shrinking of political space, 20, 105–6, 121
Peru, SRHR in: activism for, 110–14, 121; Catholic Church and, 104, 107–8, 111, 115; as complex story, 121; neoliberalism and, 120, 121; under Toledo, 115–16
Peru, sterilization program in, 20, 102–3, 104,

107–8, 219; compensation for victims of, 103–4, 117; as crimes against humanity, 120–21; effects of activism against, 117–18; IACHR ruling on, 103–4; indigenous women as focus of, 102, 108; institutional changes in response to, 117; opposition to, 111–12; quotas in, 108, 109
Peter, Fabienne, 136
pharmaceutical companies, successful challenging of, in South Africa, 21, 129, 210
Phelan, Jo, 16
Piaget, Jean, 69
Pillay, Navanethem "Navi," 156, 163–64
Pinker, Stephen, 14
Plan AUGE (Acceso Universal a Garantías Explícitas), 204
PMNCH. *See* Partnership for Maternal Newborn and Child Health
Poblete Vilches, Vinicio, 203, 222
Poblete Vilches, Vinicio Marco, 204–5, 221
Poblete Vilches v. Chile case (2018), 202–5, 221–22
Polanyi, Karl, 105
political change: necessity of transforming existing system to achieve health equality, 38; power structures, necessity of reconstructing, 6; redistribution of wealth, necessity of, 184, 195; responsible, key components of, 223. *See also* human rights as tool for progressive social change; progressive political change; social change
political determinants of health, 56, 62, 63, 74, 154–55, 180, 216
political institutions, global loss of faith in, 173–74
political participation: in CP rights concept, 37; potential broader concept of, 37. *See also* democracy
political polarization, cynicism and, 182
political space for advancing egalitarian health rights: activists' efforts to expand, 50; health activists' contesting of boundaries of, 210–11; need for expansion of, 38, 55
political space for democratic deliberation: courts' enforcement of health as human right and, 171, 220; human rights-based approaches (HRBAs) to health and, 158–59, 160–62, 173; neoliberalism's shrinking of, 7–8, 20, 105–6, 121, 145, 146, 148, 154; and vernacularization of international rights in social constitutionalism, 89–91
political unrest, current, causes of, 177, 182

population debates at UN, turn from state-centered to women-centered focus, 82–83
populism: origins of, 177, 182; and pushback against SRHR, 214; and xenophobia, misogyny, and racial discrimination, 182
Portugal, abortion law in, 47
positivism, origin of, 32
poverty as political issue, UN acceptance of, 86
power: conception of, in civil and political rights, 37; existing systems of, human rights as tool for challenging, 208; of IFIs, 209–11; of internalized norms and values, 211; (de)legitimation of, by law, 12; liberal understanding of, and civil and political rights as negative rights, 37, 209; multiplying dimensions of, 208, 209–12; of neoliberalism, potential for challenging, 211–12; pathologies of, 17; rights as tool for regulating, 187
Power, Suffering, and the Struggle for Dignity (Yamin), 5
practical progress, as element in health rights, 14
Prado, Mariana Mota, 165
private health care providers, states' legal responsibility to regulate, 150, 160
procedural justice, in Universal Health Coverage (UHC), 189–90, 200, 220
process-tracing, 8
progress, economic: as element in health rights, 14; equal distribution, necessity of, 17; social benefits of, 17
progress in medicine, as element in health rights, 14
progressive political change: decline in opportunity for, 207; youth as potential catalysts of, 221. *See also* human rights as tool for progressive social change
PromSex, 113, 121
protection writs, under transformative constitutionalism, 89
Protocol of San Salvador. *See* Additional Protocol to the American Convention on Human Rights on ESC Rights
"provincial globalism", 217
public *vs.* private space: child rights and, 68–69; effect of internet and social media on, 215; in liberal legal regime, 50; as obstacle to women's rights, 41, 42, 46, 69, 81, 213–14; and women's rights in twenty-first century, 214–16
public wealth, shrinking of, under neoliberal reforms, 154

Qatar: inequality in, 177; migrant workers' rights in, 176–77, 219; slavery in, 176
quality-adjusted life years (QALYs), Convention on the Rights of Persons with Disabilities and, 136
queer theory, 137

race, and US health inequalities, 15, 16
racial minorities, press for inclusion in 1970's, 36
rape: in armed conflict, as war crime, 112; marital, 41, 107–8, 124
Rawls, John, 33
Reagan, Ronald W., 54–55
Rede Cegonha, 158
redistribution of wealth, necessity for 184, 195
regional legal forums. *See* international and regional legal forums, rights activists turn to
representations of reality: as male constructions, 5–6; necessity of reconstructing, 6
reproductive, maternal, newborn, and child health (RMNCH) approach to maternal health, MDGs and, 157–58
reproductive rights movement, and maternal mortality, efforts to reduce, 72
ReproSalud, 108
responsibility to one another, as basis of health as human right, 13, 38
revolutionary politics: disillusionment of 1970's, 35; Marxist, damaged humanity in, 223
rights: as bounded by rights of others, 31; as inexorably tied to law, 11; as loci of contestation, 13; as terse formulations of arguments, 13; as tools for regulation power, 187
rights movements of 1970's, backlashes against, 36
Rio + 20 Conference. *See* United Nations Conference on Sustainable Development (Rio, 2012)
Ríos, Mario, 121–22
Roa, Monica, 93–94
Rodríguez Franco, Diana, 117
Rodríguez Garavito, Cesar, 117
Rodrik, Dani, 61
Roe v. Wade case (US, 1973), 45
Roosevelt, Eleanor, 121
Roosevelt, Franklin D., 54
Rosenfield, Allan, 70–71
Roser, Max, 14, 15

Rosga, Annjanette, 175
Rossi, Julieta, 168
Rousseau, Jean-Jacques, 41
Rousseff, Dilma, 153, 172
Ruger, Jennifer Prah, 33, 217
Ruggie, John, 62
Ruiz, Samuel, 111
Rwandan genocide, and international criminal liability, 92, 112

Sabel, Charles F., 169
Sachs, Albie, 223
Safe Motherhood Initiative, 70–72
SAHAYOG, 163
Salinas de Gortari, Carlos, 78, 95, 98
Sandoval, Hernán, 204, 222–23
SAPs. *See* structural adjustment programs
Satterthwaie, Margaret, 175
Section 27, 146–47
self-conception, new, as transformative, 122
self-determination, states' right to, *vs.* international human rights, 35; in South African AIDS crisis, 21, 124–25, 126–27, 131–32. *See also* global governance, conflict with national political imperatives; political space for advancing egalitarian health rights
Sen, Amartya: capabilities theory of, 58–59, 78–79; on DALYs, 136; on development as expansion of human freedoms, 55, 57–59; on health as basis of enjoying other rights, 15; on health as human right, 62; on health inequality, 1; on ITAs, 33–34; on limits of nation-state framework, 216; on population control debates, 83; on unfreedoms, 17; on view of law from critical distance, 12, 32
Sen, Gita, 132
Sendero Luminoso (Shining Path), 104
Sepúlveda, Lilián, 93–94
services, trade in, new institutions to facilitate, in 1990's, 96–97
sexual and reproductive health and rights (SRHR): activists' linking to social justice demands, 51; advancement of, strategies for, 119–20, 119t; advances and missteps, in 2000's, 125; and appeals to supranational forums, 113; backlash against, 20–21, 22, 104, 114–16, 121, 125, 137, 138, 193, 214; Beijing Conference and, 84–85; Cairo Conference and, 82–84; conservative opposition to, 83–84; court-enforceable

rights, expansion of, 150; establishment as real right, 104–5; evolving challenges of addressing, 208, 213–16; expansion of, in 1990's, 78; importance in health rights activism, 208; indicators used to measure, impact of, 23, 178, 184–85; international human rights activism and, 93–94; introduction of, as dramatic change in perspective, 83, 84; in Latin America, Catholic Church and, 104, 107–8, 111, 115; maternal mortality as element of, 157–58; Millennium Development Goals (MDGs) and, 21, 115–16; mobilizations and countermobilizations in, 36; moral economies' engagement with, as counterproductive, 7, 213; as necessary for women's sexual pleasure, 213; need for consistent frameworks for interpretation of, 193; neoliberalism's effect on, 100, 120, 121; paradigm changes required for, 208; political conflict over, 185; and prevention of maternal mortality, 133–34; progress on, 7, 99–100; SDGs and, 23, 183; strategies used to advance, 137; successes of twenty-first century, 173; Symbolic Tribunal on (Mexico City, 2016), 99–100; as tool for advancing women's health rights, 104–5; women's activism for, in Argentina, 50–51. *See also* Peru, SRHR in; Peru, sterilization program in
sexual minorities, press for inclusion in 1970's, 36
sexual orientation and gender identity (SOGI), Yogyakarta Principles and, 136–37
Shalev, Carmel, 19
Shen, Kyle, 90
Shiffman, Jeremy, 71
Sigal, Martín, 168
Sikkink, Kathryn, 93–94, 217
Simon, William H., 169
slavery: brutality of, 25; justifications for, 26; Mangapwani slave caves, 24–25, 176; in Qatar, 176
Smith, Adam, 57
Smith, Chris, 114
Smith, Stephanie, 71
Smoot-Hawley Act of 1930, 61
Socal, Mariana, 165
social change: and complex identities, preservation of, 6; law as necessary venue for, 11–12; and representations of reality, necessity of reconstructing, 6

social choice theory, in relation to health rights and UDHR, 33
social (transformative) constitutionalism, 87–89; in Brazil, 151–52; and ESC rights, 216; and health rights as real rights, 164; and local adaptation of international rights law (vernacularization), 89–91; neoliberal reforms as force opposing, 96, 97; protection writs under, 89; rise of, 87–88; and role of courts in setting policy, 88–89; in South Africa, 126
social constructivism, and child rights, 69
social contract: continuous expansions of, 208–9; extraterritorial obligations (ETOs) as extension of, 24, 179, 217–18; health care as part of, in inclusive democracy, 67; need for extension beyond borders, 208–9, 216–18; welfare programs as part of, 54
social goals, instrumentalizing women's bodies to meet, 102
social gradients, effect on health, 154–55
social inequality as cause of ill health: as basis of claim to health as human right, 56, 62, 63, 74; biomedical understanding of disease as inconsistent with, 56, 64–65, 73–74; evidence for, 63
social justice: international law required to achieve, 40; program for achievement of, 8; SRHR activism and, 51; struggle for, as Sisyphean, 101
social media, and changes to public-private distinction, 215
social policy: democratic control over, importance of, 218; inextricable link to health as human right, 31
social transformation through US courts, faded hopes for, in 1980's, 3
sodomy laws, repeal of, 137
Solari, Luis, 115
Sontag, Susan, 52
Soskice, David, 61
South Africa: Constitutional Court, on CESCR General Comment 14 core requirements, 144; corruption in, 146; economic inequality, efforts to address, 126–27, 219; growth of inequality in, 146; national political imperatives, conflicts with global governance, 124–25, 126–27; neoliberal economic policies in, 127, 146
South Africa, HIV/AIDS crisis in, 127; and ARVs, struggle to give access to, 21, 125, 126–30; and ARVs as human right, court

rulings on, 129–30; PMTCT (prevention of mother-to-child transmission) program, court ruling mandating, 21, 128–30, 150; and prohibitive cost of treatment, 128; protections for AIDS orphans, 124
Special Procedures, development in 2000's, 139
Special Rapporteur on Extreme Poverty and Human Rights, 211
Special Rapporteur on the Right to Health, 135, 138, 139, 157
Special Rapporteur on Violence against Women, 80, 81
Spinaci, Sergio, 126
SRHR. *See* sexual and reproductive health and rights
state(s): accountability for rights violations, international efforts to enforce, 91–94; capacities for crisis response, variation in, 179; obligations, shifting of public discourses on, 196; and shrinking of public wealth under neoliberal reforms, 154; transformation of moral conceptions on role of, in 1980's, 74
state responsibility for human rights: early focus on individual actors *vs.* systemic issues, 92; using international forums to define, 91–94
Steinem, Gloria, 27
sterilization. *See* Peru, sterilization program
Stiglitz, Joseph, 57, 175, 184
strategies for SRHR advancement, 119, 119t
structural adjustment programs (SAPs): commodification of health care in, 19, 56, 60, 66–67, 74; and democratic deliberation, removal of, 94–99; disproportionate effects on women and children, 59–60, 98, 179–80, 214; in global South, 55, 59–60, 105; and moral conceptions on role of state, transformation of, 74; as neoliberal, 56; and norm substitution, 94, 97; number of, by 1991, 95; policies in, 59; political unrest in response to, 95; and sharp reduction of social welfare programs, 59–60; use of indicators to remove decision-making from democratic space, 97–99
Summers, Lawrence, 15
Sunstein, Cass, 33
Supa, Hilaria, 111–12
SUS. *See* Brazilian Sistema Único de Saúde
Sustainable Development Goals (SDGs): blended finance in, 184; civil society input to, 183; on components of sustainable development, 183; development of, 183; and ESC rights, development of measures for, 186–87; inclusion of all countries in, 23, 183; indicators used to measure, redefining of goals by, 178, 183–85, 199–200; potential effectiveness of, 220; and SRHR and gender equality agenda, 23, 183; as successor goals to MDGs, 23, 153, 178, 182; Universal Health Coverage as goal of, 23, 178, 220
Symbolic Tribunal on Maternal Mortality and Obstetric Violence, 99–100, 148
Syrett, Keith, 170

Tabula Rogeriana (al-Idrisi), 175–76
TAC. *See* Treatment Action Campaign
Tamayo, Giulia, 102, 103, 108, 111, 116–17, 118, 186
Tanzania, poverty and AIDS in, 72–74
tax evasion, cross-border, need for crackdown on, 194–95
Tehranifar, Parisa, 16
Thapar-Björket, Suruchi, 70
Thatcher, Margaret, 54–55, 63
T.H. Chan School of Public Health (Harvard), 72, 85
Tiahrt Amendment (US, 1998), 114
Tipp, Tippu, 25
TMBs. *See* treaty monitoring bodies
TNCs. *See* transnational corporations
Tobin, John, 33, 142
Toledo, Alejandro, 104, 115–16
Toonen v. Australia case (1994), 137
Toussaint v. Canada case (2018), 189
trade, international: benefits of, 61; removal from democratic space, in 1990's, 97; restructuring of, in 1990's, 95–96; in services and intellectual property, new institutions in 1990's to facilitate, 20, 96–97
Trade-Related Aspects of Intellectual Property (TRIPS) Agreement, 96, 127
traditional birth attendants (TBAs): delegitimation of, 100; in Zapatista autonomous communities, 76
transfer pricing, need for crackdown on, 194–95
transformative constitutionalism. *See* social (transformative) constitutionalism
transnational corporations (TNCs): civil society pressure on, 217–18; control through public opinion, 217; ESC rights as tool for restraining, 206; health effects of actions

by, 100; new tools needed in fight against, 206; political influence of, 180; state control of, need for, 217; state control of, through ETOs, 24, 196; tax evasion by, 195; UN Global Compact and, 132
Treatment Action Campaign (TAC), 21, 127–28, 129, 146–47, 150
treaty monitoring bodies (TMBs): analytical frameworks used by, 140–41; and ETOs, 196; follow-up on legal judgments by, 149; general comments and recommendations by, 138–39; overreach of, in 2000's, 22, 144–45; power struggles underlying, 10
Treaty on Human Rights and TNCs and Other Business Enterprises, need for, 217
TRIPS. *See* Trade-Related Aspects of Intellectual Property (TRIPS) Agreement
Trump, Donald J.: and climate change, 180; as crazy, 25; election of, as discouraging, 2; hatred of Muslims, 25; origins of unrest leading to election of, 177; and tariffs, 182; upheaval caused by, as opportunity for progressive transformation, 201, 212

UDHR. *See* Universal Declaration of Human Rights
UN Special Rapporteur. *See* Special Rapporteur entries
UNAIDS. *See* Joint United Nations Programme on HIV/AIDS
UNCTAD. *See* United Nations Conference on Trade and Development
UNFPA. *See* United Nations Population Fund
Unger, Roberto, 12, 14, 221
UNICEF, 19, 60, 67, 68–70
United Nations: Decade for Women, 42, 70; development agencies, Global Compact with transnational corporations, 132; development agenda, neoliberal influence on, 104, 116; development assistance, and promotion of human rights principles, 132–33; founding goals of, 30; fragmentation as issue in, 193; human rights advocacy, bureaucratization of, in twenty-first century, 125, 139; human rights-based approach to development of, tensions with neoliberal development goals, 19, 20, 57–59, 125, 129; human rights bureaucracy, growth in twenty-first century, 125; and New International Economic Order, 35; Special Procedures of, 193; and SRHR, conservative opposition to, 138. *See also entries under* Convention; Special Rapporteur; other specific agencies and agreements
United Nations Commission for Human Rights, 35, 60–61
United Nations Common Understanding on Development Assistance (2003), 132–33
United Nations Conference on Sustainable Development (Rio, 2012) [Rio + 20 Conference], 79, 153, 183
United Nations Conference on Trade and Development (UNCTAD), 34–35
United Nations conferences on human rights and development in 1990's, 77, 78–82; focus on link between health and human rights, 85–86; and human rights promotion, 19, 79–81; and people-centered development, 79; rise of NGOs and, 80; and SRHR rights, development of, 82–85; turn from state-centered to women-centered population debates, 82–83; and women's rights, development of, 81–82
United Nations Development Programme (UNDP), and Human Development Index (HDI), 55, 78–79
United Nations Fund for Population Activities, 44
United Nations Global Fund to Fight AIDS, Malaria and Tuberculosis (Global Fund), 131
United Nations Human Rights Commission, 80
United Nations Human Rights Committee, 137, 189, 193, 194
United Nations Human Rights Council, 80, 157, 163
United Nations Population Fund (UNFPA), 44, 108
United Nations Technical Guidance on the Application of a Human Rights-Based Approach to . . . Reduce Preventable Maternal Mortality and Morbidity, 22, 157–60, 163
United States (US): and HIV/AIDS funding, 131; and climate change, 180–81; health inequalities, racial, 15, 16; inequality in, 154, 179; injustices of, social movements in, 4; pressure on South Africa regarding generic drug distribution, 127
Universal Declaration of Human Rights (UDHR): civil and political rights in, 34; civil liberties in, 32; compromise between capitalist and communist approach to

rights, 34; countries' disregard of rights in, 32; cross-cultural validity of, 33; economic, social, and cultural rights in, 32, 34; as founding document of international human rights, 30–31, 32; holistic view of rights in, 4; as incompletely theorized agreement, 33; liberal philosophical tradition and, 30–31; as male-drafted document, 32; nations not party to, 32; on universal dignity, 12, 33

Universal Health Coverage (UHC): appeals process in, 190; and cost-effectiveness, 190; and democratized decision-making, 190–92, 200; elements necessary for social justice in, 23, 188, 200, 220; employment-based benefits and, 188, 214; expensive medical conditions and, 198–99; and fair financing, 188–89, 200, 220; as goal of SDGs, 178; and immigrant rights to health care, 189; and out-of-pocket costs, 188; privatized health systems and, 178; and procedural justice, 189–90, 200, 220; regulation and oversight of, 192–93, 220; as separate from right to health, 187; and transparency, 189–90, 199; in western Europe, 67. *See also* Brazilian Sistema Único de Saúde (SUS)

Uprimny, Rodrigo, 171

Uruguay, cigarette packaging regulations in, 192

Valongueiro, Sandra, 149

Venezuela, riots in response to austerity measures, 96

vernacularization of international rights, in social constitutionalism, 89–91

Vienna Conference. *See* World Conference on Human Rights (Vienna, 1993)

Vienna Programme of Action, 80

violence against women: designation of domestic abuse as, 29; UN recognition as human rights issue, 80–82, 103, 112, 213–14. *See also* obstetric violence

Violence Against Women Act of 1994, 43

Waldman, Ronald, 133
Wang, Daniel, 165
Waris, Attiya, 188
Washington Consensus, 55, 59
Wayúu indigenous community (Colombia), 218
wealthy nations, transnational obligations of, 195–97

welfare programs (social protection), decreased support for, in 1980's–90's, 54–55. *See also* Aid to Families with Dependent Children (AFDC)

Welfare to Work Act. *See* Personal Responsibility and Work Opportunity Reconciliation Act of 1996

WEP. *See* Women's Employment Project

West, Robin, 46

Western countries (United States and Europe), focus on civil and political rights, 34

Western culture, privileging of CP rights in, 29, 34, 36–37

"We the Peoples" (UN Secretary-General), 114

WFS. *See* World Fertility Survey

Whitehall Study, 63

WHO: Alma-Ata Declaration, 63–64, 68, 143; Commission on Macroeconomics and Health, 122; Commission on Social Determinants of Health, 148, 154; on HRBA impacts, 163; preamble, definition of health in, 39

will-formation, in ensuring health as human right, 38

women: disciplining by androcentric biomedicine, 44; sexual pleasure, SRHR rights required for, 213; social construction as Other, 26. *See also* Peru, sterilization program in

Women's Employment Project (WEP), 53

Women's Federation of Anta, 112

Women's Global Network for Reproductive Rights, 72

women's health: factors beyond health system, need to address, 100; and health as human right, 85–86. *See also* violence against women

women's health care: *Alyne da Silva Pimentel* case and, 149–50; inadequacy of, in 1970's, 43–44, 70; SAPs in global South and, 60; women's access to information and, 44. *See also* Brazil, health care for women, inadequacy of; contraception; maternal health care; maternal mortality

women's movements: of global North and South, and UN conferences of 1990's, 82; in global South, ties to broader movements, 44–45; as multiple groups, 213; neoliberalism's derailing of, 116. *See also* feminists

women's rights: and anti-impunity turn in international rights activism, 93; Beijing Conference on Women and, 20, 77, 82;

contraception and, 18, 44–45; control over own bodies, as fundamental to dignity, 29; and domestic violence, 43; and formal *vs.* substantive equality, 43; need for broad measures of, 185; and nondependence as basis of dignity, 41; press for inclusion in 1970's, 36; progress in establishing, 7, 99–100; public *vs.* private distinction as obstacle to, 41, 42, 46, 69, 81, 213–14; and public *vs.* private in twenty-first century, 214–16; and regulation of intersubjective conduct, 41; and reproductive health as human right, 77; turn from social mobilization to court-centric approach, 81–82; Vienna Conference and, 81–82. *See also* abortion; Convention on the Elimination of All Forms of Discrimination against Women (CEDAW); sexual and reproductive health and rights (SRHR)

World Bank: and Brazil's corruption scandals, 172; framing as neoliberal "knowledge bank," 105; human rights pushback against, 211; and inequality measures in SDGs, 184; loans to South Africa, 127; and Peru's structural adjustment, 106; and postwar multilateralism, 39; and structural adjustment programs, 59; *World Development Report*, 58–59

World Conference on Human Rights (Tehran, 1968), 35

World Conference on Human Rights (Vienna, 1993), 79–82; civil society actors at, 80; and fall of barriers between ESC and CP rights, 19, 77; focus on people-centered development, 79–80; on poverty as violation of human dignity, 79; Programme of Action from, 80–81; and women's rights advancement, 81–82

World Conference on Women (Beijing, 1995): conservative backlash against, 20, 114; focus on people-centered development, 79; Fujimori and, 107–8; on gender as social construct, 77; NGOs at, 77; and SRHR rights, 84–85; and women's rights, 20, 77, 82

World Development Report (World Bank), 58–59

World Fertility Survey (WFS), 70

World Food Summit (Rome), 79

World Trade Organization (WTO): establishment of, 20, 96; and intellectual property protections, 96–97; ministerial meeting (1999), protest against, 126; and TRIPS, 96

xenophobia, populism and, 182

Yogyakarta Principles (2006), 136–37
youth, as architects of future political transformation, 221

Zaidi, Sarah, 77, 79
Zapatista National Liberation Army (EZLN), 75–78; autonomous communities established by, 76; autonomous health system of, 76; causes of rebellion, 93, 94, 95, 219; declaration of revolution, 75; poor health care in, 77; poverty motivating revolution by, 76
Zuma, Jacob, 146

Stanford Studies in Human Rights

Mark Goodale, editor

Editorial Board
Abdullahi A. An-Na'im
Upendra Baxi
Alison Brysk
Rosemary Coombe
Sally Engle Merry
James Nickel
Ronald Niezen
Fernando Tesón
Richard A. Wilson

The Politics of Love in Myanmar: LGBT Mobilization and Human Rights as a Way of Life
Lynette J. Chua
2018

Branding Humanity: Competing Narratives of Rights, Violence, and Global Citizenship
Amal Hassan Fadlalla
2018

Remote Freedoms: Politics, Personhood and Human Rights in Aboriginal Central Australia
Sarah E. Holcombe
2018

Letters to the Contrary: A Curated History of the
UNESCO Human Rights Survey
Mark Goodale
2018

Just Violence: Torture and Human Rights in the Eyes of the Police
Rachel Wahl
2017

Bodies of Truth: Law, Memory, and Emancipation
in Post-Apartheid South Africa
Rita Kesselring
2016

Rights After Wrongs: Local Knowledge and Human Rights in Zimbabwe
Shannon Morreira
2016

If God Were a Human Rights Activist
Boaventura de Sousa Santos
2015

Digging for the Disappeared: Forensic Science after Atrocity
Adam Rosenblatt
2015

The Rise and Fall of Human Rights:
Cynicism and Politics in Occupied Palestine
Lori Allen
2013

Campaigning for Justice: Human Rights Advocacy in Practice
Jo Becker
2012

In the Wake of Neoliberalism: Citizenship and Human Rights in Argentina
Karen Ann Faulk
2012

Values in Translation: Human Rights and the Culture of the World Bank
Galit A. Sarfaty
2012

Disquieting Gifts: Humanitarianism in New Delhi
Erica Bornstein
2012

Stones of Hope: How African Activists Reclaim Human Rights to Challenge Global Poverty
Edited by Lucie E. White and Jeremy Perelman
2011

Judging War, Judging History: Behind Truth and Reconciliation
Pierre Hazan
2010

Localizing Transitional Justice: Interventions and Priorities after Mass Violence
Edited by Rosalind Shaw and Lars Waldorf, with Pierre Hazan
2010

Surrendering to Utopia: An Anthropology of Human Rights
Mark Goodale
2009

Human Rights for the 21st Century: Sovereignty, Civil Society, Culture
Helen M. Stacy
2009

Human Rights Matters: Local Politics and National Human Rights Institutions
Julie A. Mertus
2009